The Faber book of
CHURCH AND CLERGY

What is a Mark of the Beast waistcoat? Why did John Milton hate Bishops? How does a Monsignor tear his postage stamps? And what does a congregation do when the Vicar announces that he is God?

These and a hundred similar questions are answered by this anthology, which ranges from fragments of church history to reflections on architecture, from scenes of parochial life to serious theology, from saints like George Herbert to eccentrics like the Vicar of Stiffkey.

Ever since the arrival of the first Christian missionaries in Britain, the church has been inextricably woven into the fabric of national life. Authors as diverse as the Venerable Bede and Tony Benn, Margery Kempe and Stevie Smith, W E Gladstone and Thomas Hardy have been selected in an anthology which is designed to reflect the wide range of ecclesiastical life and influence. There are twenty chapters on subjects as diverse as clergy wives, monks and nuns, preaching, clothes, pilgrimages and controversy.

A N Wilson was born in 1950. He is the Literary Editor of the *Evening Standard*. He is the author of twelve novels, including *Wise Virgin* which won the W H Smith award and *The Healing Art* which won both the Arts Council National Book Award and the Somerset Maugham Prize. He has written biographies of Belloc, Milton and Sir Walter Scott, and *Tolstoy* won the Whitbread Prize for biography.

The Faber Book of
CHURCH AND CLERGY
Edited by A. N. WILSON

faber and faber

LONDON BOSTON

First published in 1992
by Faber and Faber Limited
3 Queen Square London WC1N 3AU
This paperback edition first published in 1993

Printed.in England by Clays Ltd, St Ives Plc.

Compilation and introductions © Ruth Alexander Guilding, 1992

A. N. Wilson is hereby identified as author of this work in
accordance with Section 77 of the Copyright, Designs and
Patents Act 1988

A CIP record for this book is available from the British Library
ISBN 0-571-16975-9

2 4 6 8 10 9 7 5 3 1

CONTENTS

Introduction, vii

1 The Church, 1
2 Church Buildings, 19
3 Shrines, 40
4 Church-going, 50
5 Preaching, 78
6 Bishops, Archbishops and Cardinals, 102
7 Cathedral People, 130
8 Scenes from Clerical Life, 142
9 Clerical Attire, 165
10 Sacred and Profane Love, 173
11 Pastoralia, 194
12 Clergy Wives, 209
13 Stony Ground, 220
14 Mighty Offensive, 224
15 Some Eccentrics, 240
16 *Odium Theologicum*, 251
17 Monks and Nuns, 271
18 Lay Piety, 296
19 Doubt, 315
20 The Christian Year, 330

Bibliography of Works Consulted, 363
Acknowledgements, 369
Index, 372

INTRODUCTION

The Church has been called a household of faith. Perhaps it would be truer to say that it has many households. Those who live outside those households, as most of us do in the west, are missing something for which there is no substitute. They either do so for reasons of indifference, or because they can not force their minds to believe in the often very unpalatable doctrines of Christianity, or because they do not think that collective religious organizations have made this world a happier place. I stand outside the Church these days for all those reasons. But I recognize that for those within the household, its satisfactions have little to do with intellectual arguments. Churches, whether we define them as buildings, or organizations, or collections of people, are places where the preoccupations of every day are taken up into a world of values higher than our own. Philip Larkin, in an over-quoted poem, speaks of the Church in this way:

> A serious house on serious earth it is
> In whose blent air all our compulsions meet,
> Are recognized and robed as destinies,
> And that much never can be obsolete.

'Blent air' is awful – one of my reasons for not wishing to include this famous poem in this anthology – but the poem 'Church-going' does recognize that much more is involved, when we go to church, than a mere assent to the more improbable aspects of Christian mythology.

When I was asked to compile this book, I therefore found myself wishing to draw together pieces of prose and poetry which reflected this broad range of responses: to draw up an inventory of the mental furniture which most church members, whether or not they are

vii

religious believers, have in common. Far more than unbelievers, it is the modern Christians themselves who have been responsible for the obliteration of much of the familiar old furniture. In fact, those believers who are dubbed 'traditionalist' by the popular press have often been the reverse of traditional in their attitude to what the rest of us regard as 'the Church'. They often seem to have a violent antipathy to the older forms of church service, and the older translations of the Bible. Catholic charismatics are seldom devotees of the Tridentine Mass, which provided spiritual nourishment to Europeans for hundreds of years. The evangelicals who pack the doors of Anglican Churches know nothing of *Hymns Ancient and Modern* or *The Book of Common Prayer*. They could probably pass an exam in St Paul's Letters (in the 'Good News' translation) but they would have no sense of what – let us say – Parson Kilvert would have meant by 'the Church': the passing seasons reflected in the liturgical year; the quiet parish round of visiting the sick, instructing children, marrying the young couples and burying the dead. Fewer and fewer people have any experience of life in the old parsonages; or of those large, impoverished, intelligent clerical families which, until a generation or two ago, were the backbone of the English middle class.

Decking the church for Christmas; arranging the flowers, and the flower rotas; laughing at the eccentricities of bishops and curates and the congregations committed to their charge: such stuff would seem to have little to do with true religion to the new noddle Born Again believer. But for centuries it formed a part of the fabric of our national life. It is the world so well-evoked by Thomas Hardy in his novels and poems.

> On afternoons of drowsy calm
> We stood in the panelled pew
> Singing one-voiced a Tate and Brady psalm
> To the tune of 'Cambridge New'.
>
> We watched the elms, we watched the rooks,
> The clouds upon the breeze,
> Between the whiles of glancing at our books,
> And swaying like the trees.
>
> So mindless were these outpourings!
> Though I am not aware

That I have gained by subtle thought on things
Since we stood psalming there.

My thoughts precisely when I look back on thirty-five years or more
of 'mindless outpourings'.

I have looked mainly among my own books for extracts which
seemed worth recording for this present volume. Often enough, a
passage which seemed excellent in context was impossibly neutered
or weakened when served up as an 'extract'. Very often it was
impossible to reduce prose, particularly passages of fiction, to a
manageable length and there will be those who think that some of
the passages in this book are too long. Sometimes, I felt myself
overwhelmed by the magnitude of the task. At one stage I had
accumulated over 700 pages of stuff; and since it was not my purpose
to compile a bedside book which would break the wrists of an elderly
reader or a hospital patient, this was obviously too much.

It was necessary to exclude, exclude, exclude. If I had wished, I
could have interpreted the phrase 'Church and Clergy' to include the
whole story of Christendom, from the conversion of the first apostles
on the day of Pentecost, through the missionary journeys of St Paul,
the councils of the early church, the controversies of Popes and anti-
Popes, the fervour of Eastern hiero-monks and archpriests, the piety
of desert fathers and Western religious founders, the zeal of crusaders,
the ardour of the seventeenth-century religious wars, the quarrels of
the Jesuits with the Jansenists, the rise of Scepticism, the strength of
nineteenth-century religious reactions, the courage of missionaries,
the last death-throes of temporal power of the Papacy . . . Enough
for a small encyclopedia here. And what of that fascinating subject,
American religion? The story would have had to include the faith of
the founding fathers, Catholic and Protestant, and the flourishing of
such exotics as the Christian Scientists and the Mormons. Once
again, room for a whole book here.

With considerable cowardice and insularity I decided to limit my
scope (more or less) to British Christianity. I start with the Venerable
Bede, and most of the centuries in between his and ours have been
included. Inevitably, I find that most of my material is Victorian.

The more stuff which I accumulated, the more obvious it became
that I was not merely compiling a selection of favourite verse and
prose. Rather, I was compiling a portrait of a largely obsolete world.

The new Christianity has the character of a brand-new sect. It has no interest in the past and, despite its congregations of hundreds, I suspect that it makes no impact at all on the millions who have never heard the Word, and would not believe it if they did. Meanwhile, those millions who polish the car on Sunday morning and never go to church, have bred up two generations of children who probably have only the haziest sense of what the Church is. To this unbaptized generation – by far the greater part of the western world – Christianity is a religion as obsolete as the paganism of ancient Greece. Figures in stained-glass windows walking on waves or distributing bread to multitudes present no train of association in their minds, any more than a statue of Ariadne or Bacchus would have any meaning to a child who had not been told the meaning of classical myth. Small chance, I am afraid, that such as these will be interested in how or why the cathedrals came to be built, or in the day-to-day life of parishes in town and country from the age of Bede to that of Barbara Pym. But for those who like that sort of thing, as I do, here is a collection of it.

[1]

THE CHURCH

I can remember the time when I was priggish enough to be mildly shocked by Betjeman's 'Hymn' –

> The Church's Restoration
> In eighteen-eighty-three
> Has left for contemplation
> Not what there used to be . . .

The original hymn that he was parodying meant so much to me, that it seemed profane to allude to it in a spirit of mockery.

> The Church's one foundation
> Is Jesus Christ, her Lord . . .

Since the time of the Reformation, Christians have divided between those who believed that the visible, institutional Church on earth was indeed founded by Jesus Christ (St Matthew's Gospel, 16:18), and those who felt, like John Milton, that it was blasphemous for any human organization to claim possession of the Holy Spirit of God. Certainly, some of the cruellest persecutions and some of the bloodiest wars in history have been perpetrated by those who wished their fellow-human beings to embrace

> Her charter of salvation
> One Lord, one Faith, one Birth.

From this historical perspective, one sees why Blake's vision of institutional Christianity was of an ugly Chapel, spoiling the Garden of Love, where

Priests in black gowns were walking their rounds,
And binding with briars my joys and desires.

For many modern readers, remote from theological concerns, and
incapable of entering into the questions that exercised the likes of
John Donne, or Baron von Hügel or Austin Farrer in the following
extracts, there could be no conceivable interest, then, in wondering
to which 'Church' they should belong. The whole matter would seem
to be obsolete. Thomas Carlyle, the great Victorian sage, wrote the
life of Abbot Samson, and used it as an excuse to meditate on the
ebbing out of the 'sea of Faith', which had happened to his own
generation. For the Victorians, who so loved to imitate the Middle
Ages in architecture, the actual thought processes of medieval man
were all but irrecoverable. 'The great antique heart,' Carlyle wrote:
'how like a child in its simplicity, how like a man's in its earnest
solemnity and depth! Heaven lies over him wheresoever he goes or
stands on the Earth, making all the Earth a mystic Temple to him,
the Earth's business all a kind of worship. Glimpses of light creatures
flash in the common sunlight; angels yet hover doing God's messages
among men: that rainbow was set in the clouds by the hand of
God . . .' and yet, having lured the reader by his rhetoric to suppose
that he has discarded this 'primeval poetic element', Carlyle rounds
on us with a jerk. 'It was a Reality and it is One,' he says. 'The
garment only of it is dead; the essence of it lives through all Time
and all Eternity.'

But the Church would not be human if it were not, in Rose
Macaulay's words, 'a wonderful and most extraordinary pageant of
contradictions.' An unbeliever is given pause when so intelligent a
person as Rose Macaulay, or Michael Ramsey or Von Hügel sees
the faults of the 'pageant' so clearly, and yet elects to remain within
it.

The Church's one foundation

The Church's one foundation
  Is Jesus Christ, her Lord;
She is his new creation
  By water and the Word:
From heaven he came and sought her
  To be his holy Bride,
With his own Blood he bought her,
  And for her life he died.

Elect from every nation,
  Yet one o'er all the earth,
Her charter of salvation
  One Lord, one Faith, one Birth;
One holy name she blesses,
  Partakes one holy Food,
And to one hope she presses
  With every grace endued.

Though with a scornful wonder
  Men see her sore opprest,
By schisms rent asunder,
  By heresies distrest,
Yet Saints their watch are keeping,
  Their cry goes up, 'How long?'
And soon the night of weeping
  Shall be the morn of song.

'Mid toil, and tribulation,
  And tumult of her war,
She waits the consummation
  Of peace for evermore;
Till with the vision glorious
  Her longing eyes are blest,
And the great Church victorious
  Shall be the Church at rest.

Yet she on earth hath union
  With God the Three in One,
And mystic sweet communion
  With those whose rest is won:

3

O happy ones and holy!
Lord, give us grace that we
Like them, the meek and lowly,
On high may dwell with thee.

S. J. Stone (1839–1900)
(Tune 'Aurelia', S. S. Wesley (1810–76))

The Flight of the Sparrow

Edwin holds a council with his chief men about accepting the Faith of Christ. The high priest destroys his own altars [AD 627]

When he heard this, the king answered that it was his will as well as his duty to acept the Faith that Paulinus taught, but said that he must still discuss the matter with his principal advisers and friends, so that, if they were in agreement with him, they might all be cleansed together in Christ the Fount of Life. Paulinus agreed, and the king kept his promise. He summoned a council of the wise men, and asked each in turn his opinion of this strange doctrine and this new way of worshipping the godhead that was being proclaimed to them.

Coifi, the Chief Priest, replied without hesitation: 'Your Majesty, let us give careful consideration to this new teaching; for I frankly admit that, in my experience, the religion that we have hitherto professed seems valueless and powerless. None of your subjects has been more devoted to the service of our gods than myself; yet there are many to whom you show greater favour, who receive greater honours, and who are more successful in all their undertakings. Now, if the gods had any power, they would surely have favoured myself, who have been more zealous in their service. Therefore, if on examination you perceive that these new teachings are better and more effectual, let us not hestiate to accept them.'

Another of the king's chief men signified his agreement with this prudent argument, and went on to say: 'Your Majesty, when we compare the present life of man on earth with that time of which we have no knowledge, it seems to me like the swift flight of a single sparrow through the banqueting-hall where you are sitting at dinner on a winter's day with your thanes and counsellors. In the midst there is a comforting fire to warm the hall; outside, the storms of winter rain or snow are raging. This sparrow flies swiftly in through one door of the hall, and out through another. While he is inside,

4

he is safe from the winter storms; but after a few moments of comfort, he vanishes from sight into the wintry world from which he came. Even so, man appears on earth for a little while; but of what went before this life or of what follows, we know nothing. Therefore, if this new teaching has brought any more certain knowledge, it seems only right that we should follow it.' The other elders and counsellors of the king, under God's guidance, gave similar advice.

The Venerable Bede (c. 673–735), *Ecclesiastical History*, Bk II, ch 13

Treuthe is the beste

Thanne hadde I wonder in my wit what womman it weere
mind; might be

That swiche wise wordes Holy Writ shewed,
And halsede hire on the heighe name, er she thennes yede,
adjured; (God's) n.; went

What she were witterly that wissed me so faire.　　*certainly; counselled*
'Holi Chirche I am,' quod she, 'thow oughtest me to knowe.
recognize

I underfeng thee first and the feith taughte.　　*received; to you*
Thow broughtest me borwes my biddyng to fulfille,　　*pledges*
And to loven me leelly the while thi lif dureth.'　　*loyally; lasts*
Thanne I courbed on my knees and cried hire of grace,
bent; for mercy

And preide hire pitously to preye for my synnes,
And also kenne me kyndely on Crist to bileve,　　*teach; properl;y*
That I myghte werchen his wille that wroghte me to man:
created me a man
'Teche me to tresor, but tel me this ilke—　　*direct; same (thing)*
How I may save my soule, that seint art yholden.'
you who; holy; considered

'Whan alle tresors arn tried,' quod she, 'Treuthe is the beste.
I do it on *Deus caritas* to deme the sothe;　　*appeal to; judge*
It is dereworthe a drury as deere God hymselven　　*precious; love-gift*
Who is trewe of his tonge and telleth noon oother,　　*speaks nought else*
And dooth the werkes therwith and wilneth no man ille,
acts accordingly; intends

5

He is a god by the Gospel, agrounde and olofte,   *according to*
And ylik to Oure Lord by Seint Lukes wordes.   (cf. Lk. 12:33)
The clerkes that knowen this sholde kennen it aboute,   *make known*
For Cristen and uncristen cleymeth it echone.   *(non)Christian; claim*

William Langland (*c.* 1362–87) *Piers Plowman*

Wolves

'Hee to his own a Comforter will send,
The promise of the Father, who shall dwell
His Spirit within them, and the Law of Faith
Working through love, upon their hearts shall write,
To guide them in all truth, and also arm
With spiritual Armour, able to resist
Satan's assaults, and quench his fiery darts,
What Man can do against them, not afraid,
Though to the death, against such cruelties
With inward consolations recompens't,
And oft supported so as shall amaze
Their proudest persecutors: for the Spirit
Pour'd first on his Apostles, whom he sends
To evangelize the Nations, then on all
Baptiz'd, shall them with wondrous gifts endue
To speak all Tongues, and do all Miracles,
As did their Lord before them. Thus they win
Great numbers of each Nation to receive
With joy the tidings brought from Heav'n: at length
Their Ministry perform'd, and race well run,
Their doctrine and their story written left,
They die; but in their room, as they forewarn,
Wolves shall succeed for teachers, grievous Wolves,
Who all the sacred mysteries of Heav'n
To their own vile advantages shall turn
Of lucre and ambition, and the truth
With superstitions and traditions taint,
Left only in those written Records pure,
Though not but by the Spirit understood.
Then shall they seek to avail themselves of names,

6

Places and titles, and with these to join
Secular power, though feigning still to act
By spiritual, to themselves appropriating
The Spirit of God, promis'd alike and giv'n
To all Believers; and from that pretense,
Spiritual Laws by carnal power shall force
On every conscience; Laws which none shall find
Left them enroll'd, or what the Spirit within
Shall on the heart engrave. What will they then
But force the Spirit of Grace itself, and bind
His consort Liberty; what, but unbuild
His living Temples, built by Faith to stand,
Their own Faith not another's: for on Earth
Who against Faith and Conscience can be heard
Infallible? yet many will presume:
Whence heavy persecution shall arise
On all who in the worship persevere
Of Spirit and Truth; the rest, far greater part,
Will deem in outward Rites and specious forms
Religion satisfi'd; Truth shall retire
Bestuck with sland'rous darts, and works of Faith
Rarely be found: so shall the World go on,
To good malignant, to bad men benign,
Under her own weight groaning, till the day
Appear of respiration* to the just,
And vengeance to the wicked, at return
Of him so lately promis'd to thy aid,
The Woman's seed, obscurely then foretold,
Now amplier known the Saviour and thy Lord;
Last in the Clouds from Heav'n to be reveal'd
In glory of the Father, to dissolve
Satan with his perverted World, then raise
From the conflagrant mass, purg'd and refin'd,
New Heav'ns, new Earth, Ages of endless date
Founded in righteousness and peace and love,
To bring forth fruits Joy and eternal Bliss.'

* Respiration: freedom, the chance to breathe again.

John Milton (1608–74) *Paradise Lost*, XII

The Garden of Love

I went to the Garden of Love,
And saw what I never had seen:
A Chapel was built in the midst,
Where I used to play on the green.

And the gates of this Chapel were shut,
And 'Thou shalt not' writ over the door;
So I turn'd to the Garden of Love
That so many sweet flowers bore;

And I saw it was filled with graves,
And tomb-stones where flowers should be;
And Priests in black gowns were walking their rounds,
And binding with briars my joys & desires.

William Blake, *Songs of Experience* (1794)

Religion

My God, when I walke in those groves,
And leaves thy spirit doth still fan,
I see in each shade that there growes
An Angell taking with a man.

Under a *Juniper*, some house,
Or the coole *Mirtles* canopie,
Others beneath an *Oakes* greene boughs,
Or at some *fountaines* bubbling Eye;

Here *Jacob* dreames, and wrestles; there
Elias by a Raven is fed,
Another time by th' Angell, where
He brings him water with his bread;

In *Abr'hams* Tent the winged guests
(O how familiar then was heaven!)
Eate, drinke, discourse, sit downe, and rest
Untill the Coole, and shady *Even*;

Nay thou thy selfe, my God, in *fire*,
Whirle-winds, and *Clouds*, and the *soft voice*
Speak'st there so much, that I admire
We have no Conf'rence in these daies;

Is the truce broke? or 'cause we have
A mediatour now with thee,
Doest thou therefore old Treaties wave
And by appeales from him decree?

Or is't so, as some green heads say
That now all miracles must cease?
Though thou hast promis'd they should stay
The tokens of the Church, and peace;

No, no; Religion is a Spring
That from some secret, golden Mine
Derives her birth, and thence doth bring
Cordials in every drop, and Wine;

But in her long, and hidden Course
Passing through the Earths darke veines,
Growes still from better unto worse,
And both her taste, and colour staines,

Then drilling on, learnes to encrease
False *Ecchoes*, and Confused sounds,
And unawares doth often seize
On veines of *Sulphur* under ground;

So poison'd, breaks forth in some Clime,
And at first sight doth many please,
But drunk, is puddle, or mere slime
And 'stead of Phisick, a disease;

Just such a tainted sink we have
Like that *Samaritans* dead *Well*,
Nor must we for the Kernell crave
Because most voices like the *shell*.

Heale then these waters, Lord; or bring thy flock,
Since these are troubled, to the springing rock,
Looke downe great Master of the feast; O shine,
And turn once more our *Water* into *Wine*!

Henry Vaughan, Silex Scintillans (1650)

Divine Meditations

Show me deare Christ, thy spouse, so bright and clear.
What! is it She, which on the other shore
Goes richly painted? or which robb'd and tore
Laments and mournes in Germany and here?
Sleepes she a thousand, then peepes up one yeare?
Is she selfe truth and errs? now new, now outwore?
Doth she, and did she, and shall she evermore
On one, on seaven, or on no hill appeare?
Dwells she with us, or like adventuring knights
First travaile we to seeke and then make Love?
Betray kind husband thy spouse to our sights,
And let myne amorous soule court thy mild Dove,
Who is most trew, and pleasing to thee, then
When she'is embrac'd and open to most men.

John Donne (1572–1631), Sonnet xviii

from Jubilate Agno

Let John rejoice with Nautilus who spreads his sail and plies his
oar, and the Lord is his pilot.
*For I bless God that the CHURCH of ENGLAND is one of the
SEVEN ev'n the candlestick of the Lord.*

Let Philip rejoice with Boca, which is a fish that can speak.
For the ENGLISH TONGUE shall be the language of the WEST.

Let Bartholomew rejoice with the Eel, who is pure in proportion
to where he is found and how he is used.
*For I pray almighty CHRIST to bless the MAGDALEN HOUSE
and to forward a National purification. . .*

Let Mark rejoice with the Mullet, who is John Dore, God be
gracious to him and his family.
*For I pray for CHICHESTER to give the glory to God, and to keep
the adversary at bay.*

Let Barnabas rejoice with the Herring – God be gracious to the
Lord's fishery.
For I am making to the shore day by day, the Lord Jesus take me.

Let Cleopas rejoice with the Mackerel, who cometh in a shoal after a leader.

For I bless the Lord JESUS upon RAMSGATE PIER – the Lord forward the building of harbours...

Let Sadoc rejoice with the Bleak, who playeth upon the surface in the Sun.

For I bless God that I am not in a dungeon, but am allowed the light of the Sun.

Christopher Smart (1722–71) Fragment B, Jubilate Agno

On Being Anglican

There are many Churches; what business have you to call the Church of England *the* Church? It is time we grasped the nettle of the question. The Church of England is not *the* Church; there is only one Church, as there is only one Christ. The centre of the Church is neither Rome nor Canterbury; it is the heart of Heaven. There is a company of saints who enjoy the society of Jesus Christ more intimately than his disciples ever did on earth. We, who only know him by faith, and touch him only in sacraments, are no more than outposts and colonies of his sacred empire. The fatherland is above, and there the vast body of the citizens reside. How many in heaven, and on earth, how few!

And even these few, how scattered, how divided! The everlasting shepherd promised that his flock should be one fold: and so it will at last in the heavenly Jerusalem. But as for earthly unity, in the present state of our warfare, it is a promise which, like other divine promises, depends on human obedience for its full effect. God has promised us salvation, and pledged it to us with his sacred blood. Yet he has warned us that where many are called, few may be chosen. He has promised us unity, and made his death the bond; but our perversity has made schisms and heresies. The Church feels herself to be one, and groans to find herself divided, but there is no easy way to heal all her divisions.

Meanwhile, how can I, truly and with a good conscience, abide in the Church of God? Only by remaining in the Church of England. But why? Because the people there are visibly the most pious, or the missionary action visibly the most efficacious, the ceremonies the most dignified or the most congenial? No. It is not for me to admire or embrace, or even prefer, a sect called Anglicanism. What is it then? There are two overriding considerations. I dare not dissociate myself from the apostolic ministry, and the continuous sacramental life of the Church extending unbroken from the first days until now. That is the first point, and the second is this: I dare not profess belief in the great Papal error. Christ did not found a Papacy. No such institution appeared for several hundred years. Its infallibilist claim is a blasphemy, and never has been accepted by the oriental part of Christendom. Its authority has been employed to establish as dogmas of faith, propositions utterly lacking in historical foundation. Nor is this an old or faded scandal – the papal fact-factory has been going full blast in our own time, manufacturing sacred history after the event.

I cannot desert the apostolic ministry, I cannot submit to the Pope. And I was not born a Greek or Slavic Christian. I was born in this English-speaking world, where God's merciful providence has preserved the form and substance of the Catholic Church, and freed it from papal usurpation. At first, the Church, liberated from the Pope, fell heavily under the hand of the king, but the bondage was not lasting. That royalism is an accident to our faith, is made evident by the healthy condition of the American Episcopal Church, where prayers are not offered for Queen Elizabeth. The Crown is no part of our religion. Not that this need prevent us from wishing most fervently that God may save our royal house, to be the happy and unquestioned centre of our loyal affection, or the source of humane and Christian influences in the state. While we worship a King above, our vision will be assisted by the shadow of a throne below, and the very criticism which strips the unrealities of regal state, may discover to us the true pattern of sovereignty in him who made us.

When reunion is discussed, it is a sentiment as inevitable as it is amiable on diplomatic lips, to say that all Churches have their peculiar riches; that we disvalue no one's treasures by prizing our own, but hope that everything of worth may find its place in the final synthesis. Such sentiments are wholesome, if they lead us to look for merits rather than defects in other denominations. But the effect is less wholesome if we are led by such talk to suppose that Anglicanism should be valued as a charming or quaint or rare or beautiful species of ecclesiastical plant. We have our saints, some fostered by the

Anglican spirit, some in revolt against it. But saints belong to Christendom: our saints are not ours. And though various edifying traditions of piety, learning and social action have flourished among us, they might perhaps as well have flourished somewhere else. It will be a sad admission, if our tree has produced no flowers or fruits – an admission we are happily not obliged to make. But we are not Anglicans because of these; because of George Herbert, or Dr Donne, or Isaac Walton, or Bishop Ken, or John Wesley, or John Keble – because of Prayer-Book English, or Cathedral psalmody, or Cambridge theology, or Oxford piety. No, we are Anglicans because we can obey Christ in this Church, by abiding in the stock and root of his planting, and in the sacramental life. We may begin by making a fuss about the Church, as a clever boy may make a fuss about a telescope, admiring its mechanism of tubes and lenses, and fiddling with the gadgets. But the purpose of the telescope is to eliminate itself and leave us face to face with the object of vision. So long as you are aware of the telescope you do not see the planet. But look, suddenly the focus is perfect; there is the hard ball of silver light, there are the sloping vaporous rings, and there the clear points, the satellites. And where is the telescope? It is no more to us than the window-pane through which we look into our garden.

The Church mediates Christ: her sacraments make Christ present, her creed presents the lineaments of his face, her fellowship incorporates us in his body. To be a loyal churchman is hobbyism or prejudice, unless it is the way to be a loyal Christian. Christ is our calling, Christ our life; he whom the cross could not daunt nor the grave retain will make our dry bones live, and restore to the universal Church that peace and unity that are agreeable to his will, that we may be one in him, as he with the Father and the Holy Ghost is one life, one love, one God.

Austin Farrer, The End of Man (1973)

Letter to a Niece

You see, my Gwen, how vulgar, lumpy, material, appear great lumps of camphor in a drawer; and how ethereal seems the camphor smell all about in the drawer. How delicious, too, is the sense of bounding health, as one races along some down on a balmy spring morning;

and how utterly vulgar, rather improper indeed, is the solid breakfast, are the processes of digestion that went before! Yet the camphor lumps, and the porridge, and its digestion, they had their share, had they not? in the ethereal camphor scent, in the bounding along upon that sunlit down? And a person who would both enjoy camphor scent and disdain camphor lumps; a person who would revel in that liberal open air and condemn porridge and digestion: such a person would be ungrateful, would she not? – would have an unreal, a superfine refinement? The institutional, the Church is, in religion, especially in Christianity, the camphor lump, the porridge, etc.; and the 'detached' believers would have no camphor scent, no open air, bounding liberty, had there not been, from ancient times, those concrete, 'heavy,' 'clumsy,' 'oppressive' things – lumps, porridge, Church.

There is, most certainly, a further difficulty in this question. The Church, especially *the* Church in the most definite sense, the Roman Catholic Church, has at its worst done various kinds of harm, introduced complications and oppressions which, but for it, would not have been in the world. I know this in a detail far beyond, my Gwen, what you will ever know. But, my Dearie, let us keep our heads; and let us ask ourselves, not whether 'Church' of any kind does not open the door to certain abuses special to itself, but, primarily, only whether *as a matter of fact* it has not been through the Church or Churches that Christianity has been taught or practised; that Paganism has been vanquished; that Gnosticism and Pantheism have not carried all before them, long ago: whether indeed it is not owing to the Church and Churches – to the organized, social, historical, institutional fact and tradition, that the most independent-seeming, the most directly inspired souls, do not draw a large part of the purest of their conceptions.

Baron von Hügel, Letters to a Niece (1933)

The Last Church
to J. H. B. N.

Friend, when the dews are falling,
When the red sunset fades,
When summer owls are calling
Deep in the darkening glades;

Some day we shall see beckoning
   A spire over the hill,
A church beyond our reckoning,
   One church still;

It will be dark when we get there,
   With a dim light inside,
The lich-gate open set there,
   The west door open wide,
Twelfth century, triple moulded,
   Chevrony, billety, beak,
No church-locking clerk to be scolded,
   No keys to seek.

We shall find no organ pealing,
   No singing boys to hear,
Only twelve weepers kneeling,
   Six and six by a bier:
We shall not see their faces
   Cowled and turned to the east,
But there will be left two places
   Behind the priest.

There we shall take our places,
   Turning still to the east,
Close to the altar-paces,
   Close to the kneeling priest;
And the light from the silver candles
   Will glint on the cope on his back,
On the silver coffin handles,
   All else being black.

We shall take no heed of the prophets
   Dark in the grisaille glass,
Of panelled quatrefoil soffits,
   Of low-side window and brass;
But looking still to the altar,
   Follow the monotone,
Change and change without falter,
   Versicle, antiphone.

Dirige, de profundis,
    For churches of the past,
Deus obruimur undis,
    Is this church to be the last?
And the lights will seem to us lower,
    The altar candles dim,
And the voices softer and slower,
    A funeral hymn.

Yet our hearts shall not falter
    Kneeling behind the priest,
Turning still to the altar,
    Looking still to the east:
Illa hora admonebor,
    The present is as the past,
Tuum vultum intuebor
    In that church last.

John Meade Falkner, Poems (1933)

Minor Canon Corner

Minor Canon Corner was a quiet place in the shadow of the Cathedral, which the cawing of the rooks, the echoing footsteps of rare passers, the sound of the Cathedral bell, or the roll of the Cathedral organ, seemed to render more quiet than absolute silence. Swaggering fighting men had had their centuries of ramping and raving about Minor Canon Corner, and beaten serfs had had their centuries of drudging and dying there, and powerful monks had had their centuries of being sometimes useful and sometimes harmful there, and behold they were all gone out of Minor Canon Corner, and so much the better. Perhaps one of the highest uses of their ever having been there, was, that there might be left behind, that blessed air of tranquillity which pervaded Minor Canon Corner, and that serenely romantic state of the mind – productive for the most part of pity and forbearance – which is engendered by a sorrowful story that is all told, or a pathetic play that is played out.

Charles Dickens, The Mystery of Edwin Drood (1870)

'I hate the Church of England'

At the conclusion of one visit overseas the Archbishop's return to England seemed likely to be delayed indefinitely owing to an impending strike at Heathrow Airport, and last-minute changes of plan had to be made, necessitating a switch to an Australian aircraft due to land about ten minutes before the strike was timed to begin. The only person unperturbed was the Archbishop, who sometimes gave the impression that, given half a chance, he would never have returned to England at all. In order to report on the progress of events, his press officer entered the Archbishop's bedroom to find him stretched out on the bed, his hands clasped behind his head, repeating again and again, 'I hate the Church of England! I hate the Church of England!'

'It's a good job there's no one but me to hear you saying that!', his press officer said.

'Oh, but it's true', was Ramsey's reply. 'I do hate the Church of England. Indeed I do.'

Michael De-la-Noy, *Michael Ramsey: A Portrait* (1990)

An extraordinary pageant

Many people are troubled by the quarrels and the wars and the rivalries that raged for centuries round the Holy Sepulchre, between different sets of Christians; my mother, for instance, thought all this was a dreadful pity and disgrace, and that the whole history of the Christian Church was pretty shocking, and she liked to think that this was partly why she had left the Vicarage and my father, but really it was not this at all, but that she had grown bored and met someone else and preferred to rove about the world with him. Of course from one point of view she was right about the Church, which grew so far, almost at once, from anything which can have been intended, and became so blood-stained and persecuting and cruel and war-like and made small and trivial things so important, and tried to exclude everything not done in a certain way and by certain people, and stamped out heresies with such cruelty and rage. And this failure of the Christian Church, of every branch of it in every country, is one of the saddest things that has happened in all the world. But it is what happens when a magnificent idea has to be worked out by human beings who do not understand much of it but interpret it in their own way and think they are guided by God, whom they have not yet grasped. And yet they had grasped something, so that the Church has always had great magnificence and much courage, and people have died for it in agony, which is supposed to balance all the other people who have had to die in agony because they did not accept it, and it has flowered up in learning and culture and beauty and art, to set against its darkness and incivility and obsurantism and barbarity and nonsense, and it has produced saints and martyrs and kindness and goodness, though these have also occurred freely outside it, and it is a wonderful and most extraordinary pageant of contradictions, and I, at least, want to be inside it, though it is foolishness to most of my friends.

Rose Macaulay, *The Towers of Trebizond* (1956)

[2]

CHURCH BUILDINGS

Words are not the only language. Architects, stone-carvers, glass-makers and sculptors speak in their own way. 'The purpose of a church,' wrote Sir Ninian Comper, one of the best ecclesiastical architects of the twentieth century, 'is to move to worship, to bring a man to his knees, to refresh his soul in a weary land'. An extract from Comper's classic essay, 'Of the atmosphere of a church' is to be found in this section of the book. Those who do not share Comper's faith will perhaps find an echo of Thomas Carlyle in their hearts, and be haunted by the human memories, stretching back through hundreds of years, which are tied up in these old buildings – 'blackened shin-bone(s) of the old dead Ages'.

Modern Christian believers often seem impatient with those of us who love these old places. So long as they have a large enough, or small enough, space to gather together, first for worship, and then for drinking coffee out of plastic cups, they feel happy. A love of church buildings and church furnishings strikes them as frivolous. Unbelievers and half-believers do not always know what draws them to church buildings, but whatever it is, it is a little different from the impulse which leads them to explore other ancient monuments.

In this chapter, I have brought together a number of extracts which reflect this fact. G. K. Chesterton once wrote that 'man was a ritualist before he could speak'. Since, for historical reasons, the Church of England has most of the beautiful old ecclesiastical buildings in this country, it is not surprising that Anglicans have so many hymns celebrating the sheer physical beauty of their surroundings: 'We love the place, O Lord, Wherein Thine Honour dwells' or 'Christ is made the sure foundation'. The latter hymn is often sung at Dedication

Festivals. I remember roaring it out in a suburban church built entirely of modern brick, and noting the giggles of the visiting clergy when we came to the lines

> Many a blow of biting sculpture
> Fashioned well these stones elect.

Nowadays, with vandalistic clergy on the one hand, and an over-scrupulous zeal on behalf of the 'heritage' industry, we are in danger of losing William Barnes's innocent sense of joy in his parish church.

Many of us, on hearing the old bells peal out, feel that we would rather wait until the service is over before venturing inside. Unsure that we can assent to any of the words spoken from the lectern or the pulpit, we still return, hoping to find the place empty, and to hear what we need to hear, which, very often, is silence.

Chorus from *The Rock* III

We build in vain unless the LORD build with us.
Can you keep the City that the LORD keeps not with you?
A thousand policemen directing the traffic
Cannot tell you why you come or where you go.
A colony of cavies or a horde of active marmots
Build better than they that build without the LORD.
Shall we lift up our feet among perpetual ruins?
I have loved the beauty of Thy House, the peace of thy sanctuary,
I have swept the floors and garnished the altars.
Where there is no temple there shall be no homes,
Though you have shelters and institutions,
Precarious lodgings while the rent is paid,
Subsiding basements where the rat breeds
Or sanitary dwellings with numbered doors
Or a house a little better than your neighbour's;
When the Stranger says: 'What is the meaning of this city?
Do you huddle close together because you love each other?'
What will you answer? 'We all dwell together
To make money from each other' or 'This is a community'?

And the Stranger will depart and return to the desert.
O my soul, be prepared for the coming of the Stranger,
Be prepared for him who knows how to ask questions.

O weariness of men who turn from GOD
To the grandeur of your mind and the glory of your action,
To arts and inventions and daring enterprises,
To schemes of human greatness thoroughly discredited,
Binding the earth and the water to your service,
Exploiting the seas and developing the mountains,
Dividing the stars into common and preferred,
Engaged in devising the perfect refrigerator,
Engaged in working out a rational morality,
Engaged in printing as many books as possible,
Plotting of happiness and flinging empty bottles,
Turning from your vacancy to fevered enthusiasm
For nation or race or what you call humanity;
Though you forget the way to the Temple,
There is one who remembers the way to your door:
Life you may evade, but Death you shall not.
You shall not deny the Stranger.

T. S. Eliot, Collected Poems (1936)

St Edmundsbury

Here, sure enough, is an Abbey; beautiful in the eye of Dilettantism. Giant Pedantry also will step in, with its huge Dugdale and other enormous Monasticons under its arm, and cheerfully apprise you, That this was a very great Abbey, owner and indeed creator of St Edmund's Town itself, owner of wide lands and revenues; nay that its land were once a county of themselves; that indeed King Canute or Knut was very kind to it, and gave St Edmund his own gold crown off his head, on one occasion: for the rest, that the Monks were of such and such a genus, such and such a number; that they had so many carucates of land in this hundred, and so many in that; and then farther that the large Tower or Belfry was built by such a one, and the smaller Belfry was built by etc. etc. – Till human nature can stand no more of it; till human nature desperately take refuge in forgetfulness, almost in flat disbelief of the whole business, Monks,

Monastery, Belfries, Carucates and all! Alas, what mountains of dead ashes, wreck, and burnt bones, does assiduous Pedantry dig up from the Past Time, and name it History, and Philosophy of History; till, as we say, the human soul sinks wearied and bewildered; till the Past Time seems all one infinite incredible gray void, without sun, stars, hearth-fires, or candlelight; dim offensive dust-whirlwinds filling universal Nature; and over your Historical Library, it is as if all the Titans had written for themselves: DRY RUBBISH SHOT HERE!

And yet these grim old walls are not a dilettantism and *dubiety*; they are an earnest fact. It was a most real and serious purpose they were built for! Yes, another world it was, when these black ruins, white in their new mortar and fresh chiselling, first saw the sun as walls, long ago. Gauge not, with thy dilettante compasses, with that placid dilettante simper, the Heaven's-Watchtower of our Fathers, the fallen God's-Houses, the Golgotha of true Souls departed!

Their architecture, belfries, land-carucates? Yes – and that is but a small item of the matter. Does it never give thee pause, this other strange item of it, that men then had a *soul* – not by hearsay alone, and as a figure of speech; but as a truth that they *knew*, and practically went upon! Verily it was another world then. Their Missals have become incredible, a sheer platitude, sayest thou? Yes, a most poor platitude; and even, if thou wilt, an idolatry and blasphemy, should any one persuade *thee* to believe them, to pretend praying by them.

Another world, truly: and this present poor distressed world might get some profit by looking wisely into it, instead of foolishly. But at lowest, O dilettante friend, let us know always that it *was* a world, and not a void infinite of gray haze with fantasms swimming in it. These old St Edmundsbury walls, I say, were not peopled with fantasms; but with men of flesh and blood, made altogether as we are. Had thou and I then been, who knows but we ourselves had taken refuge from an evil Time, and fled to dwell here, and meditate on an Eternity, in such fashion as we could? Alas, how like an old osseous fragment, a broken blackened shin-bone of the old dead Ages, this black ruin looks out, not yet covered by the soil; still indicating what a once gigantic Life lies buried there! It is dead now, and dumb; but was alive once, and spake. For twenty generations, here was the earthly arena where painful living men worked out their life-wrestle – looked at by Earth, by Heaven and Hell. Bells tolled to prayers;

and men, of many humours, various thoughts, chanted vespers, matins; and round the little islet of their life rolled forever (as round ours still rolls, though we are blind and deaf) the illimitable Ocean, tinting all things with *its* eternal hues and reflexes; making strange prophetic music! How silent now; all departed, clean gone. The World Dramaturgist has written: *Exeunt.* The devouring Time-Demons have made away with it all: and in its stead, there is either nothing; or what is worse, offensive universal dust-clouds, and grey eclipse of Earth and Heaven, from 'dry rubbish shot here'!

Thomas Carlyle, Past and Present, Part II (1843)

The Young Glass-stainer

'These Gothic windows, how they wear me out
With cusp and foil, and nothing straight or square,
Crude colours, leaden borders roundabout,
And fitting in Peter here, and Matthew there!

'What a vocation! Here do I draw now
The abnormal, loving the Hellenic norm;
Martha I paint, and dream of Hera's brow,
Mary, and think of Aphrodite's form.'

Thomas Hardy, Moments of Vision (1917)

Copying Architecture in an Old Minster

(*Wimborne*)

How smartly the quarters of the hour march by
    That the jack-o'-clock never forgets;
Ding-dong; and before I have graced a cusp's eye,
Or got the true twist of the ogee over,
    A double ding-dong ricochetts.

Just so did he clang here before I came,
    And so will he clang when I'm gone
Through the Minster's cavernous hollows – the same
Tale of hours never more to be will he deliver
    To the speechless midnight and dawn.

I grow to conceive it a call to ghosts,
   Whose mould lies below and around.
Yes; the next 'Come, come,' draws them out from their posts,
And they gather, and one shade appears, and another,
   As the eve-damps creep from the ground.

See – a Courtenay stands by his quatre-foiled tomb,
   And a Duke and his Duchess near;
And one Sir Edmund in columned gloom,
And a Saxon king by the presbytery chamber;
   And shapes unknown in the rear.

Maybe they have met for a parle on some plan
   To better ail-stricken mankind;
I catch their cheepings, though thinner than
The overhead creak of a passenger's pinion
   When leaving land behind.

Or perhaps they speak to the yet unborn,
   And caution them not to come
To a world so ancient and trouble-torn,
Of foiled intents, vain lovingkindness,
   And ardours chilled and numb.

They waste to fog as I stir and stand,
   And move from the arched recess,
And pick up the drawing that slipped from my hand,
And feel for the pencil I dropped in the cranny
   In a moment's forgetfulness.

Thomas Hardy (ibid.)

The Church Windows

Lord, how can man preach thy eternall word?
  He is a brittle crazie glasse:
Yet in thy temple thou dost him afford
  This glorious and transcendent place,
  To be a window, through thy grace.

But when thou dost anneal in glasse thy storie,
  Making thy life to shine within
The holy Preachers; then the light and glorie
  More rev'rend grows, & more doth win;
  Which else shows watrish, bleak, & thin.

Doctrine and life, colours and light, in one
  When they combine and mingle, bring
A strong regard and aw: but speech alone
  Doth vanish like a flaring thing,
  And in the eare, not conscience ring.

George Herbert, *The Temple* (1633)

The Church Porch

The porch was the place in which the penitents had to wait, and in which on Holy Thursday the greater part of the ceremony of reconciliation was performed.

Several councils and synods issued decrees forbidding the trial of pleas in the church or its porches, and the number of the prohibitions is in some measure a proof that such secular uses were not unknown if indeed they were uncommon. Fairs and merchandise from time to time invaded the porches in spite of many protests. The Council of Constantinople, in 692, forbade the sale of food, drink, and ornaments in the circuit of the churches, and in support of the rule, adduced the example of Christ in clearing the Temple of its traffickers. But the church authorities found it a hard task, as a long string of ineffectual ordinances sufficiently shows. Nor were churchmen always averse from allowing the sale of certain articles, such as chaplets and medals, girdles of St Francis of Assisi, scapulars, prayer books, images of the saints, crucifixes, etc., all of which were sold close by the precincts of Notre Dame, and many other churches. It was *apropos* of a controversy on this subject that Jean Baptiste Thiers wrote his 'Dissertation sur les Porches des Eglises' (Orleans, 1679), in which there is much curious information. That the separation of the religious from the secular has never been complete, is evidenced by the notices of elections, rates, and other worldly matters, which may still be read on the doors and in the porches of churches. At Mucklestone, near Market Drayton, there hangs in the porch a frame containing engravings after Mr Hedley Fitton's clever drawings of the district.

The church porch was in former days the place often selected for the payment of dowries, legacies, and other monies. There was a manifest convenience in such an arrangement, for the names of those present could be added to the record as witnesses, and, in case of dispute, their testimony would be important.

When the porch was chambered it furnished a place for the sacristan, or for night watchers, who from it could, by looking into the church, see that it was safe from fire and sacrilege. At Malmesbury Abbey Church it was used as a school-house.

Marriages were celebrated in the porch, and there it was that the Wife of Bath was united to the five husbands whom she survived. The marriage by proxy of Charles I to Henrietta Maria was celebrated at the door of Nôtre Dame of Paris.

The mystic ceremonies of St Mark's Eve were celebrated in the church porch. Young men and young women went there between eleven at night and one o'clock on the following morning, and watched for the wraiths of those who were to die within the next twelve months.

William Andrews, Curious Church Gleanings (1896)

Morwenstow Church

Morwenstow Church stands on the steep slope of a hill.

It is a church of very great interest, consisting of nave, chancel and two aisles. The arcade of the north aisle is remarkably fine, and of two dates. Two semicircular arches are richly carved with Norman zigzag and billet; one is plain, eventually intended to be carved like the other two. The remaining two arches are transition early English pointed and plain. At the spring of the sculptured arches, in the spandrels, are very spirited projecting heads: one of a ram is remarkably well modelled. The vicar, who mused over his church, and sought a signification in everything, believed that this represented the ram caught in a thicket by the horns, and was symbolical of Christ, the true sacrifice. Another projecting head is spirited – the mouth is contorted with mocking laughter: this, he asserted, was the head of Arius. Another head, with the tongue lolling out, was a heretic deriding the sacred mysteries.

But his most singular fancy was with respect to the chevron ornamentation on the arcade. When first I visited the church, I exclaimed at the beauty of the zigzag moulding.

'Zigzag! zigzag!' echoed the vicar scornfully. 'Do you not see that it is near the font that this ornament occurs? It is the ripple of the lake of Genesareth, the Spirit breathing upon the waters of baptism. Look without the Church – there is the restless old ocean thundering with all his wakes: you can hear the roar even here. Look within – all is calm: here plays over the baptismal pool only the Dove who fans it into ripples with His healing wings.'

The font is remarkably rude, an uncouth, misshapen block of stone from the shore, scooped out, its only ornamentation being a cable twisted round it, rudely carved. The font is probably of the tenth century.

The entrance door to the nave is of very fine Norman work in three orders, but defaced by the removal of the outer order, which has been converted into the door of the porch. Mr Hawker, observing that the porch door was Norman, concluded that his church possessed a unique specimen of a Norman porch; but it was pointed out to him that his door was nothing but the outer order of that into the church, removed from its place; and then he determined, as soon as he could collect sufficient money, to restore the church, to pull down the porch and replace the Norman doorway in its original condition.

The church is dedicated to St John the Baptist. A little stream runs through the graveyard, and rushes down the hill to the porch door, where it is diverted, and carried off to water the glebe. This, he thought, was brought through the churchyard for symbolic reasons, to typify Jordan, near which the Baptist ministered. The descent into the church is by three steps. 'Every church dedicated to John the Baptiser,' he said in one of his sermons, 'is thus arranged. We go down into them, as those who were about to be baptised of John went down into the water. The Spirit that appeared when Christ descended into Jordan hovers here, over that font, over you, over me, and ever will hover here as long as a stone of Morwenna's church stands on this green slope, and a priest of God ministers in it.'

Sabine Baring-Gould, *The Vicar of Morwenstow* (1876)

'O happy Flowers'

O happy Flowers! O happy Flowers!
How quietly for hours and hours,
In dead of night, in cheerful day,
Close to my own dear Lord you stay,
Until you gently fade away.
O happy Flowers! what would I give
In your sweet place all day to live,
And then to die, my service o'er,
Softly as you do, at his door.

O happy Lights! O happy Lights!
Watching my Jesus livelong nights,
How close you cluster round His throne,
Dying so meekly, one by one,
As each its faithful watch has done.
Could I with you but take my turn,
And burn with love of Him, and burn
Till love has wasted me, like you,
Sweet Lights! what better could I do?

O happy Pyx! O happy Pyx!
Where Jesus doth His dwelling fix.
O little palace! dear and bright,
Where He, who is the world's true light,
Spends all the day, and stays all night!
Ah! if my heart could only be
A little home from Him like thee,
Such fires my happy soul would move,
I could not help but die of love!

O Pyx, and Lights, and Flowers! but I
Through envy of you will not die;
Nay, happy things! what will you do,
Since I am better off than you,
The whole day long, the whole night through?
For Jesus gives himself to me,
So sweetly and so utterly,
By rights long since I should have died
For love of Jesus Crucified.

My happy Soul! my happy Soul!
How shall I then my love control?
O sweet Communion! Feast of bliss!
When the dear Host my tongue doth kiss,
What happiness is like to this?
Oh Heaven, I think, must be alway
Quite like a First Communion Day.
With love so sweet and joy so strange, –
Only that Heaven will never change!

Frederick William Faber, *Hymns* (1861)

A-Putten the Church to Rights

Bright wer the mornen a-dimmen the moon,
Bright wer the vorenoon an' bright wer the noon,
Bright wer the road down the zunsheeny ridge,
Bright wer the water an' bright wer the bridge;
An' bright in the light wer two eyes in my zight
On the road that did wind up to Brenbury tow'r.
The eyes at my zide wer my Fanny's, my bride,
The day o' my wedden, my wedden's gaÿ hour:
Zoo if you ha' work in the church to meäke good,
Here's my bit o' zilver to buy stwone or wood.

There we took up our child when we bound en by vow
To his Seävior, a-mark'd wi' the cross on his brow,
While his little red feäce an' two hands wer in zight,
But the rest o'n a-hidden in long vwolds o' white;
An' wi' little blue eyes to the blue o' the skies

Wer a-looken up weakly, our child a fine bwoy,
That his mother'd a-call'd en, wi' noo ncäme at all,
O her dear, an' her pretty, her hope, an' her joy:
Zoo if you do put the wold builden to rights,
I'll paÿ vor a stroke, you shall have my two mites.

William Barnes, *Poems in the Dorset Dialect* (1879)

A prison chapel

The prison chapel is situated at the back of the governor's house,
the latter having no windows looking into the interior of the prison.
Whether the associations connected with the place – the knowledge
that here a portion of the burial service is, on some dreadful
occasions, performed over the quick, and not upon the dead – cast
over it a still more gloomy and sombre air than art has imparted to
it, we know not, but its appearance is very striking. There is something in a silent and deserted place of worship solemn and impressive
at any time; and the very dissimilarity of this one from any we have
been accustomed to, only enhances the impression. The meanness of
its appointments – the bare and scanty pulpit, with the paltry painted
pillars on either side – the women's gallery, with its great heavy
curtain – the men's, with its unpainted benches and dingy front –
the tottering little table at the altar, with the commandments on the
wall above it, scarcely legible through lack of paint, and dust and
damp – so unlike the velvet and gilding, the marble and wood, of a
modern church – are strange and striking. There is one object, too,
which rivets the attention and fascinates the gaze, and from which
we may turn horror-stricken in vain, for the recollection of it will
haunt us, waking and sleeping, for a long time afterwards. Immediately below the reading-desk, on the floor of the chapel, and forming
the most conspicuous object in its little area, is the *condemned pew*;
a huge black pen, in which the wretched people who are singled out
for death are placed, on the Sunday preceding their execution, in
sight of all their fellow-prisoners, from many of whom they may
have been separated but a week before, to hear prayers for their own
souls, to join in the responses of their own burial service, and to
listen to an address, warning their recent companions to take example
by their fate, and urging themselves, while there is yet time – nearly

four-and-twenty hours – to 'turn and flee from the wrath to come!' Imagine what have been the feelings of the men whom that fearful pew has enclosed, and of whom, between the gallows and the knife, no mortal remnant may now remain! Think of the hopeless clinging to life to the last, and the wild despair, far exceeding in anguish the felon's death itself, by which they have heard the certainty of their speedy transmission to another world, with all their crimes upon their heads, rung into their ears by the officiating clergyman!

At one time – and at no distant period either – the coffins of the men about to be executed were placed in that pew, upon the seat by their side, during the whole service. It may seem incredible, but it is true. Let us hope that the increased spirit of civilization and humanity which abolished this frightful and degrading custom may extend itself to other usages equally barbarous; usages which have not even the plea of utility in their defence, as every year's experience has shown them to be more and more inefficacious.

Charles Dickens, *Sketches by Boz* (1836–7)

Misericordes

Lineal descendant of the ancient satyr, the mediæval demon was a man with the legs and feet of a goat, and all the propensities towards mirthful mischief and hilarious abandon characteristic of his classic prototype. The idea of the bad hob-goblin of Saxon-English folk-lore fell in well with the design thus perpetuated by the monks, and the fact that evil is almost invariably represented under ludicrous forms, is probably due to the reflection that good men could afford to laugh; that the demons enjoyed a thousand humorous antics while burning or otherwise tormenting their victims, was of course no consolation to the wicked sufferers. In his transition from classic groves to the haunts of mediæval man, the satyr demon became slightly differentiated in form. His horns in some instances have disappeared, but in most have become those of a bull, and his goatish tail is mostly found to be elongated to that of a bull or lion; or often has the barbed end incident to the dragon form. From the same source, the dragon being a favourite embodiment of evil, is also derived the demon's bat-like wings. To these physical equipments is frequently added a human face set in the abdomen, as in the famous demon playing Luther's head as bagpipes, or more rarely at the knees. The misericorde carving of the demon rushing upon the miser at his money chest, in Beverley Minster, has these traits, while a figure of a goose-shaped dragon in the same series has the additional human face in the breast. It is not improbable that this was an arrangement brought to mind by the figures used by mummers, who inside light mimic structures representing dragons and other creatures, looked out through a hole cut in the breasts. Perhaps there is no form of mediæval dragon which cannot be found in one or another set of misericordes.

William Andrews, *Curious Church Gleanings* (1896)

Our New Church Clock

Henceforward shall our time be plainly read—
Down in the nave I catch the twofold beat
Of those full-weighted moments overhead;
And hark! the hour goes clanging down the street
To the open plain! How sweet at eventide
Will that clear music be to toil-worn men!
Calling them home, each to his own fire-side;
How sweet the toll of all the hours till then!
The cattle, too, the self-same sound shall hear,
But they can never know the power it wields
O'er human hearts, that labour, hope, and fear;
Our village-clock means nought to steed or steer;
The call of Time will share each twinkling ear
With summer flies and voices from the fields!

Charles Tennyson Turner, *Sonnets* (1872)

In a Country Church

To one kneeling down no word came,
Only the wind's song, saddening the lips
Of the grave saints, rigid in glass;
Or the dry whisper of unseen wings,
Bats not angels, in the high roof.

Was he balked by silence? He kneeled long,
And saw love in a dark crown
Of thorns blazing, and a winter tree
Golden with fruit of a man's body.

R. S. Thomas, *Song at the Year's Turning* (1955)

English churches

The English garden is proverbial for beauty; and the English cottage garden stands almost alone in the world. Except where smoke, stench, and the havoc of manufacturing and mining operations have utterly deformed the blessed face of Nature, the English cottager commonly and spontaneously provides some little pasture for his eye by clothing his home in the beauty of shrubs and flowers. And even where he has been thus violently deprived of his lifelong communion with Nature, or where his lot is cast in huge cities from which he scarcely ever escapes, he still resorts to potted flowers and to the song of caged birds for solace. This love of natural objects, which are scarcely ever without beauty or grace, ought to supply a basis on which to build all that is still wanting. But I turn to another chapter. The ancient ecclesiastical architecture of this country indicates a more copiously diffused love and pursuit of beauty, and a richer faculty for its production, in connection with purpose, than is to be found in the churches of any other part of Christendom. Not that we possess in our cathedrals and greater edifices the most splendid of all examples. But the parish churches of England are as a whole unrivalled; and it has been the opinion of persons of the widest knowledge, that they might even challenge without fear the united parish churches of Europe, from their wealth of beauty in all the particulars of their own styles of architecture.

W. E. Gladstone, *The Church of England and Ritualism* (1873)

The candlesticks

The use of a row of six candlesticks on the altar, or on its shelf or gradine, is pure Romanism, and a defiance of the Ornaments Rubric, as of all other authority in the Church of England.* From the begin-

33

ning of the thirteenth century to the end of the nineteenth every declaration on the subject has mentioned the two lights on the altar only, and to this primitive and universal use of two lights at the most every known representation bears witness. Any one within reach of a picture-gallery can verify this for himself; in the National Gallery, for instance, are many illustrations of great interest in the Flemish, German, and Italian rooms and among the drawings of the Arundel Collection in the basement. The evidence of inventories, directories, etc., is practically the same. Now the instinct which led the Church in the great ages of architecture and craftsmanship to use altar lights in this way was a true one; for an altar with two candlesticks upon it is more majestic and more beautiful than an altar with more than two. Furthermore, a row of candles hides the reredos or upper frontal, which ought to be one of the richest and most lovely things in the church: the miserable way in which priceless masterpieces are hidden in the churches of Italy by tall candlesticks and tawdry sham flowers is painfully familiar to every traveller.

* No doubt most parsons have set up this distinctively Roman Catholic feature in honest ignorance, and without any intention of converting their churches into a feeble imitation of those which Romanists have intruded into the parishes of England. But a mistake having been made, the most honest and manly course is to acknowledge and correct it. The attempt to perpetuate it by pretending that the lights, being on a gradine, are not altar lights at all, is too puerile to need further mention. Such methods only bring us into discredit.

Percy Dearmer, *The Parson's Handbook* (1903)

Draping the communion table on Good Friday

Sunday, 21 April 1871
I hear that Houseman at Bredwardine wishing to drape the Communion table with black on Good Friday and having no black drapery suitable for the purpose was misguided enough to put over the Table the old filthy parish pall. Everyone was disgusted and shocked at what they considered a piece of indecency. It is the talk of the country and Miss Newton is up in arms.

Francis Kilvert, *Diaries* (1974)

Mr Sibthorpe's Proprietary Chapel on the Isle of Wight

The refurnishing of Mr Richard Waldo Sibthorpe's S. James' Proprietary Chapel at Ryde, Isle of Wight, which was a stronghold of extreme evangelicalism in the 'forties just as it is to-day, led to some abusive criticism in *The Ecclesiologist*. We read that the chapel had been 'brought back to its original state, or to a condition even worse. The pulpit, etc. have been replaced before the Altar, the east window made to open, so as to communicate with a schoolroom adjoining, and to render the church itself useful in accommodating an audience to listen to religious speakers who occupy a platform in the said schoolroom.' At All Hallows and S. Petrock, Exeter, the altars were furnished with drawers, wherein parish papers were kept. The presence of WCs close to the altar was mentioned again and again. At S. James', Bermondsey, there were two – one for the clergy, the other for the congregation, on either side of the chancel.

Then we find a fascinating description (together with an illustration) of an 'Actual Arrangement of the Altar, Pulpit, and Reading Placc, of a Proprietary Chapel in a fashionable watering place.' Here 'the architect fixed over the Altar twin boxes or tubs for the desk and pulpit, precisely alike in size and shape, and in the very closest alliance, indeed you pass from No. 1 into No. 2. These boxes are fastened to the wall; but have no visible support and the wall itself, from its flimsy texture, must prove but a frail guardian. Should the preacher be weighty in person, and vehement in action, he will in falling cause these deformities to break from their moorings, and both he and his brother minister will be precipitated forwards at the risk of their necks and limbs.' At All Saints', Spitalfields, 'the pulpit, reading-pue, and clerk's pue, ranging one under the other, stood exactly in front of the Altar.' As to the font, it was merely a shallow square basin, like a frying-tin.

Peter Anson, *Fashions in Church Furnishings* (1960)

A hanging pyx

After dinner our host deposited Cyril Tomkinson and myself alone in the drawing-room with coffee and brandy. Cyril poured out the coffee and, taking a taste of it, gave a deep sigh of satisfaction. 'Thank God,' he said, 'for good coffee. There's far too much bad coffee about nowadays. People seem to think that God is pleased if they make it weak.' He then said that Father Raynes had no doubt told me that he was looking for a curate. Would I be interested in the job? I had indeed become very interested – I had never met a clergyman like Cyril – and I answered 'Yes.' 'I ought, then, to ask you a few questions. Do you mind?' 'Of course not,' I said. There was a slight pause, and Cyril then asked me: 'Are you the sort who falls in love with choirboys?' 'No,' I said, 'I'm afraid I'm not.' 'Don't apologize,' said Cyril, 'a clergyman's interests should never be confined to his church. Do you read Henry James?' 'No. I haven't read anything of his.' 'That's a pity. However, it can be arranged.' By this time I realized that he was enjoying playing Lady Bracknell and was observing both whether I had identified the rôle and also whether I would be crass enough to say so. I had noticed and I wasn't crass. So he offered me the job. He later told me that clergymen at All Saints, Margaret Street, had to have a certain degree of sophistication. 'Holiness is necessary. But it is not enough,' he added.

Later that week he showed me round the church. Over the high altar there is an enormous silver hanging pyx given in the early 1920s by the then Duke of Newcastle in memory of former members of the choir who had died in the First World War. At that time the pyx went up and down by electric motor. An enormous key, which looked as if it had strayed from a pantomime, had to be inserted in a lock in the surface of the altar to work the machine which made a horrible buzzing noise. 'My dear,' commented Cyril, 'in this church the good God lives in a lift.'

Harry Williams, *Some Day I'll Find You* (1986)

Ballade of Illegal Ornaments

'. . . *the controversy was ended by His Lordship, who wrote to the Incumbent ordering him to remove from the Church all Illegal Ornaments at once, and especially a Female Figure with a Child.*'

I

When that the Eternal deigned to look
   On us poor folk to make us free,
He chose a Maiden, whom He took
   From Nazareth in Galilee;

Since when the Islands of the Sea,
The Field, the City, and the Wild
  Proclaim aloud triumphantly
A Female Figure with a Child.

II

These Mysteries profoundly shook
  The Reverend Doctor Leigh, D.D.,
Who therefore stuck into a Nook
  (Or Niche) of his Incumbency
  An Image filled with majesty
To represent the Undefiled,
  The Universal Mother – She –
A Female Figure with a Child.

III

His Bishop, having read a book
  Which proved as plain as plain could be
That all the Mutts had been mistook
  Who talked about a Trinity,
  Wrote off at once to Doctor Leigh
In manner very far from mild,
  And said: 'Remove them instantly!
A Female Figure with a Child!'

Envoi

Prince Jesus, in mine Agony,
  Permit me, broken and defiled,
Through blurred and glazing eyes to see
  A Female Figure with a Child.

Hilaire Belloc, Verses (1932)

On the atmosphere of a church

The atmosphere of a church should be such as to hush the thoughtless
voice. It once was so amongst ourselves and still is so in France even
when the building may not be of arresting beauty. I have been
rebuked for talking to the organist about his music within one of the
doors of Dijon Cathedral, and I remember being told by the Vicar
at Hughenden the year Disraeli died that if anyone spoke to him in

the church he would take him out into the porch before he answered. Surely here to-day with all our new materialistic organizations we have lost something of the sense of what a church is.

'My Father's house is a house of prayer, but ye have made it a den of thieves.' It is a most stern saying; and as then, so now, it is commercialism that is at the bottom of these activities ('greed and careerism' as a modern writer has put it), though it may be disguised in such fine words that the users of them may not be conscious of it. 'The tables of the money changers' – have they not literally invaded some of our Cathedrals? And even when the money changers are not there, are we not reminded of the tables in visible shape in too many churches in England, both Anglican and Roman, for the sale of tracts of (often controversial) propaganda? Seldom are the books on these tables the Holy Gospels which I have seen in beautiful form at the west end of the Cathedral at Rheims.

But party propaganda and the sale of the Gospels (and even the preaching of the Gospel) is not the purpose of a church: for what is a church? – It is a building which enshrines the altar of Him who dwelleth not in temples made with hands and who yet has made there His Covenanted Presence on earth. It is the centre of Worship in every community of men who recognize Christ as the *Pantokrator*, the Almighty, the Ruler and Creator of all things; at its altar is pleaded the daily Sacrifice in complete union with the Church Triumphant in Heaven, of which He is the one and only Head, the High Priest for ever after the order of Melchisedech.

There is then no such thing as a Protestant church. A church is of its very nature Catholic, embracing all things. There are Protestant Meeting Houses for preaching, and for praying and hymn-singing in common, and they are not to be despised; but if they are more than a plain room, they have become a meaningless imitation of that from which of set purpose they broke away.

A church built with hands, as we are reminded at every Consecration and Dedication Feast, is the outward expression here on earth of that spiritual Church built of living stones, the Bride of Christ, *Urbs beata Jerusalem*, which stretches back to the foundation of the world and onwards to all eternity. With her Lord she lays claim to the whole of His Creation and to every philosophy and creed and work of man which His Holy Spirit has inspired. And so the temple here on earth, in different lands and in different shapes, in the East and in the West, has developed or added to itself fresh forms of beauty and, though it has suffered from iconoclasts and destroyers both within and without, and perhaps nowhere more than in this land, it has never broken with the past: it has never renounced its claim to continuity.

To enter therefore a Christian church is to enter none other than the House of God and the Gate of Heaven. It is to leave all strife, all disputes of the manner of Church government and doctrine outside – 'Thou shalt keep them secretly in Thy tabernacle from the strife of tongues' – and to enter here on earth into the Unity of the Church Triumphant in Heaven. It cannot be otherwise, since He Himself, who is the Temple of it, the Lamb slain from the foundation of the world, is there also. Such a conception of a church, however faintly realized, must put to shame the quarrels of Catholic Christians, who profess the same creeds but set up Church against Church.

Ninian Comper, *Of the Atmosphere of a Church* (1936)

[3]

SHRINES

The religious impulse has invested or discovered numinous qualities, not merely in buildings, but in places. It is noticeable how violently shrines are attacked whenever it is deemed necessary to change a people's religious persuasion, or to wipe it out altogether. One sees the same thing at work when the prophet Elijah tears down the high places of the prophets, when Henry VIII's men despoil the shrine of Our Lady at Walsingham, and when the Communist Chinese attack the monasteries of Tibet. In holy places, superstition has flourished, or, to put it another way, 'the ribs of our ancient earth are riddled with desperate pieties'. The words are those of John Cowper Powys and come from that brilliant chronicle of life in a shrine-town, *A Glastonbury Romance*.

'The builders of Stonehenge have perished,' Powys wrote, 'but there are those who worship its stones still. The builders of Glastonbury have perished; but there are people yet living among us whose eyes have seen the Grail . . . The Towers of Cybele still move in the darkness from cult to cult, from revelation to revelation. Made of a stuff more lasting than granite, older than basalt, harder than marble, and yet as insubstantial as the airiest mystery of Thought, these Towers of the journeying Mother still trouble the dreams of men with their tremulous uprising.' The over-written Powysian prose expresses something which I have felt when visiting shrines – either the well-known ones like Glastonbury or Walsingham, or little-known wells, circles and ruined chapels in Wales.

T. S. Eliot found in Little Gidding a place 'where prayer has been valid'. For many of us, it is less cerebral than that. There is some of Dean Stanley's feeling at the shrine of Becket: 'a gift of insight into the past, of loving it for its own sake, of retaining around us as much as we can of its grace and beauty'.

There is something stronger, and more elemental than that, though, in the cult of shrines, which would go some way to explain why their powerfulness can sometimes be creepy, and why there is, among those who cluster around shrines, much silliness mingled with the holiness. This quality is captured well in Colin Stephenson's account of Alfred Hope Patten, the man who restored the Shrine of Walsingham in 1931, and who, as we read here, was so obsessed by collecting relics that he attracted some absurd practical jokers – as well as inspiring the magnificently-turned indignation of the then Bishop of Durham, Hensley Henson.

Colin Stephenson was attacked by many who revered Hope Patten. His portrait was thought to be unfair, and even impious; but it was written from the point of view of a man who, deep down, took the cult of Walsingham extremely seriously – and who did more than anyone else to popularize the shrine after Hope Patten died.

Medieval pilgrimages to Walsingham

Bidderes and beggeres faste aboute yede *Beggars; went*
[Til] hire bely and hire bagge [were] bredful ycrammed, *belly; brimful*
Faiteden for hire foode, foughten at the ale. *Begged falsely; ale house*
In glotonye, God woot, go thei to bedde, *gluttony; knows*
And risen with ribaudie, tho Roberdes knaves; *obscenities; vagabonds (C)*
Sleep and sory sleuthe seweth hem evere. *wretched sloth; follow*
Pilgrymes and palmeres plighten hem togidere

vowed, pledged themselves
For to seken Seint Jame and seintes at Rome; *seek St James (C)*
Wenten forth in hire wey with many wise tales, *way; speeches*
And hadden leve to lyen al hire lif after. *leave; tell lies; life*
I seigh somme that seiden thei hadde ysought seintes: *saw; said*
To ech a tale that thei tolde hire tonge was tempred to lye

tongue; tuned
Moore than to seye sooth, it semed bi hire speche. *truth*
Heremytes on an heep with hoked staves *crowd; crooked*

Wenten to Walsyngham—and hire wenches after:
Grete lobies and longe that lothe were to swynke   *lubbers; tall; labour*
Clothed hem in copes to ben knowen from othere,

        Dressed; distinguished

And shopen hem heremytes hire ese to have.

      turned themselves into; comfort, ease

William Langland (c. 1330–86) *Piers Plowman*

A Lament for our Lady's Shrine at Walsingham

In the wrackes of Walsingam
Whom should I chuse,
But the Queene of Walsingham
   to be guide to my muse
Then thou Prince of Walsingham
   graunt me to frame,
Bitter plaintes to rewe thy wronge,
   bitter wo for thy name,
Bitter was it soe to see,
   The seely sheepe
Murdred by the raveninge wolves
   While the sheephardes did sleep,
Bitter was it oh to vewe
   the sacred vyne,
Whiles the gardiners plaied all close,
   rooted up by the swine.
Bitter bitter oh to behould,
   the grasse to growe
Where the walles of Walsingam
   so statly did shewe,
Such were the workes of Walsingam:
   while shee did stand
Such are the wrackes as now do shewe
   of that holy land,
Levell Levell with the ground
   the towres doe lye
Which with their golden glitteringe tops
   Pearsed once to the skye,

Wher weare gates no gates ar nowe,
   the waies unknowen
Wher the presse of peares did passe
   While her fame far was blowen.
Oules do scrike wher the sweetest himnes
   lately weer songe
Toades and serpentes hold ther dennes,
   Wher the Palmers did thronge.
Weepe, weepe o Walsingam
   Whose dayes are nightes
Blessinges turned to blasphemies
   Holy deedes to dispites,
Sinne is wher our Ladie sate
   Heaven turned is to Hell.
Sathan sittes wher our Lord did swaye
   Walsingam oh farewell.

Anon

Hope Patten's collection of relics

Hope was at the height of his enthusiasm about relics, having recently added greatly to his collection. Readers of the *Mirror* were told:

A letter came from a devout client of Our Lady of Walsingham offering us a relic of St Hugh BC. St Hugh is the chief patron of the Administrator. One of his great ambitions has been to have relics of St Hugh and St Thomas of Canterbury. The latter was sent to the Shrine last year from America, and now one of the great Carthusian Bishop of Lincoln has come. It seemed to be beyond one's wildest dreams ever to have these treasures at the Shrine. They are most unusual and difficult to come by. Of course, in both cases they are properly sealed and accompanied by the letters of authentication.

He had no sense of humour about this rather 'cigarette card collecting' approach, and when some of his young men in the college enclosed a feather in a reliquary and labelled it 'St Michael', so that a rather innocent nun placed it on the altar, he was furiously angry.

Colin Stephenson, *Walsingham Way* (1969)

43

Hensley Henson's indignation

The Dean and Mrs Cranage motored me to Walsingham, and showed me the Anglican shrine, and the Roman Catholick 'Slipper Chapel', now restored and enlarged. The latter was far less aggressively superstitious than the former. Nothing seemed to be omitted which could insult good sense, violate good taste, and show contempt for the English Church. The bizarre superstitions of Lourdes were moderate and reasonable beside the tawdry and vulgar improvisation of 'Anglican' Walsingham. One could almost understand the iconoclasm of a Dowsing, and brazen Protestantism of a Kensit! The Bishop of Norwich, who is known to loathe this repulsive illegality, feels himself to be impotent, and tolerates what he must needs lament, and condemn. I was reminded of the replica of the Lourdes grotto which is so conspicuous in the garden of the Vatican. It is said that this preposterous shrine at Walsingham attracts large numbers of Anglican pilgrims. Meanwhile the Papists are 'digging themselves in', buying everything they can, and preparing for the victory which they confidently expect. I was amazed at the spectacle which I beheld. The patron of Walsingham is said to be disgusted with the parochial régime, which now exists, and when the benefice becomes vacant, he may be able to make an appointment which will restore Anglican churchmanship. But that may not be easy to achieve, in the face of the opposition that such an effort would encounter.

Hensley Henson, *Retrospect of an Unimportant Life* (1940)

The hazards of visiting shrines in the wrong frame of mind

It happened in this same neighbourhood that a boy tried to steal some young pigeons from a nest in Saint David's church in Llanfaes. His hand stuck fast to the stone on which he was leaning, this being no doubt a miraculous punishment inflicted by the Saint, who was protecting the birds of his own church. For three days and nights the boy, accompanied by his parents and his friends, offered vigils, fasts and prayers at the church altar. On the third day, by God's intervention, the power which held his hand fast was loosened and he was released from the miraculous force which bound him there to the stone. I myself saw this same boy, then no longer young but

44

become an old man living in Newbury in England, for so the years had passed, when he appeared before David II, Bishop of St David's, and confirmed that these events really had occurred, the reason for this being, of course, that they had taken place in that Bishop's own diocese. The stone is preserved to this day among the relics of the church in question, with the marks of the boy's fingers pressed into the flint as though in wax and clearly visible.

In our own lifetime a miracle very similar to this happened in Bury St Edmunds. A poor woman used to visit the Saint's shrine, ostensibly to pay her devotions. She came not to give, but to take away. It was her habit to steal the gold and silver offered by others. The way she took it was extremely clever, for she would kiss it, suck it into her lips as she did so, and then carry it away hidden in her mouth. One day as she was actually doing this, such being her custom, her lips and tongue stuck fast to the altar. She was caught in the act by divine intervention, and she spat out the piece of silver which she had in her mouth. A great crowd of people came running to gape at this, some of them Jews and some of them Christians. There she remained, fixed and motionless, for the greater part of the day, so that the miracle was clear for all to see and there could be no doubt about it in anyone's mind.

In the north of England, just across the Humber, in Howden church, the parson's *belle amie* sat herself down without thinking on the wooden tomb of Saint Osana, the sister of King Osred, which jutted out in an open space as if it were a seat. When she wanted to get up, her backside stuck tight to the wood and she was unable to wrench herself free. The people came running. They cut away her clothing until she was quite naked and kept beating her hard with lashes until the blood flowed. She wept bitterly and prayed for forgiveness. In view of her repentance and the penalty which she had paid, she was freed by divine intervention and allowed to go home.

Giraldus Cambrensis (c. 1146–1220), *A Journey through Wales*

Bury St Edmunds

What a scene; shining luminous effulgent, as the lamps of St Edmund do, through the dark Night; John of Dice, with vestrymen, clambering on the roof to look through; the Convent all asleep, and the

Earth all asleep – and since then, Seven Centuries of Time mostly gone to sleep! Yes, there, sure enough, is the martyred Body of Edmund, landlord of the Eastern Counties, who, nobly doing what he liked with his own, was slain three hundred years ago: and a noble awe surrounds the memory of him, symbol and promoter of many other right noble things.

But have not we now advanced to strange new stages of Hero-worship, now in the little Church of Hampden, with our penknives out, and twelve grave-diggers with pulleys? The manner of men's Hero-worship, verily it is the innermost fact of their existence, and determines all the rest – at public hustings, in private drawing-rooms, in church, in market, and wherever else. Have true reverence, and what indeed is inseparable therefrom, reverence the right man, all is well; have sham-reverence, and what also follows, greet with it the wrong man, then all is ill, and there is nothing well. Alas, if Hero-worship become Dilettantism, and all except Mammonism be a vain grimace, how much, in this most earnest Earth, has gone and is evermore going to fatal destruction, and lies wasting in quiet lazy ruin, no man regarding it! Till at length no heavenly *Ism* any longer coming down upon us, *Isms* from the other quarter have to mount up. For the Earth, I say, is an earnest place; Life is no grimace, but a most serious fact. And so, under universal Dilettantism much having been stript bare, not the souls of men only, but their very bodies and bread-cupboards having been stript bare, and life now no longer possible – all is reduced to desperation, to the iron law of Necessity and very Fact again; and to temper Dilettantism, and astonish it, and burn it up with infernal fire, arises Chartism, *Bare-backism*, Sansculottism so-called! May the gods, and what of unworshipped heroes still remain among us, avert the omen!

But however this may be, St Edmund's Loculus, we find, has the veils of silk and linen reverently replaced, the lid fastened down again with its sixteen ancient nails; is wrapt in a new costly covering of silk, the gift of Hubert Archbishop of Canterbury: and through the sky-window John of Dice sees it lifted to its place in the Shrine, the pannels of this latter duly refixed, fit parchment documents being introduced withal – and now John and his vestry-men can slide down from the roof, for all is over, and the Convent wholly awakens to matins. 'When we assembled to sing matins,' says Jocelin, 'and understood what had been done, grief took hold of all that had not

seen these things, each saying to himself: "Alas, I was deceived."
Matins over, the Abbot called the Convent to the great Altar; and
briefly recounting the matter, alleged that it had not been in his
power, nor was it permissible or fit, to invite us all to the sight of
such things. At hearing of which, we all wept, and with tears sang
Te Deum laudamus; and hastened to toll the bells in the Choir.'

Stupid blockheads, to reverence their St Edmunds's dead Body in
this manner? Yes, brother – and yet, on the whole, who knows how
to reverence the Body of a Man? It is the most reverend phenomenon
under this Sun. For the Highest God dwells visible in that mystic
unfathomable Visibility, which calls itself 'I' on the Earth. 'Bending
before men', says Novalis, 'is a reverence done to this Revelation in
the Flesh. We touch Heaven when we lay our hand on a human
Body.' And the Body of one Dead – a temple where the Hero-soul
once was and now is not: Oh, all mystery, all pity, all mute *awe* and
wonder; *Super*naturalism brought home to the very dullest; Eternity
laid open, and the nether Darkness and the upper Light-Kingdoms,
do conjoin there, or exist nowhere!

Thomas Carlyle, *Past and Present* (1843)

Canterbury

Round it still lie the tombs of King, and Prince, and Archbishop; the
worn marks on the stones show the reverence of former ages. But
the place itself is vacant, and the lessons which that vacancy has to
teach us must now take the place of the lessons of the ancient Shrine.

There are very few probably at the present time, in whom, as they
look round on the desolate pavement, the first feeling that arises is
not one of disappointment and regret, that a monument of past times
so costly and curious should have been thus entirely obliterated.
There is probably no one, who, if the Shrine were now standing,
would dream of removing it. One such tomb, as has been said, still
remains in Westminster Abbey: the very notion of destroying it would
call out a general outcry from all educated men throughout the
kingdom. Why is it that this feeling, so familiar and so natural to
us, should then have been so completely overruled? The answer to
this question is doubly instructive. First, it reveals to us one great
difference between our age and the time, not only of the Reformation,

but of many preceding ages. In our time, there has sprung up, to a degree hitherto unprecedented, a love of what is old, of what is beautiful, of what is venerable – a desire to cherish the memorials of the past, and to keep before our eyes the vestiges of times, which are brought so vividly before us in no other way. It is, as it were, God's compensation to the world for its advancing years. Earlier ages care but little for these relics of antiquity; one is swept away after another to make room for what is yet to come; precious works of art, precious recollections, are trampled under foot; the very abundance in which they exist seems to beget an indifference towards them. But in proportion as they become fewer and fewer, the affection for them grows stronger and stronger; and the further we recede from the past, the more eager now seems our craving to attach ourselves to it by every link that remains. Such a feeling it is, which most of us would entertain towards this ancient Shrine – such a feeling as, in the mass of men, hardly existed at the time of its destruction. In this respect at least we are richer than were our fathers; other gifts they had, which we have not: this gift of insight into the past, of loving it for its own sake, of retaining around us as much as we can of its grace and beauty – we have, as they had not. It is true that reverence for the dead ought never to stand in the way of the living – that when any great evil is avoided, or any great good attained, by destroying old recollections, no historical or antiquarian tenderness can be pleaded for their preservation: but where no such reason exists, let us keep them as best we can, and as we stand on the vacant space of Becket's Shrine, let us be thankful that we have retained what we have, and cherish it accordingly.

Arthur Stanley, *Historical Memorials of Canterbury Cathedral* (1883)

Little Gidding

If you came this way,
Taking the route you would be likely to take
From the place you would be likely to come from,
If you came this way in May time, you would find the hedges
White again, in May, with voluptuary sweetness.
It would be the same at the end of the journey,
If you came at night like a broken king,

If you came by day not knowing what you came for,
It would be the same, when you leave the rough road
And turn behind the pig-sty to the dull façade
And the tombstone. And what you thought you came for
Is only a shell, a husk of meaning
From which the purpose breaks only when it is fulfilled
If at all. Either you had no purpose
Or the purpose is beyond the end you figured
And is altered in fulfilment. There are other places
Which also are the world's end, some at the sea jaws,
Or over a dark lake, in a desert or a city –
But this is the nearest, in place and time,
Now and in England.

       If you came this way,
Taking any route, starting from anywhere,
At any time or at any seasons,
It would always be the same: you would have to put off
Sense and notion. You are not here to verify,
Instruct yourself, or inform curiosity
Or carry report. You are here to kneel
Where prayer has been valid. And prayer is more
Than an order of words, the conscious occupation
Of the praying mind, or the sound of the voice praying.
And what the dead had no speech for, when living,
They can tell you, being dead: the communication
Of the dead is tongued with fire beyond the language of the living.
Here, the intersection of the timeless moment
Is England and nowhere. Never and always.

                          T. S. Eliot, *Four Quartets* (1944)

[4]

CHURCH-GOING

One Sunday morning not long ago in Istanbul, I decided that I should like to go to church, and I made my way to the Christan quarter of the city, a warren of slummy streets climbing the steep hill above the Golden Horn. I was trying to find the Greek Orthodox Patriarchate, which I had visited once before, but I lost my way. After a sign-language conversation with two amused Turkish policemen, I was led through a market, where boys held up live chickens by the legs for the inspection of potential purchasers, and where sheep milled about with human beings in a little court-yard – not dissimilar in atmosphere, I should imagine, from the Temple Courts of Jerusalem in the time of Christ. On the inner corner of this smelly little court-yard, a large door was open, and from the inside of this door, I heard the noise of Armenian worshippers at morning service.

A bearded man in a crown – a bishop? – stood at the altar, chanting, and waving incense. A number of old men in liturgical costume stood around, also bellowing like the bulls of Bashan. At another altar, one of the old men periodically stopped chanting, and carried children round the altar three times. The large, and attentive congregation occasionally joined in song, or hit the floor with their hands, or made the sign of the cross. Though reasonably experienced as a church-goer, and familiar with the rites of Rome, Moscow and Constantinople, I had no idea, at any point, what was going on. Had we reached the epistle, when, after about an hour, one of the old men in a blue robe carried a book to a lectern and bawled at us with high fervour? Or was it merely the notices, advising us of the Armenian equivalent of a meeting of the Mother's Union, to be held in the Church Hall next Tuesday? As often, when surrounded by a large crowd of religious people at worship, I was moved – but completely baffled by the proceedings. There was little or nothing in the ritual or symbolism to suggest the story of the Last Supper which was, presumably, amid all the chanting, and bowing and walking about, being re-enacted.

A similar sense of bafflement would, doubtless, be felt by an Armenian Christian attending the morning service at an Anglican cathedral. Certainly, non-Christians find the goings-on in Christian places of worship pretty incomprehensible, even when – as so often nowadays in the modern services – some helpful clergyman is providing us with stage directions: 'We will now make our confession to Almighty God and turn to Section 43 of the blue leaflet.'

from Il Penseroso

But let my due feet never fail,
To walk the studious Cloysters pale.
And love the high embowed Roof,
With antick Pillars massy proof,
And storied Windows richly dight,
Casting a dimm religious light.
There let the pealing Organ blow,
To the full voic'd Quire below,
In Service high, and Anthems cleer,
As may with sweetness, through mine ear,
Dissolve me into extasies,
And bring all Heav'n before mine eyes.
And may at last my weary age
Find out the peacefull hermitage,
The Hairy Gown and Mossy Cell,
Where I may sit and rightly spell
Of every Star that Heav'n doth shew,
And every Herb that sips the dew;
Till old experience do attain
To something like Prophetic strain.

These pleasures *Melancholy* give,
And I with thee will choose to live.

John Milton (1608–74)

An unintentional confirmation

31 March 1870
In Hadley's shop I met Dewing who told me of a most extraordinary
misfortune that befell Pope the curate of Cusop yesterday at the
Whitney Confirmation. He had one candidate Miss Stokes a farmer's
daughter and they went together by train. Pope went in a cutaway
coat very short, with his dog, and took no gown. The train was very
late. He came very late into church and sat down on a bench with
the girl cheek by jowl. When it came to his turn to present his
candidate he was told by the Rector (Henry Dew) or someone in
authority to explain why he came so late. The Bishop of Hereford
(Atlay) has a new fashion of confirming only two persons at a time,
kneeling at the rails. The Bishop had marked two young people come
in very late and when they came up to the rails he thought from
Pope's youthful appearance and from his having no gown that he
was a young farmer candidate and brother of the girl. He spoke to
them severely and told them to come on and kneel down for they
were extremely late. Pope tried to explain that he was a clergyman
and that the girl was his candidate but the Bishop was overbearing
and imperious and either did not hear or did not attend, seeming to
think he was dealing with a refractory ill-conditioned youth. 'I know,
I know,' he said. 'Come at once, kneel down, kneel down.' Poor
Pope resisted a long time and had a long battle with the Bishop, but
at last unhappily he was overborne in the struggle, lost his head,
gave way, knelt down and was *confirmed* there and then, and no
one seems to have interfered to save him, though Mr Palmer of
Eardisley and others were sitting close by and the whole Church was
in a titter. It is a most unfortunate thing and will never be forgotten
and it will be unhappily a joke against Pope all his life. The Bishop
was told of his mistake afterwards and apologized to Pope, though
rather shortly and cavalierly. He said, what was quite true, that Pope
ought to have come in his gown.

Francis Kilvert, *Diaries* (1974)

The times of services

The difficulties that remain nowadays are principally concerned with the hour of the service. The intention of the Prayer Book undoubtedly is that when there is only one Communion on a Sunday, this should be the principal service of the day, and that at which the sermon is preached. Our present habit is to fix the principal morning service so late that fasting communion is difficult; but this habit has come down to us from the days of infrequent Communions, and it is very probable that with improved ideas the principal service will tend towards an earlier hour. It is also probable that this will become necessary owing to the increasing practice of bicycling, etc., on Sundays.

Percy Dearmer, *The Parson's Handbook* (1903)

The Bugler's First Communion

A Bugler boy from barrack (it is over the hill
There) – boy bugler, born, he tells me, of Irish
    Mother to an English sire (he
Shares their best gifts surely, fall how things will),

This very very day came down to us after a boon he on
My late being there begged of me, overflowing
    Boon in my bestowing,
Came, I say, this day to it – to a First Communion.

Here he knelt then in regimental red.
Forth Christ from cupboard fetched, how fain I of feet
    To his youngster take his treat!
Low-latched in leaf-light housel his too huge godhead.

There! and your sweetest sendings, ah divine,
By it, heavens, befall him! as a heart Christ's darling, dauntless;
    Tongue true, vaunt- and tauntless;
Breathing bloom of a chastity in mansex fine.

Frowning and forefending angel-warder
Squander the hell-rook ranks sally to molest him;
    March, kind comrade, abreast him;
Dress his days to a dexterous and starlight order.

How it dóes my heart good, visiting at that bleak hill,
When limber liquid youth, that to all I teach
    Yields tender as a pushed peach,
Hies headstrong to its wellbeing of a self-wise self-will!

Then though I should tread tufts of consolation
Dáys áfter, só I in a sort deserve to
    And do serve God to serve to
Just such slips of soldiery Christ's royal ration.

Nothing élse is like it, no, not all so strains
Us: fresh youth fretted in a bloomfall all portending
    That sweet's sweeter ending;
Realm both Christ is heir to and thére réigns.

O now well work that sealing sacred ointment!
O for now charms, arms, what bans off bad
    And locks love ever in a lad!
Let mé though see no more of him, and not disappointment

Those sweet hopes quell whose least me quickenings lift,
In scarlet or somewhere of some day seeing
    That brow and bead of being,
An our day's God own Galahad. Though this child's drift

Seems by a divíne doom chánnelled, nor do I cry
Disaster there; but may he not rankle and roam
    In backwheels though bound home? –
That left to the Lord of the Eucharist, I here lie by;

Recorded only, I have put my lips on pleas
Would brandle adamantine heaven with ride and jar, did
    Prayer go disregarded:
Forward-like, but however, and like favourable heaven heard these.

Gerard Manley Hopkins (1844–89)

Seventeenth-century high church

That night Mr Crashaw, Inglesant, and one or two others, remained
in the Church from nine till twelve, during which time they said over
the whole Book of Psalms in the way of antiphony, one repeating

one verse and the rest the other. The time of their watch being ended they returned to the house, went to Mr Ferrar's door and bade him good-morrow, leaving a lighted candle for him. They then went to bed, but Mr Ferrar arose according to the passage of Scripture 'at midnight I will arise and give thanks,' and went into the Church, where he betook himself to religious meditation.

Early on the Sunday morning the family were astir and said prayers in the oratory. After breakfast many people from the country around and more than a hundred children came in. These children were called the Psalm children, and were regularly trained to repeat the Psalter, and the best voices among them to assist in the service on Sundays. They came in every Sunday, and according to the proficiency of each were presented with a small piece of money, and the whole number entertained with a dinner after Church. The Church was crowded at the morning service before the Sacrament. The service was beautifully sung, the whole family taking the greatest delight in Church music, and many of the gentlemen from Cambridge being amateurs. The Sacrament was administered with the greatest devotion and solemnity. Impressed as he had been with the occupation of the preceding day and night, and his mind excited with watching and want of sleep and with the exquisite strains of the music, the effect upon Inglesant's imaginative nature was excessive. Above the altar, which was profusely bedecked with flowers, the antique glass of the east window, which had been carefully repaired, contained a figure of the Saviour of an early and severe type. The form was gracious and yet commanding, having a brilliant halo round the head, and being clothed in a long and apparently seamless coat; the two fore-fingers of the right hand were held up to bless. Kneeling upon the half-pace, as he received the sacred bread and tasted the holy wine, this gracious figure entered into Inglesant's soul, and stillness and peace unspeakable, and life, and light, and sweetness, filled his mind. He was lost in a sense of rapture, and earth and all that surrounded him faded away. When he returned a little to himself, kneeling in his seat in the Church, he thought that at no period of his life, however extended, should he ever forget that morning or lose the sense and feeling of that touching scene, of that gracious figure over the altar, of the bowed and kneeling figures, of the misty autumn sunlight and the sweeping autumn wind. Heaven itself seemed to have opened to him, and one fairer than the fairest of the angelic hosts to have come down to earth.

Henry Shorthouse, *John Inglesant* (1881)

No gum boots in Church

Sunday 26th February
Thaw and slush. Impossible to go to Church except in gum boots, and I still retain enough of the Irish Protestant leaven to regard that as a somewhat sacrilegious proceeding. So stopped at home.

W. H. Lewis, *Brothers and Friends* (1987)

Anti-ritualist

Palm Sunday 1934
To church in the morning where there was a distribution of palm crosses: Thomas came down to the steps at the top of the nave, accompanied by a server with a basket of palms, and we all went up and got one, except J[ack].* I too would have liked to avoid doing so, for I do not find that sort of thing is of any help to me from a devotional point of view: and I think there is a quite real risk that an imaginative child may get the impression that its bit of palm is in some way a magical charm: however, I hadn't the nerve not to go up for mine. I burnt it as soon as I got home. [This evening I went] with J to Evensong, where, oddly enough, the Bursar of Cuddesdon College preached on Prayer. We did not quite agree about the sermon: I thought it on the whole good, and J thought it on the whole bad – but we agreed that it was at any rate not dull . . . [O]ne of his stories I was however glad to hear: how St Theresa wrote to a friend that she never finished her prayers without saying to herself, 'Well thank goodness that's over'.

W. H. Lewis, *Brothers and Friends* (1987)

* i.e. C. S. Lewis.

Anglican church-going

How dignified, how stately, how elegant, with ranks of tapers waver-
ing gold against a dim background, while boys' voices lift the psalm
Audite hæc, omnes high above the pealing organ to the high
embowed roof, to linger and wander there among ten thousand cells.
Through the windows richly dight, slant crimson, violet and deep
blue rays of October evening sunshine; it touches the round heads
and white surplices of little singing boys; it glints on the altar, dim-
ming the tall, flickering flames, gleaming on the heads of thoughtful
clergymen who listen to the quire's chant. *For he shall carry nothing
away with him when he dieth: neither shall his pomp follow him.
For while he lived he counted himself an happy man: and so long as
thou doest well unto thyself, men will speak good of thee. He shall
follow the generation of his fathers: and shall never see light. Man
being in honour hath no understanding: but is compared unto the
beasts that perish*. . .

The soft and melancholy chant dies on a falling lilt. The clergy,
quire and people sit down in deep oak seats, all but the lector, who
rustles to the lectern, adjusts his pince-nez, and says gently, '*Here
beginneth the first verse of the sixth chapter of the Book of Micah.
Hear ye now what the Lord saith: Arise, contend thou before the
mountains, and let the hills hear thy voice* . . .'

The musical Eton-and-Cambridge monotone, just not parsonically
pitched, strolls on, relating the Lord's controversy in the mountains
with his people. I turn the pages of my Prayer Book, read the charming rubics, read the Preface, of 1662, so gentlemanlike, so suavely
urbane. *It hath been the wisdom of the Church of England, ever
since the first compiling of her Publick Liturgy, to keep the mean
between the two extremes*. . .

And then, Of Ceremonies, why some be abolished and some
retained. . . . *And moreover, they be neither dark nor dumb ceremonies, but are so set forth, that every man may understand what
they do mean, and to what use they do serve*. . . . *And in these our
doings we condemn no other Nations, nor prescribe anything but to
our own people only: For we think it convenient that every Country
should use such Ceremonies as they shall think best to the setting
forth of God's honour and glory, and to the reducing of the people
to a most perfect and godly living*. . .

57

Meanwhile, the Eton-and-Cambridge voice is gently putting searching inquiries, becoming reluctantly menacing. *Are there yet*, it asks, *the treasures of wickedness in the house of the wicked, and the scant measure that is abominable? Shall I count them pure with the wicked balances, and with the bag of deceitful weights? . . . Therefore also will I make thee sick in smiting thee, in making thee desolate because of thy sins. Thou shalt eat, but not be satisfied. . . Thou shalt sow, but thou shalt not reap; thou shalt tread the olives, but thou shalt not anoint thee with oil, and sweet wine, but shalt not drink wine. . . That I should make thee a desolation, and the inhabitants thereof a hissing. . .*

It has grown too violent, this mountain controversy. *Here endeth the first Lesson*, and so to the Magnificat. One feels that it was time.

These violent Hebrews: they break in strangely, with hot Eastern declamation and gesture, into our tranquil Anglican service, our so ordered and so decent Common Prayer. A desolation and a hissing: those are not threats that our kindly clergy like to quote, even against those of their flock who have abominable scant measures and wicked balances. Milton railed against 'the oppressions of a simonious, decimating clergy,' but, though they cannot help (since they must live) being decimating, they are no longer so simonious, and are a kindly race.

As to these services, which they long since so gracefully adapted, so fitly, beautifully, and ceremoniously translated and assembled, they are, as Sir John Suckling pointed out three centuries ago, fit for the attendance of even the fastidious Cato, who was disgusted by those of his own age and country. 'Then,' complained the shocked Sir John, 'the Ceremonies of *Liber Pater* and *Ceres*, how obscene! and those Days which were set apart for the Honour of the Gods, celebrated with such shews as *Cato* himself was ashamed to be present at. On the contrary, our Services are such, as not only *Cato*, but God himself may be there.'

Or so, at least, we hope. No doubt the Romans hoped too that Liber Pater and Ceres were present with them at worship, and that their lectisternia were enjoyed by the reclining and feasting deities. Be that as it may, and whatever the gods may think of it (and one must endeavour not to fall into arrogance in this matter of divine attendance at our worship), for my part I greatly admire and enjoy the Anglican order.

Though of course there is, from time to time, a sermon. . . . But it seems that this cannot, in any Church, be helped.

Rose Macaulay, *Personal Pleasures* (1935)

An encounter with a Protestant in a London church

Well, I attended the S. Thomas's Mass, and managed this time to catch the right moment to [go] up to the altar; in front of me was one of those helpful women who know all the answers to unspoken versicles by the priest, and she even rang a little bell at the right moments. When I came out, another woman who had been there accosted me, with some ferocity. The dialogue ran like this:

'Is this a *Roman* church?'
'No, it's Church of England.'
'What about the 39 articles?'
'Well, how do you mean what about them? They never say them at early service anywhere, I think.'
'And what about all those *images?*'
'Well, churches do have images, don't they.'
'Not *Protestant* churches. This is more like a Catholic one.'
'Well, the C. of E. is both, I suppose.'
'I call it a SCANDAL. Something should be *done* about it.'

She departed in dudgeon; but what can she or will she do about it? Inform the National Union of Protestants, perhaps. I'm sure Fr Irvine and the others would be delighted if they sent a spy along and had a protest in church. . . . Poor old C. of E., with Romans to right of it, Protestants to left of it, volleying and thundering. It does indeed stand to be shot at.

Rose Macaulay, *Letters to a Friend* (1962)

Christ Church, Oxford

On the whole, of important places and services for the Christian souls of England, the choir of Christ Church was at that epoch of English history virtually the navel, and seat of life. There remained in it the traditions of Saxon, Norman, Elizabethan, religion unbroken – the memory of loyalty, the reality of learning, and, in nominal obedience at least, and in the heart of them with true docility, stood every morning, to be animated for the highest duties owed to their country, the noblest of English youth. The greater number of the peers of England, and, as a rule, the best of her squirealty, passed necessarily through Christ Church.

The cathedral itself was an epitome of English history. Every stone, every pane of glass, every panel of woodwork, was true, and of its time – not an accursed sham of architect's job. The first shrine of St Frideswide had indeed been destroyed, and her body rent and scattered on the dust by the Puritan; but her second shrine was still beautiful in its kind – most lovely English work both of heart and hand. The Norman vaults above were true English Norman; bad and rude enough, but the best we could do with our own wits, and no French help. The roof was true Tudor – grotesque, inventively constructive, delicately carved; it, with the roof of the hall staircase, summing the builder's skill of the fifteenth century. The west window, with its clumsy painting of the Adoration of the Shepherds, a monument of the transition from window to picture which ended in Dutch pictures of the cattle without either shepherds or Christ – but still, the best men could do of the day; and the plain final woodwork of the stalls represented still the last art of living England in the form of honest and comfortable carpentry.

In this choir, written so closely and consecutively with indisputable British history, met every morning a congregation representing the best of what Britain had become – orderly, as the crew of a man-of-war, in the goodly ship of their temple. Every man in his place, according to his rank, age, and learning; every man of sense or heart there recognizing that he was either fulfilling, or being prepared to fulfil, the gravest duties required of Englishmen. A well-educated foreigner, admitted to that morning service, might have learned and judged more quickly and justly what the country had been, and still had power to be, than by months of stay in court or city. There, in his stall, sat the greatest divine of England – under his commandant niche, her greatest scholar – among the tutors the present Dean Liddell, and a man of curious intellectual power and simple virtue, Osborne Gordon. The group of noblemen gave, in the Marquis of Kildare, Earl of Desart, Earl of Emlyn, and Francis Charteris, now Lord Wemyss – the brightest types of high race and active power. Henry Acland and Charles Newton among the senior undergraduates, and I among the freshmen, showed, if one had known it, elements of curious possibilities in coming days. None of us then conscious of any need or chance of change, least of all the stern captain, who, with rounded brow and glittering dark eye, led in his old thunderous Latin the responses of the morning prayer.

For all that I saw, and was made to think, in that cathedral choir, I am most thankful to this day.

John Ruskin, *Præterita* (1886–9)

Morning Service

July 19, Sunday [1789]. . . . Mr Du Quesne and self walked this morning to Bruton Church, sat in the large Seat in the Chancel. We were misinformed about the time Divine Service began, as we were informed that it began at 11 instead of that it began at 10 this morning, consequently we were one Hour behind, and did not get to Church till just before the Communion Service. A Mr Roberts read Prayers and Preached there. A large Congregation attended at Church. Mr Robert White and Wife dined and spent the Afternoon at Cole, they came over on foot from Ansford. Fanny Woodforde from the Parsonage came over with them. Old Mrs Pounsett dined and spent the After. with us. In the Afternoon Mr Du Quesne, Mr Pounsett, self and Mr Robert White walked up to Mr Samuel Pounsetts and smoked a Pipe with him at Cole-Style and he gave us some Cocka-gee-Cyder. We returned back to Coffee and Tea. We had for Dinner some Fish, Trout, Whitings and Eels, some boiled Beef and a Loin of Veal &c. Mr White and Wife and Fanny Woodforde left us ab^r 8.

James Woodforde, *The Diary of a Country Parson* (1926)

Life of Dr Johnson

Next day we got to Harwich, to dinner; and my passage in the packet-boat to Helvoetsluys being secured, and my baggage put on board, we dined at our inn by ourselves. I happened to say, it would be terrible if he should not find a speedy opportunity of returning to London, and be confined in so dull a place. JOHNSON. 'Don't, Sir, accustom yourself to use big words for little matters. It would *not* be *terrible*, though I *were* to be detained some time here.' The practice of using words of disproportionate magnitude, is, no doubt, too frequent every where; but, I think, most remarkable among the French, of which, all who have travelled in France must have been struck with innumerable instances.

We went and looked at the church, and having gone into it, and walked up to the altar, Johnson, whose piety was constant and fervent, sent me to my knees, saying, 'Now that you are going to leave your native country, recommend yourself to the protection of your CREATOR and REDEEMER.'

After we came out of the church, we stood talking for some time together of Bishop Berkeley's ingenious sophistry to prove the non-existence of matter, and that every thing in the universe is merely ideal. I observed, that though we are satisfied his doctrine is not true, it is impossible to refute it. I never shall forget the alacrity with which Johnson answered, striking his foot with mighty force against a large stone, till he rebounded from it – 'I refute it *thus*.'

James Boswell, *The Life of Samuel Johnson* (1791)

At worship

. . . we entered a small low-arched door, secured by a wicket, which a grave-looking person seemed on the point of closing, and descended several steps as if into the funeral vaults beneath the church. It was even so; for in these subterranean precincts – why chosen for such a purpose I knew not – was established a very singular place of worship.

Conceive, Tresham, an extensive range of low-browed, dark, and twilight vaults, such as are used for sepulchres in other countries, and had long been dedicated to the same purpose in this, a portion of which was seated with pews, and used as a church. The part of the vaults thus occupied, though capable of containing a congregation of many hundreds, bore a small proportion to the darker and more extensive caverns which yawned around what may be termed the inhabited space. In those waste regions of oblivion, dusky banners and tattered escutcheons indicated the graves of those who were once, doubtless, 'princes in Israel'. Inscriptions, which could only be read by the painful antiquary, in language as obsolete as the act of devotional charity which they employed, invited the passengers to pray for the souls of those whose bodies rested beneath. Surrounded by these receptacles of the last remains of mortality, I found a numerous congregation engaged in the act of prayer. The Scotch perform this duty in a standing instead of a kneeling posture – more, perhaps, to take as broad a distinction as possible from the ritual of Rome than for any better reason; since I have observed, that in their family worship, as doubtless in their private devotions, they adopt, in their immediate address to the Deity, that posture which other Christians use as the humblest and most reverential. Standing, therefore, the men being uncovered, a crowd of several hundreds of both sexes, and all ages, listened with great reverence and attention to the extempore, at least the unwritten, prayer of an aged clergyman, who was very popular in the city. Educated in the same religious persuasion, I seriously bent my mind to join in the devotion of the day; and it was not till the congregation resumed their seats, that my attention was diverted to the consideration of the appearance of all around me.

At the conclusion of the prayer, most of the men put on their hats or bonnets, and all who had the happiness to have seats sate down.

Sir Walter Scott, Rob Roy (1817)

Eccentric and eclectic church-going habits

The years immediately following the First War witnessed the emergence in London of a whole host of thaumaturges and mystagogues both lay and clerical, and of the latter there can have been few at whose feet my mother did not at one time or another sit. As I grew older my unenthusiastic presence beside her was more frequently insisted on, but of all these innumerable Magi I retain clear recollections of only one or two. There was the Reverend Fearon who had at one time been curate to Archdeacon Wilberforce, a prelate for whom my mother always retained a peculiar reverence, and who presided over the destinies of the Church Mystical Union in a particularly depressing brick church in Norfolk Square wearing a scarlet cassock and a short, blond bob. In his sermons, which were long and largely incomprehensible, the word 'anthropomorphic' used exclusively in a pejorative sense, was of frequent occurrence, and the ritual was marked by long, long pauses of total silence during which we were exhorted to empty our minds of all extraneous thoughts and concentrate on Perfect Oneness. Try as I would, despite clouds of encouraging incense, the successful accomplishment of this feat always eluded me and, long before I came within spitting distance of Perfect Oneness, extraneous thoughts came crowding back, most of them lubricious.

After my mother finally broke with the Church Mystical Union, for reasons which I have long since forgotten, there followed a period spiritually dominated by a portly faith-healer who was also, I think, a lay-preacher whose services, to which mercifully I was only infrequently taken, consisted, as far as I can remember, almost entirely of silent prayer. Of his successor, however, the Bishop of Basil Street, my memories are vivid. This ecclesiastical ham whose charlatanism was, even for a schoolboy, palpable, claimed to have been consecrated by the Old Catholic Archbishop of Utrecht and wore the conventional purple-piped soutane and skull cap of a Roman bishop. His cathedral, known, if I remember rightly, as The Sanctuary, a Jacobean-style hall tucked away behind Harrods, was furnished, along with more familiar *bondieuseries*, with statues of Buddha, Zoroaster and Pythagoras, and boasted in addition a lavishly gilded bishop's throne in Wardour-Street Gothic which had once belonged, so the Bishop claimed, to Sarah Bernhardt. The congregation, numerous and well-heeled, was largely feminine but included one or two prominent merchant bankers whose credulity, so naïvely exalted was my childish estimate of Lombard Street shrewdness, never ceased to astonish me; the services were liturgically elaborate but despite the Bishop's wide experience and carefree borrowings there always clung to them a faint suggestion of improvisation inducing an embarrassment which at length out-weighed the fascinated curiosity which first acquaintance had aroused. On the whole, therefore, it was a great relief when my mother finally abandoned The Sanctuary and joined a Lodge of female Freemasons from attendance at whose rites my sex debarred me.

Osbert Lancaster, *All Done from Memory* (1953)

Afternoon Service at Mellstock
(*Circa* 1850)

On afternoons of drowsy calm
We stood in the panelled pew,
Singing one-voiced a Tate-and-Brady psalm
To the tune of 'Cambridge New.'

We watched the elms, we watched the rooks,
The clouds upon the breeze,
Between the whiles of glancing at our books,
And swaying like the trees.

So mindless were those outpourings! –
Though I am not aware
That I have gained by subtle thought on things
Since we stood psalming there.

Thomas Hardy, *Moments of Vision* (1917)

A dire Good Friday service

29 *March* [1975] A dire Good Friday service – the Bible (the gospel narrative) lamely paraphrased and meditations, so far from the old days when the preacher for the Three Hours Service would draw such a large congregation that extra chairs had to be brought in. A year now since my stroke and *Deo gratias* for my recovery.

Barbara Pym, *A Very Private Eye* (1985)

from Summoned by Bells

All silvery on frosty Sunday nights
Were City steeples white against the stars.
And narrowly the chasms wound between
Italianate counting-houses, Roman banks,
To this church and to that. Huge office-doors,
Their granite thresholds worn by weekday feet
(Now far away in slippered ease at Penge),
Stood locked. St Botolph this, St Mary that

Alone shone out resplendent in the dark.
I used to stand by intersecting lanes
Among the silent offices, and wait,
Choosing which bell to follow: not a peal,
For that meant somewhere active; not St Paul's,
For that was too well-known. I liked things dim –
Some lazy Rector living in Bexhill
Who most unwillingly on Sunday came
To take the statutory services.
A single bell would tinkle down a lane:
My echoing steps would track the source of sound –
A cassocked verger, bell-rope in his hands,
Called me to high box pews, to cedar wood
(Like incense where no incense ever burned),
To ticking gallery-clock, and charity bench,
And free seats for the poor, and altar-piece –
Gilded Commandment boards – and sword-rests made
For long-discarded aldermanic pomp.
A hidden organist sent reedy notes
To flute around the plasterwork. I stood,
And from the sea of pews a single head
With cherries nodding on a black straw hat
Rose in a neighbouring pew. The caretaker?
Or the sole resident parishioner?
And so once more, as for three hundred years,
This carven wood, these grey memorial'd walls
Heard once again the Book of Common Prayer,
While somewhere at the back the verger, now
Turned Parish Clerk, would rumble out 'Amen.'
'Twas not, I think, a conscious search for God
That brought me to these dim forgotten fanes.
Largely it was a longing for the past,
With a slight sense of something unfulfilled;
And yet another feeling drew me there,
A sense of guilt increasing with the years –
'When I am dead you will be sorry, John' –
Here I could pray my mother would not die.
Thus were my London Sundays incomplete
If unaccompanied by Evening Prayer.

How trivial used to seem the Underground,
How worldly looked the over-lighted west,
How different and smug and wise I felt
When from the east I made my journey home!

John Betjeman, Summoned by Bells (1960)

St James's, Piccadilly

6 September [1970]. Bob and I met at Green Park station to go to
the Chapel Royal (11.15 Sung Eucharist), but when we got there
found it was closed until October. '*And* you're too late for the
Guards' Chapel,' said the man. So we made our way to St James
Piccadilly where Matins had started. The rector (the Rev. William
Pye Baddeley – brother of Hermione and Angela) was in the middle
of reading the 2nd lesson in a modern version, where Mary Magdalen
breaks the box of precious ointment over Jesus . . . 'Here endeth that
perfectly lovely lesson,' he declared. The congregation was mostly
elderly and well dressed. We prayed for visitors to London, especially
those from the USA and there were some dollar bills in the plate.

Barbara Pym, A Very Private Eye (1985)

Matins at St Mary Abbots, Kensington

Sunday 28 March 1897
In the morning we three went to Church at St Mary Abbots! This
was the last Sunday on which the banns were to be read, so that we
had resolved to go – It began at 11.30, and finished at 1.15 – We
had rummaged the house for prayer books and hymn books, our
search produced two hymn books (tonic sol fa) and one prayer book.
This last however was left behind. A little black gentleman showed
us into seats at the top of the church. Soon music and singing began,
the row in front of us rose, and behind a wheezy old lady began to
follow the choristers in a toothless tuneless whistle – so on for the
rest of the performance. At certain parts we stood, then sat, and
finally knelt – this I refused to do – My neighbour looked so miserable
and uncomfortable – In the middle the banns of John Waller Hills
and Stella Duckworth along with several others were read, and no

one pronounced any reasons why etc. etc. Our prayers and psalms were rather guess work – but the hymns were splendid – We had a sermon from a new pastor – he said we shall never hear the beloved voice again, alluding to the departed vicar* – the old ladies snuffled and sobbed . . .

* The Hon. Edward Carr Glyn (1843–1928), Vicar of Kensington since 1878 and from 1897–1916 Bishop of Peterborough.

Virginia Woolf, *A Passionate Apprentice: The Early Journals* (1990)

St Saviour's, Aberdeen Park, Highbury, London, N

With oh such peculiar branching and over-reaching of wire
   Trolley-bus standards pick their threads from the London sky
Diminishing up the perspective, Highbury-bound retire
   Threads and buses and standards with plane trees volleying by
And, more peculiar still, that ever-increasing spire
   Bulges over the housetops, polychromatic and high.

Stop the trolley-bus, stop! And here, where the roads unite
   Of weariest worn-out London – no cigarettes, no beer,
No repairs undertaken, nothing in stock – alight;
   For over the waste of willow-herb, look at her, sailing clear,
A great Victorian church, tall, unbroken and bright
   In a sun that's setting in Willesden and saturating us here.

These were the streets my parents knew when they loved and won –
   The brougham that crunched the gravel, the laurel-girt paths that wind,
Geranium-beds for the lawn, Venetian blinds for the sun,
   A separate tradesman's entrance, straw in the mews behind,
Just in the four-mile radius where hackney carriages run,
   Solid Italianate houses for the solid commercial mind.

These were the streets they knew; and I, by descent, belong
   To these tall neglected houses divided into flats.
Only the church remains, where carriages used to throng
   And my mother stepped out in flounces and my father stepped out in spats
To shadowy stained-glass matins or gas-lit evensong
   And back in a country quiet with doffing of chimney hats.

Great red church of my parents, cruciform crossing they knew —
  Over these same encaustics they and their parents trod
Bound through a red-brick transept for a once familiar pew
  Where the organ set them singing and the sermon let them nod
And up this coloured brickwork the same long shadows grew
  As these in the stencilled chancel where I kneel in the presence
    of God.

Wonder beyond Time's wonders, that Bread so white and small
  Veiled in golden curtains, too mighty for men to see,
Is the Power which sends the shadows up this polychrome wall,
  Is God who created the present, the chain-smoking millions and
    me;
Beyond the throb of the engines is the throbbing heart of all —
  Christ, at this Highbury altar, I offer myself To Thee.

John Betjeman, Summoned by Bells (1960)

Two backsides

May 1871

Mr Marsden entertained me with some reminiscences of his own. 'A public house in the village, haven't we?' he said. 'We just have, and they keep a fearful noise there sometimes. Then I put my head out of my bedroom window and holla to them and they fly like the wind. When I was curate of Llangorse,' he said, 'the Vicar of Talgarth was ill and I had to procure an assistant curate. So I wrote to Llewellyn, now Dean of St. David's — then Principal of Lampeter — to send me a man who wanted a title for orders and could speak Welsh and English. Llewellyn wrote that he had the very man for me, *doctus utriusque linguae*. The man came. I saw his Welsh was very shaky.

Once he was publishing Banns. He meant to say, 'Why these two persons may not lawfully be joined together in holy Matrimony'. But what he did say was, 'Why these two backsides may not lawfully be joined together in Holy Matrimony'. Everyone in the Church hid their faces. When he came out of the Church I said, 'Well, you *have* done it now'. 'What?' said he. I told him. 'God forbid,' said he. 'It is true,' I said.

Francis Kilvert, Diaries (1974)

Church and Chapel

Here is a fashionable church, where the service commences at a late hour, for the accommodation of such members of the congregation – and they are not a few – as may happen to have lingered at the Opera far into the morning of the Sabbath; an excellent contrivance for poising the balance between God and Mammon, and illustrating the ease with which a man's duties to both may be accommodated and adjusted. How the carriages rattle up, and deposit their richly-dressed burdens beneath the lofty portico! The powdered footmen glide along the aisle, place the richly-bound prayer-books on the pew desks, slam the doors, and hurry away, leaving the fashionable members of the congregation to inspect each other through their glasses, and to dazzle and glitter in the eyes of the few shabby people in the free seats. The organ peals forth, the hired singers commence a short hymn, and the congregation condescendingly rise, stare about them, and converse in whispers. The clergyman enters the reading-desk – a young man of noble family and elegant demeanour, notorious at Cambridge for his knowledge of horse-flesh and dancers, and celebrated at Eton for his hopeless stupidity. The service commences. Mark the soft voice in which he reads, and the impressive manner in which he applies his white hand, studded with brilliants, to his perfumed hair. Observe the graceful emphasis with which he offers up the prayers for the King, the Royal Family, and all the Nobility; and the nonchalance with which he hurries over the more uncomfortable portions of the service, the seventh commandment for instance, with a studied regard for the taste and feeling of his auditors, only to be equalled by that displayed by the sleek divine who succeeds him, who murmurs, in a voice kept down by rich feeding, most comfortable doctrines for exactly twelve minutes, and then arrives at the anxiously expected 'Now to God,' which is the signal for the dismissal of the congregation. The organ is again heard; those who have been asleep wake up, and those who have kept awake, smile and seem greatly relieved; bows and congratulations are exchanged, the livery servants are all bustle and commotion, bang go the steps, up jump the footmen, and off rattle the carriages: the inmates discoursing on the dresses of the congregation, and congratulating themselves on having set so excellent an example to the community in general, and Sunday-pleasures in particular.

Enter a less orthodox place of religious worship and observe the contrast. A small close chapel with a whitewashed wall, and plain deal pews and pulpit, contains a close-packed congregation, as different in dress as they are opposed in manner, to that we have just quitted. The hymn is sung – not by paid singers, but by the whole assembly at the loudest pitch of their voices, unaccompanied by any musical instrument, the words being given out, two lines at a time, by the clerk. There is something in the sonorous quavering of the harsh voices, in the lank and hollow faces of the men, and the sour solemnity of the women, which bespeaks this a stronghold of intolerant zeal and ignorant enthusiasm: The preacher enters the pulpit. He is a coarse, hard-faced man of forbidding aspect, clad in rusty black, and bearing in his hand a small plain Bible from which he selects some passage for his text, while the hymn is concluding. The congregation fall upon their knees, and are hushed into profound stillness as he delivers an extempore prayer, in which he calls upon the Sacred Founder of the Christian faith to bless his ministry, in terms of disgusting and impious familiarity not to be described. He begins his oration in a drawling tone, and his hearers listen with silent attention. He grows warmer as he proceeds with his subject, and his gesticulation becomes proportionately violent. He clenches his fists, beats the book upon the desk before him, and swings his arms wildly about his head. The congregation murmur their acquiescence in his doctrines: and a short groan occasionally bears testimony to the moving nature of his eloquence. Encouraged by these symptoms of approval, and working himself up to a pitch of enthusiasm amounting almost to frenzy, he denounces sabbath-breakers with the direst vengeance of offended Heaven. He stretches his body half out of the pulpit, thrusts forth his arms with frantic gestures, and blasphemously calls upon the Deity to visit with eternal torments those who turn aside from the word, as interpreted and preached by – himself. A low moaning is heard, the women rock their bodies to and fro, and wring their hands; the preacher's fervour increases, the perspiration starts upon his brow, his face is flushed, and he clenches his hands convulsively, as he draws a hideous and appalling picture of the horrors preparing for the wicked in a future state. A great excitement is visible among his hearers, a scream is heard, and some young girl falls senseless on the floor. There is a momentary rustle, but it is only for a moment – all eyes are turned towards the preacher.

He pauses, passes his handkerchief across his face, and looks complacently round. His voice resumes its natural tone, as with mock humility he offers up a thanksgiving for having been successful in his efforts, and having been permitted to rescue one sinner from the path of evil. He sinks back into his seat, exhausted with the violence of his ravings; the girl is removed, a hymn is sung, a petition for some measure for securing the better observance of the Sabbath, which has been prepared by the good man, is read; and his worshipping admirers struggle who shall be the first to sign it.

Charles Dickens (1812–70), *Reprinted Pieces*

Mass in a Dublin church

Same notice on the door. Sermon by the very reverend John Conmee SJ on saint Peter Claver SJ and the African Mission. Prayers for the conversion of Gladstone they had too when he was almost unconscious. The protestants are the same. Convert Dr William J. Walsh DD to the true religion. Save China's millions. Wonder how they explain it to the heathen Chinee. Prefer an ounce of opium. Celestials. Rank heresy for them. Buddha their god lying on his side in the museum. Taking it easy with hand under his cheek. Josssticks burning. Not like Ecce Homo. Crown of thorns and cross. Clever idea Saint Patrick the shamrock. Chopsticks? Conmee: Martin Cunningham knows him: distinguishedlooking. Sorry I didn't work him about getting Molly into the choir instead of that Father Farley who looked a fool but wasn't. They're taught that. He's not going out in bluey specs with the sweat rolling off him to baptise blacks, is he? The glasses would take their fancy, flashing. Like to see them sitting round in a ring with blub lips, entranced, listening. Still life. Lap it up like milk, I suppose.

The cold smell of sacred stone called him. He trod the worn steps, pushed the swingdoor and entered softly by the rere.

Something going on: some sodality. Pity so empty. Nice discreet place to be next some girl. Who is my neighbour? Jammed by the hour to slow music. That woman at midnight mass. Seventh heaven. Women knelt in the benches with crimson halters round their necks, heads bowed. A batch knelt at the altarrails. The priest went along by them, murmuring, holding the thing in his hands. He stopped at each, took out a communion, shook a drop or two (are they in water?) off it and put it neatly into her mouth. Her hat and head sank. Then the next one. Her hat sank at once. Then the next one: a small old woman. The priest bent down to put it into her mouth, murmuring all the time. Latin. The next one. Shut your eyes and open your mouth. What? *Corpus*: body. Corpse. Good idea the Latin. Stupefies them first. Hospice for the dying. They don't seem to chew it: only swallow it down. Rum idea: eating bits of a corpse. Why the cannibals cotton to it.

He stood aside watching their blind masks pass down the aisle, one by one, and seek their places. He approached a bench and seated himself in its corner, nursing his hat and newspaper. These pots we have to wear. We ought to have hats modelled on our heads. They were about him here and there, with heads still bowed in their crimson halters, waiting for it to melt in their stomachs. Something like those mazzoth: it's that sort of bread: unleavened shewbread. Look at them. Now I bet it makes them feel happy. Lollipop. It does. Yes, bread of angels it's called. There's a big idea behind it, kind of kingdom of God is within you feel. First communicants. Hokypoky penny a lump. Then feel all like one family party, same in the theatre, all in the same swim. They do. I'm sure of that. Not so lonely. In our confraternity. Then come out a bit spreeish. Let off steam. Thing is if you really believe in it. Lourdes cure, waters of oblivion, and the Knock apparition, statues bleeding. Old fellow asleep near that confessionbox. Hence those snores. Blind faith. Safe in the arms of kingdom come. Lulls all pain. Wake this time next year.

He saw the priest stow the communion cup away, well in, and kneel an instant before it, showing a large grey bootsole from under the lace affair he had on. Suppose he lost the pin of his. He wouldn't know what to do. Bald spot behind. Letters on his back: INRI? No: IHS. Molly told me one time I asked her. I have sinned: or no: I have suffered, it is. And the other one? Iron nails ran in.

Meet one Sunday after the rosary. Do not deny my request. Turn up with a veil and black bag. Dusk and the light behind her. She might be here with a ribbon round her neck and do the other thing all the same on the sly. Their character. That fellow that turned queen's evidence on the invincibles he used to receive the, Carey was his name, the communion every morning. This very church. Peter Carey, yes. No, Peter Claver I am thinking of. Denis Carey. And just imagine that. Wife and six children at home. And plotting that murder all the time. Those crawthumpers, now that's a good name for them, there's always something shiftylooking about them. They're not straight men of business either. O, no, she's not here: the flower: no, no. By the way, did I tear up that envelope? Yes: under the bridge.

The priest was rinsing out the chalice: then he tossed off the dregs smartly. Wine. Makes it more aristocratic than for example if he drank what they are used to Guinness's porter or some temperance beverage Wheatley's Dublin hop bitters or Cantrell and Cochrane's ginger ale (aromatic). Doesn't give them any of it: shew wine: only the other. Cold comfort. Pious fraud but quite right: otherwise they'd have one old booser worse than another coming along, cadging for a drink. Queer the whole atmosphere of the. Quite right. Perfectly right that is.

Mr Bloom looked back towards the choir. Not going to be any music. Pity. Who has the organ here I wonder? Old Glynn he knew how to make that instrument talk, the *vibrato*: fifty pounds a year they say he had in Gardiner street. Molly was in fine voice that day, the *Stabat Mater* of Rossini. Father Bernard Vaughan's sermon first. Christ or Pilate? Christ, but don't keep us all night over it. Music they wanted. Footdrill stopped. Could hear a pin drop. I told her to pitch her voice against that corner. I could feel the thrill in the air, the full, the people looking up:

Quis est homo

Some of that old sacred music splendid. Mercadante: seven last words. Mozart's twelfth mass: *Gloria* in that. Those old popes keen on music, on art and statues and pictures of all kinds. Palestrina for example too. They had a gay old time while it lasted. Healthy too, chanting, regular hours, then brew liqueurs. Benedictine. Green Chartreuse. Still, having eunuchs in their choir that was coming it a bit thick. What kind of voice is it? Must be curious to hear after their own strong basses. Connoisseurs. Suppose they wouldn't feel anything after. Kind of placid. No worry. Fall into flesh, don't they? Gluttons, tall, long legs. Who knows? Eunuch. One way out of it.

He saw the priest bend down and kiss the altar and then face about and bless all the people. All crossed themselves and stood up. Mr Bloom glanced about him and then stood up, looking over the risen hats. Stand up at the gospel of course. Then all settled down on their knees again and he sat back quietly in his bench. The priest came down from the altar, holding the thing out from him, and he and the massboy answered each other in Latin. Then the priest knelt down and began to read off a card:

—O God, our refuge and our strength . . .

Mr Bloom put his face forward to catch the words. English. Throw them the bone. I remember slightly. How long since your last mass? Glorious and immaculate virgin. Joseph, her spouse. Peter and Paul. More interesting if you understood what it was all about. Wonderful organisation certainly, goes like clockwork. Confession. Everyone wants to. Then I will tell you all. Penance. Punish me, please. Great weapon in their hands. More than doctor or solicitor. Woman dying to. And I schschschschschsch. And did you chachachachacha? And why did you? Look down at her ring to find an excuse. Whispering gallery walls have ears. Husband learn to his surprise. God's little joke. Then out she comes. Repentance skindeep. Lovely shame. Pray at an altar. Hail Mary and Holy Mary. Flowers, incense, candles melting. Hide her blushes. Salvation army blatant imitation. Reformed prostitute will address the meeting. How I found the Lord. Squareheaded chaps those must be in Rome: they work the whole show. And don't they rake in the money too? Bequests also: to the P. P. for the time being in his absolute discretion. Masses for the repose of my soul to be said publicly with open doors. Monasteries and convents. The priest in that Fermanagh will case in the witness-box. No browbeating him. He had his answer pat for everything. Liberty and exaltation of our holy mother the church. The doctors of the church: they mapped out the whole theology of it.

The priest prayed.

—Blessed Michael, archangel, defend us in the hour of conflict. Be our safeguard against the wickedness and snares of the devil (may God restrain him, we humbly pray!): and do thou, O prince of the heavenly host, by the power of God thrust Satan down to hell and with him those other wicked spirits who wander through the world for the ruin of souls.

The priest and the massboy stood up and walked off. All over. The women remained behind: thanksgiving.

Better be shoving along.

James Joyce, Ulysses (1922)

Why are the Clergy . . . ?

Why are the clergy of the Church of England
Always altering the words of the prayers in the Prayer Book?
Cranmer's touch was surer than theirs, do they not respect him?
For instance last night in church I heard
(I italicize the interpolation)
'The Lord bless you and keep you *and all who are dear unto you*'
As the blessing is a congregational blessing and meant to be
This is questionable on theological grounds
But is it not offensive to the ear and also ludicrous?
That 'unto' is a particularly ripe piece of idiocy
Oh how offensive it is. I suppose we shall have next
'Lighten our darkness we beseech thee oh Lord *and the darkness*
    of all who are dear to us.'
It seems a pity. Does Charity object to the objection?
Then I cry, and not for the first time to that smooth face
Charity, have pity.

Stevie Smith, Collected Poems (1975)

The Alternative Service Book

The Reformation had set out to create the first genuinely lay piety,
a magnificent ambition. But what did it achieve? It said to the lay
person, 'You'll go on worshipping like a monk, only instead of
looking up to the heavenly world you'll be taught to look up to your
betters in general and to the King in particular.' If you think this
verdict one-sided, inspect the interiors of English churches abroad in
countries like India or Ireland. They are monuments to the crown,
the gentry and the military. It is not surprising that the long-term
historical results of all this have been so disappointing. And if the
Established Protestant churches of Northern Europe have a particularly dismal record, *all* churches share many of the same problems
with worship. It is too other-worldly, too extra-historical and too
quietistic. There is a natural suspicion that the great ones who author-
ized these forms of worship for our use stood to gain by encouraging
us to mistrust ourselves, to be apolitical and to look to another
world. And in any case, since all human life is lived inside language
and society and history, the form of consciousness involved is

illusory. Today, lay Christian worship should not purport to be taking place in an antechamber of heaven, a step outside historical time. The point is obvious; and yet the situation is getting worse, not better. *The Book of Common Prayer* (1662) gives a rather vivid impression of the cultural and political world that produced it. Its replacement, the *Alternative Service Book* (1980), floats in a social vacuum, its pages containing no reference anywhere to any of the distinctive features of modern civilization such as democracy, industry, growing knowledge, religious pluralism, feminism and historical change. The book moves in a Heritage limbo, pseudo-traditional and outside real history. In relation to the lives we are actually living and what is making news at the end of the twentieth century, the *ASB* services are purest fantasy. Morally speaking, we might just as well be spending our time in church reading *The Lord of the Rings*.

Don Cupitt, Only Human (1989)

George VI's Coronation

She was standing next to her grandmother, Queen Mary, as the ceremony went on and on . . . 'At the end, the service got rather boring as it was all prayers. Grannie and I were looking to see how many more pages to the end, and we turned one more and then I pointed to the word at the bottom of the page and it said "Finis". We both smiled at each other and turned back to the service.'

The Times, 8 March 1990, quoting from Princess Elizabeth's 1937 diary

[5]

PREACHING

I have been cursed with a curious mental quirk: I always remember sermons. I wish that my memory were as sharp when attending the theatre, and then I should know all the plays of Shakespeare by heart. Instead, if I wake in the small hours, I can remember sermons preached by booming Old Rugbeian bishops in my school chapel, or homilies by droning dryasdust mattins-sermons mumbled by superannuated prebendaries from cobwebby cathedral pulpits; or fatuous evensong sermons in once-visited country churches; and, of course, a high proportion of extremely good sermons. The clergy in my experience are generally much better public speakers than politicians, and I have heard as many good sermons as bad.

Preaching

When he preacheth, he procures attention by all possible art, both by earnestness of speech, it being natural to men to think, that where is much earnestness, there is somewhat worth hearing: and by a diligent and busy cast of his eye on his auditors, with letting them know that he observes who marks, and who not; and with particularizing of his speech now to the younger sort, then to the elder, now to the poor, and now to the rich. This is for you, and This is for you; for particulars ever touch, and awake more than generals. Herin also he serves himself of the judgments of God, as of those of ancient times, so especially of the late ones; and those most, which are nearest to his Parish; for people are very attentive at such discourses, and think it behoves them to be so, when God is so near them, and even over their heads. Sometimes he tells them stories, and sayings of others, according as his text invites him; for them also men heed, and remember better than exhortations; which though earnest, yet often die with the Sermon, especially with Country people; which are thick, and heavy, and hard to raise to a point of Zeal, and fervency, and need a mountain of fire to kindle them; but stories and sayings they will well remember. He often tells them, that Sermons are dangerous things, that none goes out of Church as he came in, but either better or worse; that none is careless before his Judge, and that the Word of God shall judge us. By these and other means the Parson procures attention; but the character of his Sermon is Holiness; he is not witty, or learned, or eloquent, but Holy.

George Herbert, *A Priest to the Temple* (1652)

An altercation with a friar

Then came a friar to Lynne who was held a holy man and a good preacher. His name and his perfection in preaching spread, and sprung wonder wide.

Then came good men to the said creature in good charity and said:

'Margery, now shall ye have preaching enough, for there is coming one of the most famous friars in England to this town, to be here in residence.'

Then was she merry and glad and thanked God with all her heart that so good a man was coming to dwell amongst them. In a short time after, he said a sermon in a chapel of Saint James in Lynne, where many people were gathered to hear the sermon; and ere the friar went to the pulpit, the parish priest of the same place where he would preach, went to him and said:

'Sir, I pray you be not displeased. Here will come a woman to your sermon, who oftentimes, when she heareth of the Passion of Our Lord, or of any high devotion, weepeth, sobbeth, and crieth, but it lasts not long. Therefore, good sir, if she makes any noise at your sermon, suffer it patiently and be not abashed thereof.'

The good friar went forth to say the sermon and preached full holily and devoutly, and spoke much of Our Lord's Passion, so that the said creature could not longer bear it. She kept herself from crying as long as she might, and then at last she burst out with a great cry, and cried wondrous sore.

The good friar suffered it patiently and said no word thereto, at that time.

In a short time after, he preached again in the same place, the said creature being present, and, beholding how fast the people came running to hear the sermon, she had great joy in her soul, thinking in her mind:

'Ah! Lord Jesus, I trow, if Thou wert here to preach in Thine own Person, the people would have great joy to hear Thee. I pray Thee, Lord, make Thy holy word settle in their souls as I would it should do in mine, and that as many may be turned by his voice, as would be by Thy voice, if Thou preachedest Thyself.'

And with such holy thoughts and holy mind, she asked grace for the people at that time and afterwards; and what with the sermon, and what with her own meditation, the grace of devotion wrought so sore in her mind that she fell into boisterous weeping.

Then said the good friar: 'I would this woman were out of the church; she annoyeth the people.'

Some that were her friends, answered him: 'Sir, hold her excused. She cannot withstand it.'

Then many people turned against her and were full glad that the good friar held against her. Then said some men that she had a devil within her, and so had they said many times before, but now they were more bold, for they thought that their opinion was well strengthened or fortified by this good friar. Nor would be suffer her at his sermon unless she would leave off her sobbing and her crying.

Margery Kempe (c. 1373–1439), The Book of Margery Kempe

The eloquence of the preacher

Burley, who had now returned from the pursuit, found his followers in this distracted state. With the ready talent of one accustomed to encounter exigencies, he proposed that one hundred of the freshest men should be drawn out for duty – that a small number of those who had hitherto acted as leaders, should constitute a committee of direction until officers should be regularly chosen – and that, to crown the victory, Gabriel Kettledrummle should be called upon to improve the providential success which they had obtained, by a word in season addressed to the army. He reckoned very much, and not without reason, on this last expedient, as a means of engaging the attention of the bulk of the insurgents, while he himself, and two or three of their leaders, held a private council of war, undisturbed by the discordant opinions, or senseless clamour, of the general body.

Kettledrummle more than answered the expectations of Burley. Two mortal hours did he preach at a breathing; and certainly no lungs, or doctrine, excepting his own, could have kept up, for so long a time, the attention of men in such precarious circumstances. But he possessed in perfection a sort of rude and familiar eloquence peculiar to the preachers of that period, which, though it would have been fastidiously rejected by an audience which possessed any portion of taste, was a cake of the right leaven for the palates of those whom he now addressed. His text was from the forty-ninth chapter of Isaiah, 'Even the captives of the mighty shall be taken away, and the prey of the terrible shall be delivered: for I will contend with him that contendeth with thee, and I will save thy children.

'And I will feed them that oppress thee with their own flesh; and they shall be drunken with their own blood, as with sweet wine: and all flesh shall know that I the Lord am thy Saviour and thy Redeemer, the Mighty One of Jacob.'

. . . Kettledrummle had no sooner ended his sermon, and descended from the huge rock which had served him for a pulpit, than his post was occupied by a pastor of a very different description. The reverend Gabriel was advanced in years, somewhat corpulent, with a loud voice, a square face, and a set of stupid and unanimated features, in which the body seemed more to predominate over the spirit than was seemly in a sound divine. The youth who succeeded him in exhorting this extraordinary convocation, Ephraim Macbriar by name, was hardly twenty years old; yet his thin features already indicated that a constitution, naturally hectic, was worn out by vigils, by fasts, by the rigour of imprisonment, and the fatigues incident to a fugitive life. Young as he was, he had been twice imprisoned for several months, and suffered many severities, which gave him great influence with those of his own sect. He threw his faded eyes over the multitude and over the scene of battle; and a light of triumph arose in his glance, his pale yet striking features were coloured with a transient and hectic blush of joy. He folded his hands, raised his face to heaven, and seemed lost in mental prayer and thanksgiving ere he addressed the people.

... 'Your garments are dyed – but not with the juice of the wine-press; your swords are filled with blood,' he exclaimed – 'but not with the blood of goats or lambs; the dust of the desert on which ye stand is made fat with gore – but not with the blood of bullocks, for the Lord hath a sacrifice in Bozrah, and a great slaughter in the land of Idumea ... Heaven has been with you, and has broken the bow of the mighty; then let every man's heart be as the heart of the valiant Maccabeus, every man's hand as the hand of the mighty Samson, every man's sword as that of Gideon, which turned not back from the slaughter; for the banner of Reformation is spread abroad on the mountains in its first loveliness, and the gates of hell shall not prevail against it ...'

... The eloquence of the preacher was rewarded by the deep hum of stern approbation which resounded through the armed assemblage at the conclusion of an exhortation so well suited to that which they had done, and that which remained for them to do. The wounded forgot their pains, the faint and hungry their fatigues and privations, as they listened to doctrines which elevated them alike above the wants and calamities of the world, and identified their cause with that of the Deity.

Sir Walter Scott, Old Mortality (1816)

Letter about Wesley preaching

10 October 1766

My health advances faster than my amusement. However, I have been at one opera, Mr Wesley's. They have boys and girls with charming voices, that sing hymns, in parts, to Scotch ballad tunes; but indeed so long, that one would think they were already in eternity, and knew how much time they had before them. The chapel is very neat, with true Gothic windows (yet I am not converted); but I was glad to see that luxury is creeping in upon them before persecution; they have very neat mahogany stands for branches, and brackets of the same in taste. At the upper end is a broad *hautpas* of four steps, advancing in the middle: at each end of the broadest part are two of *my* eagles, with red cushions for the parson and clerk. Behind them rise three more steps, in the midst of which is a third eagle for pulpit. Scarlet armed chairs to all three. On either hand, a balcony for elect ladies. The rest of the congregation sit on forms. Behind the pit, in a dark niche, is a plain table within rails; so you see the throne is for the apostle. Wesley is a lean elderly man, fresh-coloured, his hair smooth combed, but with a *soupçon* of curl at the ends. Wondrous clean, but as evidently an actor as Garrick. He spoke his sermon, but so fast, and with so little accent, that I am sure he has often uttered it, for it was like a lesson. There were parts and eloquence in it; but towards the end he exalted his voice, and acted very ugly enthusiasm; decried learning, and told stories, like Latimer, of the fool of his college, who said, 'I *thanks* God for everything.' Except a few from curiosity, and *some honourable women*, the congregation was very mean. There was a Scotch Countess of Buchan, who is carrying a pure rosy vulgar face to heaven, and who asked Miss Rich, if that was *the author of the poets*. I believe she meant me and the 'Noble Authors'.

Horace Walpole letter to John Chute, *Selected Letters* (1968)

Preaching

Every attempt, in a sermon, to cause emotion, except as the consequence of an impression made on the reason, or the understanding, or the will, I hold to be fanatical and sectarian.

No doubt preaching, in the proper sense of the word, is more effective than reading; and, therefore, I would not prohibit it, but leave a liberty to the clergyman who feels himself able to accomplish it. But, as things now are, I am quite sure I prefer going to church to a pastor who reads his discourse: for I never yet heard more than one preacher without book, who did not forget his argument in three minutes' time; and fall into vague and unprofitable declamation, and generally, very coarse declamation too. These preachers never progress; they eddy round and round. Sterility of mind follows their ministry.

Samuel Taylor Coleridge, *Table Talk* (1836)

from The Prelude

Nor did the Pulpit's oratory fail
To achieve its higher triumph. Not unfelt
Were its admonishments, nor light heard
The awful truths delivered thence by tongues
Endowed with various power to search the soul;
Yet ostentation, domineering, oft
Poured forth harangues, how sadly out of place! –
There have I seen a comely bachelor,
Fresh from a toilette of two hours, ascend
His rostrum, with seraphic glance look up,
And, in a tone elaborately low
Beginning, lead his voice through many a maze
A minuet course; and, winding up his mouth,
From time to time, into an orifice
Most delicate, a lurking eyelet, small,
And only not invisible, again
Open it out, diffusing thence a smile
Of rapt irradiation, exquisite.
Meanwhile, the Evangelists, Isaiah, Job,
Moses, and he who penned, the other day,
The Death of Abel, Shakespeare, and the Bard
Whose genius spangled o'er a gloomy theme
With fancies thick as his inspiring stars,
And Ossian (doubt not – 'tis the naked truth)
Summoned from streamy Morven – each and all
Would, in their turns, lend ornaments and flowers
To entwine the crook of eloquence that helped
This pretty Shepherd, pride of all the plains,
To rule and guide his captivated flock.

William Wordsworth, *The Prelude* (1850)

The Rev. Mr Irving

Mr Irving, then, is no common or mean man. He has four or five qualities, possessed in a moderate or in a paramount degree, which, added or multiplied together, fill up the important space he occupies in the public eye. Mr Irving's intellect itself is of a superior order;

he has undoubtedly both talents and acquirements beyond the ordinary run of every-day preachers. These alone, however, we hold, would not account for a twentieth part of the effect he has produced: they would have lifted him perhaps out of the mire and slough of sordid obscurity, but would never have launched him into the ocean-stream of popularity, in which he 'lies floating many a rood' – but to these he adds uncommon height, a graceful figure and action, a clear and powerful voice, a striking, if not a fine face, a bold and fiery spirit, and a most portentous obliquity of vision, which throw him to an immeasurable distance beyond all competition, and effectually relieve whatever there might be of common-place or bombast in his style of composition. Put the case that Mr Irving had been five feet high – Would he ever have been heard of, or, as he does now, have 'bestrode the world like a Colossus?' No, the thing speaks for itself. He would in vain have lifted his Lilliputian arm to Heaven, people would have laughed at his monkey-tricks. Again, had he been as tall as he is, but had wanted other recommendations, he would have been nothing.

> 'The player's province they but vainly try,
> Who want these powers, deportment, voice, and eye.'

Conceive a rough, ugly, shock-headed Scotchman, standing up in a Caledonian Chapel, and dealing 'damnation round the land' in a broad northern dialect, and with a harsh, screaking voice, what ear polite, what smile serene would have hailed the barbarous prodigy, or not consigned him to utter neglect and derision? But the Rev. Edward Irving, with all his native wildness, 'hath a smooth aspect framed to make women' saints; his very unusual size and height are carried off and moulded into elegance by the most admirable symmetry of form and ease of gesture; his sable locks, his clear iron-grey complexion, and firm-set features, turn the raw, uncouth Scotchman into the likeness of a noble Italian picture; and even his distortion of sight only redeems the otherwise 'faultless monster' within the bounds of humanity, and, when admiration is exhausted and curiosity ceases, excites a new interest by leading to the idle question whether it is an advantage to the preacher or not. Farther, give him all his actual and remarkable advantages of body and mind, let him be as tall, as strait, as dark and clear of skin, as much at his ease, as silver-tongued, as eloquent and as argumentative as he is, yet with all these, and without a little charlatanry to set them off he had been nothing. He might, keeping within the rigid line of his duty and professed calling, have preached on for ever; he might have divided the old-fashioned doctrines of election, grace, reprobation, predestination, into his sixteenth, seventeenth, and eighteenth heads, and his *lastly* have been looked for as a 'consummation devoutly to be wished'; he might have defied the devil and all his works, and by the help of a loud voice and strong-set person –

'A lusty man to ben an Abbot able;' –

have increased his own congregation, and been quoted among the godly as a powerful preacher of the word; but in addition to this, he went out of his way to attack Jeremy Bentham, and the town was up in arms. The thing was new. He thus wiped the stain of musty ignorance and formal bigotry out of his style. Mr Irving must have something superior in him, to look over the shining close-packed heads of his congregation to have a hit at the *Great Jurisconsult* in his study. He next, ere the report of the former blow had subsided, made a lunge at Mr Brougham, and glanced an eye at Mr Canning; *mystified* Mr Coleridge, and *stultified* Lord Liverpool in his place – in the Gallery. It was rare sport to see him, 'like an eagle in a dovecote, flutter the Volscians in Corioli.' He has found out the secret of attracting by repelling. Those whom he is likely to attack are curious to hear what he says of them: they go again, to show that they do not mind it. It is no less interesting to the bystanders, who like to witness this sort of *onslaught* – like a charge of cavalry, the shock, and the resistance. Mr Irving has, in fact, without leave asked or a licence granted, converted the Caledonian Chapel into a Westminster Forum or Debating Society, with the sanctity of religion added to it... He literally sends a challenge to all London in the name of the KING OF HEAVEN, to evacuate the streets, to disperse its population, to lay aside its employments, to burn its wealth, to renounce its vanities and pomp; and for what? – that he may enter in as the *King of Glory*; or after enforcing his threat with the battering-ram of logic, the grape-shot of rhetoric, and the cross-fire of his double vision, reduce the British metropolis to a Scottish heath, with a few miserable hovels upon it, where they may worship God according to *the root of the matter*, and where an old man with a blue bonnet, a fair-haired girl, and a little child would form the flower of his flock!

William Hazlitt, The Spirit of the Age (1825)

The Oxford Counter-reformation

The hearts of men vibrate in answer to one another like the strings of musical instruments. These sermons were, I suppose, the records of Newman's own mental experience. They appear to me to be the outcome of continued meditation upon his fellow-creatures and their positions in the world; their awful responsibilities; the mystery of their nature, strangely mixed of good and evil, of strength and weakness. A tone, not of fear, but of infinite pity runs through them all, and along with it a resolution to look facts in the face; not to fly to evasive generalities about infinite mercy and benevolence, but to examine what revelation really has added to our knowledge, either of what we are or of what lies before us. We were met on all sides with difficulties; for experience did not confirm, it rather contradicted, what revelation appeared distinctly to assert. I recollect a sermon from him – I think in the year 1839 – I have never read it since; I may not now remember the exact words, but the impression left is ineffaceable. It was on the trials of faith, of which he gave different illustrations. He supposed, first, two children to be educated together, of similar temperament and under similar conditions, one of whom was baptized and the other unbaptized. He represented them as growing up equally amiable, equally upright, equally reverent and God-fearing, with no outward evidence that one was in a different spiritual condition from the other; yet we were required to believe, not only that their condition was totally different, but that one was a child of God, and his companion was not.

Again, he drew a sketch of the average men and women who made up society, whom we ourselves encountered in daily life, or were connected with, or read about in newspapers. They were neither special saints nor special sinners. Religious men had faults, and often serious ones. Men careless of religion were often amiable in private life – good husbands, good fathers, steady friends, in public honourable, brave, and patriotic. Even in the worst and wickedest, in a witch of Endor, there was a human heart and human tenderness.

None seemed good enough for heaven, none so bad as to deserve to be consigned to the company of evil spirits, and to remain in pain and misery for ever. Yet all these people were, in fact, divided one from the other by an invisible line of separation. If they were to die on the spot as they actually were, some would be saved, the rest would be lost – the saved to have eternity of happiness, the lost to be with the devils in hell.

Again, I am not sure whether it was on the same occasion, but it was in following the same line of thought, Newman described closely some of the incidents of our Lord's passion; he then paused. For a few moments there was a breathless silence. Then, in a low, clear voice, of which the faintest vibration was audible in the farthest corner of St Mary's, he said, 'Now, I bid you recollect that He to whom these things were done was Almighty God.' It was as if an electric stroke had gone through the church, as if every person present understood for the first time the meaning of what he had all his life been saying. I suppose it was an epoch in the mental history of more than one of my Oxford contemporaries.

J. A. Froude, Short Studies of Great Subjects (1867–83)

John Henry Newman in the pulpit

The name of Cardinal Newman is a great name to the imagination still; his genius and his style are still things of power. But he is over eighty years old; he is in the Oratory at Birmingham; he has adopted, for the doubts and difficulties which beset men's minds to-day, a solution which, to speak frankly, is impossible. Forty years ago he was in the very prime of life; he was close at hand to us at Oxford; he was preaching in St Mary's pulpit every Sunday; he seemed about to transform and to renew what was for us the most national and natural institution in the world, the Church of England. Who could resist the charm of that spiritual apparition, gliding in the dim afternoon light through the aisles of St Mary's, rising into the pulpit, and then, in the most entrancing of voices, breaking the silence with words and thoughts which were a religious music – subtle, sweet, mournful? I seem to hear him still, saying: 'After the fever of life, after weariness and sicknesses, fightings and despondings, languor and fretfulness, struggling and succeeding; after all the changes and chances of this troubled, unhealthy state, – at length comes death, at length the white throne of God, at length the beatific vision.' Or, if we followed him back to his seclusion at Littlemore, that dreary village by the London road, and to the house of retreat and the church which he built there – a mean house such as Paul might have lived in when he was tent-making at Ephesus, a church plain and thinly sown with worshippers – who could resist him there either, welcoming back to the severe joys of church-fellowship, and of daily worship and prayer, the firstlings of a generation which had wellnigh forgotten them? Again I seem to hear him: ' . . . True faith does not covet comforts; they who realise that awful day, when they shall see Him face to face whose eyes are as a flame of fire, will as little bargain to pray pleasantly now as they will think of doing so then.'

Matthew Arnold, *Discourses in America* (1885)

Mr Brontë's blindness

During this summer of 1846, while her literary hopes were waning, an anxiety of another kind was increasing. Her father's eyesight had become seriously impaired by the progress of the cataract which was forming. He was nearly blind. He could grope his way about, and recognize the figures of those he knew well when they were placed against a strong light; but he could no longer see to read, and thus his eager appetite for knowledge and information of all kinds was severely balked. He continued to preach. I have heard that he was led up into the pulpit, and that his sermons were never so effective as when he stood there, a grey, sightless old man, his blind eyes looking out straight before him, while the words that came from his lips had all the vigour and force of his best days. Another fact has been mentioned to me, curious as showing the accurateness of his sensation of time. His sermons had always lasted exactly half an hour. With the clock right before him, and with his ready flow of words, this had been no difficult matter so long as he could see. But it was the same when he was blind. As the minute-hand came to the point, marking the expiration of the thirty minutes, he concluded his sermon.

Elizabeth Gaskell, *The Life of Charlotte Brontë* (1857)

Thomas Arnold

More than either matter or manner of his preaching, was the impression of himself. Even the mere readers of his sermons will derive from them the history of his whole mind, and of his whole management of the school. But to his hearers it was more than this. It was the man himself, there more than in any other place, concentrating all his various faculties and feelings on one sole object, combating face to face the evil, with which directly or indirectly he was elsewhere perpetually struggling. He was not the preacher or the clergyman, who had left behind all his usual thoughts and occupations as soon as he had ascended the pulpit. He was still the scholar, the historian, and theologian, basing all that he said, not indeed ostensibly, but consciously, and often visibly, on the deepest principles of the past and present. He was still the instructor and the schoolmaster, only teaching and educating with increased solemnity and energy. He was still the simple-hearted and earnest man, labouring to win others to share in his own personal feelings of disgust at sin, and love of goodness, and to trust to the same faith, in which he hoped to live and die himself.

It is difficult to describe, without seeming to exaggerate, the attention with which he was heard by all above the very young boys. Years have passed away, and many of his pupils can look back to hardly any greater interest than that with which, for those twenty minutes, Sunday after Sunday, they sat beneath that pulpit, with their eyes fixed upon him, and their attention strained to the utmost to catch every word that he uttered. It is true, that, even to the best, there was much, and to the mass of boys, the greater part of what he said, that must have passed away from them as soon as they had heard it, without any corresponding fruits. But they were struck, as boys naturally would be, by the originality of his thoughts, and what always impressed them as the beauty of his language; and in the substance of what he said, much that might have seemed useless, because for the most part impracticable to boys, was not without its effect in breaking completely through the corrupt atmosphere of school opinion, and exhibiting before them once every week an image of high principle and feeling, which they felt was not put on for the occasion, but was constantly living amongst them. And to all it must have been an advantage, that, for once in their lives, they had listened to sermons, which none of them could associate with the thought of weariness, formality, or exaggeration. On many there was left an impression to which, though unheeded at the time, they recurred in after life. Even the most careless boys would sometimes, during the course of the week, refer almost involuntarily to the sermon of the past Sunday, as a condemnation of what they were doing. Some, whilst they wonder how it was that so little practical effect was produced upon themselves at the time, yet retain the recollection (to give the words of one who so described himself,) that, 'I used to listen to them from first to last with a kind of awe, and over and over again could not join my friends at the chapel door, but would walk home to be alone; and I remember the same effects being produced by them, more or less, on others, whom I should have thought as hard as stones, and on whom I should think Arnold looked as some of the worst boys in the school.'

Dean Stanley, The Life of Dr Arnold (1844)

The gift of using words

I must make a protest against the pretence, so often put forward by the working clergy, that they are overburdened by the multitude of sermons to be preached. We are all too fond of our own voices, and a preacher is encouraged in the vanity of making his heard by the privilege of a compelled audience. His sermon is the pleasant morsel of his life, his delicious moment of self-exaltation. 'I have preached nine sermons this week,' said a young friend to me the other day, with hand languidly raised to his brow, the picture of an overburdened martyr. 'Nine this week, seven last week, four the week before. I have preached twenty-three sermons this month. It is really too much.' 'Too much, indeed,' said I, shuddering; 'too much for the strength of any one.' 'Yes,' he answered meekly, 'indeed it is; I am beginning to feel it painfully.' 'Would,' said I, 'you could feel it – would that you could be made to feel it.' But he never guessed that my heart was wrung for the poor listeners.

There was, at any rate, no tedium felt in listening to Mr Slope on the occasion in question. His subject came too home to his audience to be dull; and, to tell the truth, Mr Slope had the gift of using words forcibly. He was heard through his thirty minutes of eloquence with mute attention and open ears; but with angry eyes, which glared round from one enraged parson to another, with wide-spread nostrils from which already burst forth fumes of indignation, and with many shufflings of the feet and uneasy motions of the body, which betokened minds disturbed, and hearts not at peace with all the world.

Anthony Trollope, *Barchester Towers* (1857)

The Bishop of London preaching

20th January 1867 – Now to look back along the years. The first part of my Episcopate was marked by my taking more share than I have done lately in direct missionary work in the diocese – preaching continually in the east of London, often preaching where necessary in the open air. I think this was wise. It gave the impetus to the clergy and encouraged them to break through the old routine rules which cramped their energy, and to put an end to that fear, which was at one time real, that the Church of England might die of its dignity. I helped, I think, to let it be understood that its true dignity consisted in its doing in every proper way, after Christ's example, Christ's work. I may consider this period of my work as marked by the establishment of the Diocesan Home Mission – a great movement, raising up what is indispensable as supplementary to the parochial system in such a place as London. But our efforts were long difficult to bring to pass. It was a good idea to send missionary clergy from the bishop to all sorts of work in London which the parochial clergy could not undertake – the care of navvies, the densely peopled lanes of huge parishes, etc. All that we were able to do at first was to impress on the public mind that this was a legitimate Church of England work. I bore my own part in such work, preaching, for example, to the half gypsy population of the Potteries, Kensington, in the open air almost by moonlight, to the omnibus men in their yard at Islington by night, to the people assembled by Covent Garden Market on a Sunday afternoon in summer, and once to a great assemblage in the quadrangle here at Fulham, while our church was closed. I was not neglectful, I hope, of my other work, preaching steadily at St James's, Piccadilly, in the spring, and in the various churches in the diocese; attending the House of Lords and speaking on all fit occasions; and I did my best in Convocation. My first

Visitation and Charge belongs to this period (1858). My second Visitation and Charge (1862) marks a second stage. The endeavour to evangelize this vast metropolis soon showed that organization far more systematic than anything hitherto tried was necessary.

Samuel Waldegrave, Life of Archbishop Tait (1891)

Old Mr Thomas of Disserth

14 July 1871

I got out at Whitney and went to the Rectory. I dined with the girls and their father. He told me of the sermons which old Mr Thomas the Vicar of Disserth used to preach as they were described to him by the Venables. He would get up in the pulpit without an idea about what he was going to say, and would begin thus. 'Ha, yes, here we are. And it is a fine day. I congratulate you on the fine day, and glad to see so many of you here. Yes indeed. Ha, yes, very well. Now then I shall take for my text so and so. Yes. Let me see. You are all sinners and so am I. Yes indeed.' Sometimes he would preach about 'Mr Noe'. 'Mr Noe, he did go on with the ark, thump, thump, thump. And the wicked fellows did come and say to him "Now, Mr Noe, don't go on there, thump, thump, thump, come and have a pint of ale at the Red Lion. There is capital ale at the Red Lion, Mr Noe." For Mr Noe was situated just as we are here, there was the Red Lion close by the ark, just round the corner. Yes indeed. But Mr Noe he would not hearken to them, and he went on thump, thump, thump. Then another idle fellow would say, "Come Mr Noe – the hounds are running capital, yes indeed. Don't go on there thump, thump, thump." But Mr Noe he did never heed them, he just went on with his ark, thump, thump, thump.'

Francis Kilvert, Diaries (1974)

An answer to prayer

Mr Hawker was walking one day on the cliffs near Morwenstow, with the Rev. W. Vincent, when a gust of wind took off Mr Vincent's hat, and carried it over the cliff.

Within a week or two a Methodist preacher at Truro was discoursing on prayer, and in his sermon he said: 'I would not have you, dear brethren, confine your supplications to spiritual blessings, but ask also for temporal favours. I will illustrate my meaning by narrating an incident, a fact, that happened to myself ten days ago. I was on the shore of a cove near a little, insignificant place at North Cornwall, named Morwenstow, and about to proceed to Bude. Shall I add, my Christian friends, that I had on my head at the time a shocking bad hat, and that I somewhat blushed to think of entering the harbour, town and watering-place, so ill-adorned as to my head? Then I lifted up my prayer to the Almighty, that He would pluck me out of the great strait in which I found myself, and clothe me suitably as to my head; for He painteth the petals of the polyanthus, and colours the calyx of the coreopsis. At that solemn moment I raised my eyes to heaven; and I saw, in the spacious firmament on high, the blue, etheral sky, a black spot. It approached, it largened, it widened, it fell at my feet. It was a brand-new hat, by a distinguished London maker. I cast my battered beaver to the waves, and walked into Bude as fast as I could, with the new hat on my head.'

Sabine Baring-Gould, The Vicar of Morwenstow (1876)

The Importance of Being Earnest

Enter JACK *from back of garden* R.; *he comes* C., *is dressed entirely in black;* MISS PRISM *shakes his hand;* JACK *takes out his handkerchief and puts it to his eyes.*

PRISM: Mr Worthing!

CHAS: Mr Worthing.

PRISM: This is indeed a surprise. We did not look for you till Monday afternoon.

JACK: (*shakes* PRISM'S *hand in a tragic manner*) I have returned sooner than I expected. Dr Chasuble, I hope you are well.

CHAS: Dear Mr Worthing. I trust this garb of woe does not betoken some terrible calamity.

JACK: My brother!

PRISM: More shameful debts and extravagancies?

CHAS: Still leading his life of pleasure?

JACK: (*shaking his head*) Dead! (*putting handkerchief to his eyes*)

CHAS: Your brother Ernest dead?

JACK: Quite dead.

PRISM: What a *lesson* for him. I trust he will profit by it. (*sit* R.)

CHAS: Mr Worthing, I offer you my sincere condolences. You have at least the consolation of knowing that you were always the most generous and forgiving of brothers.

JACK: (*handkerchief business*) Poor Ernest. He had many faults, but it is a sad blow.

CHAS: Very sad indeed. Were you with him at the end?

JACK: No, he died abroad in Paris. I had a telegram last night from the manager of the Grand Hotel.

CHAS: Was the cause of his death mentioned?

JACK: A severe chill, it seems.

CHAS: (*raising his hand*) None of us are perfect. I myself am particularly susceptible to draughts. Will the – interment take place here?

JACK: No. He seems to have expressed the desire to be buried in Paris. (CHASUBLE *helps* JACK *to sit* C.)

CHAS: In Paris. (*shakes his head*) I fear that hardly points to any very serious state of mind at the last. You would no doubt wish me to make some slight allusion to this tragic domestic affliction next Sunday. (JACK *presses his hand convulsively*.) My sermon on the meaning of the manna in the Wilderness can be adapted to almost any occasion, joyful, or, as in the present case, distressing. (*long pause.*) I have preached it at Harvest celebrations, christenings, confirmations, on days of humiliation and festal days. The last time I delivered it was in the Cathedral, as a charity sermon on behalf of the Society for the Prevention of Discontent Among the Upper Classes. The Bishop, who was present, was much *struck* by some of the analogies I drew.

Oscar Wilde, The Importance of Being Earnest (1895)

Queen Victoria's taste in sermons

When I began at Windsor, the Queen used to give me minute instructions as to what ought and ought not to be done with respect to the services in her Private Chapel, the relation of the Domestic Chaplain to the servants, both indoor and outdoor, and the management of occasional functions, such as a baptism or a marriage. The curious aloofness of her life from the ordinary current of English ways showed itself in her wishes and arrangements about Divine Service. When she came to the Throne, English Ritual, in the large sense of the word, was at its lowest ebb and ordinary Church services were dreary in the extreme. The Prince Consort brought with him the traditions of Lutheran services, which he liked, and what was called the Ritual Revival, then in its mildest forms, surplices, chanted psalms, eastward position, turning eastward at the creed, found no recognition or even toleration in the Royal chapel.

Forty years later, when I began my Windsor life, these things had become usual elsewhere, but the Queen never saw them, and I remember her incredulous surprise one day when I was discussing these matters with her and contrasted the usages of the Private Chapel at Windsor with common usages elsewhere. Even the very Protestant ritual of Whippingham Parish Church was thought by herself to be rather advanced because the clergy preached in a surplice. The black gown never departed from the Private Chapel at Windsor, though bishops of course preached in their episcopal dress. In the Private Chapel we used Mercer's hymn-book, a most dreary compilation. Fortunately she took a fancy to some special hymn *tunes* in *Hymns Ancient and Modern*, and I suggested incidentally one day that we might have both hymn-books in the Chapel. She agreed, the new hymn-books came and Mercer was never used again. She was however very particular about the hymns and would deprecate or forbid any that she disliked. It was the custom, still maintained I believe by King Edward, that the preacher should write out his text and that it should be placed in her seat, together with a paper showing the hymns to be sung.

With regard to sermons, and her likes and dislikes thereon, a great deal of nonsense has been talked by people who knew little about it. She was in my opinion a very reasonable and sensible judge of sermons. She actively disliked to have in the Private Chapel sermons of an ambitious public character, dealing largely with great affairs. On the other hand she always wished that some allusion should be made to personal incidents, specially those connected with the Royal household and it was her constant use to send to the preacher an intimation, perhaps ten minutes before service, that she wished an allusion made to the death of so-and-so, or the illness of somebody else. This was very disquieting to many men. What I used to urge upon preachers who asked my advice was that they should preach as they would to the household, simple sermons with something to attract attention or awaken interest. It was her very common habit to ask to have in writing a copy of a sermon which had interested her.

Randall Davidson and William Benham, *The Life of Archibald Campbell Tait* (1891)

In Church

'And now to God the Father,' he ends,
And his voice thrills up to the topmost tiles:
Each listener chokes as he bows and bends,
And emotion pervades the crowded aisles.
Then the preacher glides to the vestry-door,
And shuts it, and thinks he is seen no more.

The door swings softly ajar meanwhile,
And a pupil of his in the Bible class,
Who adores him as one without gloss or guile,
Sees her idol stand with a satisfied smile
And re-enact at the vestry-glass
Each pulpit gesture in deft dumb-show
That had moved the congregation so.

Thomas Hardy, *Satires of Circumstance* (1911)

Arthur Wagner's sermons in Brighton

Arthur Wagner must have been a man of extraordinary imagination for he brought into being these basilica-like churches and when the Brighton Corporation, horrified by the height of St Bart's, refused permission for another building of the same proportions, he excavated for the Church of the Resurrection so that one entered at the head of a mighty flight of steps. It did not withstand the damp very well and by the time I knew it it had already been turned into a refrigerated meat store. No wonder his father, the Vicar of Brighton, seeing his son pouring away the family fortune in these extraordinary buildings preached from the text: 'Lord have mercy on my son, for he is a lunatic.' It was a time when texts were much used in this way and it is recounted that once when after some trouble Fr Wagner sacked both his curates the sermon was preached on the text: 'Stay ye here with the ass, while I and the lad go yonder.'

I am sorry I never knew him for I owe him a lot for the monuments he left behind, which to a great extent formed my opinion of what the Church of England ought to look like. He lived to a ripe old age having built churches with careless abandon and founded a Sisterhood, which in those days was a *sine qua non* for any Anglo-Catholic priest worth his salt. He became rather senile and it is nice to think that when the statue of Queen Victoria was erected to commemorate her Diamond Jubilee he died happy in the thought that his life's work had been crowned and the Brighton Corporation, who had prevented some of his more ambitious schemes, had erected an image of Our Blessed Lady.

Colin Stephenson, *Merrily on High* (1971)

A dismal sermon

Sunday, August 26th, 1934

We went to church for the morning service, and heard a sermon which suggested some reflections. The preacher appeared to be on the verge of middle age; he may well have another quarter of a century of active ministry before him. What kind of a preacher will he have become by the time his course is run? He *must* deteriorate, for we all do that as we decline into old age; but how pitifully small will be his stock of thought and knowledge which will have been running out without replenishment on the way! Mannerisms such as his may soon develop into incapacitating and ineradicable faults. Surely a little modesty, a little industry, a little effort could have corrected them; but, most probably, these are now, in his own view, distinctive excellencies. He is rather proud of them than otherwise! Some observations in Archbishop Whately's Autobiography about the easy degeneration of Evangelical preachers – with whom extemporaneous preaching is a tradition, and almost a principle – into the dreariest of windbags came to my mind as I listened to the discourse.

Hensley Henson, *Retrospect of an Unimportant Life* (1945)

A Jewish refugee preaches at the time of Munich

Chamberlain flew to Munich and with Hitler, Daladier, and Mussolini signed the infamous piece of paper. It is now no longer fashionable to identify the leaders and their henchmen who tainted their names by the smiling betrayal of Czechoslovakia. A witchhunt after these many years serves no purpose, but the shame of a false theology remains. Here was an exquisite example of false prophecy. Every ingredient of pious treachery, in the name of God, could be heard, seen, and felt. The darkness lay over the whole land, and only a very few lights remained. The piece of paper which promised 'Peace in our Time' was shown, admired, and believed in. Protests were not reported, but pictures of hysterical and jubilant crowds filled the pages. Never was so much relief felt for so little easing of pain. Delusion fed upon delusion. God, it was said, had come to our aid. On the Sunday following the news the Dean of Lincoln preached at a solemn thanksgiving service. He held the congregation spellbound by ascribing the turn of events to God's wonderful providence. I ran out of my stall and feeling sick to the point of convulsion I gazed at the great west façade of the cathedral. The façade, in all its magnificence, is a sham, for it is not integral to the nave behind it. I saw in it the empty gesture of false prophecy.

The year which followed – in which I was ordained and recovered from the collapse – is perhaps the most interesting of our spiritual history. It is also the most hidden. The political and military development somehow went against the expectation of Chamberlain and Halifax. The country slowly woke up from its dreams and accepted rearmament. Spitfires and Hurricanes began to come off the production line. The rehearsal for evacuation in 1938 had prepared the civilian population for another crisis. The whole feeling changed. But the Church still dragged its feet. On the parochial level I endured the whole of the muddle. At the Armistice Service, attended by the British Legion, I was produced as an exhibit for reconciliation with the Germans. The real cause why I was in the English pulpit would have been suppressed if I had not invoked St Paul's 'Are they Hebrews? So am I'. Curiously enough, this outburst was well received, and even the clergy did not protest. Their pacific attitude was based as much upon ignorance as on bad theology, and once they heard my cause they were quite ready to be swayed. But the battle was prolonged, for the Vicar was bitten with the bug of the Oxford Group Movement, and this strange and somewhat formidable organization wanted to include Hitler and Himmler in its Moral Rearmament. The Vicar, therefore, offered from the heart prayers for the conversion of the German leadership. Such a prayer fed the illusion that such men had still to make a choice. It was also dangerous ammunition because it contained a parallel clause in which we prayed for the conversion of our own men, who favoured war instead of peace. In this manner Churchill was put on the same moral level as Hitler.

Ulrich Simon, *Sitting in Judgement* (1978)

A Billy Graham rally

I told him how I had been to Harringay arena one evening with my friend Joe, who was a literary editor, because we had press tickets lent us by John Betjeman, so we drove down, and because of the press tickets, we were shown right to the front of the arena, and sat on chairs just below the platform, where all the thousands of people behind could see us, which was embarrassing, and when we looked up Dr Graham was above us, holding up his Bible and being eloquent and the whole arena hanging on his words, which were about Immorality, for he was taking the ten commandments, and that night he had got to the seventh, which was the only one, he said, that was about Immorality, and Immorality was worse than all the other sins. He said it happened continually everywhere, in the streets and in the fields and on the beaches, and at the Judgment Day God would say 'You thought no one saw you that evening on the beach, but I saw you, I took a picture of you.' Joe wanted to go out, but I said we couldn't as we were right in front, so he had to bear it. Later Dr Graham told every one who wished to decide for Christ to come forward, and slow religious music played, and many hundreds or thousands of people left their seats and came forward and stood under the platform. I thought it would be very nice if Joe decided for Christ, it might improve the literary world, which is full of Immorality and other faults, but he wouldn't. He said why didn't I; but when I decide for Christ (which I sometimes do, but it does not last) it is always in an Anglican church (high), and I didn't think I would care to decide thus in the Harringay arena, so neither of us got up.

I wondered what effect Dr Graham's disciples would have on Turks, and if they would come forward when he told them, but I thought that if they did they would probably only be deciding for the Prophet, and the missioners would send them back to the mosques they attended, with notes for their Imams.

Rose Macaulay, *The Towers of Trebizond* (1956)

Sermons in Pimlico

My final reminiscence of Pimlico shall be of a parade of church scout troops drawn from southwest London (north of the river – we were not without standards) for a service in St Martin in the Fields. I had to march down Whitehall in shorts as scout uniform in those days demanded. I hoped that none of my contemporaries, working in this or the other government department, would see me. The preacher at the service was Father Farrington, at that time vicar of St Gabriel's, Pimlico. His sermon was completely above the heads of the boys, but they behaved well and looked extremely solemn throughout, especially at Father Farrington's opening words: 'Hallo, scouts. I'm going to begin by telling you a parable. You know what a parable is? It's a heavenly story with no earthly meaning.' I can't remember any more of the sermon.

Harry Williams, CR, *Some Day I'll Find You* (1986)

[6]

BISHOPS, ARCHBISHOPS
AND CARDINALS

Even among the ranks of the higher clergy, there have been some
good men – perhaps few better than the saintly Bishop Thomas
Wilson of Sodor and Man. I love the almost Blakean story, which is
to be found in the following chapter, of Bishop Wilson reading the
Greek Testament with one of his theological students, and exclaiming, 'Don't you see them? Don't you see them?' 'See what, my lord?'
asked the student. 'The angels ascending and descending upon those
trees.' Hooker, the great founder of Anglicanism, contemplated the
angels on his death bed – 'the number and nature of Angels, and
their blessed obedience and order, without which, peace could not
be in Heaven: and Oh! that it might be so on earth!'

I once heard the late Archbishop of Canterbury, Michael Ramsey,
quote those words. I should not be surprised to know that he saw
the angels ascending and descending from the trees, nor that he
contemplated their order and their glory as he lay dying. This would
perhaps account for his celebrated absent-mindedness and his
inability to indulge in 'small talk'.

But not all the bishops have been saints. Some, like Thomas Cranmer, have been a strange mixture of strength and weakness, and
others have been as self-serving and uninspired as the senior officials
in any other human organization.

I have included one of John Milton's famous attacks on episcopacy
in general, and on the bishops in particular. 'Most certain it is (as
all our Stories bear witness) that ever since their coming to the See
of Canterbury, for nearly twelve hundred years, to speak of them in
general, they have been in England to our Souls a sad and doleful
succession of illiterate and blind guides.'

Alas, I am prepared to believe that this has been true. It is certainly very striking that even now, in the latter-days of institutional Christianity, there are many excellent parochial clergy but so few good bishops. Most of the bishops nowadays seem only too anxious to keep up the tradition of being 'doleful and illiterate'. At least they are not threatening figures, as they were in Milton's day.

After ten years or so during which the Church of England had been abolished, or at least put 'on ice', there were many, like Samuel Pepys, who began to nurse rather romantic feelings about the bishops. At the time of Charles II's restoration, many people who had hardly ever set eyes on a bishop queued to see them processing into Westminster. Pepys cannot have been the only witness of this scene to be unimpressed. And yet, only twenty-eight years later, the Trial of the Seven Bishops provoked an enormous and natural swell of popular support for the Church of England.

Since those days, bishops have proliferated. There are more diocesans in England, each with their suffragans and assistants; and there is, of course, a complete rival, or complementary, set of bishops and archbishops in the Catholic Church. The modern ecclesiastical scene recalls the Gilbert and Sullivan song in which 'bishops in their shovel-hats/Were plentiful as tabby-cats/In point of fact – too many!' Only, they don't, unfortunately, any longer wear shovel-hats.

Bishop Stokesley of London confronts his clergy

Leaving disaffection to mature itself, we return to the struggle between the House of Commons and the bishops, which recommenced in the following winter; first pausing to notice a clerical interlude of some illustrative importance which took place in the close of the summer. The clergy, as we saw, were relieved of their premunire on engaging to pay 118,000 pounds within five years. They were punished for their general offences; the formal offence for which they were condemned being one which could not fairly be considered an offence at all. When they came to discuss therefore the manner in which the money was to be levied, they naturally quarrelled among themselves as to where the burden of the fine should fairly rest, and a little scene has been preserved to us by Hall, through which, with momentary distinctness, we can look in upon those poor men in their perplexity. The bishops had settled among themselves that each diocese should make its own arrangements; and some of these great persons intended to spare their own shoulders to the utmost decent extremity. With this object, Stokesley, Bishop of London, who was just then very busy burning heretics, and therefore in bad odour with the people, resolved to call a meeting of five or six of his clergy, on whom he could depend; and passing quietly with their assistance such resolutions as seemed convenient, to avoid in this way the more doubtful expedient of a large assembly.

The necessary intimations were given, and the meeting was to be held on the 1st of September, in the Chapter-house of St Paul's. The bishop arrived at the time appointed, but unhappily for his hopes, not only the chosen six, but with them six hundred of the clergy of Middlesex, accompanied by a mob of the London citizens, all gathered in a crowd at the Chapter-house door, and clamouring to be admitted.

The bishop, trusting in the strength of the chains and bolts, and still hoping to manage the affair officially, sent out a list of persons who might be allowed to take part in the proceedings, and these with difficulty made their way to the entrance. A rush was made by the others as they were going in, and there was a scuffle, which ended for the moment in the victory of the officials: but the triumph was of brief duration; the excluded clergy were now encouraged by the people; they returned vigorously to the attack, broke down the doors, 'struck the bishop's officers over the face,' and the whole crowd, priests and laity, rushed together, storming and shouting, into the Chapter-house. The scene may be easily imagined; dust flying, gowns torn, heads broken, well-fed faces in the hot September weather steaming with anger and exertion, and every voice in loudest outcry. At length the clamour was partially subdued, and the bishop, beautifully equal to the emergency, arose bland and persuasive.

'My brethren,' he said, 'I marvel not a little why ye be so heady. Ye know not what shall be said to you, therefore I pray you keep silence, and hear me patiently. My friends, ye all know that we be men, frail of condition and no angels; and by frailty and lack of wisdom we have misdemeaned ourselves towards the king our sovereign lord and his laws; so that all we of the clergy were in premunire, by reason whereof all our promotions, lands, goods, and chattels were to him forfeit, and our bodies ready to be imprisoned. Yet his Grace, moved with pity and compassion, demanded of us what we could say why he should not extend his laws upon us.

'Then the fathers of the clergy humbly besought his Grace for mercy, to whom he answered he was ever inclined to mercy. Then for all our great offences we had but little penance; for when he might, by the rigour of his laws, have taken all our livelihoods, he was contented with one hundred thousand pounds, to be paid in five years. And though this sum may be more than we may easily bear, yet, by the rigour of his law, we should have borne the whole burden; whereupon, my brethren, I charitably exhort you to bear your parts of your livelihood and salary towards payment of this sum granted.'

J. A. Froude, *The History of England from the Fall of Wolsey to the Death of Elizabeth* (1862–6)

The death of Cranmer

The morning broke in a storm of rain, and the crowds which thronged St Mary's came out to see a reed shaken with the wind. The reed was bent and sorely bruised, but it was not broken yet; even now it might be fashioned into a rod. To St Mary's Cranmer was led in procession between two friars, and as they approached the doors a significant *Nunc Dimittis* was raised. Inside, Cranmer was placed on a stage opposite the pulpit, from which Dr Cole was to preach a sermon. Cranmer had given no sign to Cole or the friars who visited him in the morning; but he had told a poor woman, on whom he bestowed some money, that he would sooner have the prayers of a good layman than those of a bad priest. That boded ill for his final profession, and both Romanists and Reformers passed from hope to fear and from fear to hope as they witnessed Cranmer's demeanour. He was made the touchstone of truth, and his foes themselves had determined that his conduct should test the strength of the two forms of faith.

He stood there, 'an image of sorrow,' while Cole delivered his not unmerciful sermon. With more kindliness than consistency he recalled for Cranmer's comfort the fate of the three faithful children of Israel, who refused to bow before the false god which the King had set up, and passed through the fire unscathed. When he had ended he asked them all to pray for the contrite sinner. Cranmer knelt with the congregation. Then he rose and gave thanks for their prayers, and began to read from a paper he held in his hand. It was his seventh recantation – amended. First came a prayer – 'the last and sublimest of his prayers'; then followed four exhortations. He besought his hearers to care less for this world and more for God and the world to come; to obey the King and Queen, not for fear of them only, but much more for the fear of God, for whosoever resisted them resisted God's ordinance; to love one another like brothers and sisters and do good to all men; and finally he reminded the rich how hard it was for them to enter the kingdom of heaven, and moved them to charity; for what was given to the poor was given to God.

'And now,' he went on, 'forasmuch as I have come to the last end of my life, whereupon hangeth all my life past and all my life to come, either to live with my Saviour Christ for ever in joy, or else to be in pains ever with the wicked devils in hell; and I see before mine eyes presently either heaven ready to receive me, or else hell ready to swallow me up: I shall therefore declare unto you my faith without colour or dissimulation; for now is no time to dissemble whatsoever I have written in time past.'

Then Cranmer began the real work of that day. Having recited the Lord's Prayer in English he began the profession of faith contained in the seventh recantation; but now he declared no unlimited belief in General Councils. He had completely re-covered the ground lost in his recantations and re-gained the position of 1552. If his audience perceived the drift of these changes, the tension must have grown almost unbearable. The climax was reached; his trial was over, his triumph began.

'And now I come to the great thing that so troubleth my conscience, more than any other thing that I said or did in my life: and that is my setting abroad of writings contrary to the truth, which here now I renounce and refuse as things written with my hand contrary to the truth which I thought in my heart, and written for fear of death, and to save my life, if it might be; and that is all such bills which I have written or signed with mine own hand since my degradation; wherein I have written many things untrue. And forasmuch as my hand offended in writing contrary to my heart, it shall be first burned. And as for the Pope, I refuse him as Christ's enemy and Antichrist, with all his false doctrine. And as for the Sacrament – '

He got no farther; his foes had been dumb with amazement, but now their pent-up feelings broke loose. 'Stop the heretic's mouth!' cried Cole, 'take him away!' 'Play the Christian man,' said Lord

Williams; 'remember your recantations and do not dissemble.' 'Alas, my lord,' replied Cranmer, 'I have been a man that all my life loved plainness, and never dissembled till now against the truth; which I am most sorry for'; and he seized the occasion to add that as for the Sacrament he believed as he had taught in his book against the Bishop of Winchester. The tumult redoubled. Cranmer was dragged from the stage and led out towards the stake.

A. W. Pollard, *Thomas Cranmer and the English Reformation* (1905)

Cranmer and the Bread of Heaven

'. . . the bread had nothing to do with the Body – that was what he was dying
for –'

DOM GREGORY DIX ON CRANMER

Dear master, was it really for this you died?
   To make that separation clear
   That heaven is elsewhere, nowise here?
That the divine bitter yeast is not inside
   Our common bread; this body, loved so
In its young crocus light, and the full orb of manhood,
   And the paean of sound, all that our senses know
Is not the matter of God?

The 'last enchantments of the Middle Ages'
   In this case, were a faggot fire
   And rubbish pitched beside the pyre;
A couple of burnt doors, from this so-intellectual rage
   Remain, and the proposition (if dying made it plain)
Flesh turns to ashes, bread cannot turn to God.
   Yet how if the question that cost so much pain
Itself was wrongly made?

A change takes place: to this all can assent;
   But question 'what place does it take?
   Or none at all?' – there's the mistake,
There we confuse our terms. For this is an event,
   Not subject to a physical experiment
As water is split for energy; no gain
   In splitting hairs. We know that God can enter
To what He first contained;

We know the kingdom of heaven suffers violence,
    But not atomic. Who can weigh
    Love in a man's heart? So we still say
'Body and soul' as though they were at variance.
    Who can weigh Love? Yet sensibly he burns,
His conflagration is eyes, hands, hearts:
    So is he sensed, but in and out of the eternal,
Because the sense departs.

Anne Ridler, A Matter of Life and Death (1959)

Marmaduke Middleton, Bishop of Waterford 1579

His relations with the clergy and inhabitants of the diocese generally were so strained, and their hostility towards himself so intense, that it is more than probable that his rule was harsh and arbitrary. Indeed, an attempt to kill him, as he was 'at evening prayer with candlelight,' was made by some villains who had been instigated to the crime by one of his own archdeacons, 'John Pratt, clerk.' They 'sore wounded two of the bishop's servants,' and the bishop 'was himself in danger of killing.' The cause of offence had been his insisting on the archdeacon, who was a non-resident pluralist, residing at one of his cures. Such at least is Middleton's account of the matter set forth in a memorial to the queen, but after the falsehood he dictated to his secretary it would seem to be necessary to hear the other side.

The hatred against him, which had been long growing, at length showed itself in 1587, soon after his Visitation of the diocese, in charges brought against him before the Court of High Commission, and which embraced treason, murder, bigamy, and theft. The bishop, however, was acquitted through the 'contrarieties' of the evidence, as he was on the renewal of the Articles of Accusation three years afterwards, when the promoter renounced them in open court. Then followed a cessation of hostilities for two years, when Bishop Middleton was cited to appear before the Archbishop of Canterbury and other commissioners to answer the same charges, but this time with a very different result.

F. O. White, Lives of the Elizabethan Bishops (1898)

The death of Hooker

About one day before his death, Dr Saravia, who knew the very secrets of his soul – for they were supposed to be confessors to each other – came to him, and, after a conference of the benefit, the necessity, and safety of the Church's absolution, it was resolved the Doctor should give him both that and the Sacrament the following day. To which end the Doctor came, and, after a short retirement and privacy, they two returned to the company; and then the Doctor gave him and some of those friends which were with him, the blessed Sacrament of the body and blood of our Jesus. Which being performed, the Doctor thought he saw a reverend gaiety and joy in his face; but it lasted not long; for his bodily infirmities did return suddenly, and became more visible, insomuch that the Doctor apprehended death ready to seize him; yet, after some amendment, left him at night, with a promise to return early the day following; which he did, and then found him better in appearance, deep in contemplation, and not inclinable to discourse; which gave the Doctor occasion to require his present thoughts. To which he replied, 'That he was meditating the number and nature of Angels, and their blessed obedience and order, without which, peace could not be in Heaven: and Oh! that it might be so on Earth!' After which words, he said, 'I have lived to see this world is made up of perturbations; and I have been long preparing to leave it, and gathering comfort for the dreadful hour of making my account with God, which I now apprehend to be near: and though I have by his grace loved him in my youth, and feared him in mine age, and laboured to have a conscience void of offence to him, and to all men; yet if thou, O Lord! be extreme to mark what I have done amiss, who can abide it? And therefore, where I have failed, Lord, shew mercy to me; for I plead not my righteousness, but the forgiveness of my unrighteousness, for His merits, who died to purchase pardon for penitent sinners. And since I owe thee a death, Lord, let it not be terrible, and then take thine own time: I submit to it: let not mine, O Lord! but let thy will be done.' With which expression he fell into a dangerous slumber; dangerous as to his recovery, yet recover he did, but it was to speak only these few words: 'Good Doctor, God hath heard my daily petitions, for I am at peace with all men, and he is at peace with me; and from that blessed assurance I feel that inward joy,

which this world can neither give nor take from me: my conscience
beareth me this witness, and this witness makes the thoughts of death
joyful. I could wish to live to do the Church more service; but cannot
hope it, for my days are past as a shadow that returns not.' More
he would have spoken, but his spirits failed him; and, after a short
conflict betwixt Nature and Death, a quiet sigh put a period to his
last breath, and so he fell asleep.

Izaak Walton, *Lives* (1665)

'A sad and doleful succession of illiterate and blind guides'

Most certain it is (as all our Stories bear witness) that ever since their
coming to the See of Canterbury for near twelve hundred years, to
speak of them in general, they have been in England to our Souls a
sad and doleful succession of illiterate and blind guides: to our purses,
and goods a wasteful band of robbers, a perpetual havoc, and rapine:
to our state a continual Hydra of mischief, and molestation, the forge
of discord and Rebellion: This is the Trophy of their Antiquity, and
boasted Succession through so many Ages. And for those Prelate-
Martyrs they glory of, they are to be judged what they were by the
Gospel, and not the Gospel to be tried by them.

And it is to be noted that if they were for Bishoprics and Ceremonies, it was in their prosperity, and fulness of bread, but in their
persecution, which purified them, and near their death, which was
their garland, they plainly disliked and condemned the Ceremonies,
and threw away those Episcopal ornaments wherein they were
installed, as foolish and detestable, for so the words of Ridley at his
degradement, and his letter to Hooper expressly shew. Neither doth
the Author of our Church History spare to record sadly the fall (for
so he terms it) and infirmities of these Martyrs, though we would
deify them. And why should their Martyrdom more countenance
corrupt doctrine, or discipline, than their subscriptions justify their
Treason to the Royal blood of this Realm by diverting and entailing
the right of the Crown from the true heirs, to the houses of Northumberland and Suffolk, which had it took effect, this present King had
in all likelihood never sat on this Throne, and the happy union of
this Island had been frustrated.

Lastly, whereas they add that some the learnedest of the reformed abroad admire our Episcopacy, it had been more for the strength of the Argument to tell us that some of the wisest Statesmen admire it, for thereby we might guess them weary of the present discipline, as offensive to their State, which is the bug we fear; but being they are Churchmen, we may rather suspect them for some Prelatizing-spirits that admire our Bishoprics, not Episcopacy. The next objection vanishes of itself, propounding a doubt, whether a greater inconvenience would not grow from the corruption of any other discipline, than from that of Episcopacy. This seems an unseasonable foresight, and out of order to defer, and put off the most needful constitution of one right discipline, while we stand balancing the discommodities of two corrupt ones. First constitute that which is right, and of itself it will discover, and rectify that which swerves, and easily remedy the pretended fear of having a Pope in every Parish, unless we call the zealous, and meek censure of the Church, a Popedom, which whoso does let him advise how he can reject the Pastorly Rod, and Sheep-hook of Christ, and those cords of love, and not fear to fall under the iron Sceptre of his anger that will dash him to pieces like a Potsherd.

John Milton, 'Of Reformation in England and the Causes that Hitherto Have
Hindered It' (1651)

Upon Bishop Andrewes his Picture before his Sermons

This reverend shadow cast that setting Sun,
Whose glorious course through our Horizon run,
Left the dimme face of this dull Hemisphæare,
All one great eye, all drown'd in one great Teare.
Whose faire illustrious soule, led his free thought
Through Learnings Universe, and (vainely) sought
Roome for her spatious selfe, untill at length
Shee found the way home, with an holy strength
Snatch't her self hence, to Heaven: fill'd a bright place,
Mongst those immortall fires, and on the face
Of her great maker fixt her flaming eye,
There still to read true pure divinity.
And now that grave aspect hath deign'd to shrinke

Into this lesse appearance; If you thinke,
'Tis but a dead face, art doth here bequeath:
Looke on the following leaves, and see him breathe.

Richard Crashaw, *The Delights of the Muses* (1646)

The trial of the seven bishops

On the 29th of June, the day appointed for the trial, the Bishops, attended by thirty-five Lords, and a number of other friends, took their seats in Westminster Hall. The Court was thronged with a multitude of anxious spectators: every eye seemed rivetted on these Confessors for the rights of the Church, as they sat in front of the Bench, conscious of their innocence, cheered by a unversal sympathy, and prepared to incur any penalty that might be inflicted upon them for the cause of truth. The Judges had already declared the King's prerogative to be above all law. One of them was a Roman Catholic, and the Lord Chief Justice a creature of the Court. At every stage of the trial, which lasted ten hours, whenever the Crown lawyers failed in their proof, or any other circumstance occurred advantageous to the prisoners, the Court resounded with a shout of laughter, or an exclamation of joy, from the crowded audience, which all the menaces of the Judge could not repress.

At seven o'clock in the evening, the jury withdrew to consider their verdict. Three loud cheers were given for the Bishops, who retired with all the privacy they could to their houses; but wherever the people met with them, 'they huzza'd and humm'd them in great abundance.'

One of their friends wrote a note to the Archbishop, dated 6 o'clock the next morning, and before the Court opened; he says,

We have watched the jury all night, carefully attending without the door, on the stair head. They have, by order, been kept all night without fire or candle, bread, drink, tobacco, or any other refreshment whatever, save only some basons of water and towels this morning about 4. The officers, and our own servants, and others hired by us to watch the officers, have and shall constantly attend, but must be supplied with fresh men to relieve our guards, if need be. I am informed by my servant, that about midnight they were very loud one among another: and the like happened about three this morning; which makes me collect they are not yet agreed: they beg a candle to light their pipes, but are denied.

In a postscript, he says,

Just now the officer brings me word they are all agreed, and are sending to my Lord Chief Justice to know when he pleases to take their verdict.

At ten o'clock the Bishops, attended as before, and the Judges, took their seats in Court to hear the all-important verdict. It is impossible to describe the keen interest that held all parties in breathless suspense, as the crier called over the names of the jury. The cause not of the Bishops only, but of the nation, seemed to hang on the next few minutes: the safety of the Reformed religion – the vitality of the law – the very existence of liberty were involved in the result. We may imagine the gravity, and thoughtful collectedness of mind, depicted on the countenances of the Bishops, as they awaited the verdict – themselves the objects of an intense solicitude. The Judges, the officers of the Court, the Counsel, the Peers, and the multitude of spectators – were hushed into silence.

SIR SAMUEL ASTREY: Gentlemen, are you agreed on your verdict?
JURY: Yes.
SIR SAMUEL ASTREY: Who shall say for you.
JURY: Our foreman.
SIR SAMUEL ASTREY: Do you find the Defendants or any of them Guilty of the misdemeanour, whereof they are impeached, or not Guilty?
FOREMAN: NOT – GUILTY.

The first word was enough – the last was almost drowned in a tumultuous and eager burst of irrepressible triumph: 'there was a most wonderful shout, that one would have thought the Hall had crack'd.' 'Not Guilty! Not Guilty!' resounded from side to side, with loud and long huzzas, which were re-echoed from without. 'It passed with electrical rapidity from voice to voice along the infinite multitude who waited in the streets. It reached the Temple in a few minutes. For a short time no man seemed to know where he was. No business was done for hours. The Solicitor General informed Lord Sunderland, in the presence of the Nuncio, that never within the remembrance of man had there been heard such cries of applause, mingled with tears of joy.' 'The acclamations,' says Sir John Reresby, 'were a very rebellion in noise.'

James in his Memoirs relates, that,

'As the Verdict of Acquittal was given, there was such prodigious acclamations of joy, as seem'd to set the King's authority at defyance: it spread itself not only into the Citie, but even to Hounslo Heath, where the soldiers, upon the news of it, gave up a great shout, tho' the King was then actually at dinner in the Camp; which surprised him extreamly, not on account of the Bishops' acquittal – but what gave his Majesty great disquiet was to see such industry used to inflame the multitude, and set the people's heartes against him, and that this infection had spread itself even amongst those, from whom he expected his chief security: and that the Church partie instead of obedience, and duty which he had hoped for, and which he thought his protection justly merited, should be now the ringleaders of the faction.

Startled at the acclamations of the army, he sent Feversham out to know what was the matter. The Earl came back, and told the King, 'It was nothing but the soldiers shouting upon the news of the Bishops being acquitted.' The King replied 'And do you call that nothing? but so much the worse for them.'

The jury were received with the loudest applause; hundreds, with tears in their eyes, embraced them as deliverers. The Bishops escaped from the huzzas of the people as privately as possible, and exhorted them to fear God and honour the King. 'Ken came with the Archbishop of Canterbury, in his Coach to Lambeth, over London Bridge and through Southwark, which took them up several hours, as the concourse of the people were innumerable, the whole way hanging upon the Coach, and insisting on the being blessed by those two Prelates, who with much difficulty and patience at last got to Lambeth House.' James accuses the Bishops of 'heightening the discontent by all their little artifices to render his intentions suspected: for as they went through Westminster Hall, the people falling on their knees in mighty crowds to aske their blessing, they cry'd out to them "Keep your Religion." '

It had been well for him if he could more truly have appreciated their motives, or more clearly have traced to their cause these tokens of sympathy between the Bishops and the people, – an affection for their common religion.

'A Layman', *Life of Thomas Ken* (1854)

The Epitaph upon Gilbert Glanvill Bishop of Rochester, as written in Rochester Cathedral. Translated

Gilbertus Glanvil whose heart was as hard as an Anvil
Always litigious when he should have been highly religious,
Still charg'd with Law suits he to that Court aptly descended
Where quiet appears not and quarrells never are ended.

Matthew Prior (1721)

Bishop Wilson and the angels

'Give Thy holy angels charge concerning us,' was his petition each night. 'For the guard Thy holy angels keep over me, I thank Thy good providence,' was his morning thanksgiving. No wonder that God should vouchsafe a visible fulfilment to a prayer offered daily by one of his saints for almost a whole century.

When sitting one morning in his study, listening to a clerical student who was reading to him out of the Greek Testament, probably one of the many passages which bear upon the ministry of angels, the bishop exclaimed, 'Don't you see them? don't you see them?' 'See what, my lord,' answered the student. 'The angels ascending and descending upon those trees.' Doubtless those ministering spirits were hovering around this heir of salvation, ready to convey his departing spirit to that paradise of God 'where,' to use his own words, 'the souls of the faithful enjoy rest and felicity in hopes of a blessed resurrection.'

Notwithstanding this token of divine favour, that self-abasement which was the characteristic of his whole life continued to the end. One day, not long before his death, he was heard to exclaim in secret prayer, 'God be merciful to me a sinner – a vile sinner – a miserable sinner.'

He died blessing God, and praising Him in ejaculations from the Prayer-book, on the 7th of March, 1755, in the ninety-third year of his age, and the fifty-eight of his consecration. He was buried in the churchyard of St Michael; and it need not be added that the day of his interment was a day of mourning throughout his diocese. His tenantry had been appointed to bear his remains to their humble resting-place, but the whole multitude pressed forward to share the precious burden. The coffin was made out of one of the elm-trees which he had planted soon after coming to the island, and which, some years before his death, had been cut down and sawed into planks, to be in a state of readiness to receive his corpse. It is observable that his uncle, to whom allusion in the course of this memoir has often been made, 'some years before his death, caused his gravestone to be laid in that place where his body was afterwards buried.'

Such was Bishop Wilson – 'a name justly revered by the members of that Church of which he was in his day, and has been since, in sacred language, "a burning and a shining light." '

William Henry Teale, Lives of English Divines (1846)

The Bishop of Ripon visits Haworth

In March the quiet parsonage had the honour of receiving a visit from the then Bishop of Ripon. He remained one night with Mr Brontë. In the evening some of the neighbouring clergy were invited to meet him at tea and supper; and during the latter meal, some of the 'curates' began merrily to upbraid Miss Brontë with 'putting them into a book'; and she, shrinking from thus having her character as authoress thrust upon her at her own table, and in the presence of a stranger, pleasantly appealed to the Bishop as to whether it was quite fair thus to drive her into a corner. His Lordship, I have been told, was agreeably impressed with the gentle, unassuming manners of his hostess, and with the perfect propriety and consistency of the arrangements in the modest household. So much for the Bishop's recollection of his visit. Now we will turn to hers.

March 4th.

The Bishop has been, and is gone. He is certainly a most charming Bishop – the most benignant gentleman that ever put on lawn sleeves; yet stately too, and quite competent to check encroachments. His visit passed capitally well; and at its close, as he was going away, he expressed himself thoroughly gratified with all he had seen. The Inspector has been also in the course of the past week; so that I have had a somewhat busy time of it. If you could have been at Haworth to share the pleasures of the company, without having been inconvenienced by the little bustle of the preparation, I should have been *very* glad. But the house was a good deal put out of its way, as you may suppose; all passed, however, orderly, quietly, and well. Martha waited very nicely, and I had a person to help her in the kitchen. Papa kept up, too, fully as well as I expected, though I doubt whether he could have borne another day of it. My penalty came on in a strong headache as soon as the Bishop was gone: how thankful I was that it had patiently waited his departure! I continue stupid to-day. Of course, it is the reaction consequent on several days of extra exertion and excitement. It is very well to talk of receiving a Bishop without trouble, but you *must* prepare for him.'

Elizabeth Gaskell, *The Life of Charlotte Brontë* (1857)

The Bishop of Oxford drinks sherry-cobbler through a straw

The success of the first volume of 'Modern Painters' of course gave me entrance to the polite circles of London; but at that time, even more than now, it was a mere torment and horror to me to have to talk to big people whom I didn't care about. Sometimes, indeed, an incident happened that was amusing or useful to me; – I heard Macaulay spout the first chapter of Isaiah, without understanding a syllable of it – saw the Bishop of Oxford taught by Sir Robert Inglis to drink sherry-cobbler through a straw – and formed one of the worshipful concourse invited by the Bunsen family, to hear them 'talk Bunsenese' (Lady Trevelyan), and *see* them making presents to – each other – from their family Christmas tree, and private manger of German Magi. But, as a rule, the hours given to the polite circles were an angering penance to me – until, after I don't know how many, a good chance came, worth all the penitentiary time endured before.

John Ruskin, *Præterita* (1912)

A dream about Cardinal Newman

There were indeed times when the more fundamental question thrust itself forward: 'If you are to be ordained to the priesthood, are you sure it ought to be priesthood in the Anglican Church and not priesthood in the Roman Church?'

'Here I may recall a very vivid dream in which these questions took shape and which for a time vaguely troubled me. With the inconsequence of dreams I was at Exeter station, possessed of a first-class ticket to London, and a warm rug, waiting for the London express and pleasurably anticipating a comfortable journey. When the train drew up and I was slipping into my first-class carriage, a hand was laid on my shoulder from behind and a voice of singular sweetness and yet decisiveness said: "I think you must turn and come third-class with me." I looked round and saw a figure holding a cloak before its face. I could not but obey the voice. I followed the figure into a third-class carriage. It sat down in front of me, withdrew the cloak from its face, and disclosed the features of – John Henry, Cardinal Newman! Moral – leave the security and comfort of the Anglican Establishment and face the strangeness and ascetic discipline of Rome. No man, I suppose, who has had to think out his religious position for himself, and who is by temperament inclined to the Catholic position, can ever have failed to feel the immense attractiveness of that august and world-wide communion. But a liberal bent of mind and the evangelical strain in my blood prevented me from yielding to it. I soon came to be convinced that the Anglican Church, *if true to its ideal*, stands for a truer, higher, more spiritual Catholicism than Rome. I must emphasize 'if true to its ideal,' for then and ever since then I have felt here a difference from many at least who have been born and bred in the Church of England. It is not to that Church *as it is* at any particular time or in any particular place that my loyalty is given, but to that Church in its ideal, *as it might be*, as I believe it is meant to be, as it is capable of becoming. And after all, it is to the ideal of any institution – the State, marriage, political party – that ultimate loyalty is due and right.

J. G. Lockhart, Cosmo Gordon Lang (1949)

Cardinal Newman's corpse

August 13th – 'While at luncheon received telegram from Father Neville to say that if I wished to see Cardinal Newman's remains I must come at once. So caught the 2.10 train. Arrived at the Oratory at 5. Met Father Neville who took me to the Church, then to the little sitting-room and tiny oratory, where he produced a good portrait of the Cardinal which the Cardinal had proposed to give me when he heard I had been disappointed of Millais's, and had been over-ruled, I suppose, very naturally: then to his admirably planned library. The sitting-room a mere cell filled with books.

'The Cardinal just like a saint's remains over a high altar, waxy, distant, emaciated, in a mitre, rich gloves whereon the ring (which I kissed), rich slippers. With the hat at the foot.

'And this was the end of the young Calvinist, the Oxford don, the austere Vicar of St Mary's. It seemed as if a whole cycle of human thought and life were concentrated in that august repose. That was my overwhelming thought. Kindly light had led a guided Newman to this strange, brilliant, incomparable end.

'Seeing him on his right side in outline one saw only an enormous nose and chin almost meeting – a St Dominic face. The left side was inconceivably sweet and soft, with that gentle corner of the mouth so greatly missed in the other view. The body, so frail and slight that it had ceased to be a body terrestrial.'

Marquis of Crewe, *Lord Rosebery* (1931)

Cardinal Manning and the dock strike of 1898

Apart from the moral effects of his action in intervening in the memorable crisis of the autumn of 1889, between the Directors of the London Docks and the men on Strike, the vigour and vitality displayed by Cardinal Manning offered another singular illustration of the power of mind over matter; of the impulse of heart and soul over-mastering the feebleness of age and the infirmities of illness. Force of will, tenacity of purpose, which through life were the most marked elements in Manning's character, were never more conspicuous than in the supreme effort to fight the battle of the men on Strike at the London Docks. He stood up almost singlehanded as the champion of Labour. The odds against him were immense. The Dock Directors resented the interference of an outsider, ignorant of the customs of the Trade, of the merits of the facts in dispute, of the principles, as their supporters in the press or on the platform contended, of political economy.* A weaker man than Manning would have fallen back abashed, as some of his colleagues did, in the face of opposition. Self-confidence, however, never forsook him. Benevolence, sympathy, pity for the men on Strike and their wives and children filled his heart. A noble ambition prompted him to perform the part of a public benefactor as peacemaker at a serious crisis. For after the victory over the Dock Directors had been practically secured, the Strike Committee, flushed with success and with large funds still at their command, threatened to keep up the Strike for an indefinite period. The plea put forward by the Leaders of the Strike was as to the date at which the new scale of payment conceded by the Directors was to come into operation. It had been fixed for the first of the following January. The Strike Committee, breaking the agreement which they had provisionally accepted, now demanded that the date should be advanced to the first of October, a fortnight from the date of their new demand. The Dock Directors absolutely refused the exorbitant demand. Now was the time for Cardinal Manning to show his skill as a diplomatist, and a peacemaker. His first business was to endeavour to obtain concessions on the part of the Dock Directors as to the date of introducing the new scale of wages, in the view of inducing the men on Strike to abate their extravagant demands. The Directors were obdurate. They insisted on the observance of the date as originally arranged. Cardinal Manning, with the Lord Mayor and the Bishop of London, who had come up to town, met the Leaders of the Strike at the Mansion House and drew up the terms agreed to by the Directors of the Docks, namely an advance on the rate of wages of sixpence per day from the first of January. The Leaders of the Strike were fair-spoken and plausible, and promised to submit the terms to the men, and report without delay the result to the Mansion House. The Committee of Conciliation, as it was called, waited at the Mansion House till ten o'clock in the evening; no answer was given. But next morning, Sunday, as Cardinal Manning has recorded, 'appeared a manifesto repudiating terms, negotiations, and negotiators.' In the afternoon, a meeting of the men on Strike in Hyde Park passed a Resolution declaring that they would accept the Directors' terms only on condition that the date of the new scale of wages should be advanced from 1st January to 1st October.

A dead-lock ensued. The dangers attending the prolongation of the Strike were incalculable. The Bishop of London, indignant at what he considered the duplicity of the Leaders of the Strike, shook the dust from off his feet and left the Committee of Conciliation in the lurch. Had Cardinal Manning followed his faint-hearted example what dangers, what calamities to the community, what evils might not have ensued.

At this crisis the value of Cardinal Manning's intervention was seen at its full. The Leaders of the Strike were elated at what they considered to be their victory over the Directors. They desired to push things to extremes. They were careless of consequences. They rejected with scorn terms of concilation. It was Cardinal Manning's aim and object to bring them to reason, and in order to do so he knew that he must first win the confidence of the men and then gain their hearts. In this view, Cardinal Manning and Mr Buxton met the various Strike Committees at Poplar, in their headquarters, at 'Wade's Arms.' The Conference lasted three and a half hours. The meeting was attended by about sixty or seventy men. They were excited and obstinate. They insisted on the full fruits of their victory. Two hours were spent in hopeless discussion. At last, Cardinal Manning made a final appeal to the men. He spoke with earnestness and out of the fulness of his heart. He implored them not to prolong the Strike, not to add to the sufferings of their wives and children, not to imitate the cruelty and hardness of heart of the Directors, not to reject the advice and disappoint the hopes of their friends and champions. Cardinal Manning proposed to split the difference and make the first Monday in November the date for the introduction of the new scale of wages. The hearts of the men were moved at last by his touching appeals and eloquent remonstrances. They began to give way. One of the Leaders of the Strike moved a Resolution, adopting Cardinal Manning's proposal, and empowering him to treat with the Directors. After still further discussion and delay the Resolution was at last carried – nineteen men not voting – by twenty-eight to fifteen.

The final difficulty was to induce the Directors to accept the terms of the men and ratify the compromise. Empowered by the Lord Mayor, who was absent from London, Cardinal Manning and Mr Buxton saw the Directors with the view of inducing them to accept the proposition of the men. No immediate or definite answer could be given. Collateral issues had to be considered. Several days were spent in negotiations with the wharfingers and lightermen and others still on Strike. At last, late on Saturday evening, the remnant of the men on Strike gave in, and the Directors signed the agreement. The Strike was at an end.

The putting an end to this dispute, which was producing disastrous consequences to all concerned, directly or indirectly – to the port of London, to the community at large – seemed to justify Cardinal Manning's interposition. He may have been ignorant of the customs of the Trade, of the merits of the questions in dispute; he may have lacked the technical knowledge essential to the part of an arbitrator; yet, in spite of these shortcomings, and of his, maybe, somewhat crude theories, he succeeded where others failed.

* In the beginning of the Strike Cardinal Manning was under the impression that the Directors of the London Docks were reaping enormous profits. He only learned subsequently, from inquiries made by one of his secretaries, of the unfortunate pecuniary position of the two principal Dock Companies who were the first objects of attack on the part of the Strikers.

Edmund Sheridan Purcell, *Life of Cardinal Manning* (1895)

Whispered at the church-opening

In the bran-new pulpit the bishop stands,
And gives out his text, as his gaze expands
To the people, the aisles, the roof's new frame,
And the arches, and ashlar with coloured bands.

'Why – he's the man,' says one, 'who came
To preach in my boyhood – a fashion then –
In a series of sermons to working-men
On week-day evenings, a novelty
Which brought better folk to hear and see.
They preached each one each week, by request:
Some were eloquent speakers, among the best
Of the lot being this, as all confessed.'

'I remember now. And reflection brings
Back one in especial, sincerest of all;
Whose words, though unpicked, gave the essence of things; –
And where is he now, whom I well recall?'

'Oh, he'd no touches of tactic skill:
His mind ran on charity and good will:
He's but as he was, a vicar still.'

Thomas Hardy, *Winter Words* (1928)

Bishop Barnes of Birmingham

The adjoining church was, of course, very high, with the little red light of the reserved Sacrament always aglow, the pungency of incense always in the air, Holy Water in good supply, and confessionals available like telephone kiosks as and when required. All this led to an acrimonious controversy with the then Bishop of Birmingham, Dr Barnes, who regarded the Eucharist as a distasteful form of magic. A sometime *Daily News* columnist, he was one of Ramsay MacDonald's clerical appointments, another being Dr Hewlett Johnson, Dean of Canterbury, who over the years preached Stalin and him sanctified from the pulpit of the Anglican Church's senior cathedral. Thus MacDonald, least revolutionary of Socialists, all unconsciously delivered a body blow at institutional Christianity far more destructive in its consequences than all the efforts of overtly anti-Christian crusades. The best demolition work is done by such unlikely agents; bourgeois society being a Prometheus fated to gorge its own entrails. Was it not two bourgeois Jews – a typical Viennese general practitioner, and a British Museum Reading Room *enragé* – Freud and Marx – who undermined the whole basis of Western European civilization as no avowedly insurrectionary movement ever has or could, by promoting the notion of determinism, in the one case in morals, in the other in history, thereby relieving individual men and women of all responsibility for their personal and collective behaviour?

When I was working on the *Manchester Guardian*, I met Dr Barnes, a friend of C. P. Scott. He turned out to be a rather holy-looking man. Clergymen, in my experience, tend to get holier and holier-looking as they move farther and farther away from their faith; rather in the same way that a certain type of womaniser gets more ethereal looking the more women he seduces. It must be some kind of inner adjustment mechanics, like a thermostat. There never was a more deaconal dean than Dr Hewlett Johnson when, in his gaiters and with a large cross adorning his waistcoat, he sat beaming beatifically among his church's foremost enemies. Dr Barnes's rig was also elegantly clerical, and he had a gentle, purring, exaggeratedly meek manner of addressing one. At the time I met him he was much exercised about a new telescope which had just been developed. Telescopes, he seemed to imply, were getting so powerful that before long they'd be looking into heaven itself. Then all doubts would be set at rest, and science and faith come together in one blessed consummation. When Scott died, Barnes conducted his funeral service in Manchester Cathedral. In the course of his address on that occasion he remarked that some might consider it strange that he, an Anglican bishop, should be presiding over the obsequies of a distinguished Unitarian in an Anglican cathedral; but to him it seemed the most natural thing in the world, since Scott, like himself, had been a puzzled theist. This appeared in *The Times* report as 'puzzled atheist'. It confirmed my feeling that misprints, like the foolishness of men, are the wisdom of God.

Malcolm Muggeridge, *The Green Stick* (1967)

A bishop takes Mulliner's Buck-U-Uppo

'My dear bishop,' said old General Bloodenough, the Chairman of the College Board of Governors, shaking his hand at the conclusion of the unveiling, 'your magnificent oration put my own feeble efforts to shame, put them to shame, to shame. You were astounding!'

'Thanks awfully,' mumbled the bishop, blushing and shuffling his feet.

The weariness which had come upon the bishop as the result of the prolonged ceremony seemed to grow as the day wore on. By the time he was seated in the headmaster's study after dinner he was in the grip of a severe headache.

The Rev Trevor Entwhistle also appeared jaded.

'These affairs are somewhat fatiguing, bishop,' he said, stifling a yawn.

'They are, indeed, Headmaster.'

'Even the '87 port seems an inefficient restorative.'

'Markedly inefficient. I wonder,' said the bishop, struck with an idea, 'if a little Buck-U-Uppo might not alleviate our exhaustion. It is a tonic of some kind which my secretary is in the habit of taking. It certainly appears to do him good. A livelier, more vigorous young fellow I have never seen. Suppose we ask your butler to go to his room and borrow the bottle? I am sure he will be delighted to give it to us.'

'By all means.'

The butler, dispatched to Augustine's room, returned with a bottle half full of a thick, dark coloured liquid. The bishop examined it thoughtfully.

'I see there are no directions given as to the requisite dose,' he said. 'However, I do not like to keep disturbing your butler, who has now doubtless returned to his pantry and is once more settling down to the enjoyment of a well-earned rest after a day more than ordinarily fraught with toil and anxiety. Suppose we use our own judgment?'

'Certainly. Is it nasty?'

The bishop licked the cork warily.

'No. I should not call it nasty. The taste, while individual and distinctive and even striking, is by no means disagreeable.'

'Then let us take a glassful apiece.'

The bishop filled two portly wine-glasses with the fluid, and they sat sipping gravely.

'It's rather good,' said the bishop.

'Distinctly good,' said the headmaster.

'It sort of sends a kind of glow over you.'

'A noticeable glow.'

'A little more, Headmaster?'

'No, I thank you.'

'Oh, come.'

'Well, just a spot, bishop, if you insist.'

'It's rather good,' said the bishop.

'Distinctly good,' said the headmaster.

Now you, who have listened to the story of Augustine's previous adventures with the Buck-U-Uppo, are aware that my brother Wilfred invented it primarily with the object of providing Indian Rajahs with a specific which would encourage their elephants to face the tiger of the jungle with a jaunty sang-froid: and he had advocated as a medium dose for an adult elephant a teaspoonful stirred up with its morning bran-mash. It is not surprising, therefore, that after they had drunk two wine-glassfuls apiece of the mixture the outlook on life of both the bishop and the headmaster began to undergo a marked change.

Their fatigue had left them, and with it the depression which a few moments before had been weighing on them so heavily. Both were conscious of an extraordinary feeling of good cheer, and the odd illusion of extreme youth which had been upon the bishop since his arrival at Harchester was now more pronounced than ever. He felt a youngish and rather rowdy fifteen.

'Where does your butler sleep, Catsmeat?' he asked, after a thoughtful pause.

'I don't know. Why?'

'I was only thinking that it would be a lark to go and put a booby-trap on his door.'

The headmaster's eyes glistened.

'Yes, wouldn't it!' he said.

They mused for awhile. Then the headmaster uttered a deep chuckle.

'What are you giggling about?' asked the bishop.

'I was only thinking what a priceless ass you looked this afternoon, talking all that rot about old Fatty.'

In spite of his cheerfulness, a frown passed over the bishop's fine forehead.

'It went very much against the grain to speak in terms of eulogy – yes, fulsome eulogy – of one whom we both know to have been a blighter of the worst description. Where does Fatty get off, having statues put up to him?'

'Oh well, he's an Empire builder, I suppose,' said the headmaster, who was a fair-minded man.

'Just the sort of thing he would be,' grumbled the bishop. 'Shoving himself forward! If ever there was a chap I barred, it was Fatty.'

'Me, too,' agreed the headmaster. 'Beastly laugh he'd got. Like glue pouring out of a jug.'

'Greedy little beast, if you remember. A fellow in his house told me he once ate three slices of brown boot-polish spread on bread after he had finished the potted meat.'

'Between you and me, I always suspected him of swiping buns at the school shop. I don't wish to make rash charges unsupported by true evidence, but it always seemed to me extremely odd that, whatever time of the term it was, and however hard up everybody else might be, you never saw Fatty without his bun.'

'Catsmeat,' said the bishop, 'I'll tell you something about Fatty that isn't generally known. In a scrum in the final House Match in the year 1888 he deliberately hoofed me on the shin.'

'You don't mean that?'

'I do.'

'Great Scott!'

'An ordinary hack on the shin,' said the bishop coldly, 'no fellow minds. It is part of the give and take of normal social life. But when a bounder deliberately hauls off and lets drive at you with the sole intention of laying you out, it – well, it's a bit thick.'

'And those chumps of Governors have put up a statue to him!'

The bishop leaned forward and lowered his voice.

'Catsmeat.'

'What?'

'Do you know what?'

'No, what?'

'What we ought to do is to wait till twelve o'clock or so, till there's no one about, and then beetle out and paint that statue blue.'

'Why not pink?'

'Pink, if you prefer it.'

'Pink's a nice colour.'

'It is. Very nice.'

'Besides, I know where I can lay my hands on some pink paint.'

'You do?'

'Gobs of it.'

'Peace be on thy walls, Catsmeat, and prosperity within thy palaces,' said the bishop. 'Proverbs cxxi. 6.'

P. G. Wodehouse, Mulliner Nights (1933)

A modernist bishop

'Faith is such a personal matter, especially in these days,' said the Bishop vaguely.

'He may have been pulling my leg,' said Marcus.

'You know quite well he wasn't,' said Norah. 'He was being downright cynical. A priest, calmly announcing that he doesn't believe in God!'

'Well, if I may say so without frivolity, it rather depends on the tone that is used! I understand you are writing a book on the subject, Marcus?'

'Not exactly, sir,' said Marcus. He felt like a schoolboy being interrogated and noted with annoyance his conditioned reactions.

'I'm not writing about God. I'm writing about morality. Though I am going to devote a chapter to the ontological argument.'

'Excellent, excellent. The only sound argument in the whole of theology, in my humble view, only don't quote me! I'm so glad. We need all the help we can get.'

'But I'm not a Christian,' said Marcus.

'Well, you know, the dividing lines are not by any means as clear as they used to be. Passion, Kierkegaard said, didn't he, passion. That's the necessary thing. We must remember that the Holy Spirit bloweth where it listeth. It's not the gale, it's the windless calm that is Godless. "Where's the bloody horse?" if you follow me!'

'But there's still a difference between believing in God and not believing in God,' said Norah.

'Oh, certainly. But perhaps this difference is not quite what we once thought it was.'

Iris Murdoch, The Time of the Angels (1960)

An interview with Cardinal Heenan

MUGGERIDGE: I always feel that almost the only reason that I'd like to become a Cardinal would be to be waited on by nuns.

CARDINAL: I think you'd make a very good Cardinal as a matter of fact.

MUGGERIDGE: I doubt it strongly. Not a Cardinal, perhaps a bishop.

CARDINAL: Well, you've got to start somewhere.

MUGGERIDGE: I always like lunching on Fridays because we don't have meat.

CARDINAL: You're not getting any fish, by the way, you're getting an omelette.

MUGGERIDGE: No, no, it's very nice. This would be part of the Catholic life that I would find least difficult. I suppose it dates from a time when eating meat was a tremendously important thing.

CARDINAL: Well, you know what they say. They say that it was an example of the Jewish instinct of the twelve Apostles; they were all fishermen, and they decided that if they made a rule about fish on Fridays, it would be good business. But I don't think that's theological doctrine.

Malcolm Muggeridge, Muggeridge through the Microphone (1968)

Michael Ramsey's lap

The new Archbishop of Canterbury has a lovely lap for a cat.

Barbara Pym, *A Very Private Eye* (1985)

An Archbishop's lack of small talk

At the bishop of Chichester's dinner table, Mrs Phipps had earlier experienced an unnerving introduction to Ramsey. Simon Phipps was at that time suffragan bishop of Horsham, and as he had a previous engagement he was unable to go to dinner one evening with Ramsey's cousin Roger Wilson and his wife, Joyce, so Mary Phipps, a psycho-analyst by profession and only recently married to Simon, went alone. The Ramseys were staying, and Joyce Wilson warned Mary Phipps the conversation might be stilted. Mary was placed on Ramsey's right. After the soup had been served, Ramsey asked her if she thought depression was the same thing as the dark night of the soul. She said, 'No'. After some fifteen minutes of further silence, and the serving of the next course, the Archbishop again turned to her, and said, 'Good. Neither do I.'

Michael De-la-Noy, *Michael Ramsey: A Portrait* (1990)

[7]

CATHEDRAL PEOPLE

The Russians have a word which means 'cathedral people'. Indeed, it is the title of one of the finest nineteenth-century novels, by Leskov. No book of 'church and clergy' could be complete without a glimpse at the world of cathedrals. So, in this chapter we meet deans, archdeacons and even an apostolic protonotary.

  Two of the most interesting writers in the English language, Jonathan Swift and William Ralph Inge, have been the deans of cathedrals. As the diary of Dean Inge makes clear, he enjoyed the prestige of being Dean of St Paul's, but the cathedral services – which for many of us are the most uplifting and beautiful experiences – were a source of perpetual irritation. Dean Swift was a much greater writer, of course: arguably the greatest writer that the Church of Ireland ever produced, and one of the most destructively original geniuses in the English language. I hope that justifies my having included a lot of Dean Swift. Unlike Dean Inge, he was a very good dean; and he enjoyed the seemly and restrained traditions of Anglican worship. During his lifetime and since, readers of Swift have tried to reconcile the 'savage indignation' of his imagination and the Christianity which, as a clergyman, he was bound to profess. Few writers have ever entertained a bleaker or less charitable view of the human race and its follies; but the essence of his paradoxical creed is perhaps to be found in his *Thoughts on Religion*.

A Dean defends his daughter's honour

When he got to Piccadilly he put himself into a cab, and had himself driven to the corner of Munster Court. It was a little street, gloomy to look at, with dingy doors and small houses, but with windows looking into St James's Park. There was no way through it, so that he who entered it must either make his way into some house, or come back. He walked up to the door, and then taking out his watch, saw that it was half-past six. It was almost too late for calling. And then this thing that he intended to do required more thought than he had given it. Would it not be well for him that there should be something holy, even to him, in spite of that Devil's advocate who had been so powerful with him? So he turned and, walking slowly back towards Parliament Street, got into another cab, and was taken to his club. 'It has come out,' said Major M'Mickmack to him, immediately on his entrance, 'that when the Dean went to see Brotherton at the hotel, Brotherton called Lady George all the bad names he could put his tongue to.'

'I dare say. He is blackguard enough for anything,' said De Baron.

'Then the old Dean took his lordship in his arms, and pitched him bang into the fireplace. I had it all from the police myself.'

'I always liked the Dean.'

'They say he is as strong as Hercules,' continued M'Mickmack. 'But he is to lose his deanery.'

'Gammon!'

'You just ask any of the fellows that know. Fancy a clergyman pitching a Marquis into the fire!'

'Fancy a father not doing so if the Marquis spoke ill of his daughter,' said Jack De Baron.

Anthony Trollope, Is He Popenjoy? (1878)

'The little games that go on in Cathedrals'

Wednesday, 21 December 1870

Coming into the Vicarage from the school I found Sir Gilbert Lewis pacing round the gravel walk round the lawn in gloves and stick and great coat trying to get warm before starting on his cold journey to Harpton. He told me a good deal about Maria Kilvert of Worcester whom he knew, as he is a Canon of Worcester. He said she was tall and thin. She used to come rapidly into Church (into the Cathedral) to receive the sacrament two or three times a month, but for the last three years she had not attended the other services. She used to come in a respirator. She shut herself up almost entirely ever since he had been Canon of Worcester, 15 years. Lady Lewis used to call and was sometimes admitted. Sir Gilbert had not called for three years. The house looked most melancholy and dreary, like a house of the dead, no movement, the blinds never drawn up, no carriage ever stopping at the gate, scarcely any one ever going out or in at the door. Sir Gilbert does not believe she had the slightest acquaintance with Lord Lyttelton, or that she even knew him by sight. He said mad people are apt to come to Cathedrals. There was a mad woman who came to Worcester Cathedral and gave him a great deal of trouble by screeching out. There was a Mr Quarrell who used to make antics at the time of the Communion. At a certain point in the service this man would bow down till he got his head on the pavement and his movements were so extraordinary that all they could do was to look at him and watch him. The authorities did not know what to do with him. They could not say, 'You shall not be a Communicant', but they let him know indirectly that they thought his proceedings very ridiculous. 'Ah,' said Sir Gilbert, 'you don't know all the little games that go on in Cathedrals.'

Francis Kilvert, Diaries (1974)

An unsuitable guest for a deanery

Nell Gwyn also was one of the Court circle, and to be provided for, though not so handsomely. Strange to say, this was the occasion of placing Ken in a difficulty. He had a good prebendal house in the Cathedral Close, opposite to the Deanery where the King used to lodge. When the 'Harbinger,' whose duty it was to provide lodgings in a royal progress, 'came to Winton, he marked the Doctor's house, which he held in right of his prebend, for the use of Mrs Gwin.' But Ken's fearless heart at once prompted him to vindicate the holiness of his office. 'He absolutely refused her admittance, declaring that a woman of ill repute ought not to be endured in the house of a clergyman, especially the King's Chaplain.' This must have excited no small surprise among the courtiers; but as he was peremptory, 'she was forced to seek other lodgings.' A small room was built for her at the south end of the Deanery. 'It was ever afterwards known by the name of "Nell Gwyn," and has only been removed within the present century.'

He could not enter into worldly considerations of policy and prudence, which so often outweigh the clear dictates of conscience. His was no false or partial rule of conduct. How could he preach to his poor ones in the Soke of the sanctity of God's law, and receive a harlot into his own dwelling? The same simplicity of character and straight-forward zeal which had prompted him, in the palace at the Hague, to protect the honour of Jane Wroth, at the risk of offending the Prince of Orange, at once made him reject Nell Gwyn, though it should expose him to the King's resentment, which he could not but expect, as the natural consequence, for Hawkins says, his refusal 'was publickly known.' Humble as he was, he had, in his measure, the holy courage of the Baptist, which made him reprove adultery even in a palace. But Ken did not meet the Evangelist's reward; for Charles, so far from taking offence, appears to have admired the Christian boldness of his chaplain, and shortly after engaged him in a secret expedition to Tangier, in Africa, which about that time occupied much of his thoughts.

'A Layman', *Life of Thomas Ken* (1845)

Dean Donne poses for his monument

It is observed, that a desire of glory or commendation is rooted in the very nature of man; and that those of the severest and most mortified lives, though they may become so humble as to banish self-flattery, and such weeds as naturally grow there; yet they have not been able to kill this desire of glory, but that like our radical heat, it will both live and die with us; and many think it should do so; and we want not sacred examples to justify the desire of having our memory to outlive our lives; which I mention, because Dr Donne, by the persuasion of Dr Fox, easily yielded at this very time to have a monument made for him; but Dr Fox undertook not to persuade him how, or what monument it should be; that was left to Dr Donne himself.

A monument being resolved upon, Dr Donne sent for a Carver to make for him in wood the figure of an Urn, giving him directions for the compass and height of it; and to bring with it a board, of the just height of his body.

'These being got, then without delay a choice Painter was got to be in readiness to draw his picture, which was taken as followeth – Several charcoal fires being first made in his large study, he brought with him into that place his winding-sheet in his hand, and having put off all his clothes, had this sheet put on him, and so tied with knots at his head and feet, and his hands so placed as dead bodies are usually fitted, to be shrowded and put into their coffin, or grave. Upon this Urn he thus stood,with his eyes shut, and with so much of the sheet turned aside as might shew his lean, pale, and death-like face, which was purposely turned towards the East, from whence he expected the second coming of his and our Saviour Jesus.' In this posture he was drawn at his just height; and when the picture was fully finished, he caused it to be set by his bed-side, where it continued and became his hourly object till his death, and was then given to his dearest friend and executor Dr Henry King, then chief Residentiary of St Paul's, who caused him to be thus carved in one entire piece of white marble, as it now stands in that Church . . .

Isaak Walton, *The Life of Dr John Donne* (1640)

Promotion

(Reply to a letter of congratulation, in verse, from the Very Rev C. A. Alington)

I'm the sort of man they make an Apostolic Protonotary –
I've written reams and reams of prose, and quite a lot of potery;
To walk on garden-rollers is among my minor glories,
And I used to be prevailed upon to write detective stories;
I can also punt canoes (or, as they say in Greenland) kayaks,
And had quite a flair at one time for composing elegiacs;
I can look up trains in Bradshaw, on occasions locomotory,
As undoubtedly becomes an Apostolic Protonotary.

In short, when I've unravelled all the complicated mystery
About what the Holy Office does, the Rota, the Consistory;
When I've studied more theology, and don't get quite so drowsy
    on
Attending learned lectures which discuss the Homoousion;

When I've somehow put behind me (with my poor command of
   French) a list
Of authors whose philosophy is known as Existentialist,
When my learning on a multitude of themes is less bucolic –
There's ne'er a Protonotary will be so Apostolic.

November, 1951

Ronald Knox, *In Three Tongues* (1959)

Advice to Archbishop Campbell Tait upon his appointment to the Deanery of Carlisle

'I do hope that in your hands the post of Dean will prove not to be
a completely useless office. For, indeed, it seems to me that if a man
has judgment and courage, a Dean might prove an invaluable person
in a Cathedral town. Not only might he take the lead in the works
of mercy and in the business of education, but he might also be the
foremost man in preaching the Gospel to the people. But this last
will require that he should step out of the beaten path by instituting
some such thing as an Evening Service, or a service at some suitable
hour for the poor. Often as I walk in the nave of our Cathedral do
I wish that our Dean had the health and the inclination to make the
large building available for the poor. . . . How good would it be for
you to take the lead in such a work – good for the people and good
for yourself. . . . Of course I know that you must wait and feel your
way, and gain the confidence of others before you act; but all I wish
to impress upon you is the importance of attempting some such
thing, and of not being deterred by the numerous lions which the
slothful habits of chapters put in the way of any attempt to make
Cathedrals of use. I remember well your effort to save the poor
College servants, and I cannot but hope that you will prove that you
have still the same mind, now that you are not a College but a
Cathedral Don. Again, may I ask you to forgive me if I suggest
another subject for serious thought? Cannot you as Dean be kind to
some of the poorer clergy? It is quite painful to see how great people
forget our Lord's command to invite those who cannot repay them.
At Salisbury, if a Bible or Missionary Meeting bring the poor clergy
in, they may (except in one or two cases, as when the Bishop happens
to take the chair) seek refreshment at inns. Now, this ought not to be;

for great luncheons are provided when the rich come in to infirmary sermons, to which they and their wives and their daughters go, while the utmost a poor clergyman can expect is a dinner for himself occasionally, while his wife and children may go anywhere. Do, my dear Tait, be kind to the poor clergy. And if the Whigs carry you up higher, and make you a Bishop, never forget the advice of a truly affectionate friend, who does long to see you breaking through the miserably unchristian customs of most Cathedral dignitaries, and proving yourself to be one who is willing, not to make a show in society, but by simple-minded preaching of the Gospel, by self-denying simplicity of habits and tastes, by self-humbling endeavours, to show kindness to the poor in all classes, to earn from your Master the name in your Deanery of a good and faithful servant.'

Samuel Waldegrave, Life of Archbishop Tait (1891)

A visit to Alice in the deanery

I never went to official dinners in Oxford if I could help it; not that I was ever really wanted at them, but sometimes it became my duty to go, as an Art Professor; and when the Princess of Wales came, one winter, to look over the Art Galleries, I had of course to attend, and be of what use I could: and then came commands to the dinner at the Deanery – where I knew no more how to behave than a marmot pup! However, my place was next but one to D'Israeli's, whose head, seen close, interested me; the Princess, in the centre of the opposite side of the table, might be glanced at now and then – to the forgetfulness of the evils of life. Nobody wanted *me* to talk about anything; and I recovered peace of mind enough, in a little while, to hear D'Israeli talk, which was nice; I think we even said something to each other, once, about the salmon. Well – then, presently I was aware of a little ripple of brighter converse going round the table, and saw it had got at the Princess, and a glance of D'Israeli's made me think it must have something to do with *me*. And so it had, thus: – It had chanced either the day before, or the day before that, that the Planet Saturn had treated me with his usual adversity in the carrying out of a plot with Alice in Wonderland. For, that evening, the Dean and Mrs Liddell dined by command at Blenheim: but the girls were not commanded; and as I had been complaining of never getting a sight of them lately, after knowing them from the nursery,

Alice said that she thought, perhaps, if I would come round after papa and mamma were safe off to Blenheim, Edith and she might give me a cup of tea and a little singing, and Rhoda show me how she was getting on with her drawing and geometry, or the like. And so it was arranged. The night was wild with snow, and no one likely to come round to the Deanery after dark. I think Alice must have sent me a little note, when the eastern coast of Tom Quad was clear. I slipped round from Corpus through Peckwater, shook the snow off my gown, and found an armchair ready for me, and a bright fireside, and a laugh or two, and some pretty music looked out, and tea coming up.

Well, I think Edith had got the tea made, and Alice was just bringing the muffins to perfection – I don't recollect that Rhoda was there; (I never did, that anybody else was there, if Edith was; but it is all so like a dream now, I'm not sure) – when there was a sudden sense of some stars having been blown out by the wind, round the corner; and then a crushing of the snow outside the house, and a drifting of it inside; and the children all scampered out to see what was wrong, and I followed slowly – and there were the Dean and Mrs Liddell standing just in the middle of the hall, and the footmen in consternation, and a silence – and –

'How sorry you must be to see us, Mr Ruskin!' began at last Mrs Liddell.

'I never was more so,' I replied. 'But what's the matter?'

'Well,' said the Dean, 'we couldn't even get past the parks; the snow's a fathom deep in the Woodstock Road. But never mind; we'll be very good and quiet, and keep out of the way. Go back to your tea, and we'll have our dinner downstairs.'

And so we did; but we couldn't keep papa and mamma out of the drawing-room when they had done dinner, and I went back to Corpus, disconsolate.

Now, whether the Dean told the Princess himself, or whether Mrs Liddell told, or the girls themselves, *somehow* this story got all round the dinner-table, and D'Israeli was perfect in every detail, in ten minutes, nobody knew how. When the Princess rose, there was clearly a feeling on her part of some kindness to me; and she came very soon, in the drawing-room, to receive the report of the Slade Professor.

John Ruskin, *Præterita* (1886–9)

On the Death of Dr Swift

The Time is not remote, when I
Must by the Course of Nature dye:
When I foresee my special Friends,
Will try to find their private Ends:
Tho' it is hardly understood,
Which way my Death can do them good;
Yet, thus methinks, I hear 'em speak;
See, how the Dean begins to break:
Poor Gentleman, he droops apace,
You plainly find it in his Face:
That old Vertigo in his Head,
Will never leave him, till he's dead:
Besides, his Memory decays,
He recollects not what he says;
He cannot call his Friends to Mind;
Forgets the Place where last he din'd:
Plyes you with Stories o'er and o'er,
He told them fifty Times before.
How does he fancy we can sit,
To hear his out-of-fashion'd Wit?
But he takes up with younger Fokes,
Who for his Wine will bear his Jokes:
Faith, he must make his Stories shorter,
Or change his Comrades once a Quarter:
In half the Time, he talks them round;
There must another Sett be found. . . .

From *Dublin* soon to *London* spread,
'Tis told at Court, the Dean is dead.

Kind Lady *Suffolk* in the Spleen,
Runs laughing up to tell the [Queen,]
The [Queen] so Gracious, Mild, and Good,
Cries, 'Is he gone? 'Tis time he shou'd.
'He's dead you say; [Why, let him] rot;
'I'm glad [the medals were] forgot.
'I promis'd [him, I own, but] when?
'I only [was a Princess] then;

'But now as Consort of [a King]
'You know 'tis quite a different Thing.' . . .

    Suppose me dead; and then suppose
A Club assembled at the *Rose;*
Where from Discourse of this and that,
I grow the Subject of their Chat:
And, while they toss my Name about,
With Favour some, and some without;
One quite indiff'rent in the Cause,
My Character impartial draws. . . .

    'Perhaps I may allow, the Dean
'Had too much Satyr in his Vein;
'And seem'd determin'd not to starve it,
'Because no Age could more deserve it.
'Yet, Malice never was his Aim;
'He lash'd the Vice, but spar'd the Name.
'No Individual could resent
'Where Thousands equally were meant.
'His Satyr points at no Defect,
'But what all Mortals may correct:
'For he abhorr'd that senseless Tribe,
'Who call it Humour when they jibe:
'He spar'd a Hump, or crooked Nose,
'Whose Owners set not up for Beaux.
'True genuine Dullness move'd his Pity,
'Unless it offer'd to be witty.
'Those, who their Ignorance confess'd,
'He ne'er offended with a Jest;
'But laugh'd to hear an Idiot quote,
'A Verse from *Horace*, learn'd by Rote.

    'He knew an hundred pleasant Stories,
'With all the Turns of *Whigs* and *Tories:*
'Was chearful to his dying Day,
'And Friends would let him have his Way.'

Jonathan Swift, *On the Death of Doctor Swift* (1739)

Thought on religion

It is impossible that anything so natural, so necessary, and so universal as death, should ever have been designed by providence as an evil to mankind.

Jonathan Swift, Poetical Works (1967)

The Epitaph on Swift's Tomb in Saint Patrick's Cathedral Dublin

WRITTEN BY HIMSELF
HIC DEPOSITVM EST CORPVS
JONATHAN SWIFT, S.T.P.
HVIVS ECCLESIAE CATHEDRALIS
DECANI,
VBI SAEVA INDIGNATIO
VLTERIVS COR LACERARE NEQUIT.
ABI, VIATOR,
ET IMITARE, SI POTERIS,
STRENVVM PRO VIRILI LIBER-
TATIS VINDICEM.
OBIIT ANNO MDCCXLV
MENSIS OCTOBRIS DIE 19
AETATIS ANNO LXXVIII

Jonathan Swift, (ibid.)

Distaste for church music

... my diary abounds with petulant and almost profane lunges against the dreary and interminable musical services which I had to attend. I can and do pray when I 'enter into my chamber and shut the door'; but in the midst of howling and caterwauling I cannot. 'Melodies heard are sweet, but those unheard are sweeter. Quite right, John Keats; they are.' 'Music hath charms to soothe the savage breast. It has the opposite effect on me who am not a savage.' 'If I believed that I shall listen through all eternity to the seraphim blowing their loud uplifted trumpets, it would almost deter me from the practice of virtue.' 'They turned the Nicene Creed into an anthem;

before the end I had ceased to believe anything.' 'Use not vain repetitions. For ten minutes today the choir repeated the words "I wrestle and pray".' 'Are we quite sure that the Deity enjoys being serenaded'? Such were the groans of a much suffering unmusical man.

W. R. Inge, *Diary of a Dean*, (1949)

[8]

SCENES FROM CLERICAL LIFE

There can not be many rectories in England like that of Hurstmon-ceaux, described in Augustus Hare's *Memorials of a Quiet Life*, with its vast library, and its quiet, innocent, scholarly routines. Nor can many archdeacons today live in houses as well appointed as that of Archdeacon Grantly at Plumstead Episcopi (from Trollope's *The Warden*). Most of the vicarages and rectories of England have now been sold off to businessmen and the parson lives in a small modern house, in which there would scarcely be room for a tenth of the books and furniture which a Victorian clergyman would have deemed necessary to carry on his existence.

The 'clerical class' has vanished too. From the mid-twentieth century, most of those young university men who might, in the old days, have become parsons, opted instead for a job in school or university teaching, or in other professions. In country districts, the clergy have not one, but several parishes to look after. It is not unusual, in a county like Norfolk, for the parson to have four or five churches in his care. Latter-day Archdeacon Grantlys or Francis Kilverts would spend their Sunday mornings dashing from church to church. The early service at Plumstead Magna; 'Family service' at Plumstead Parva; a late Mattins at Puddingdale on the fourth Sunday in the month – otherwise they must make do with having the service taken by a lay reader.

With the decline of religion, there has gone a decline in a whole way of life – the sort of life which Charlotte Mary Yonge and Trollope wrote about in their novels, and which Francis Kilvert so brilliantly painted in his immortal diaries.

Yet, as we are reminded by the extracts which follow – as far apart in time as Chaucer and Oliver Goldsmith, there has always been a trickle of good parsons, in town and country, to keep the church from absolute collapse; as well as the unimpressive curates described by the novelists D. H. Lawrence, Virginia Woolf and Mollie Panter-Downes. The saddest extract in this section is the not unfeline letter written by John Henry Newman about his old friends from the 'Oxford Movement', John Keble and Edward Bouverie Pusey. Keble is nearly dead. As for the revered Dr Pusey: 'He has, I think, a paunch.' After their painfully stilted exchange, Newman rises to go back to his rather unhappy Roman Catholic life in Birmingham. The bell chimes for Evensong, reminding him of a comfortable world from which he had heroically excluded himself.

The parson

A good man was ther of religioun,
And was a povre PERSOUN OF A TOUN,
But riche he was of hooly thoght and werk.
He was also a lerned man, a clerk,
That Cristes gospel trewely wolde preche;
His parisshens devoutly wolde he teche.
Benygne he was, and wonder diligent,
And in adversitee ful pacient,
And swich he was ypreved ofte sithes.
Ful looth were hym to cursen for his tithes,
But rather wolde he yeven, out of doute,
Unto his povre parisshens aboute
Of his offryng and eek of his substaunce.
He koude in litel thyng have suffisaunce.
Wyd was his parisshe, and houses fer asonder,
But he ne lefte nat, for reyn ne thonder,
In siknesse nor in meschief to visite
The ferreste in his parisshe, muche and lite,
Upon his feet, and in his hand a staf.
This noble ensample to his sheep he yaf,
That first he wroghte, and afterward he taughte.

Out of the gospel he tho wordes caughte,
And this figure he added eek therto,
That if gold ruste, what shal iren do?
For if a preest be foul, on whom we truste,
No wonder is a lewed man to ruste;
And shame it is, if a prest take keep,
A shiten shepherde and a clene sheep.
Wel oghte a preest ensample for to yive,
By his clennesse, how that his sheep sholde lyve.
He sette nat his benefice to hyre
And leet his sheep encombred in the myre
And ran to Londoun unto Seinte Poules
To seken hym a chaunterie for soules,
Or with a bretherhed to been withholde;
But dwelte at hoom, and kepte wel his folde,
So that the wolf ne made it nat myscarie;
He was a shepherde and noght a mercenarie.
And though he hooly were and vertuous,
He was to synful men nat despitous,
Ne of his speche daungerous ne digne,
But in his techyng discreet and benygne.
To drawen folk to hevene by fairnesse,
By good ensample, this was his bisynesse.
But it were any persone obstinat,
What so he were, of heigh or lough estat,
Hyn wolde he snybben sharply for the nonys.
A bettre preest I trowe that nowher noon ys.
He waited after no pompe and reverence,
Ne maked him a spiced conscience,
But Cristes loore and his apostles twelve
He taughte, but first he folwed it hymselve.

Geoffrey Chaucer (*c*. 1343–1400) 'General Prologue', *Canterbury Tales*

The parson in his house

The Parson is very exact in the governing of his House, making it a Copy and model for his Parish. He knows the temper and pulse of every person in his house, and accordingly either meets with their vices, or advanceth their virtues. His wife is either religious, or night and day he is winning her to it. Instead of the qualities of the world, he requires only *three* of her; *First*, a training up of her children and maids in the fear of God, with prayers, and catechizing and all religious duties. *Secondly*, a curing and healing of all wounds and sores with her own hands; which skill either she brought with her, or he takes care she shall learn it of some religious neighbour. *Thirdly*, a providing for her family in such sort, as that neither they want a competent sustentation, nor her husband be brought in debt. His children he first makes Christians, and then Commonwealth's men; the one he owes to his heavenly Country, the other to his earthly, having no title to either, except he do good to both. Therefore having seasoned them with all piety, not only of words in praying, and reading; but in actions, in visiting other sick children, and tending their wounds, and sending his charity by them to the poor, and sometimes giving them a little money to do it of themselves, that they get a delight in it, and enter favour with God, who weighs even children's actions. I *Kings* xiv. 12, 13. He afterwards turns his care to fit all their dispositions with some calling, not sparing the eldest, but giving him the prerogative of his father's profession, which happily for his other children he is not able to do. Yet in binding them Apprentices (in case he think fit to do so) he takes care not to put them into vain trades, and unbefitting the reverence of their Father's calling, such as are Taverns for men, and Lace-making for women; because those trades, for the most part, serve but the vices and vanities of the world, which he is to deny and not augment.

George Herbert, *A Priest to the Temple* (1652)

The parson and his pipe

The repast, of which the rector of the seventeenth century invited his tithe-payers to partake at his private board, was an entertainment of homely fare, though cordial welcome. The dishes consisted of the solid joints and substantial puddings, which even the aristocracy of the time regarded as the choicest of food; and though the principal toasts were drunk in canary, the cloth was no sooner removed than the guests looked for no more delicate drink than sound home-brewed ale and steaming punch. The conversation turned chiefly on agricultural matters, the affairs of the parish, and the political interests of the Church; and whilst his reverence and the church-wardens exchanged sentiments on such familiar topics, their admiring and less enlightened auditors nodded their heads approvingly over their tobacco-pipes. That the clergy of the Restoration Period were habitual, if not excessive, smokers, and saw no sin in the delight which comes from the fumes of the aromatic weed, may be inferred from the arrangements made for clerical smokers at Lambeth Palace during Sheldon's primacy. 'It was a practice,' writes Eachard's biographer, 'I suppose, from time immemorial, when any guests dined at Lambeth, for the archbishop, when dinner was over, and after drinking two or three loyal toasts, to invite some of the company into a withdrawing chamber. The rest went up with the chaplains into their own room, situated in the highest tower of the palace, where they amused themselves with a pipe of tobacco, as honest Wood says, and a sober glass, till the bell invited the family to prayers.'

John Cordy Jeafferson, *A Book about Clergy* (1870)

The parson and his games

Whether we find the clergy of old time generally and openly playing bowls* or foot-ball – two favourite sports with the rectors and curates of the sixteenth and seventeenth centuries – or diverting themselves with games of skill and chance, which have dropped into neglect or disrepute in the present day, it is safe for us to infer that such pastimes were deemed appropriate to clergy, and that, in having recourse to them for daily recreation, ecclesiastics no more violated public decorum than the younger clergy of our time offend against prevailing opinion when they play in cricket-matches, or indulge in athletic sports. At the present date many of the ancient diversions of the English home are forbidden to ecclesiastical persons; but it is worthy of observation, that nearly every curtailment of the trivial pleasures of the clergy in one direction has been attended with a corresponding extension of them in another. The Victorian rector may not play with dice, save upon a backgammon-board; but he has free leave to provide himself with a billiard-table, and try to surpass Roberts in the difficult art of making breaks. He is thought to derogate from his dignity if he drive wooden spheres over the parish bowling-green, but society is well pleased to see him play croquet on his own lawn. He may not keep hounds, but no one thinks him precluded by official obligation from lavishing money on a handsome equipage and well-filled stable.

Of the diversions still popular with our clergy, chess is one of the very few which 'the cloth' favoured in old time. In clerical biographies of the Elizabethan period, and the later days of the seventeenth century, the reader continually comes upon passages that record in language of sympathy and approval the prowess of clerical chess-players. But Baxter and other Puritan divines of the Commonwealth period discerned evil in the game which prelates and deans, rectors and vicars, had played to their own delight and with the approbation of beholders from time immemorial. In 'A Letter from a Minister to a Friend concerning the Game of Chess' (1680) – a broadside pre-served in the Harleian Miscellany – a conscientious and too scrupu-lous pastor, bewailing the faults into which an enthusiastic love of chess has betrayed him, observes, 'It hath not done with me, when I have done with it. It hath followed me into my study, into my pulpit; when I have (in my thoughts) been playing at chess: then I have had, as it were, a chess-board before my eyes: then I have been thinking how I might have obtained the strategems of my antagonist, or make such and such motions to his disadvantage; nay, I have heard of one who was playing at chess in his thoughts (as appeared by his words) when he lay a-dying. . . . It hath wounded my con-science, and broken my peace. I have had sad reflections upon it, when I have been most serious. I find, if I were now to die, the remembrance of this game would greatly trouble me, and stare me in the face. I have read in the life of the famous John Huss, how he was greatly troubled for his using of this game a little before his death.'

* During his confinement in Christ Church Deanery, the aged Cranmer was permitted to amuse himself with bowls, whilst his subtle and merciless enemies were enticing him to abjure Protestantism. 'In this mean time,' says Foxe, 'while the Archbishop was thus remaining in durance (whom they kept now in prison almost the space of three years), the doctors and divines of Oxford busied themselves all that ever they could about Master Cranmer to have him recant, essaying, by all crafty practices and allurements they might devise, how to bring their purpose to pass. And to the intent they might win him easily, they had him to the Dean's house of Christ's Church, in the said university; where he lacked no delicate fare, *played at the bowls*, had his pleasure for walking, and all other things that might bring him from Christ.'

John Cordy Jeafferson (ibid.)

Dr SWIFT
The Happy Life of a COUNTRY PARSON

Parson, these things in thy possessing
Are better than the Bishop's blessing.
A Wife that makes conserves; a Steed
That carries double when there's need:
October store, and best Virgina,
Tythe-Pig, and mortuary Guinea:
Gazettes sent gratis down, and frank'd,
For which thy Patron's weekly thank'd:
A large Concordance, bound long since:
Sermons to Charles the First, when Prince;
A Chronicle of ancient standing;
A Chrysostom to smooth thy band in.
The Polygott – three Parts – my Text,
Howbeit – likewise – now to my next.
Lo here the Septuagint, – and Paul,
To *sum the whole,* – the *Close of all.*
    He that has these, may pass his life,
Drink with the 'Squire, and kiss his wife;
On Sundays preach, and eat his fill;
And fast on Fridays – if he will;
Toast Church and Queen, explain the News,
Talk with Church-Wardens about Pews,
Pray heartily for some new Gift,
And shake his head at Doctor Swift.

Alexander Pope, *Imitations of English Poets* (1738)

from The Deserted Village

Near yonder copse, where once the garden smil'd,
And still where many a garden flower grows wild;
There, where a few torn shrubs the place disclose,
The village preacher's modest mansion rose.
A man he was, to all the country dear,
And passing rich with forty pounds a year;
Remote from towns he ran his godly race,
Nor e'er had changed, nor wished to change his place;

Unpractised he to fawn, or seek for power,
By doctrines fashioned to the varying hour;
Far other aims his heart had learned to prize,
More skilled to raise the wretched than to rise.
His house was known to all the vagrant train,
He chid their wanderings, but relieved their pain;
The long remembered beggar was his guest,
Whose beard descending swept his aged breast;
The ruined spendthrift, now no longer proud,
Claimed kindred there, and had his claims allowed;
The broken soldier, kindly bade to stay,
Sate by his fire, and talked the night away;
Wept o'er his wounds, or tales of sorrow done,
Shouldered his crutch, and shewed how fields were won.
Pleased with his guests, the good man learned to glow,
And quite forgot their vices in their woe;
Careless their merits, or their faults to scan,
His pity gave ere charity began.
    Thus to relieve the wretched was his pride,
And even his failings leaned to Virtue's side;
But in his duty prompt at every call,
He watched and wept, he prayed and felt, for all.
And, as a bird each fond endearment tries,
To tempt its new fledged offspring to the skies;
He tried each art, reproved each dull delay,
Allured to brighter worlds, and led the way.
    Beside the bed where parting life was layed,
And sorrow, guilt, and pain, by turns dismayed,
The reverend champion stood. At his control,
Despair and anguish fled the struggling soul;
Comfort came down the trembling wretch to raise,
And his last faultering accents whispered praise.
    At church, with meek and unaffected grace,
His looks adorned the venerable place;
Truth from his lips prevailed with double sway,
And fools, who came to scoff, remained to pray.
The service past, around the pious man,
With steady zeal each honest rustic ran;
Even children followed with endearing wile,

And plucked his gown, to share the good man's smile.
His ready smile a parent's warmth exprest,
Their welfare pleased him, and their cares distrest;
To them his heart, his love, his griefs were given,
But all his serious thoughts had rest in Heaven.
As some tall cliff that lifts its awful form,
Swells from the vale, and midway leaves the storm,
Tho' round its breast the rolling clouds are spread,
Eternal sunshine settles on its head.

Oliver Goldsmith, *The Deserted Village* (1770)

Doughty Street in 1808

Meanwhile, there was much quiet happiness in a certain unpretending house in Doughty Street, Russell Square, and though there was strict economy visible in all its arrangements, fine taste and loving care were equally conspicuous; and if the rooms were small and modestly furnished, they were none the less bright and pleasant places. Sydney Smith kept not willingly, but of necessity, the plainest of tables, yet no man was worthy to share the hospitality of that home who felt inclined to grumble at its simple fare. Once a week, keeping up in London the old custom of his Edinburgh days, he gave a supper-party to his friends; and there was probably more merry laughter behind the closed shutters of No. 8, Doughty Street, on those occasions than in any other house – size at discretion – in the whole of London. Sometimes, however, he was inclined to wish either that 'smiles were meat for children, or kisses could be bread,' and it was the remembrance of his own early struggles which led him to say on one occasion, with dry humour, 'The observances of the Church concerning feasts and fasts are tolerably well kept, upon the whole, since the rich keep the feasts and the poor the fasts!'

Stuart J. Reid, *The Life and Times of the Rev. Sydney Smith* (1884)

Combe-Florey

Dec. 11th, 1842.

DEAR MISS MARTINEAU – I am seventy-two years of age, at which period there comes over one a shameful love of ease and repose, common to dogs, horses, clergymen, and even to *Edinburgh Reviewers*. Then an idea comes across me sometimes that I am entitled to five or six years of quiet before I die. I fought with beasts at Ephesus for twenty years. Have not I contributed my fair share for the establishment of important truths, and for the discomfiture of quacks and fools? Is not the spirit gone out of me? Can I now mix ridicule with reason, so as to hit at once every variety of opposition? Is not there a story about Gil Blas and the Archbishop of Granada?

I am just come from London, where I have been doing duty at St Paul's, and preaching against the Puseyites – I. Because they lessen the aversion to the Catholic faith, and the admiration of Protestantism, which I think one of the greatest improvements the world ever made. II. They inculcate the preposterous surrender of the understanding to bishops. III. They make religion an affair of trifles, of postures, and of garments.

Nothing is talked of in London but China. I wrote to Lord Fitzgerald, who is at the head of the Board of Control, to beg, now that the army was so near, that he would conquer Japan. I utterly deny the right of those exclusive Orientals to shut up the earth in the way they are doing, and I think it one of the most legitimate causes of war. But this argument we will have out when we meet.

I believe Peel to be a philosopher disguised in a Tory fool's-cap, who will do everything by slow degrees which the Whigs proposed to do at once. Whether the delay be wise or mischievous is a separate question, but such I believe to be the man in whom the fools of the earth put their trust.

I am living here, with my wife and one son, in one of the prettiest parsonages in England. I am at my ease in point of income, tolerably well for an old man, giving broth and physic to the poor, but no metaphysical dissertations on the Thirty-nine Articles. I have many friends, and always pronounce violent panegyrics on you whenever your name is mentioned.

SYDNEY SMITH

Stuart J. Reid (ibid.)

Revisiting Keble in old age

To Ambrose St John

Buckland Grange Ryde Septr 13. 1865

My dear A

. . . Scarcely had I left Birmingham, when it struck me that, since Pusey was to be at Keble's that evening, there was no manner of doubt that he would get into my train at Oxford and journey down with me. I was sure of this. When he did not get into my carriage at Oxford, I felt sure we should recognize each other when we were thrown off the train at Reading – but no, he did not turn up – as it happened, he went by an earlier train. However, this expectation put me upon thinking on the subject – and I made up my mind to go to Keble's next morning and see him – and I did. I slept at the Railway Hotel at Southampton Dock – a very reasonable house, and good too – my bed only 2/6 – (they are building close by a grand Imperial Hotel) and then yesterday morning (Tuesday) I retraced my steps to Bishopstoke, left my portmanteau there, and went over to Hursley. I had forgotten the country and was not prepared for such beauty, in the shape of Woods. Keble was at the door, he did not know me, nor I him. How mysterious that first sight of friends is! for when I came to contemplate him, it was the old face and manner, but the first effect and impression was different. His wife had been taken ill again in the night, and at the first moment he, I *think*, and *certainly* I, wished myself away. Then he said, Have you missed my letters? meaning Pusey is here, and I wrote to stop your coming. He then said I must go and prepare Pusey. He did so, and then took me into the room where Pusey was. I went in rapidly, and it is strange how action overcomes pain. Pusey, as being passive, was evidently shrinking back into the corner of the room – as I should have done if he had rushed in upon me. He could not help contemplating the look of me narrowly and long – Ah, I thought, you are thinking how old I am grown, and I see myself in you – though you, I do think, are more altered than I am. Indeed, the alteration in him shocked me (I would not say this to every one) – it pained and grieved me. I should have known him any where – his face is not changed, but it is as if you looked at him through a prodigious magnifier. I recollect him short and small – with a round head – smallish features – flaxen curly hair – huddled up together from his shoulders downward –

and walking fast. This was as a young man – but comparing him even when last I saw him in 1846, when he was slow in his motions and staid in his figure, still there is a wonderful change. His head and his features are half as large again – his chest is very broad (*don't say all this*) – and he has, I think, a paunch – His voice is the same – were my eyes shut, I should not have been sensible of any lapse of time. As we three sat together at one table, I had as painful thoughts as I ever recollect, though it was a pain, not acute, but heavy. There were three old men, who had worked together vigorously in their prime. This is what they have come to – poor human nature – after 20 years they meet together round a table, but without a common cause, or free outspoken thoughts – but, though kind yet subdued, and antagonistic in their mode of speaking, and all of them with broken prospects. Pusey is full of his book which is all but out – against Manning; and full of his speech on the relations between physical science and the Bible, which he is to deliver at the Church Congress at Norwich. He is full of polemics and of hope. Keble is as different as possible; he is as delightful as ever – and, it *seemed* to me as if he felt a sympathy and intimacy with me which he did not find with Pusey. At least he spoke to me of him – and I don't think in the same tone he would have spoken to him of me. I took an early dinner with them, and when the bell chimed for evensong at 4 o'clock, I got into my gig . . .

Ever Yrs affly John H Newman

John Henry Newman *Letters and Diaries* (1956)

Breakfast at Plumstead Episcopi

And now let us observe the well-furnished breakfast-parlour at Plumstead Episcopi, and the comfortable air of all the belongings of the rectory. Comfortable they certainly were, but neither gorgeous nor even grand; indeed, considering the money that had been spent there, the eye and taste might have been better served; there was an air of heaviness about the rooms which might have been avoided without any sacrifice of propriety; colours might have been better chosen and lights more perfectly diffused; but perhaps in doing so the thorough clerical aspect of the whole might have been somewhat marred; at any rate, it was not without ample consideration that those thick, dark, costly carpets were put down; those embossed, but sombre papers hung up; those heavy curtains draped so as to half exclude the light of the sun: nor were these old-fashioned chairs bought at a price far exceeding that now given for more modern goods, without a purpose. The breakfast-service on the table was equally costly and equally plain; the apparent object had been to spend money without obtaining brilliancy or splendour. The urn was of thick and solid silver, as were also the tea-pot, coffee-pot, cream-ewer, and sugar-bowl; the cups were old, dim dragon china, worth about a pound a piece, but very despicable in the eyes of the uninitiated. The silver forks were so heavy as to be disagreeable to the hand, and the bread-basket was of a weight really formidable to any but robust persons. The tea consumed was the very best, the coffee the very blackest, the cream the very thickest; there was dry toast and buttered toast, muffins and crumpets; hot bread and cold bread, white bread and brown bread, home-made bread and baker's bread, wheaten bread and oaten bread; and if there be other breads than these, they were there; there were eggs in napkins, and crispy bits of bacon under silver covers; and there were little fishes in a little box, and devilled kidneys frizzling on a hot-water dish; which, by-the-by, were placed closely contiguous to the plate of the worthy archdeacon himself. Over and above this, on a snow-white napkin, spread upon the sideboard, was a huge ham and a huge sirloin; the latter having laden the dinner table on the previous evening. Such was the ordinary fare at Plumstead Episcopi.

Anthony Trollope, *The Warden* (1855)

Zunday

In zummer, when the sheädes do creep
    Below the Zunday steeple, round
The mossy stwones, that love cut deep
    Wi' neämes that tongues noo mwore do sound,
The leäne do lose the stalken team,
    An' dry-rimm'd waggon-wheels be still,
An' hills do roll their down-shot stream
    Below the resten wheel at mill.
O holy day, when tweil do cease,
Sweet day o' rest an' greäce an' peace!

The eegrass, vor a while unwrung
  By hoof or shoe, 's a-sheenen bright,
An' clover flowers be a-sprung
  On new-mow'd knaps in beds o'white,
An' sweet wild rwoses, up among
  The hedge-row boughs, do yield their smells,
To aïr that do bear along
  The loud-rung peals o' Zunday bells,
Upon the day o' days the best,
The day o' greäce an' peace an' rest.

By brightshod veet, in peäïr an' peäïr,
  Wi' comely steps the road's a-took
To church, an' work-free han's do bear
  Woone's walken stick or sister's book;
An' there the bloomen niece do come
  To zee her aunt, in all her best;
Or married daughter do bring hwome
  Her vu'st sweet child upon her breast,
As she do seek the holy pleäce,
The day o' rest an' peace an' greäce.

William Barnes, Poems in the Dorset Dialect (1879)

Clerical anecdotes

Sometimes the parson obtains strange answers to his questions in the
services. One day a clergyman was taking a baptism, and an elderly
churchwoman was standing as godmother for the infant. He asked
the usual question, 'Dost thou in the name of this child renounce the
devil and all his works,' &c., and received the strange and unexpected
reply, 'I recommend them all.' On another occasion a parson was
burying a stranger, and not being quite sure of the sex of the deceased
turned to a conspicuous mourner and asked *sotto voce*, 'Is it a
"brother," or a "sister"?' The mourner replied in stentorian tones,
'No relation, sir,' which did not help the parson's perplexity, and
was not exactly the answer he wanted.

    If the people trouble the parson, he sometimes troubles and per-
plexes them, especially if age or eccentricity render him peculiar. Old

Dr Routh, the centenarian, sometimes gave out the banns in the presence of a couple who had been married several months. He read the Burial Service over a woman who came to be churched, and frequently lost his place in the services, usually falling back upon the Apostles' Creed.

P. H. Ditchfield, *The Old-time Parson* (1908)

Hawker of Morwenstow

It will be seen that nothing but his intense grasp of the doctrine of the Incarnation saved him from drifting into the wildest vagaries of mysticism.

He would never open out to any one who he thought was not spiritually minded.

A commonplace neighbouring parson, visiting him once, asked him what were his views and opinions.

Mr Hawker drew him to the window. 'There,' said he, 'is Henna-cliff, there the Atlantic stretching to Labrador, there Morwenstow crag, here the church and graves: these are my views. As to my opinions, I keep them to myself.'

Sabine Baring-Gould, *The Vicar of Morwenstow* (1876)

Water of baptism

April 1874
Then the Vicar of Fordington told us of the state of things in his parish when he first came to it nearly half a century ago. No man had ever been known to receive the Holy Communion except the parson, the clerk and the sexton. There were 16 women communicants and most of them went away when he refused to pay them for coming. They had been accustomed there at some place in the neighbourhood to pass the cup to each other with a nod of the head. At one church there were two male communicants. When the cup was given to the first he touched his forelock and said, 'Here's your good health, Sir'. The other said, 'Here's the good health of our Lord Jesus Christ'.

One day there was christening and no water in the Font. 'Water, Sir!' said the clerk in astonishment. 'The last parson never used no water. He spit into his hand.'

Francis Kilvert, Diaries (1974)

The parson and his people

Residence in the parish is, of course, required of those who desire their banns to be proclaimed, and an expectant bride and bridegroom must qualify themselves by staying several nights in the parish where such banns are published.

'Do you sleep in the parish?' asked a rector of an intending benedict.

'Yes, sir, I have slept through several of your sermons,' was the surprising answer.

The parson when baptizing the children of his flock is often troubled by the names which are given at the font. One poor babe whom I baptized had six names; they were too heavy a burden for the little one, who soon passed away from earth. You can never be quite sure whether you are intended to christen a child Ellen or Helen. I have given examples of curious names in my former book. An old rector was exasperated by some fine names which were given in answer to his query, 'Name this child,' and exclaimed, 'I'll have no more of these fine names; I shall christen it plain "John." ' He afterwards regretted his rashness, when told in the vestry that the child was a girl.

P. H. Ditchfield, The Old-time Parson (1908)

Hurstmonceaux Rectory

... instead of the farmhouse-like rectory in which Augustus had lived, the home of Julius was, even externally, quite different to the ordinary type of country rectories, but rather like a good country house, well placed in grounds of considerable extent.

'The rectory,' wrote Arthur Stanley, 'stood far removed from church, and castle, and village. . . . Of all the peculiarities of English life, none perhaps is so unique as an English parsonage. But how peculiar even amongst English parsonages was the rectory of Hurstmonceaux. The very first glance at the entrance-hall revealed the character of its master. It was not merely a house with a good library – the whole house was a library. The vast nucleus which he brought with him from Cambridge grew year by year, till not only study, and drawing-room, and dining-room, but passage, and antechamber, and bedrooms were overrun with the ever advancing and crowded book-shelves. At the time of his death it had reached the number of more than twelve thousand volumes; and it must be further remembered that these volumes were of no ordinary kind. Of all libraries which it has been our lot to traverse, we never saw any equal to this in the combined excellence of quantity and quality; none in which there were so few worthless, so many valuable works. Its original basis was classical, and philological; but of later years the historical, philo-sophical, and theological elements outgrew all the rest.

'In the few spaces which this tapestry of literature left unoccupied were hung the noble pictures which he had brought with him from Italy. To him they were more than mere works of art; they were companions and guests; and they were the more remarkable from their contrast with the general plainness and simplicity of the house and household, so unlike the usual accompaniments of luxury and grandeur, in which we should usually seek and find works of such costly beauty.

'In this home – now hard at work with his myriad volumes around him at his student's desk – now wandering to and fro, book in hand, between the various rooms, or up and down the long garden walk overlooking the distant Level with its shifting lights and shades – he went on year by year extending the range and superstructure of that vast knowledge of which the solid basis had been laid in the classical studies of his beloved university, or correcting, with an elaborate minuteness which to the bystanders was at times almost wearisome to behold, the long succession of proofs which, during the later years of his life, were hardly ever out of his hands.'

Augustus Hare, Memorials of a Quiet Life (1891)

Rectory gardens

My most successful speech at our Ruri-decanal Chapter was on the subject of rectory gardens. We meet once a quarter, presided over by the Rural Dean, to discuss a paper written by one of the clergy and to consider matters of importance to the deanery. On this particular morning the agenda contained a proposal from the Church Assembly that all vicarage and rectory gardens should be entrusted to the care of the Parish Church Council. Now as men we had suffered many humiliations under the tyranny of the Church Assembly; but that our gardens should be taken from us and placed under the charge of officious Church-workers, was a thing that no self-respecting rector or vicar could tolerate.

When I arrived and looked round the room I saw that no one from the deanery was absent. There was the Vicar of Penzance, whom all the children knew as Daddy Rogers; Trymer Bennett, the Rector of St Levan, who would boast he was so old that no man living knew his age and would on occasions refer to himself as 'a deathshead on a mop-stick'; Stona from the moorland parish of Sancreed, who had once 'put the weight for Oxford'; and Thomas Taylor, the quiet scholar from St Just. All these were assembled, and many others, for Penwith is a large deanery and, as I have said, none of the clergy was absent. Boscawen, the Rector of Ludgvan, a celebrated horticulturist, was in the chair and, after having read the resolution, said that he would leave it to the brethren to express their opinions on such a proposal.

I saw several of the clergy exchanging glances as to who should be the first to speak as I rose to my feet.

'Mr Rural Dean,' I said.

The Rural Dean held up his hand and the clergy sitting in front turned round to view the speaker. The Rural Dean, still holding up his hand to enjoin silence, then said, 'Will Mr Walke come to the table so that the brethren may hear him the better?'

With this encouragement I walked to the table and began to speak, my subject being the expulsion of our first parents Adam and Eve from the garden of Eden for partaking of the fruit of the tree of knowledge. I am no gardener, but I successfully introduced the names of several rare trees grown in Cornish gardens that were presumably in the garden of Eden.

'Now,' I said, 'we of the clergy have sinned in many ways and on many occasions, but we have never committed the sin of which our first parents were guilty. So it is our duty to resist the attempt of the Church Assembly to deprive us of our gardens, and to bash this

monstrous proposal on the head.' Any implied criticism of the learning of the clergy was overlooked in the joy of discovering a phrase
which so adequately expressed our feelings. Boscawen rose and said
with passion, 'Walke has told us what we must do,' and then turning
to me inquired, 'What was it you said we must do, Walke?'

'I think I said, "Bash it on the head," Mr Rural Dean,' I answered.

'Yes,' said Boscawen. 'Bash it on the head – that is the thing to
do – bash it on the head.'

Other Chapters must have also 'bashed it on the head', for we
heard no more from the Church Assembly of this sacrilegious proposal.

We found an excellent garden at St Hilary. But it was not our
garden; it was a gardener's garden with circular and diamond-shaped
beds, filled in the summer with lobelias, calceolarias and other bed-
ding-out plants. We were ruthless that first spring in our determination to make the garden our own, and to reduce to some kind
of pattern, what to our eyes appeared a meaningless collection of
geometrical-shaped beds. It was a very difficult task as the house and
walls encircling the front of the garden were built at an angle which
it seemed impossible to reconcile with the garden beyond. Possibly
our best contribution has been the planting of many rare flowering
trees given to us by Compton Mackenzie when he left England for
the Island of Capri.

Bernard Walke, *Twenty Years at St Hilary* (1935)

An East-end Curate

A small blind street off East Commercial Road;
  Window, door; window, door;
  Every house like the one before,
Is where the curate, Mr Dowle, has found a pinched abode.
Spectacled, pale, moustache straw-coloured, and with a long thin
    face,
Day or dark his lodgings' narrow doorstep does he pace.

A bleached pianoforte, with its drawn silk plaitings faded,
Stands in his room, its keys much yellowed, cyphering, and abraded,
'Novello's Anthems' lie at hand, and also a few glees,
And 'Laws of Heaven for Earth' in a frame upon the wall one sees.

He goes through his neighbours' houses as his own, and none
   regards,
And opens their back-doors off-hand, to look for them in their
   yards:
A man is threatening his wife on the other side of the wall,
But the curate lets it pass as knowing the history of it all.

Freely within his hearing the children skip and laugh and say:
   'There's Mister Dow-well! There's Mister Dow-well!' in their
   play;
   And the long, pallid, devoted face notes not,
But stoops along abstractedly, for good, or in vain, God wot!

Thomas Hardy, Human Shows (1925)

The new vicar's standing

The Reverend Ernest Lindley, aged twenty-seven, and newly married, came from his curacy in Suffolk to take charge of his church. He was just an ordinary young man, who had been to Cambridge and taken orders. His wife was a self-assured young woman, daughter of a Cambridgeshire rector. Her father had spent the whole of his thousand a year, so that Mrs Lindley had nothing of her own. Thus the young married people came to Aldecross to live on a stipend of about a hundred and twenty pounds, and to keep up a superior position.

They were not very well received by the new, raw, disaffected population of colliers. Being accustomed to farm labourers, Mr Lindley had considered himself as belonging indisputably to the upper or ordering classes. He had to be humble to the county families, but still, he was of their kind, whilst the common people were something different. He had no doubts of himself.

He found, however, that the collier population refused to accept this arrangement. They had no use for him in their lives, and they told him so, callously. The women merely said: 'they were throng,' or else: 'Oh, it's no good you coming here, we're Chapel.' The men were quite good-humoured so long as he did not touch them too nigh, they were cheerfully contemptuous of him, with a preconceived contempt he was powerless against.

At last, passing from indignation to silent resentment, even, if he dared have acknowledged it, to conscious hatred of the majority of his flock, and unconscious hatred of himself, he confined his activities to a narrow round of cottages, and he had to submit. He had no particular character, having always depended on his position in society to give him position among men. Now he was so poor, he had no social standing even among the common vulgar tradespeople of the district, and he had not the nature nor the wish to make his society agreeable to them, nor the strength to impose himself where he would have liked to be recognized. He dragged on, pale and miserable and neutral.

D. H. Lawrence, 'Daughters of the Vicar', *Collected Short Stories* (1971)

A Huntingdonshire curate

10 or 11 August 1899
We had the Curate to dinner last night, which deserves full mention because I have never sat down to a meal with a curate in my life, nor had one, to my knowledge in the house. My interest was awakened in him very easily; I had a dim idea of mythical curates, dwelling in the pages of novels, & receiving satire at the hands of all wielders of Pens – but the fact that a Black Coated gentleman could be a Human Being & not a Hypocrite (outwardly at least – I cannot answer for the condition of the Curate's morals on the strength of one dinner party) was quite strange to me. This young man seems to be largely a person of intelligence with a rather peculiar gift of humorous sarcasm. Occasionally his judgments & stories are bitter; but on the whole, he is merely good humoured & muscular. This would all be explicable; or not needing explanation; but the surprising thing is that he is a Clergyman. He is moreover a Ritualist, which I take to be a strict creed; & yet the first 5 minutes of his talk with us he declared that the only thing that made life in the country bearable was rabbit shooting. What a life he must have – here especially. He makes no secret of his dislike to Mrs Way, which he conveys to one in cumbrous irony; this lady evidently rules her husband, & would like to dictate to the Curate; certainly thinks him a most inferior creature – she is a kind of small Mrs Proudie. The young man however not having much in common with Mr Slope their hostility is open – expressed on his acerbic side, I expect, by sarcastic civility;

& on Mrs Way's by nagging [?] pretensions; the young man (I know not how to spell his name) has been here 10 months – nine months too many he says. The people about here are a peculiar race. So imbedded are they in their own delving pursuits, living lonely self contained lives, with a few strong religious opinions that only serve to narrow their minds, that a stranger is in their eyes a most contemptible creature. They are solid conservatives, & resent a stranger or an innovation in their lives. The Schoolmaster, who has been here 25 years, says he still feels out in the cold; they do not look upon him as one of themselves. The curate is a man of humour but humour has a hard battle of it in such surroundings. Nevertheless he told his Curates Recollections with great glee – jumping & jerking in a peculiar way he has when something amuses him.

Well, the state of mind of a man like this must be odd. Better lodging in a London slum than gossiping over here –

Virginia Woolf, A Passionate Apprentice: The Early Journals (1990)

Mr Vyner

See-saw, said the clock. In a quarter of an hour she had launched Mrs Porter with a Neapolitan lover on the bright bay, made George's fortune, sent Mavis sliding to meet her light destiny. She laughed at herself. Being much alone encouraged such fancies. As though the See-saw! had released him like a carved wooden figure from a weather-house, Mr Vyner shot from the church porch, saw her, and waved a hand.

'Hallo, hallo!' he called.

He ran down the steps and crossed the road, lowering his voice as he said, 'You've been visiting my bad patch, I see. Who was it, Prouts or Porters? The Porters?' He shook his head, smiled, and sighed. 'Young George is leaving, his sister told me. I'm sorry. We could do with more of him in Wealding. But they really are – they *really* are – '

He made a vague, helpless gesture, he laughed helplessly, looking towards the Porters's hump-backed roof as though they overpowered him even at that distance. The Vicar, thought Laura, the traditional butt of kindly comedy, the chevalier of spinsters, crowned with the wilting cucumber sandwiches of a thousand garden parties. And it was Mr Vyner's fate to look and sound the part of the fruity-voiced churchman, the hearty curer of souls, destined to lose his trousers before the curtain fell on the second act of the roaring farce. He boomed and brayed through the village. He had served in India for many years as an Army chaplain, and he made religion sound like a sort of church parade, with God as the C.O. counting the boots as they clumped in. But he was really good, a saint who had the misfortune to sound like a bore. Laura liked him immensely. He sweated from one end of the village to the other, no distance too long, no hour too late to bring comfort to one of the poor human souls over whom he yearned with such compassion. But the times were out of joint, the healing virtue had gone from his cloth. They did not need him. They did not hold, quoth Mrs Prout, wrapping her arms in her apron, they did not believe, they did not have any truck with. The grapes in the vineyard had grown thorns to defend themselves against the labourer. Was he sometimes despairing, the weatherman in his ancient house, in the powers of which few fully believed any longer? Difficult to tell, with his high varnished colour, his jolly smile.

Mollie Panter-Downes, *One Fine Day* (1947)

A shy curate

For his refreshment he played hockey vigorously in the local team or cycled in the fen country. He would walk a long distance out to some pub, often the Malcolm Arms at Anton's Gowt, and have lunch in the bar on beer and bread and cheese. On his walks he could sometimes be observed waving his hat about and talking to himself. The oddity which the fellow-curates remarked was that as he walked in the procession from the vestry up the aisle he could be heard whistling. No one minded. They took it for granted that this was Ramsey. The most famous story of Ramsey's absent-mindedness comes from Boston. It sounds like legend but there is excellent evidence of its truth. He went out without his front-door key. When he came back he rang the bell. His landlady was nervous of strangers and called through the door, 'I'm sorry, Mr Ramsey is out.' Ramsey: 'I'll return later.'

Owen Chadwick, *Michael Ramsey: A Life* (1990)

[9]

CLERICAL ATTIRE

Almost all clergy, regardless of denominational or theological allegiance, nowadays dress alike, with black or grey shirts and what used to be called 'Roman' or 'dog' collars. Even the most Protestant ministers of the Presbyterian Church of Northern Ireland like to sport Roman collars which – a hundred years ago – would have been thought very surprising.

A clergyman friend who worked in the East End of London (Bethnal Green) during the 1930s as a Church of England curate told me that a rumour had gone round the parish that the vicar was a Roman Catholic. The reason for this supposition on the part of the parishioners was that, to do his parish visiting, the priest wore a black suit instead of a flowing soutane.

Probably, the clergy themselves take less interest in clothes than they used to – though there will probably always be some High Church young 'spikes' who, like the curate in Compton Mackenzie's novel quoted here, believe 'No maniple, no mass'. The fact that the majority of their congregation, let alone the human race, do not know what a maniple is, would not deter their enthusiasm; perhaps the reverse. There have been those, as the extract from *The Ritual Reason Why* reveals, who consider that each item of clerical attire, particularly a garment worn in liturgical functions, is full of significance. For such as these, the bishop's mitre signifies the helmet of salvation, cloven in the midst like the tongues of fire which came down upon the heads of the apostles on the first day of Pentecost. For others, like John Milton, there is something inherently ludicrous in clerical costume, 'and we would burst our mid-riffes, rather than laugh to see them under sayl in all their lawn, and Sarcenet, their shrouds and tackle, with a geometricall rhomboides upon their heads'.

———

Parsons' wigs

It was not very thoughtful of the Reformation to allow the tonsure, which after all can be undone by Nature, to be covered by a wig, and yet to deprive a tonsured wig, which is much more difficult to restore, of the covering of the monk's hood, which would have concealed all deficiency. In Germany we have not the least idea of what the English clergyman's wig is like. Haven't we really – No! And if anyone tries to contradict me, I shall say outright that in Germany we simply do not know at all what a wig is. Ours are mere anatomical specimens of wigs. In short: as regards dignity and impressiveness they are the exact counterpart of the beard of the ancients, with this difference only, that the hair is fixed on the other side of the face. And the form of it? Very well, I will describe the clergyman's wig, in its flowering time of course, in the manner of Linnaeus. Everyone knows how onions blossom. The little flowers form together a sort of sphere which is set high and firmly at the end of a long stem, as if on a spit. Now imagine the hollow stem to be the neck, and imagine from that sphere as many little flowers cut away in front as would be needful to accommodate a mask, and from the top as many as needful to accommodate a hat, but with no mask or hat there, and you have exactly the shape and even the colour of the Englishman's wig. I do not know whether it is a deranged imagination or some other metastasis of the poetic gift in me, but often on fine summer evenings, when I could no longer clearly discern the thin, hollow stems, I could not help comparing a field of onions in flower with an English Church Convention.

Georg Christoph Lichtenberg, *Commentaries on Hogarth's Engravings* (1794)

The Mark of the Beast

A costume for the clergy is as much connected with discipline and self-respect as an uniform for the army, and is no small guarantee for conduct. The disuse of clerical costume was a recent innovation; but thirty-five or forty years ago the abuse had become almost universal. It was consummated by the change in lay fashions – a very singular one – to a nearly exclusive use by men of black. The reaction began in the cut of the waistcoat, which, as worn by the innovators, was buttoned all the way up to the cravat. This was deemed so distinctly Popish, that it acquired the nickname of 'The Mark of the Beast'; and it is a fact that, among the tailors of the west-end of London, this shape of waistcoat was familiarly known as 'the M.B. waistcoat.' Any one who will now take the pains to notice the dress of the regular Presbyterian or Dissenting minister will, I think, find that, in a great majority of instances, he too, when in his best, wears, like the clergyman, the M.B. waistcoat.

W. E. Gladstone, *The Church of England and Ritualism* (1873)

The curate's petticoats

Wednesday, 9 June 1875
Foxham seems to be in a sad state ecclesiastically. Mrs Peglin told us that the Curate, Mr Rivett-Carnac, who walks about in a cassock, was attacked one day by their gander which tore a grievous rent in his 'petticoats'. He said he should tell his friends what a 'ferocious house guardian' Mrs Peglin kept. 'Perhaps, Sir,' suggested the old lady slyly, 'the gander was excited by some peculiarity in the dress.'

Francis Kilvert, *Diaries* (1974)

What is the 'biretta'?

A square cap of black silk or other stuff, worn by persons in Holy Orders at processions and other out-door functions.

The *biretta* is the non-episcopal form of the *mitre*, and both signify the helmet of salvation and the glory of the Priesthood. The mitre is cloven in the midst, like the 'tongues of fire' which fell upon the Apostles (Acts ii. 3), to shew that the wearer is a successor of the

Apostles, and shares with them in the Pentecostal gift. It is a question whether the use of the mitre is of extreme antiquity. Some even assign its introduction to the 10th century. But Bona (*Rer. Lit.* lib. i. c, xxiv.), while admitting the possibility of the fact, shews that *some* ornament of the head was worn from the earliest ages. The reader will remember that under the old law a 'mitre' (or turban) of fine linen was appointed for the high priest (Exod. xxviii. 4), and 'bonnets' for the priests and Levites (ver. 41). The fathers mention that S. James the Just, first bishop of Jerusalem, and also the Apostle S. John, were in the habit of wearing the golden plate which was prescribed for the mitre of the high priest in the Jewish ritual.

In the Eastern Church the actual mitre is unknown, but the clergy wear a particular kind of cap, over which they arrange the hood.

A. W. Mowbray, *The Ritual Reason Why* (1863)

Parson Hawker's clothes

Mr Hawker, as has been already intimidated, was rather peculiar in his dress. At first, soon after his induction to Morwenstow, he wore his cassock; but in time abandoned this inconvenient garb, in which he found it impossible to scramble about his cliffs. He then adopted a claret-coloured coat, with long tails. He had the greatest aversion to anything black: the only black things he would wear were his boots. These claret-coloured coats would button over the breast, but were generally worn open, displaying beneath a knitted blue fisherman's jersey. At his side, just where the Lord's side was pierced, a little red cross was woven in the jersey. He wore fishing-boots reaching above his knee.

The claret-coloured cassock coats, when worn out, were given to his servant-maids, who wore them as morning-dresses when going about their dirty work.

'See there! the parson is washing potatoes!' or, 'See there! the parson is feeding the pigs!' would be exclaimed by the villagers, as they saw his servant girls engaged on their work, in their master's house.

At first he went about in a college cap; but after speedily made way for a pink or plum-coloured beaver hat without a brim, the colour of which rapidly faded to a tint of pink, the blue having disappeared. When he put on a coat, jersey or hat he wore it till it was worn out: he had no best suit.

Sabine Baring-Gould, The Vicar of Morwenstow (1876)

Vestments

With regard to all ornaments and vestments one precaution is most necessary. The parson must make it clearly understood that he will not accept a single thing for the church unless the advice has first been sought of that person who overlooks the decoration of the church. Who that person is will depend on circumstances, but he must be a competent judge; and committees are useless unless their members are modest.

If this precaution be not taken, the services of the church are certain in time to be vulgarized. Some kind friend will work an impossible stole; another will compose a ruinous frontal, and, without warning any one, present it as a pleasant surprise when it is finished; another will be attracted by some brass-work of the gilt gingerbread order in a shop-window, and with a smile of kindly triumph will deposit it one day in the vestry. It will be too late then for the parson to protest: all these good people will be hurt (and one cannot blame them) if their presents are rejected. But if it be publicly explained beforehand that beauty of effect is a most difficult task, for which a lifelong training is required – and that a church must suffer if left to the chance of a multitude of individual tastes, this catastrophe will be avoided.

Sometimes one is tempted to think that folk consider anything good enough for a church. But this is not generally the case. It simply is that the elements of artistic knowledge have not yet entered the heads of many people – and will not, unless the Church educate them by its example. Simplicity, unity, proportion, restraint, richness of colour, ecclesiastical propriety, these things are simply not understood by a vast number. It is not their fault; they have had no opportunity of learning: they want to help the church, and they will do so well if they are only taught; but, if not, it will not cross their minds that decoration without harmony is just as excruciating as music without harmony.

Percy Dearmer, The Parson's Handbook (1903)

No maniple, no Mass

Mark arranged with Dorward to come and sleep in his tent and say Mass on the feast of the Nativity of the Blessed Virgin at six o'clock. In order to promote the fellowship of the occasion, he arranged a concert on the previous evening, which lasted from dusk till nearly midnight, a rousing concert with camp fires crackling and a starry sky above. Dorward sang a comic song, which had a great success not because the song was particularly comic, but because Dorward sang it so incredibly out of tune. Accordion solos provided most of the instrumental music; but there was a banjo and a one-stringed fiddle as well, not to mention the mouth-organs and a penny whistle. When the concert was over and silence, save for the intermittent crying of a baby, had fallen upon the caravans and tents and sleepers in the hedgerows, Dorward and Mark erected an altar by the light of a late moon.

In the morning at sunrise Mark was woken by Dorward's throwing various articles on his camp-bed and muttering to himself in evident agitation:

'Can't say Mass this morning. Can't say Mass. I've forgotten to bring the maniple. No maniple. No Mass. It's that muddle-headed Mrs Gladstone. I told her to be sure she packed all my vestments. And she's forgotten the maniple.'

'Well, you'll have to say Mass without it,' Mark replied firmly.

'My dear boy, it couldn't be done.'

'Don't be so ridiculous, Dorward. You can't disappoint these poor people at the last minute. Besides, if it comes to that, you'd be restoring the original use of the maniple by tying an ordinary dinner-napkin to your left arm. You haven't forgotten anything else? Have you brought the chalice?'

Mark knew that Dorward was not serious in refusing to say Mass, and after a short argument it was agreed that the absence of a maniple would not invalidate the Mass.

'Have you got the cassock and cotta for the server?' Mark asked.

'No cassock,' said Dorward. 'Don't be so High Church, Mark. You never see the servers in France or Flanders bothering about cassocks.'

Compton Mackenzie, *The Parson's Progress* (1923)

Bishop Jewel

He consented to wear the episcopal dress though disapproving of it, and submitted to the ceremonies used at his consecration, while at the same time he regarded them as silly if not worse. For the employment of 'ornaments' in the worship of God, Jewel felt only amused contempt. Engaged to argue against the use of the crucifix in churches, he wrote thus of its defenders, 'I smile when I think with what grave and solid reasons they will defend their little cross.' But he wrote more seriously when there seemed a prospect of its restoration, and he was prepared to resign his bishopric rather than yield, the ground of his objection being that 'the ignorant and superstitious multitude' were 'in the habit of paying adoration to this idol above all others.'

But Jewel was now called to a task far more congenial, and indeed much more important, than arguing against crucifixes. He was fully conscious that the great end of the ministry was the preaching of the gospel, and by the aid of the Holy Spirit impregnating the souls of men with the Word of Life, and if he turned aside to deal with the 'fooleries' of ceremonies, ornaments, habits, and gestures, it was but because, and so far as, they interfered with and hindered the progress of truth. No wearer of the rochet and chimere ever possessed a loftier, and yet a more tolerant, contempt for these 'ridiculous trifles,' as he called them. They were, at the best, but the baubles of children which would be put away when manhood was reached. The soul that was built up in knowledge and piety had, if it were sane, an imperishable safeguard against these things. For a man, because he claimed to be a descendant of the Apostles, to wear a distinctive vesture of satin and lawn, was in his opinion a practice grotesquely contemptible.

F. O. White, *Lives of the Elizabethan Bishops* (1898)

Geometrical rhomboides

They intreate us that we would not be weary of those insupportable greevances that our shoulders have hitherto crackt under, they beseech us that we would think 'em fit to be our Justices of peace, our Lords, our highest officers of State, though they come furnish't with no more experience then they learnt betweene the *Cook*, and the *manciple*, or more profoundly at the Colledge *audit*, or the *regent house*, or to come to their deepest insight, at their *Patrons Table*; they would request us to indure still the russling of their Silken Cassocks, and that we would burst our *mid-riffes* rather then laugh to see them under Sayl in all their Lawn, and Sarcenet, their shrouds, and tackle, with a *geometricall rhomboides* upon their heads.

John Milton, 'Of Reformation in England and the Causes that
Hitherto Have Hindered It' (1641)

[10]

SACRED AND PROFANE LOVE

One of the most implausible theories you ever hear advanced to 'explain' the nature of religious psychology is the notion that religion is only a substitute, in the mind of the believer, for the gratifying of carnal appetite. If so, there would seem, in the history of religion, to have been a lot of men and women who have enjoyed the 'substitute' as well as the real thing.

A pious lady of my acquaintance, unmarried, once attended a retreat. On the first evening, the men and women attending the retreat assembled in the convent chapel for the first address. A note was passed along the front row to her. It came from a man who had come to the retreat in all sincerity to say his prayers, but his attention had been distracted by her beauty.

There is nothing surprising or shocking in this story. Passionate men and women are the ones who are the most likely to be pious, just as their emotions and bodily appetites are easily aroused by love and erotic desire. It is only vulgar newspapers who find this sort of thing surprising, with their prurient, and at the same time oddly innocent amazement whenever they discover a clergyman who has been unable to conceal his amorous preferences.

For some Christians, the tug between the love of God and the worship of Eros will be a lifelong and painful dilemma, a source of torment, not least because their failures in chastity are so eagerly seized upon by unbelievers as evidence that religion is itself a sham. For others, like John Betjeman in his splendid poem, 'Lenten Thoughts of a High Anglican', there need not really be as much of a dilemma as puritans might suppose.

One of Coventry Patmore's acquaintances in the last century was

173

repelled by the mingling, in that brilliant poet's soul, 'of piety and concupiscence'. Repellent it may have been in Patmore's case. Certainly, the Reverend J. H. Smyth-Pigott, of Clapton in London, had an uncontrolled erotic appetite, as well as an overexcited religious imagination. There can have been few Anglican clergy with as many concubines – whom Smyth-Pigott named sisters – who gave birth to children with exciting names like Comet and Life. But then, equally, it has been a rare clergyman who has persuaded large numbers of people, as Smyth-Pigott did, that he was divine.

But this is not just the chapter of randy parsons. As the first extract shows, from *Henry Esmond*, sometimes love itself is stimulated by a religious setting. Esmond and Lady Castlewood are helped to realize how much they love one another by the cathedral choir singing the Evensong psalms. As Skrebensky says to Ursula in *The Rainbow* when he leads her into the church, 'What a perfect place for a rendezvous.'

Henry Esmond

There was scarce a score of persons in the Cathedral besides the Dean and some of his clergy, and the choristers, young and old, that performed the beautiful evening prayer. But Mr Tusher was one of the officiants, and read from the eagle in an authoritative voice, and a great black periwig; and in the stalls, still in her black widow's hood, sat Esmond's dear mistress, her son by her side, very much grown, and indeed a noble-looking youth, with his mother's eyes, and his father's curling brown hair, that fell over his *point de Venise* – a pretty picture such as Vandyke might have painted. Mons. Rigaud's portrait of my Lord Viscount, done at Paris afterwards, gives but a French version of his manly, frank, English face. When he looked up there were two sapphire beams out of his eyes such as no painter's palette has the colour to match, I think. On this day there was not much chance of seeing that particular beauty of my young lord's countenance; for the truth is, he kept his eyes shut for the most part, and, the anthem being rather long, was asleep.

But the music ceasing, my lord woke up, looking about him, and his eyes lighting on Mr Esmond, who was sitting opposite him, gazing with no small tenderness and melancholy upon two persons who had had so much of his heart for so many years, Lord Castlewood, with a start, pulled at his mother's sleeve (her face had scarce been lifted from her book), and said, 'Look, mother!' so loud that Esmond could hear on the other side of the church, and the old Dean on his throned stall. Lady Castlewood looked for an instant as her son bade her, and held up a warning finger to Frank. Esmond felt his whole face flush, and his heart throbbing, as that dear lady beheld him once more. The rest of the prayers were speedily over. Mr Esmond did not hear them; nor did his mistress, very likely, whose hood went more closely over her face, and who never lifted her head again until the service was over, the blessing given, and Mr Dean, and his procession of ecclesiastics, out of the inner chapel.

Young Castlewood came clambering over the stalls before the clergy were fairly gone, and running up to Esmond eagerly embraced him. 'My dear, dearest old Harry!' he said, 'are you come back? Have you been to the wars? You'll take me with you when go again? Why didn't you write to us? Come to mother!'

Mr Esmond could hardly say more than a 'God bless you, my boy!' for his heart was very full and grateful at all this tenderness on the lad's part; and he was as much moved at seeing Frank as he was fearful about that other interview which was now to take place, for he knew not if the widow would reject him as she had done so cruelly a year ago.

'It was kind of you to come back to us, Henry,' Lady Esmond said. 'I thought you might come.'

'We read of the fleet coming to Portsmouth. Why did you not come from Portsmouth?' Frank asked, or my Lord Viscount, as he now must be called.

Esmond had thought of that too. He would have given one of his eyes so that he might see his dear friends again once more; but believing that his mistress had forbidden him her house, he had obeyed her, and remained at a distance.

'You had but to ask, and you knew I would be here,' he said.

She gave him her hand, her little fair hand; there was only her marriage ring on it. The quarrel was all over. The year of grief and estrangement was past. They never had been separated. His mistress had never been out of his mind all that time. No, not once. No, not in the prison; nor in the camp; nor on shore before the enemy; not at sea under the stars of solemn midnight; nor as he watched the glorious rising of the dawn; not even at the table where he sat carousing with friends, or at the theatre yonder where he tried to fancy that other eyes were brighter than hers. Brighter eyes there might be, and faces more beautiful, but none so dear; no voice so sweet as that of his beloved mistress, who had been sister, mother, goddess to him during his youth: goddess now no more, for he knew of her weaknesses, and by thought, by suffering and that experience it brings, was older now than she; but more fondly cherished as woman perhaps than ever she had been adored as divinity. What is it? Where lies it? the secret which makes one little hand the dearest of all? Whoever can unriddle that mystery? Here she was, her son by his side, his dear boy. Here she was, sweeping and happy. She took his hand in both hers; he felt her tears. It was a rapture of reconciliation.

William Makepeace Thackeray, *The History of Henry Esmond* (1852)

The character of a clergyman

I mentioned a cause in which I had appeared as counsel at the bar of the General Assembly of the Church of Scotland, where a *Probationer* (as one licensed to preach, but not yet ordained, is called) was opposed in his application to be inducted, because it was alledged that he had been guilty of fornication five years before. JOHNSON. 'Why, Sir, if he has repented, it is not a sufficient objection. A man who is good enough to go to heaven, is good enough to be a clergyman.' This was a humane and liberal sentiment. But the character of a clergyman is more sacred than that of an ordinary Christian. As he is to instruct with authority, he should be regarded with reverence, as one upon whom divine truth has had the effect to set him above such transgressions, as men, less exalted by spiritual habits and yet upon the whole not to be excluded from heaven, have been betrayed into by the predominance of passion. That clergymen may be considered as sinners in general, as all men are, cannot be denied; but this reflection will not counteract their good precepts so much, as the absolute knowledge of their having been guilty of certain specific immoral acts. I told him, that by the rules of the Church of Scotland,

in their 'Book of Discipline,' if a *scandal* as it is called, is not pros-
ecuted for five years, it cannot afterwards be proceeded upon, 'unless
it be *of a heinous nature*, or again become flagrant;' and that hence
a question arose, whether fornication was a sin of a heinous nature;
and that I had maintained, that it did not deserve that epithet, in as
much as it was not one of those sins which argue very great depravity
of heart: in short, was not, in the general acceptation of mankind, a
heinous sin. JOHNSON. 'No, Sir, it is not a heinous sin. A heinous sin
is that for which a man is punished with death or banishment.'
BOSWELL. 'But, Sir, after I had argued that it was not a heinous
sin, an old clergyman rose up, and repeating the text of scripture
denouncing judgement against whoremongers, asked, whether, considering this, there could be any doubt of fornication being a heinous
sin.' JOHNSON. 'Why, Sir, observe the word *whoremonger*. Every sin,
if persisted in, will become heinous. Whoremonger is a dealer in
whores, as ironmonger is a dealer in iron. But as you don't call a
man an ironmonger for buying and selling a penknife; so you don't
call a man a whoremonger for getting one wench with child.'*

* It must not be presumed that Dr Johnson meant to give any countenance to
licentiousness, though in the character of an Advocate he made a just and subtle
distinction between occasional and habitual transgression.

James Boswell, *The Life of Samuel Johnson* (1791)

Mr Collins proposes marriage

'Almost as soon as I entered the house I singled you out as the
companion of my future life. But before I am run away with by my
feelings on this subject, perhaps it will be advisable for me to state
my reasons for marrying – and moreover for coming into Hertford-
shire with the design of selecting a wife, as I certainly did.'

The idea of Mr Collins, with all his solemn composure, being run
away with by his feelings, made Elizabeth so near laughing that she
could not use the short pause he allowed in any attempt to stop him
farther, and he continued:

'My reasons for marrying are, first, that I think it a right thing for
every clergyman in easy circumstances (like myself) to set the example
of matrimony in his parish. Secondly, that I am convinced it will add
very greatly to my happiness; and thirdly – which perhaps I ought

to have mentioned earlier, that it is the particular advice and recom-
mendation of the very noble lady whom I have the honour of calling
patroness. Twice has she condescended to give me her opinion
(unasked too!) on this subject; and it was but the very Saturday night
before I left Hunsford – between our pools at quadrille, while Mrs
Jenkinson was arranging Miss de Bourgh's foot-stool, that she said,
"Mr Collins, you must marry. A clergyman like you must marry. –
Chuse properly, chuse a gentlewoman for *my* sake; and for your
own, let her be an active, useful sort of person, not brought up high,
but able to make a small income go a good way. This is my advice.
Find such a woman as soon as you can, bring her to Hunsford, and
I will visit her." Allow me, by the way, to observe, my fair cousin,
that I do not reckon the notice and kindness of Lady Catherine de
Bourgh as among the least of the advantages in my power to offer.
You will find her manners beyond any thing I can describe; and your
wit and vivacity I think must be acceptable to her, especially when
tempered with the silence and respect which her rank will inevitably
excite. Thus much for my general intention in favour of matrimony;
it remains to be told why my views were directed to Longbourn
instead of my own neighbourhood, where I assure you there are
many amiable young women. But the fact is, that being, as I am, to
inherit this estate after the death of your honoured father (who,
however, may live many years longer) I could not satisfy myself
without resolving to chuse a wife from among his daughters, that
the loss to them might be as little as possible, when the melancholy
event takes place – which, however, as I have already said, may not
be for several years. This has been my motive, my fair cousin, and I
flatter myself it will not sink me in your esteem. And now nothing
remains for me but to assure you in the most animated language of
the violence of my affection. To fortune I am perfectly indifferent,
and shall make no demand of that nature on your father, since I am
well aware that it could not be complied with; and that one thousand
pounds in the 4 per cents which will not be yours till after your
mother's decease, is all that you may ever be entitled to. On that
head, therefore, I shall be uniformly silent; and you may assure
yourself that no ungenerous reproach shall ever pass my lips when
we are married.'

It was absolutely necessary to interrupt him now.

'You are too hasty, Sir,' she cried. 'You forget that I have made no answer. Let me do it without farther loss of time. Accept my thanks for the compliment you are paying me. I am very sensible of the honour of your proposals, but it is impossible for me to do otherwise than decline them.'

'I am not now to learn,' replied Mr Collins, with a formal wave of the hand, 'that it is usual with young ladies to reject the addresses of the man whom they secretly mean to accept, when he first applies for their favour; and that sometimes the refusal is repeated a second or even a third time. I am therefore by no means discouraged by what you have just said, and shall hope to lead you to the altar ere long.'

'Upon my word, Sir,' cried Elizabeth, 'your hope is rather an extraordinary one after my declaration. . . .'

Mrs Bennet rang the bell, and Miss Elizabeth was summoned to the library.

'Come here, child,' cried her father as she appeared. 'I have sent for you on an affair of importance. I understand that Mr Collins has made you an offer of marriage. Is it true?' Elizabeth replied that it was. 'Very well – and this offer of marriage you have refused?'

'I have, Sir.'

'Very well. We now come to the point. Your mother insists upon your accepting it. Is not it so, Mrs Bennet?'

'Yes, or I will never see her again.'

'An unhappy alternative is before you, Elizabeth. From this day you must be a stranger to one of your parents – Your mother will never see you again if you do *not* marry Mr Collins, and I will never see you again if you *do*.'

Jane Austen, Pride and Prejudice (1813)

The amorous Brother Augustine

'*To the Editor of the Norfolk News*
'SIR – The following letter was brought home by my son from the monastery on Wednesday night, and handed by him to me before he himself had read it. It was put into his hands, he says, as he was leaving by "Augustine" himself. As a distressed mother, I beg of you to give insertion to this letter that other parents and the public generally may see by what arts these monks are striving to beguile and fascinate our dear children and to supplant us in their

affections. If such letters are written to a boy what may we
conjecture are written to the young of the other sex?

'Yours respectfully,

'L. Hase.'

'Feast Sancti Crucis 1864.

'MY DARLING CHILD — I want you to promise me that during the
Superior's absence you will strive as much as possible to keep
from doing wrong, and that you will daily pray for God's grace
and help to fulfil the same.

'You will not be allowed to be here much, if at all, as I rather
expected you would, so that I am obliged to write that which I
should have preferred saying to you in person, but oh! my dearest
one! you will *never* realise how much I really love you, and how
wretched I am all day without seeing you. My love for you is *so*
deep, *so* tender, that I cannot bear even to be separated from you,
and when I do see you I have such a heavy weight at my heart, and
you seem *so* careless and light-hearted and *so* taken up with others,
and all this makes me worse.

'Then the Superior, who is always having fresh favourites and
likings, seems so dreadfully afraid even of one's looking at you,
that I am perfectly obliged to look calm and indifferent when my
heart is literally burning for you.

'*This* love I NEVER felt for a living creature beside yourself, it
seems to consume me, and it is quite a comfort to write it down
to you.

'Sometimes I think you know your power over me, you give me
such searching looks and what do you meet with in return? What
but the most *earnest burning*, tender look of love, as pure as that
of angels.

'Were I and you in the world I would lavish every care, every
affection upon you that money or time could procure, every wish
should be gratified if possible.

'Sometimes on Sundays you have sat in your cassock and cotta
looking so like an angel I could have worshipped you. . . .

'What I am now going to say must be a secret to *everyone* if you
don't wish me to be troubled. I want you one day (I will tell you
the time) to go to Mason's St Giles to have your portrait taken.

Dear mama shall send the postage stamps so that it will not be with any money from here.

'I will manage you having a cotta and cassock without anyone's knowing here what you want it for.

'Burn *this*. I would not have anyone know anything about it for the world, and if you have the slightest respect for me you will do so. I do not ask it out of love for I know and feel you have none for me, and this, indeed, is the reason of my misery. Good bye, dear, sweet child, and my prayers shall ever be for your peace and happiness.

'Your affectionate brother in Xt.,
'+ AUGUSTINE, O.S.B.'

Arthur Calder Marshall, *The Enthusiast* (1962)

A doting curate

Mr Nicholls was one who had seen her almost daily for years – seen her as a daughter, a mistress and a friend. He was not a man to be attracted by any kind of literary fame. I imagine that this, by itself, would rather repel him when he saw it in the possession of a woman. He was a grave, reserved, conscientious man, with a deep sense of religion, and of his duties as one of its ministers.

In silence he had watched her, and loved her long. The love of such a man – a daily spectator of her manner of life for years – is a great testimony to her character as a woman.

How deep his affection was I scarcely dare to tell, even if I could in words. She did not know – she had hardly begun to suspect – that she was the object of any peculiar regard on his part, when, in this very December, he came one evening to tea. After tea, she returned from the study to her own sitting-room, as was her custom, leaving her father and his curate together. Presently she heard the study-door open, and expected to hear the succeeding clash of the front door. Instead, came a tap; and, 'like lightning, it flashed upon me what was coming. He entered. He stood before me. What his words were you can imagine; his manner you can hardly realize, nor can I forget it. He made me, for the first time, feel what it costs a man to declare affection when he doubts response . . . The spectacle of one, ordinarily so statue-like, thus trembling, stirred, and overcome, gave

181

me a strange shock. I could only entreat him to leave me then, and promise a reply on the morrow. I asked if he had spoken to Papa. He said he dared not. I think I half-led, half-put him out of the room.'

So deep, so fervent, and so enduring was the affection Miss Brontë had inspired in the heart of this good man! It is an honour to her; and, as such, I have thought it my duty to say thus much, and quote thus fully from her letter about it. And now I pass to my second reason for dwelling on a subject which may possibly be considered by some, at first sight, of too private a nature for publication. When Mr Nicholls had left her, Charlotte went immediately to her father and told him all. He always disapproved of marriages, and constantly talked against them. But he more than disapproved at this time; he could not bear the idea of this attachment of Mr Nicholls to his daughter. Fearing the consequences of agitation to one so recently an invalid she made haste to give her father a promise that, on the morrow, Mr Nicholls should have a distinct refusal. Thus quietly and modestly did she, on whom such hard judgments had been passed by ignorant reviewers, receive this vehement, passionate declaration of love – thus thoughtfully for her father, and unselfishly for herself, put aside all consideration of how she should reply, excepting as he wished!

Elizabeth Gaskell, *The Life of Charlotte Brontë* (1857)

Oh Daisy

Shrove Tuesday, 13 February 1872
Dined at the Vicarage at 5.30 and at 7 drove with the Venables and Crichton to the Rifle Volunteer Concert in the National Schoolroom at Hay. We had tickets for the first row, and in the third row I immediately espied Daisy and Charlotte. I had the good fortune to get a chat with Daisy before the seats were filled up, and she was so nice and I was so happy. She told me she had been to two balls and I told her how disappointed I was not to meet her at the Crichtons' ball. She said she had enjoyed her balls very much, and I said I heard that the young ladies who 'came out' at the Hereford Hunt Ball (of whom she was one) had all looked very pretty and been very much admired. She smiled and blushed and looked pleased. I told her how

well I remembered the last time I saw her nearly 3 months ago. 'It's a long time since you have been over to Llan Thomas. I suppose you have been very busy. If you come over you will find some of us at home. We don't usually go out till half past three.' 'I am afraid,' I said, 'that you have all quite forgotten me.' 'Oh, no,' she said.

I was so happy talking to her. I had been hoping and thinking all day that I might meet her at the concert this evening. But now the seats began to fill. Fanny Bevan her great and inseparable friend sat on one side of her and her father on the other. I sat in the row before them. Henry sang.

Oh Daisy.

Francis Kilvert, Diaries (1974)

'The Messiah'

In 1890 and for a few years afterwards there was a remarkable revival of interest in the Agapemone. Several prominent members of the Salvation Army joined. At Clapton, in the north-east of London, the 'Children of the Resurrection' as they called themselves, built in 1892 a magnificent Ark of the Covenant seating about 400 persons, at a cost of some £16,000. The preacher at the opening ceremony in 1896 was the Rev J. H. Smyth-Pigott, the successor to Brother Prince.

He had been born in 1852, of an old Somersetshire county family. After a varied career as a university man, sailor before the mast, soldier, coffee-planter, curate in the Church of England and Evangelist in the Salvation Army, he was converted in about 1897 to the views of Prince. In his opening sermon at Clapton he declared that he expected Christ to return that very day and to descend upon the congregation.

The Ark was (and still is) a massive church with a graceful spire, built to the designs of J. Morris of Reading. At the base of the spire are four winged figures in bronze, representing the beasts to be found in Chapter iv of the Book of Revelation. Over the porchway at the entrance to the church are the words which sum up the beliefs of the Agapemonites: 'Love in Judgment and Judgment unto Victory.'

It was on Sunday, September 7th, 1902, that Smyth-Pigott stood before a crowded congregation in the Ark and publicly announced his divinity. According to one report he revealed that he was going to walk across the water. Some of his believers fell on their knees and shouted for joy. On the following Sunday some 6,000 people waited from dawn until the evening to see the new Messiah arrive in his carriage. When he appeared he was greeted with loud hisses and cat-calls, hundreds of people swarming over the railings to enter the church, but the doors were closed. The Messiah at once drove back to his home, Cedar Lodge, followed by a shower of stones, bricks and umbrellas. . .

The Ark at Clapton seemed rather hot, so Mr Smyth-Pigott went down to Spaxton, where in July 1904 an attractive girl named Ruth Annie Preece went to live with him and his wife. Smyth-Pigott had been married since August 1886, but his wife seemed to accept Miss Preece, who was one of three sisters whose father had left them comfortably provided for. A year later a male child was born to Miss Preece, the records at Somerset House showing that the father was John Hugh Smyth-Pigott, Clerk in Holy Orders. The name given to the baby boy was Glory. At this time a London reporter who visited Spaxton described Smyth-Pigott as being a 'short, dark, thin-featured man, wearing pince-nez, with bright eyes of coal black'. He was wearing a grey lounge suit and clergyman's black felt hat. When the reporter's car broke down at the gates of the Abode, Smyth-Pigott asked in a soft, melodious, low-pitched voice if he could be of any assistance. Not suspecting that the driver was a reporter, he attempted to help repair the car, but when another reporter appeared, he disappeared into the house and stayed there.

On January 20th, 1909, Smyth-Pigott was found guilty of 'immorality, uncleanness and wickedness of life'. Neither he nor the Bishop of Bath and Wells was present in court. The proceedings were held in the old chapter-house of Wells Cathedral, the Chancellor of the Diocese sitting at a table beneath the Bishop's empty throne. Smyth-Pigott had been served notice by registered post. . .

Smyth-Pigott was unconcerned when he was finally inhibited by the Bishop in March 1909. 'I am God,' he said. 'It does not matter what they do. There is no such thing as marriage at the Agapemone. We are all brothers and sisters in God!'

Less than a year later a daughter was born to Smyth-Pigott and 'Sister Ruth', the name at first being 'Comet', to synchronise with the appearance in the sky of Halley's famous visitor. Afterwards the child was named Life, but her birth was kept secret for as long as possible. It was considered, behind the high walls at Spaxton, that the outside world would not understand.

John Montgomery, *Abodes of Love* (1962)

Mr Beebe's dip

Mr Beebe, who was hot, and who always acquiesced where possible, looked around him. He could detect no parishioners except the pine-trees, rising up steeply on all sides, and gesturing to each other against the blue. How glorious it was! The world of motor-cars and Rural Deans receded illimitably. Water, sky, evergreens, a wind – these things not even the seasons can touch, and surely they lie beyond the intrusion of man?

'I may as well wash too'; and soon his garments made a third little pile on the sward, and he too asserted the wonder of the water.

It was ordinary water, nor was there very much of it, and, as Freddy said, it reminded one of swimming in a salad. The three gentlemen rotated in the pool breast high, after the fashion of the nymphs in Götterdämmerung. But either because the rains had given a freshness, or because the sun was shedding a most glorious heat, or because two of the gentlemen were young in years and the third young in the spirit – for some reason or other a change came over them, and they forgot Italy and Botany and Fate. They began to play. Mr Beebe and Freddy splashed each other. A little deferentially, they splashed George. He was quiet: they feared they had offended him. Then all the forces of youth burst out. He smiled, flung himself at them, splashed them, ducked them, kicked them, muddied them, and drove them out of the pool.

'Race you round it, then,' cried Freddy, and they raced in the sunshine, and George took a short cut and dirtied his shins, and had to bathe a second time. Then Mr Beebe consented to run – a memorable sight.

They ran to get dry, they bathed to get cool, they played at being Indians in the willow-herbs and in the bracken, they bathed to get clean. And all the time three little bundles lay discreetly on the sward, proclaiming:

'No. We are what matters. Without us shall no enterprise begin. To us shall all flesh turn in the end.'

'A try! A try!' yelled Freddy, snatching up George's bundle and placing it beside an imaginary goalpost.

'Socker rules,' George retorted, scattering Freddy's bundle with a kick.

'Goal!'

'Goal!'

'Pass!'

'Take care my watch!' cried Mr Beebe.

Clothes flew in all directions.

'Take care my hat! No, that's enough, Freddy. Dress now. No, I say!'

But the two young men were delirious. Away they twinkled into the trees, Freddy with a clerical waistcoat under his arm, George with a wideawake hat on his dripping hair.

'That'll do!' shouted Mr Beebe, remembering that after all he was in his own parish. Then his voice changed as if every pine-tree was a Rural Dean. 'Hi! Steady on! I see people coming, you fellows!'

Yells, and widening circles over the dappled earth.

'Hi! hi! *Ladies!*'

E. M. Forster, *A Room with a View* (1908)

In the church

'What a perfect place for a *rendezvous*,' he said, in a hushed voice, glancing round.

She too glanced round the familiar interior. The dimness and stillness chilled her. But her eyes lit up with daring. Here, here she would assert her indomitable gorgeous female self, here. Here she would open her female flower like a flame, in this dimness that was more passionate than light.

They hung apart a moment, then wilfully turned to each other for the desired contact. She put her arms round him, she cleaved her body to his, and with her hands pressed upon his shoulders, on his back, she seemed to feel right through him, to know his young, tense body right through. And it was so fine, so hard, yet so exquisitely subject and under her control. She reached him her mouth and drank his full kiss, drank it fuller and fuller.

And it was good, it was very, very good. She seemed to be filled with his kiss, filled as if she had drunk strong, glowing sunshine. She glowed all inside, the sunshine seemed to beat upon her heart underneath, she had drunk so beautifully.

She drew away, and looked at him radiant, exquisitely, glowingly beautiful, and satisfied, but radiant as an illumined cloud.

To him this was bitter, that she was so radiant and satisfied. She laughed upon him, blind to him, so full of her own bliss, never doubting but that he was the same as she was. And radiant as an angel she went with him out of the church, as if her feet were beams of light that walked on flowers for footsteps.

He went beside her, his soul clenched, his body unsatisfied. Was she going to make this easy triumph over him? For him, there was now no self-bliss, only pain and confused anger.

D. H. Lawrence, *The Rainbow*, (1915)

Myfanwy at Oxford

Pink may, double may, dead laburnum
   Shedding an Anglo-Jackson shade,
Shall we ever, my staunch Myfanwy,
   Bicycle down to North Parade?
Kant on the handle-bars, Marx in the saddlebag,
   Light my touch on your shoulder-blade.

Sancta Hilda, Myfanwyatia
   Evansensis – I hold your heart,
Willowy banks of a willowy Cherwell a
   Willowy figure with lips apart,
Strong and willowy, strong to pillow me,
   Gold Myfanwy, kisses and art.

Tubular bells of tall St Barnabas,
   Single clatter above St Paul,
Chasuble, acolyte, incense-offering,
   Spectacled faces held in thrall.
There in the nimbus and Comper tracery
   Gold Myfanwy blesses us all.

Gleam of gas upon Oxford station,
   Gleam of gas on her straight gold hair,

Hair flung back with an ostentation,
  Waiting alone for a girl friend there.
Second in Mods and a Third in Theology
  Come to breathe again Oxford air.

Her Myfanwy as in Cadena days,
  Her Myfanwy, a schoolgirl voice,
Tentative brush of a cheek in a cocoa crush,
  Coffee and Ulysses, Tennyson, Joyce,
Alpha-minded and other dimensional,
  Freud or Calvary? Take your choice.

Her Myfanwy? *My* Myfanwy.
  Bicycle bells in a Boar's Hill Pine,
Stedman Triple from All Saints' steeple,
  Tom and his hundred and one at nine,
Bells of Butterfield, caught in Keble,
  Sally and backstroke answer '*Mine!*'

John Betjeman, Collected Poems (1958)

Lenten Thoughts of a High Anglican

Isn't she lovely, 'the Mistress'?
  With her wide-apart grey-green eyes,
The droop of her lips and, when she smiles,
  Her glance of amused surprise?

How nonchalantly she wears her clothes,
  How expensive they are as well!
And the sound of her voice is as soft and deep
  As the Christ Church tenor bell.

But why do I call her 'the Mistress'
  Who know not her way of life?
Because she has more of a cared-for air
  Than many a legal wife.

How elegantly she swings along
  In the vapoury incense veil;
The angel choir must pause in song
  When she kneels at the altar rail.

The parson said that we shouldn't stare
  Around when we come to church,
Or the Unknown God we are seeking
  May forever elude our search.

But I hope the preacher will not think
  It unorthodox and odd
If I add that I glimpse in 'the Mistress'
  A hint of the Unknown God.

[This is about a lady I see on Sunday mornings in a London church.]

John Betjeman, *A Nip in the Air* (1974)

On the bus

We discussed the expedition further as we rode along Piccadilly on the top of a bus. The sun was out and there were still people sitting on chairs in the park.

'It looks odd to see a clergyman holding somebody's hand in public,' said Dora chattily. 'I don't know why, but it does.'

'Where?' I asked.

'Look – there,' she said, pointing out a couple lolling in deckchairs.

'Oh, but it *can't* be!' I exclaimed, but there was no doubt that the clergyman was Julian Malory and that the hand he was holding was Allegra Gray's.

'How do you mean it can't be?' said Dora looking again. 'He certainly was holding her hand. Why, isn't it Julian Malory? What a joke! Who's he with?'

'She's a widow, a Mrs Gray, who's come to live in the flat at the vicarage.'

'Oh, I see. Well, I suppose there's nothing wrong in that?'

'No, of course there isn't,' I said rather sharply. It was just thoroughly unsuitable, sitting there for everyone to see, not even on the hard iron chairs but lolling in deckchairs. 'Fancy going into the park to hold hands, though, it seems rather an odd thing to do.'

'Well, I don't suppose they went there expressly for that purpose,' said Dora stubbornly. 'They probably went for a walk and decided to sit down and then somehow it came about. After all, holding hands is quite a natural affectionate gesture.'

'How do *you* know?' I heard myself say.

'Mildred! What *is* the matter with you? Are *you* in love with the vicar or what?' she said, so loudly that the people in front of us nudged each other and sniggered.

'No, of course not,' I said in a low angry tone, 'but it seems so unsuitable, the whole thing. Winifred and everything, oh, I can't explain now.'

'Well, I don't see what you're making such a fuss about,' said Dora, maddeningly calm. 'It's a lovely day and she's very attractive and a widow and he's not married, so it's all right. I see quite a little romance blowing up.'

By the time we had got off the bus we were arguing quite openly. It was foolish and pointless but somehow we could not stop. I saw us in twenty or thirty years' time, perhaps living together, bickering about silly trifles. It was a depressing picture.

'After all a clergyman is a man and entitled to human feelings,' Dora went on.

It was obvious to me now that she was in the kind of mood to disagree automatically with everything I said, for usually she maintained that clergymen didn't count as men and therefore couldn't be expected to have human feelings.

'Julian isn't the marrying sort,' I persisted. 'Anyway, Mrs Gray wouldn't be at all suitable for him.'

'Oh, I think you've had your eye on him for yourself all this time,' said Dora in an irritating jocular tone. '*That's* why you've been smartening yourself up.'

It was useless to deny it, once she had got the idea into her head. I was grateful to see the grey bulk of Sister Blatt looming before us as we reached the church.

'Hullo,' she said as we came up to her. 'What on earth's happened to Father Malory?' she asked. 'Evensong's in five minutes and there's no sign of him. Miss Malory said he was going to a meeting at S.P.G. House this afternoon. It must have been a very long one.' She laughed. 'You don't think he's had a sudden call to the Mission Field, do you?'

'Surely he would have come back here first and let us know?' I said.

'Oh, well, I dare say Father Greatorex will turn up,' said Sister Blatt cheerfully and went into church.

Dora giggled.'*We* could tell her where Father Malory is, couldn't we, Mildred? I think we should blackmail him.'

We went into the house. Dora decided to do some washing before supper and within half an hour the kitchen was festooned with lines of depressing-looking underwear – fawn locknit knickers and petticoats of the same material. It was even drearier than mine.

At supper we talked about our old school, William, and matters of general interest. Julian Malory was not mentioned again. I was in the kitchen making some tea when there was a knock at the door and Rocky's head peeped round.

'Helena has gone to hear a paper about pygmies,' he said, 'and I'm all alone. May I come in?'

'Yes, do,' I said, in a confused way, embarrassed by the washing hanging up.

'My friend Dora Caldicote is here,' I said, as he threaded his way through the lines of dripping garments.

'Oh, what fun!' he said lightly. 'Are you going to give me some coffee?'

'Well, we were having tea,' I said, feeling a little ashamed, both of the tea and of myself for feeling ashamed of it, 'but I can easily make you some coffee.'

'No, indeed you won't. I love tea.'

'You are Mildred's old school chum,' he said to Dora in a teasing way. 'I've heard all about you.'

Dora flushed and smiled. Oh, the awkward Wren officers, I thought, seeing them standing on the balcony at the Admiral's villa. How they must have blossomed under that charm!

Rocky was standing by the window. 'There's your vicar,' he said. 'Would there be a service now?'

'Is he alone?' asked Dora.

'Yes, very much so, and wearing rather a becoming cloak. I always think I should look rather well in one of those.'

'We saw him holding somebody's hand in the park this afternoon and Mildred was rather upset,' said Dora gaily. 'Poor man, *I* didn't see why he shouldn't.'

'Oh, but we can't have that,' said Rocky. 'I always look on him as Mildred's property. But never mind,' he turned towards me, 'I don't suppose his hand would be very pleasant to hold. We'll find somebody better for you.'

'He was supposed to be in church taking Evensong,' said Dora, who would not leave the subject.

'Oh, the poor man, I can imagine nothing more depressing on a fine weekday evening. Wondering if anybody will come or getting tired of seeing just the same faithful few. Why don't we go out and have a drink?' he asked in a bored way.

'Not after drinking tea, thank you. I don't think I should feel like it,' I said.

'Dear Mildred, you must learn to feel like drinking at *any* time. I shall make myself responsible for your education.'

So of course we did go. Dora had cider and got rather giggly with Rocky, telling him stories about our schooldays which I found embarrassing. I, in my wish to be different and not to be thought a school-marm, had said I would have beer, which turned out to be flat and bitter, with a taste such as I imagine washing-up water might have.

'Mildred is sad about her vicar,' said Rocky. 'We'll find her an anthropologist.'

'I don't want anyone,' I said, afraid that I was sounding childish and sulky but quite unable to do anything about it.

'If Everard Bone were here we might persuade him to hold your hand,' he went on teasingly. 'How would you like that?'

For a moment I almost did wish that Everard Bone could be with us. He was quiet and sensible and a church-goer. We should make dull stilted conversation with no hidden meanings to it. He would accept the story of Julian and Mrs Gray in the park without teasing me about it; he might even understand that it was a worrying business altogether. For it was. If Julian were to marry Mrs Gray what was to happen to Winifred? I was quite sure now that he did intend to marry her and could not imagine why I had not seen it all along. Clergymen did not go holding people's hands in public places unless their intentions were honourable, I told myself, hoping that I might perhaps be wrong, for clergymen were, as Dora had pointed out, human beings, and might be supposed to share the weaknesses of normal men. I worried over the problem in bed that night and wondered if I ought to do anything. I suddenly remembered some of the 'Answers to Correspondents' in the *Church Times*, which were so obscure that they might very well have dealt with a problem like this. 'I saw our vicar holding the hand of a widow in the park —

what should I do?' The question sounded almost frivolous put like that; what kind of an answer could I expect? 'Consult your Bishop immediately'? Or, 'We feel this is none of your business'?

Barbara Pym, Excellent Women (1958)

Sydney Smith on bishops flirting

Someone asked Sydney Smith whether a certain bishop was going to get married. 'Perhaps he may,' was the answer; 'yet how can a bishop marry? How can he flirt? The most he can say is, "I will see you in the vestry after service." '

Hesketh Pearson, The Smith of Smiths (1958)

[11]

PASTORALIA

Students for the priesthood used to have lectures in something called 'Pastoralia'. I do not know if the subject is still on the curriculum in seminaries. It meant those functions of a parish minister's life which were most important – how to visit the sick, the housebound, the lonely; what help, if any, could be given to those in material or spiritual distress.

A hero of mine is a man called Father Wainwright. He could have had a comfortable Archdeacon-Grantly-ish existence in some fat country living, but instead he chose to go to work in the slums of Wapping, a hundred years and more before that part of London was redeveloped to house 'yuppies' and newspaper offices. In those days, Wapping was little better than the most foetid areas of Calcutta.

Wainwright was not an intellectual heavyweight. He was a very bad preacher – in fact, he mumbled inaudibly from the pulpit, and never had anything 'interesting' or clever to say. But he gave his entire life to other people. Wainwright was a saint, who owned nothing, and who even gave the shirt off his own back to a poor man who had need of it. His was an example which few parish clergymen have been able to emulate, but I should say that he was not unique. From the beginnings of the church, the best priests have not been those who have achieved fame as controversialists, or social reformers or eloquent preachers, but those who have remained in their parishes, visiting the sick and the infirm, preparing children for confirmation, baptizing, marrying and burying their people.

Since the best have been the most unassuming, it has been hard to compile a chapter of 'Pastoralia'; but the book would not be complete without it, and this short section contains a number of examples of the clergy doing what they promise to do in the awesome ordination service on the day when they first become priests.

The parson's life

The Country Parson is exceeding exact in his Life, being holy, just, prudent, temperate, bold, grave, in all his ways. And because the two highest points of Life, wherein a Christian is most seen, are Patience, and Mortification; Patience in regard of afflictions, Mortification in regard to lusts and affections, and the stupifying and deading of all the clamorous powers of the soul, therefore he hath thoroughly studied these, that he may be an absolute Master and Commander of himself, for all the purposes which God hath ordained him. Yet in these points he labours most in those things which are most apt to scandalize his Parish. And first, because Country people live hardly, and therefore as feeling their own sweat, and consequently knowing the price of money, are offended much with any, who by hard usage increase their travail, the Country Parson is very circumspect in avoiding all covetousness, neither being greedy to get, nor niggardly to keep, nor troubled to lose any worldly wealth; but in all his words and actions slighting, and disesteeming it, even to a wondering, that the world should so much value wealth, which in the day of wrath hath not one dram of comfort for us. Secondly, because Luxury is a very visible sin, the Parson is very careful to avoid all the kinds thereof, but especially that of drinking, because it is the most popular vice; into which if he come, *he prostitutes himself* both to shame, and sin, and by having *fellowship with the unfruitful works of darkness*, he disableth himself of authority to *reprove them*: For sins make all equal, whom they find together; and then *they are worst*, who ought to be best. Neither is it for the servant of Christ to haunt Inns, or Taverns, or Alehouses, *to the dishonour of his Person and Office*. The Parson doth not so, but orders his Life in such a fashion, that when death takes him, as the Jews and *Judas* did Christ, he may say as He did, *I sat daily with you teaching in the Temple*. Thirdly, because Country people (as indeed all honest men) do much esteem their word, it being the Life of buying and selling, and dealing in the world; therefore the parson is very strict in keeping his word, though it be to his own hindrance, as knowing, that if he be not so, he will quickly be discovered and disregarded: neither will they believe him in the Pulpit, whom they cannot trust in his Conversation. As for oaths, and apparel, the disorders thereof are also very manifest. The parson's *yea* is *yea*, and *nay, nay*; and his apparel plain, but reverend, and clean, without spots, or dust, or smell; the purity of his mind breaking out, and dilating itself even to his body, clothes, and habitation.

George Herbert, *A Priest to the Temple* (1652)

A sad victory

But, oh! the wicked wastry of life in war. In less than a month after, the news came of a victory over the French fleet, and by the same post I got a letter from Mr Howard, that was the midshipman who came to see us with Charles, telling me that poor Charles had been mortally wounded in the action, and had afterwards died of his wounds. 'He was a hero in the engagement,' said Mr Howard, 'and he died as a good and a brave man should.' – These tidings gave me one of the sorest hearts I ever suffered, and it was long before I could gather fortitude to disclose the tidings to poor Charles's mother. But the callants of the school had heard of the victory, and were going shouting about, and had set the steeple bell a-ringing, by which Mrs Malcolm heard the news; and knowing that Charles's ship was with the fleet, she came over to the manse in great anxiety to hear the particulars, somebody telling her that there had been a foreign letter to me by the postman.

When I saw her I could not speak, but looked at her in pity, and, the tear fleeing up into my eyes, she guessed what had happened. After giving a deep and sore sigh, she enquired, 'How did he behave? I hope well, for he was aye a gallant laddie!' – and then she wept very bitterly. However, growing calmer, I read to her the letter; and, when I had done, she begged me to give it to her to keep, saying, 'It's all that I have now left of my pretty boy; but it's mair precious to me than the wealth of the Indies'; and she begged me to return thanks to the Lord for all the comforts and manifold mercies with which her lot had been blessed, since the hour she put her trust in him alone; and that was when she was left a penniless widow, with her five fatherless bairns.

It was just an edification of the spirit to see the Christian resignation of this worthy woman. Mrs Balwhidder was confounded, and said, there was more sorrow in seeing the deep grief of her fortitude than tongue could tell.

Having taken a glass of wine with her, I walked out to conduct her to her own house; but in the way we met with a severe trial. All the weans were out parading with napkins and kailblades on sticks, rejoicing and triumphing in the glad tidings of victory. But when they saw me and Mrs Malcolm coming slowly along, they guessed what had happened, and threw away their banners of joy; and standing all up in a row, with silence and sadness, along the kirkyard wall as we passed, showed an instinct of compassion that penetrated to my very soul. The poor mother burst into fresh affliction, and some of the bairns into an audible weeping; and, taking one another by the hand, they followed us to her door, like mourners at a funeral. Never was such a sight seen in any town before. The neighbours came to look at it as we walked along, and the men turned aside to hide their faces; while the mothers pressed their babies fondlier to their bosoms, and watered their innocent faces with their tears.

I prepared a suitable sermon, taking as the words of my text, 'Howl, ye ships of Tarshish, for your strength is laid waste.' But when I saw around me so many of my people clad in complimentary mourning for the gallant Charles Malcolm, and that even poor daft Jenny Gaffaw, and her daughter, had on an old black riband; and when I thought of him, the spirited laddie, coming home from Jamaica with his parrot on his shoulder, and his limes for me, my heart filled full, and I was obliged to sit down in the pulpit, and drop a tear.

After a pause, and the Lord having vouchsafed to compose me, I rose up, and gave out that anthem of triumph, the 124th psalm, the singing of which brought the congregation round to themselves; but still I felt that I could not preach as I had meant to do; therefore I only said a few words of prayer, and, singing another psalm, dismissed the congregation.

John Galt, *Annals of the Parish* (1871)

197

An indigent priest

June 18, Friday [1802]. We breakfasted, dined, &c. again at home. Recd. of Betty this Morning for Butter sold to Betty Cary at ˢ1/0½ᵈ per Pint o. 8. 10¼. This Morn a Person by name Richard Page, dressed as a Clergyman, walked up boldly to our Front Door through the Garden and knocked. I went and let him in, and walked into my Study and there informed me before Nancy, that he was a reduced Clergyman from Oxfordshire, was born at Bath in Somersetshire, had read Prayers &c. at the Abbey Church there for 12 Years. That a Dr Lawrence of Doctors Commons was his great Friend &c. He seemed well acquainted with Oxford and with many of my old Contemporaries there, was formerly of Baliol College or at St Edmund Hall, a short Man and thin, talked rather fast and made a plausible Story. Shewed me his Letters of Orders, signed by the late Dr Lowthe when Bishop of Oxford &c. He stayed about half an Hour with us, drank a Glass of Table Beer and then walked away. I gave him before he went, half a Guinea o. 10. 6. After he was gone we heard by Ben, that he had a Companion who talked with Ben all the time the other Man was with me, and that he saw the Man that was with me give the other the Money that I had given to him. That Man asked Ben many Questions about me. I do not know what to make of them. I saw Mr. Maynard's Name on his Petition. Marquiss Townsend's Name was also on the same.

Parson Woodforde, *The Diary of a Country Parson* (1926)

Advice to a lady suffering from depression

Foston, February 16th, 1820.
DEAR LADY GEORGIANA – *** Nobody has suffered more from low spirits than I have done – so I feel for you. 1st. Live as well as you dare. 2nd. Go into the shower-bath with a small quantity of water at a temperature low enough to give you a slight sensation of cold, 75° or 80°. 3rd. Amusing books. 4th. Short views of human life – not further than dinner or tea. 5th. Be as busy as you can. 6th. See as much as you can of those friends who respect and like you. 7th. And of those acquaintances who amuse you. 8th. Make no secret of low spirits to your friends, but talk of them freely – they are always worse for dignified concealment. 9th. Attend to the effects tea and

coffee produce upon you. 10th. Compare your lot with that of other people. 11th. Don't expect too much from human life – a sorry business at the best. 12th. Avoid poetry, dramatic representations (except comedy), music, serious novels, melancholy, sentimental people, and everything likely to excite feeling or emotion, not ending in active benevolence. 13th. *Do good,** and endeavour to please everybody of every degree. 14th. Be as much as you can in the open air without fatigue. 15th. Make the room where you commonly sit, gay and pleasant. 16th. Struggle by little and little against idleness. 17th. Don't be too severe upon yourself, or underrate yourself, but do yourself justice. 18th. Keep good blazing fires. 19th. Be firm and constant in the exercise of rational religion. 20th. Believe me, dear Lady Georgiana,

Very truly yours,

SYDNEY SMITH.

* The italics are of course Sydney Smith's, and are rendered the more significant by the fact that, in looking through several hundred autograph letters, the above is almost the only instance of their usage which I have found. – S.J.R.

Stuart J. Reid, *The Life and Times of the Rev. Sydney Smith* (1884)

The death of a royal child

Canon Fleming left London on Saturday 23rd January for Sandringham. He had no time for preparation, and he prepared his sermon in the train. He had no materials but his wonderful memory to draw upon. He had seen a letter which Tennyson had written to a friend who had lost a son. In this letter Tennyson said: 'My own belief is that the son whom you so loved is not really what we call dead, but more actually living than when alive here.' These words were running in Canon Fleming's mind as the train journeyed to Sandringham. He did not use them, however, when he stood in the pulpit. His sermon was from the text, 'I shall go to him' (2 Samuel xii. 23), King David's statement when he lost his son. He turned towards the Princess of Wales, who heard distinctly every word. After the service the Princess, in an interview with Canon Fleming, mentioned to him that just before his death Prince Eddy was lying as if in a sleep. The doctors and nurses had retired to an adjoining room. The Princess was sitting beside her son. Suddenly the Prince raised himself from his pillow and said twice, 'Who's that calling me? who's that calling me?' The Princess said gently, 'It's Jesus calling you, Eddy;' and she added, 'I hope he heard me.' Canon Fleming replied, 'Will you allow me to say, Ma'am, that the most experienced clergyman could not have given a more apt answer.'

On the same occasion the Queen said: 'In 1888 all my five children received the Holy Communion with me, and I gave Eddy a little book, and wrote in it:

> "Nothing in my hand I bring,
> Simply to Thy Cross I cling";

and also:

> "Just as I am, without one plea,
> But that Thy blood was shed for me,
> And that Thou bidd'st me come to Thee,
> O Lamb of God, I come."

When he was gone, and lay like one sleeping, we laid a cross of flowers on his breast, and after we had done so I turned to the table at his bedside and saw the little book in which were written these words, and I could not help feeling that he did cling to the Cross, and that it had all come true.' The Queen subsequently granted Canon Fleming her gracious permission to make this touching story public.

Arthur R. M. Finlayson, *Life of Canon Fleming* (1909)

The Curate's Kindness

A workhouse irony

I

I thought they'd be strangers aroun' me,
  But she's to be there!
Let me jump out o' waggon and go back and drown me
  At Pummery or Ten-Hatches Weir.

II

I thought: 'Well, I've come to the Union –
  The workhouse at last –
After honest hard work all the week, and Communion
  O' Zundays, these fifty years past.

III

''Tis hard; but,' I thought, 'never mind it:
  There's gain in the end:
And when I get used to the place I shall find it
  A home, and may find there a friend.

IV

'Life there will be better than t'other,
  For peace is assured.
The men in one wing and their wives in another
  Is strictly the rule of the Board.'

V

Just then one young Pa'son arriving
  Steps up out of breath
To the side o' the waggon wherein we were driving
  To Union; and calls out and saith:

VI

'Old folks, that harsh order is altered,
  Be not sick of heart!
The Guardians they poohed and they pished and they paltered
  When urged not to keep you apart.

VII

' "It is wrong," I maintained, "to divide them,
  Near forty years wed."
"Very well, sir. We promise, then, they shall abide them
  In one wing together," they said.'

VIII

Then I sank – knew 'twas quite a foredone thing
  That misery should be
To the end! . . . To get freed of her there was the one thing
  Had made the change welcome to me.

IX

To go there was ending but badly;
  'Twas shame and 'twas pain;
'But anyhow,' thought I, 'thereby I shall gladly
  Get free of this forty years' chain.'

X

I thought they'd be strangers aroun' me,
  But she's to be there!
Let me jump out o' waggon and go back and drown me
  At Pummery or Ten-Hatches Weir.

Thomas Hardy, Time's Laughingstocks (1909)

The country parson

'Amongst others, I believe that he was the first instrument under God in awakening serious thoughts for her soul in Jane Jennings. She told me that that which first made her feel a sorrow for sin was a sermon which he preached in Alton-Priors Church. She said, "I was standing by the door, and as he was earnestly asking us what we came to church for – whether we prayed with our *hearts*, whether we prayed at home and with our families – I felt as I had never done before, and when I went home, where I never prayed at all, I told our folks I was sure we were living in a very different way to what we ought to live and that it cut me to the heart to see our minister labouring so much to teach us, and that we paid no attention to his words." And then she added, "You cannot think how anxiously I looked through the sermon-books afterwards, to see if that sermon was amongst them, and when I found it I was so very glad." She also told me that soon after this Mr Hare made a rule that before the baptism of any child its parents should go to him for advice and instruction, and it so happened that Jane and her husband were the first summoned for this purpose. She said she had never before dreaded anything so much in her life, having been told by her neighbours she would be puzzled with hard questions. Her minister saw by her trembling how frightened she was, and, as he kindly put a chair for her in the study, said, "Don't be frightened, or think I keep a large dog to bark and jump out at you." But his words afterwards made too deep an impression ever to be forgotten, for, turning to the parents, he said with much solemnity, "Do you wish your child to become an angel in heaven, or a *devil in hell*? If I were going to give your child a large present in money, say twenty pounds perhaps, you would be ready and willing to thank me; how much more then should you thank God for allowing you to bring your child to the font at baptism, where He promises to give him his Holy Spirit, and make him happy for ever, if you will only heartily and earnestly pray for his blessing?" After these words (which first awakened in the mother's heart that feeling of responsibility she now so largely possesses for her children) he knelt down with them, earnestly praying both for them and their child, and Jane said to me, "God knows, and at the Last Day I shall know too, but I always think that prayer was answered, for none of my other six children ever asked me the questions which this little boy does – for always, when I have him alone with me, he begins talking of Jesus, and asking what he must do to please Him, and when he can go to see Him."

'When Prudence Tasker, who had been one of the first received into his newly-formed Sunday-school, was seized with violent illness, how tenderly did Mr Hare daily visit her dying-bed, obtaining for her the advice of an eminent physician in addition to that of the village doctor, often himself administering her medicines, applying her leeches himself, and trying to overcome the repugnance she felt to bleeding by telling her it was her "pastor" who desired it; and how often since have her parents dwelt upon the prayers which he offered up in that little chamber of death!

'I remember David King telling me once that nothing ever "*cut*" him so much as the words which Mr Hare preached after his recovery from illness, and that once while working in his garden, his minister, whilst talking to him, in order to illustrate the wonderful love of Christ in taking man's fallen nature upon him, asked David how he should like to become a toad, convincing him thereby that however loathsome such a change would be to him, yet it was nothing compared to that which the Son of God underwent when He laid aside his glory.'

Augustus Hare, *Memorials of a Quiet Life* (1891)

Catechizing children

Friday, 15 January 1875
Speaking to the children at the school about the Collect for the 2nd Sunday after the Epiphany and God's peace I asked them what beautiful image and picture of peace we have in the xxiii Psalm. 'The Good Shepherd,' said I, 'leading His sheep to –?' 'To the slaughter,'

said Frederick Herriman promptly. One day I asked the children to
what animal our Saviour is compared in the Bible. Frank Matthews
confidently held out his hand. 'To an ass,' he said.

Francis Kilvert, *Diaries* (1974)

Hearing confessions

Rose could just see the old head bent towards the grille. The priest
had a whistle in his breath. He listened – patiently – whistling,
while she painfully brought out her whole agony. She could hear the
exasperated women creak their chairs outside waiting for confession.
She said: 'It's *that* I repent. Not going with him.' She was defiant
and tearless in the stuffy box; the old priest had a cold and smelt of
eucalyptus. He said gently and nasally: 'Go on, my child.'

She said: 'I wish I'd killed myself. I oughta 'ave killed myself.' The
old man began to say something, but she interrupted him. 'I'm not
asking for absolution. I don't want absolution. I want to be like him
– damned.'

The old man whistled as he drew in his breath; she felt certain he
understood nothing. She repeated monotonously: 'I wish I'd killed
myself.' She pressed her hands against her breasts in the passion of
misery; she hadn't come to confess, she had come to think, she
couldn't think at home when the stove hadn't been lit and her father
had got a mood and her mother – she could tell it in her sidelong
questions – was wondering how much money Pinkie . . . She would
have had the courage now to kill herself if she hadn't been afraid
that somewhere in that obscure countryside of death they might miss
each other – mercy operating somehow for one and not for the other.
She said with breaking voice: 'That woman. *She* ought to be damned.
Saying he wanted to get rid of me. She doesn't know about love.'

'Perhaps she was right,' the old priest murmured.

'And you don't either!' she said furiously, pressing her childish
face against the grille.

The old man suddenly began to talk – whistling every now and
then and blowing eucalyptus through the grille. He said: 'There was
a man, a Frenchman, you wouldn't know about him, my child, who
had the same idea as you. He was a good man, a holy man, and he
lived in sin all through his life, because he couldn't bear the idea that

any soul could suffer damnation.' She listened with astonishment. He said: 'This man decided that if any soul was going to be damned, he would be damned too. He never took the sacraments, he never married his wife in church. I don't know, my child, but some people think he was – well, a saint. I think he died in what we are told is mortal sin – I'm not sure; it was in the war; perhaps . . .' He sighed – and whistled, bending his old head. He said: 'You can't conceive, my child, nor can I or anyone – the . . . appalling . . . strangeness of the mercy of God.'

Outside the chairs creaked again and again – people impatient to get their own repentance, absolution, penance finished for the week. He said: 'It was a case of greater love hath no man than this, that he lay down his soul for his friend.'

He shivered and sneezed. 'We must hope and pray,' he said, 'hope and pray. The Church does not demand that we believe any soul is cut off from mercy.'

She said with sad conviction: 'He's damned. He knew what he was about. He was a Catholic too.'

He said gently: 'Corruptio optimi est pessima.'

'Yes, Father?

'I mean – a Catholic is more capable of evil than anyone. I think perhaps – because we believe in him – we are more in touch with the devil than other people. But we must hope,' he said mechanically, 'hope and pray.'

'I want to hope,' she said, 'but I don't know how.'

'If he loved you, surely,' the old man said, 'that shows . . . there was some good . . .'

'Even love like that?'

'Yes.'

She brooded on the idea in the little dark box. He said: 'And come back soon – I can't give you absolution now – but come back – tomorrow.'

She said weakly: 'Yes, Father . . . And if there's a baby . . . ?'

He said: 'With your simplicity and his force . . . Make him a saint – to pray for his father.'

A sudden feeling of immense gratitude broke through the pain – it was as if she had been given the sight a long way off of life going on again. He said:

'Pray for me, my child.'

She said: 'Yes, oh yes.'

Outside she looked up at the name on the confessional box – it wasn't any name she remembered. Priests come and go.

She went out into the street – the pain was still there; you couldn't shake it off with a word; but the worst horror, she thought, was over – the horror of the complete circle; to be back at home, back at Snow's – they'd take her back – just as if the Boy had never existed at all. He had existed and would always exist. She had a sudden conviction that she carried life – and she thought proudly: Let them get over that if they can; let them get over that. She turned out on to the front opposite the Palace Pier and began to walk firmly away from the direction of her home towards Billy's. There was something to be salvaged from that house and room, something else they wouldn't be able to get over – his voice speaking a message to her: if there was a child, speaking to the child, 'If he loved you,' the priest had said, 'that shows . . .' She walked rapidly in the thin June sunlight towards the worst horror of all.

Graham Greene, Brighton Rock (1938)

Father Wainwright's forgiveness

He could be very forgiving. One night on going home, when he opened his front door he saw a man creeping catlike down the stairs from his own room, the mantelpiece clock under the visitor's arm. He tried to escape through the back entrance. But the Father stopped him and took him up to his room. There he gently rebuked him, made him put the clock back on the mantelpiece and gave him half a crown.

Lucy Menzies, Father Wainwright: A Record (1947)

Father Wainwright in Wapping

If he had a friend dangerously ill in St George's Hospital, close at hand, he would sometimes wait for the call, sitting outside on the steps of the clergy house. Not long before he died a policeman found him curled up, asleep on a doorstep near the hospital. 'What's the matter, sir?' asked the policeman. 'I'm quite comfortable, thank you,'

Fr Wainwright replied: 'I've got to be at the hospital again in an hour to see someone who is dying and I was afraid if I went home I might not wake up!' Sometimes when he did wait at the hospital for an expected call into the ward the sisters and nurses would comment on the little bowed figure sitting there on a hard bench through the watches of the night, his reward that of helping some soul 'on to the further shore.'

His favourite time to give communion to grave cases was just after midnight. But he was constantly in the wards at all hours, both at the London Hospital and St George's.

The now legendary story of the shirt happened at the 'London.' The Father was visiting a man about to be discharged who confided in him that he had no shirt to go out in. Fr Wainright simply went behind a screen, took off his own shirt and gave it to the man. That happened not once but several times. Indeed, shirts often come into the story. The reason was the prevailing unemployment; the need to pawn everything that could be pawned to buy food. The Father writes (1909):

> We have got so low now that not only do people want feeding up before they are fit for work, but in many cases boots and clothing, all they have being either in pawn or worn out.
>
> Last night a man appeared with no shirt at all under his coat; happily I found one that had just been sent. So he came to my room and attired himself to his great satisfaction and comfort. This was about 10.30 p.m. when I found him waiting for me. . . . You will understand a shirt is necessary when the coat, such as it is, is taken off for work.

When some work-party asked what would be most useful, he eagerly replied:

Might I suggest shirts? men's and boys'. Not seldom, men come to my room for shirts, who unless that want is supplied would find it impossible to take work even if offered. No one can work with his coat on, so that a shirt in fair repair is essential.

Lucy Menzies (ibid.)

An Anglo-Catholic country curate

He was surely as strange a curate as ever came to a remote agricultural parish. An old man with a long, grey beard which he buttoned inside his long, close-fitting, black overcoat. Fervour and many fast days had worn away his flesh, and he had hollow cheeks and deep-set, dark eyes which glowed with the flame of fanaticism. He was a fanatic where his Church and his creed were concerned; otherwise he was the kindest and most gentle of men. Too good for this world, some of the women said when they came to know him.

He was what is now known as an Anglo-Catholic. Sunday after Sunday he preached 'One Catholic Apostolic Church' and 'our Holy Religion' to his congregation of rustics. But he did not stop at that: he dealt often with the underlying truths of religion, preaching the gospel of love and forgiveness of sins and the brotherhood of man. He was a wonderful preacher. No listener nodded or 'lost the thread' when he was in the pulpit, and though most of his congregation might not be able to grasp or agree with his doctrine, all responded to the love, sympathy, and sincerity of the preacher and every eye was upon him from his first word to his last. How such a preacher came to be in old age but a curate in a remote country parish is a mystery. His eloquence and fervour would have filled a city church. . .

He once gave the very shoes off his feet to a woman who had pleaded that she could not go to church for want of a pair, and had added, meaningly, that she took a large size and that a man's pair of light shoes would do very well. He gave her the best of the two pairs he possessed, which he happened to be wearing, stipulating that he should be allowed to walk home in them. The wearing of them home was a concession to convention, for he would have enjoyed walking barefoot over the flints as a follower of his beloved St Francis of Assisi, towards whom he had a special devotion twenty years before the cult of the Little Poor Man became popular. He gave away so much that he could only have kept just enough to keep himself in bare necessaries. His black overcoat, which he wore in all weathers, was threadbare, and the old cassock he wore indoors was green and falling to pieces.

Flora Thompson, *Lark Rise to Candleford* (1939)

[12]

CLERGY WIVES

The days have passed when a parson's wife was expected to be like the consort of the Reverend Frank Milvey in Dickens's *Our Mutual Friend* – 'a pretty, bright little woman, something worn by anxiety, who had repressed many pretty tastes and bright fancies, and substituted in their stead, schools, soup, flannel, coats and all the weekday cares and Sunday coughs of a large population'. Instead of being the unpaid flower-arranger, social worker, secretary and housewife, the consort of the modern parish priest is very likely to be pursuing a career of her own. She might be a lawyer, or a businesswoman, or even herself a member of the clergy. It is a far cry from the days of Anthony Trollope, who occupies most of this section.

Trollope's ecclesiastical novels reveal the clergy as human beings, never more human than in their marriages. I think one of the most brilliant things in the whole of nineteenth-century English fiction is the way that Mrs Proudie (in *The Last Chronicle of Barset*) changes from being a figure whom we regard in a purely comic light – 'the bishop jumped out of his chair at hearing the wife of his bosom called a woman' – to being a person whom we recognize, in her death, as almost tragic.

I hope that some of the younger generation of clergy wives will try to keep alive the old tradition of the parsonage wife – difficult as that must be in today's economic climate. As the following glimpses of modern bishops' wives make plain, they are a striking bunch.

———

A Priest to the Temple

If he be married, the choice of his wife was made rather by his ear, than by his eye; his judgment, not his affection, found out a fit wife for him, whose humble and liberal disposition he preferred before beauty, riches, or honour. *He knew that (the good instrument of God to bring women to heaven) a wife and loving husband could, out of humility, produce any special grace of faith, patience, meekness, love, obedience, &c. and out of liberality make her fruitful in all good works.*

George Herbert, *A Priest to the Temple* (1652)

Good with zips

By good fortune the Archbishop of Canterbury, Dr Donald Coggan, joined me in East Berlin for two days as he was on a European tour. It was the festival of the Ascension. He celebrated Communion and I preached. As we were walking up the aisle, Donald said, 'Let's take off our robes here and we'll go straight in to breakfast.' I told him it was impossible as the zip fastener of my trousers had disintegrated during the service. To which Donald said, 'Come to our room. Jean is very good with zips.'

Mervyn Stockwood, *Chanctonbury Ring* (1982)

All bachelor clerygmen misbehave themselves

They were sitting, talking over their sorrows, in the drawing-room before dinner on the day after Mr Slope's departure for London; and on this occasion Mrs Grantly spoke out her mind freely. She had opinions of her own about parish clergymen, and now thought it right to give vent to them.

'If you would have been led by me, archdeacon, you would never have put a bachelor into St Ewold's.'

'But, my dear, you don't mean to say that all bachelor clergymen misbehave themselves.'

'I don't know that clergymen are so much better than other men,' said Mrs Grantly. 'It's all very well with a curate whom you have under your own eye, and whom you can get rid of if he persists in improprieties.'

'But Mr Arabin was a fellow, and couldn't have had a wife.'

'Then I would have found some one who could.'

'But, my dear, are fellows never to get livings?'

'Yes, to be sure they are, when they get engaged. I never would put a young man into a living unless he were married, or engaged to be married. Now here is Mr Arabin. The whole responsibility lies upon you.'

'There is not at this moment a clergyman in all Oxford more respected for morals and conduct than Arabin.'

'Oh, Oxford!' said the lady, with a sneer. 'What men choose to do at Oxford, nobody ever hears of. A man may do very well at Oxford who would bring disgrace on a parish: and, to tell you the truth, it seems to me that Mr Arabin is just such a man.'

The archdeacon groaned deeply, but he had no further answer to make.

'You really must speak to him, archdeacon. Only think what the Thornes will say if they heard that their parish clergyman spends his whole time philandering with this woman.'

The archdeacon groaned again. He was a courageous man, and knew well enough how to rebuke the younger clergymen of the diocese, when necessary. But there was that about Mr Arabin which made the doctor feel that it would very difficult to rebuke him with good effect.

'You can advise him to find a wife for himself, and he will understand well enough what that means,' said Mrs Grantly.

The archdeacon had nothing for it but groaning.

Anthony Trollope, Barchester Towers (1857)

Mr and Mrs Milvey

So Mr Milvey called, 'Margaretta, my dear!' and Mrs Milvey came down. A pretty, bright little woman, something worn by anxiety, who had repressed many pretty tastes and bright fancies, and substituted in their stead, schools, soup, flannel, coals, and all the week-day cares and Sunday coughs of a large population, young and old. As gallantly had Mr Milvey repressed much in himself that naturally belonged to his old studies and old fellow-students, and taken up among the poor and their children with the hard crumbs of life.

'Mr and Mrs Boffin, my dear, whose good fortune you have heard of.'

Mrs Milvey, with the most unaffected grace in the world, congratulated them, and was glad to see them. Yet her engaging face, being an open as well as a perceptive one, was not without her husband's latent smile.

'Mrs Boffin wishes to adopt a little boy, my dear.'

Mrs Milvey looking rather alarmed, her husband added:

'An orphan, my dear.'

'Oh!' said Mrs Milvey, reassured for her own little boys.

'And I was thinking, Margaretta, that perhaps old Mrs. Goody's grandchild might answer the purpose.'

'Oh, my *dear* Frank! I *don't* think that would do!'

'No?'

'Oh *no*!'

The smiling Mrs Boffin, feeling it incumbent on her to take part in the conversation, and being charmed with the emphatic little wife and her ready interest, here offered her acknowledgements and inquired what there was against him?

'I *don't* think,' said Mrs Milvey, glancing at the Reverend Frank – 'and I believe my husband will agree with me when he considers it again – that you could possibly keep that orphan clean from snuff. Because his grandmother takes so *many* ounces, and drops it over him.'

'But he would not be living with his grandmother then, Margaretta,' said Mr Milvey.

'No, Frank, but it would be impossible to keep her from Mrs Boffin's house; and the *more* there was to eat and drink there, the oftener she would go. And she *is* an inconvenient woman. I *hope* it's not uncharitable to remember that last Christmas Eve she drank eleven cups of tea, and grumbled all the time. And she is *not* a grateful woman, Frank. You recollect her addressing a crowd outside this house, about her wrongs, when, one night after we had gone to bed, she brought back the petticoat of new flannel that had been given her, because it was too short.'

'That's true,' said Mr Milvey. 'I don't think that would do. Would little Harrison –'

'Oh, *Frank!*' remonstrated his emphatic wife.

'He has no grandmother, my dear.'

'No, but I *don't* think Mrs Boffin would like an orphan who squints so *much*.'

'That's true again,' said Mr Milvey, becoming haggard with perplexity. 'If a little girl would do – '

'But, my *dear* Frank, Mrs Boffin wants a boy.'

'That's true again,' said Mr Milvey. 'Tom Bocker is a nice boy' (thoughtfully).

'But I *doubt*, Frank,' Mrs Milvey hinted, after a little hesitation, 'if Mrs Boffin wants an orphan *quite* nineteen, who drives a cart and waters the roads.'

Mr Milvey referred the point to Mrs Boffin in a look; on that smiling lady's shaking her black velvet bonnet and bows, he remarked, in lower spirits, 'That's true again.'

'I am sure,' said Mrs Boffin, concerned at giving so much trouble, 'that if I had known you would have taken so much pains, sir – and you too, ma'am – I don't think I would have come.'

'*Pray* don't say that!' urged Mrs Milvey.

'No, don't say that,' assented Mr Milvey, 'because we are so much obliged to you for giving us the preference.' Which Mrs Milvey confirmed; and really the kind, conscientious couple spoke as if they kept some profitable orphan warehouse and were personally patronized. 'But it is a responsible trust,' added Mr Milvey, 'and difficult to discharge. At the same time, we are naturally very unwilling to lose the chance you so kindly give us, and if you could afford us a day or two to look about us – you know, Margaretta, we might carefully examine the workhouse, and the Infant School, and your District.'

'To be *sure!*' said the emphatic little wife.

Charles Dickens, Our Mutual Friend (1865)

Mrs Augustus Hare

'I am amused to think how little most women would have suited him, and how exactly I do. His love for ruminating by himself, to anybody without resources of their own, would be so dull, and he would not like that eternal interruption which many wives would give; then their being fussy about trifles, talking about their neighbours' concerns, vagueness, and the *very least* regard to appearances or show, would annoy him so much; and yet, without liking a wife to be troublesome in fondness, he would ill have borne with the slightest coldness; so that, without vanity, I certainly am more adapted to his *wants* than most could have been. Perhaps I might equally say of myself that, indulged as I have always been, I should have borne ill any person of more irritable nature, and less tender and considerate. Putting aside all other considerations, I never saw anybody so easy to live with, by whom the daily petty things of life were passed over so lightly; and then there is a charm in the *refinement* of feeling, which is not to be told in its influence upon trifles.

'*July* 27 – A new parcel of books has just arrived, and Augustus having seized upon one, I have no chance of a word for some time, and so you shall hear all what you are wishing to know about his expedition. At Salisbury he went through all the forms of institution with the bishop. Saturday, with difficulty, he found his way by cross-roads to Alton-Barnes, put his hand upon the church key, rang the bell three times, and on Sunday went through the morning service with all the Articles and other necessary declarations – the evening service, prayers, and sermon; which latter, not being prepared, he was obliged to borrow a sermon, and says it was the worst he ever read. This all done, he was duly inducted rector of Alton-Barnes.'

Augustus Hare, Memorials of a Quiet Life (1891)

'A bishop's wife but still myself'

We started the handshakes and went on for what seemed hours. We tried to have a little conversation with as many as possible. Ronald, needless to say, was much better than I was, but by the time we had finished we were both nearly in hysterics from sheer fatigue. Kaye Almey, women's page editor of the *Leicester Mercury*, used her whole column to give me a write-up. It began, 'What does a bishop's wife wear at her first reception . . . ?' Kaye Almey is always generous and was more than kind on this occasion. If only she had known the vintage of that suit! Perhaps she did. The column ended by remarking that I remained fresh and smiling to the end and that helped me a lot; I felt I hadn't completely let the show down. Since then one of our nicest vicar's wives has confided to me that they all thought I looked too small and too young to have such a burden laid upon me.

We were of course constantly doing things for the first time; they were not without their difficult moments. There was, for instance, Ronald's first institution of a vicar. This is a complicated service and he had studied it with considerable care. There is a happy custom in Leicester diocese whereby the wife of the Archdeacon generally accompanies her husband on these occasions. We had already decided that we too should go together to most things, so I met Mrs Matthews at the church door and we were conducted to seats in the front. The Bishop's chair stood at the chancel steps; it had uncommonly short legs. The procession came up the aisle to a hearty hymn. Ronald approached his chair while clergy and churchwardens bowed and scraped. He sat down at last, a foot lower than he had expected, with a resounding bump. A broad grin suffused his face and I burst into uncontrollable giggles. Mrs Matthews nudged me sympathetically. I turned my giggles into coughs and the service continued without a hitch. It was just one of those things . . .

When we were not at confirmations we seemed to be at inductions, followed, of course, by the inevitable bun fight, which I found always included no less than four speeches. I was for ever getting involved in the most complicated situations at these inductions. The churchwardens were generally informed that I was coming and if I entered the church with Ronald they greeted me and escorted me to my allotted place. But if I came in by a different door anything might happen. At a beautiful little church on the outskirts of the diocese I went in by myself by the west door. The church was already nearly full and a harassed sidesman approached me.

'Where are you from, dear?' he asked me anxiously.

'From Leicester,' I answered, wondering why he should want to know. He scratched his head and scanned the seething mass jamming the pews.

'We'll have to try and fit you in here,' he mumbled, grasping my arm and leading me in a determined manner to the back of the church.

'There's room for a little 'un there,' he explained, indicating a narrow gap between two very well-developed ladies. 'Move up a bit will you and let her in.'

I tumbled over feet and hassocks and sent prayer books crashing to the ground and eventually wedged myself between my two companions, who regarded me in stolid silence. I knelt down and said my prayers and, when I was balanced once more on my perch, I observed my sidesman friend in excited consultation with the churchwarden. After much gesticulation and many hissed comments the churchwarden plodded up to my pew.

'Be you the Bishop's wife?' he enquired plaintively.

I admitted that such was the case.

'Then you must come along with me,' he announced, more in sorrow than in anger.

Amid much consternation I was handed back to the end of the pew and the churchwarden, armed with his staff, since he was already overdue in the vestry, set off at the double towards an empty pew at the front. Terrified that I should collide with the procession, I pursued him at speed and was bowed into my place, where I took my seat in solitary state. Here I was faced with a frightful dilemma – ought I to say a second set of prayers? If I did not, those who had not witnessed my earlier arrival would conclude that the Bishop's wife was undoubtedly a complete pagan; if I did, my former companions at the back would imagine me to be over-pious. Deciding that it was perhaps better to err on the side of piety rather than paganism I knelt down once more, but I was much too embarrassed to formulate any kind of prayer except that I might be saved from falling asleep from sheer exhaustion.

Cicely Williams, *A Bishop's Wife but Still Myself* (1961)

A good thing

In a country where a married archbishop was so strange, they asked him whether marriage is a good thing for an archbishop. He said only, 'It is a good thing. It is a good thing.'

Owen Chadwick, *Michael Ramsey: A Life* (1990)

Reverend Mother

It is recalled that Archbishop Ward made a striking figure when he went shopping in New Barnet, wearing a scarlet cassock, cape and biretta.* Very often he was accompanied by his wife, whose costume was much more glamorous than what she might have worn had she been a member of the Anglican Deaconess Community of St Andrew, or of the Order of Deaconesses formally restored by the Convocation of Canterbury in 1923. Far more in keeping with her status of Reverend Mother of the mixed Confraternity was the picturesque white habit, coif, and veil, set off by a large gold pectoral cross suspended on a gold chain.† Their frequent companion on such walks was a certain Fra Filius Domini (in the world, Colin Mackenzie Chamberlain), who wore a brown quasi-Franciscan habit, although the male members of the Confraternity had been raised to the rank of Canons Regular.

* A friend, who was in close touch with Ward at this time, remembers his attending Masonic meetings in London, robed as a major prelate of the Latin rite; and that to see a collar and apron over a scarlet cassock, and a scarlet biretta hanging on a peg in the anteroom, added an unusual note of colour on such occasions.

† Reverend Mother seems to have acted as a Medium, receiving orders and messages from Saints and Angels. This enabled her to control the members of the Confraternity, including Reverend Father.

Peter Anson, Bishops at Large (1964)

The wife of his bosom

'Had I been Mr Thumble,' said Mrs Proudie, 'I would have read from that desk and I would have preached from that pulpit.'

Mr Crawley waited a moment, thinking that the bishop might perhaps speak again; but as he did not, but sat expectant as though he had finished his discourse, and now expected a reply, Mr Crawley got up from his seat and drew near to the table. 'My lord,' he began, 'it has all been just as you have said. I did answer your first letter in haste.'

'The more shame for you,' said Mrs Proudie.

'And therefore, for aught I know, my letter to your lordship may be so worded as to need some apology.'

'Of course it needs an apology,' said Mrs Proudie.

'But for the matter of it, my lord, no apology can be made, nor is any needed. I did refuse to your messenger permission to perform the services of my church, and if you sent twenty more, I shall refuse them all – till the time may come when it will be your lordship's duty, in accordance with the laws of the Church, as borne out and backed by the laws of the land, to provide during my constrained absence for the spiritual wants of those poor people at Hogglestock.'

'Poor people, indeed,' said Mrs Proudie. 'Poor wretches!'

'And, my lord, it may be, that it shall soon be your lordship's duty to take due and legal steps for depriving me of my benefice at Hogglestock – nay, probably, for silencing me altogether as to the exercise of my sacred profession!'

'Of course it will, sir. Your gown will be taken from you,' said Mrs Proudie. The bishop was looking with all his eyes up at the great forehead and great eyebrows of the man, and was so fascinated by the power that was exercised over him by the other man's strength that he hardly now noticed his wife.

'It may well be so,' continued Mr Crawley. 'The circumstances are strong against me; and, though your lordship has altogether misunderstood the nature of the duty performed by the magistrates in sending my case for trial – although, as it seems to me, you have come to conclusions in this matter in ignorance of the very theory of our laws – '

'Sir!' said Mrs Proudie.

'Yet I can foresee the probability that a jury may discover me to have been guilty of theft.'

'Of course the jury will do so,' said Mrs Proudie.

'Should such verdict be given, then, my lord, your interference will be legal, proper, and necessary. And you will find that, even if it be within my power to oppose obstacles to your lordship's authority, I will oppose no such obstacle. There is, I believe, no appeal in criminal cases.'

'None at all,' said Mrs Proudie. 'There is no appeal against your bishop. You should have learned that before.'

'But till that time shall come, my lord, I shall hold my own at Hogglestock as you hold your own here at Barchester. Nor have you more power to turn me out of my pulpit by your mere voice, than I have to turn you out of your throne by mine. If you doubt me, my lord, your lordship's ecclesiastical court is open to you. Try it there.'

'You defy us, then?' said Mrs Proudie.

'My lord, I grant your authority as bishop to be great, but even a bishop can only act as the law allows him.'

'God forbid that I should do more,' said the bishop.

'Sir, you will find that your wicked threats will fall back upon your own head,' said Mrs Proudie.

'Peace, woman,' Mr Crawley said, addressing her at last. The bishop jumped out of his chair at hearing the wife of his bosom called a woman. But he jumped rather in admiration than in anger.

Anthony Trollope, *The Last Chronicle of Barset* (1879)

The death of Mrs Proudie

She had in some ways, and at certain periods of his life, been very good to him. She had kept his money for him and made things go straight, when they had been poor. His interests had always been her interests. Without her he would never have been a bishop. So, at least, he told himself now, and so told himself probably with truth. She had been very careful of his children. She had never been idle. She had never been fond of pleasure. She had neglected no acknowledged duty. He did not doubt that she was now on her way to heaven. He took his hands down from his head, and clasping them together, said a little prayer. It may be doubted whether he quite knew for what he was praying. The idea of praying for her soul, now that she was dead, would have scandalized him. He certainly was not praying for his own soul. I think he was praying that God might save him from being glad that his wife was dead.

Anthony Trollope (ibid.)

[13]

STONY GROUND

Every parish priest, however successful, must have had moments during his life when he felt that he was a failure. John Betjeman wrote a poem called 'Blame the Vicar', and if it were a better poem, I should have included it here. 'Blame the vicar' is the flavour of the few pieces which follow.

Palm Sunday

Friday, 8 March 1872
At the Scripture Lesson at the School this morning asking Eleanor Williams of Paradise, 'What happened on Palm Sunday?' she replied, '*Jesus Christ went up to heaven on an ass*'. This was the promising result of a long struggle to teach her something about the Festivals of the Church.

Francis Kilvert, Diaries (1974)

Help from the new curate

A young clergyman went down to work as curate in a Devonshire village and his 'ministrations were very acceptable', as they say. One day he met one of the old women in the village street and she said: 'Oh, Mr Brown, us be zo glad yu've come down yur! Ef yu daon' mind my zayin' so, zur, yu rade them prayers up prapper, an' as fur

the Lessons, us can yur every wurd ov 'em: an' as fur prachin' –
wull, us 'ave never 'ad nobody prache laike yu! Do yu know, us
didn' know wot sin was till yu came intu the parish!'

Rev. W. P. Besley, 1930s newspaper cutting

Cosmo Gordon Lang in Yorkshire

At Leeds he had had his first taste of Yorkshire outspokenness. Now
he renewed acquaintance with it, to his never-failing delight.

The excellent vicar of a North Riding parish had retired after eighteen years.
He had every reason to know that he had been respected and liked, and was
just a little surprised that when he left little notice was taken. A year afterwards
he had a letter from his old churchwarden asking him to come, as the parishioners wished to give him a testimonial. When he came and met them in the
school, he was surprised to see that his successor was not present. The reason
was soon obvious. This was the speech of the churchwarden who presided:
'When you were here, Mr So-and-so, we often said: "Well, we might 'ave a
worse." *And so we 'ave.* So we thowt we'd like to give ye a testimonial.'
This was the reward for eighteen years of most faithful service, but, as often
in Yorkshire, more was meant than was said.

The country people were not always responsive to new enterprises.

To a parish which had gone asleep I appointed an energetic young incumbent.
The Rural Dean was returning from a visit to the parish, driven by a farmer
churchwarden in his gig. The Rural Dean asked how he liked the new Vicar.
The good man replied: 'Afore 'e coom we were left to ourselves. But now it's
woon thing woon day and another thing the next. Ah'll tell tha what Ah think
of him' – here he took his whip and flogged his old horse – 'Ah say, damn him
– damn him – damn him' – and pointing each 'damn' with a stroke of his whip.
But I think the young Vicar gradually won his way.

J. G. Lockhart, *Cosmo Gordon Lang* (1949)

A Priest to his People

Men of the hills, wantoners, men of Wales,
With your sheep and your pigs and your ponies, your sweaty
    females,
How I have hated you for your irreverence, your scorn even
Of the refinements of art and the mysteries of the Church,
I whose invective would spurt like a flame of fire

To be quenched always in the coldness of your stare.
Men of bone, wrenched from the bitter moorland,
Who have not yet shaken the moss from your savage skulls,
Or prayed the peat from your eyes,
Did you detect like an ewe or an ailing wether,
Driven into the underground by the nagging flies,
My true heart wandering in a wood of lies?

You are curt and graceless, yet your sudden laughter
Is sharp and bright as a whipped pool,
When the wind strikes or the clouds are flying;
And all the devices of church and school
Have failed to cripple your unhallowed movements,
Or put a halter on your wild soul.
You are lean and spare, yet your strength is a mockery
Of the pale words in the black Book,
And why should you come like sparrows for prayer crumbs,
Whose hands can dabble in the world's blood?

I have taxed your ignorance of rhyme and sonnet,
Your want of deference to the painter's skill,
But I know, as I listen, that your speech has in it
The source of all poetry, clear as a rill
Bubbling from your lips; and what brushwork could equal
The artistry of your dwelling on the bare hill?
You will forgive, then, my initial hatred,
My first intolerance of your uncouth ways,
You who are indifferent to all that I can offer,
Caring not whether I blame or praise.
With your pigs and your sheep and your sons and holly-cheeked
    daughters
You will still continue to unwind your days
In a crude tapestry under the jealous heavens
To affront, bewilder, yet compel my gaze.
R. S. Thomas, *Song at the Year's Turning* (1966)

Seditious meetings of Letters

'Twas an happy time when all Learning was in Manuscript, and some little Officer, like our Author, did keep the Keys of the Library. When the Clergy needed no more knowledg then to read the Liturgy, and the Laity no more Clerkship than to save them from Hanging. But now, since Printing came into the World, such is the mischief, that a Man cannot write a Book but presently he is answered. Could the Press but once be conjured to obey only an *Imprimatur*, our Author might not disdain *perhaps* to be one of its most zealous Patrons. There have been wayes found out to banish Ministers, to fine not only the People, but even the Grounds and Fields where they assembled in Conventicles: But no Art yet could prevent these seditious meetings of Letters. Two or three brawny Fellows in a Corner, with meer Ink and Elbow-grease, do more harm than an *hundred Systematical Divines* with their *sweaty Preaching*.

Andrew Marvell, *The Rehearsal Transpros'd* (1672)

[14]

MIGHTY OFFENSIVE

Thoroughgoing anti-clericalism, of the sort which has always been a feature of life in France, has never been a conspicuous part of the English scene. The fervour of Milton's *Lycidas* is perhaps out of place in this section, in which I have tried to convey the manner in which the clergy have been found 'mighty offensive' by the laity. Samuel Johnson would certainly have seen what prompted Anthony Powell to record the conversation of the army padres in the extract from *A Valley of Bones*. There are few passages in modern literature which convey the embarrassingness of the clergy better than this vignette from Mr Powell's masterpiece. The point is less that the matter of their talk is shocking, than that it is inapposite, and because they know this, they overdo things. By assuming 'the lax jollity of men of the world', as Johnson calls it, clergymen never get it quite right. His comments on their attempts at foppish *mufti* continue to hit their target. We have all, perhaps, met clergymen whose garish neckties or shirts, on a day off from parochial toil, proclaim him to be 'but half a beau'.

It is hard, however, for the clergy either to do right, socially, or to be seen to do right. Those of us who ourselves drink, smoke, visit pubs or enjoy ribald conversation, might become arch-puritans on behalf of our vicar and object if he were seen doing such things, even though they are perhaps all in themselves harmless. On the other hand, who would not echo James Anthony Froude's objection to the sort of priggishness and narrowness of which he accuses John Keble?

Nor are the clergy themselves innocent of the vice of expecting clergymen to be perfect. Parson Woodforde would not have felt so aggrieved by his guest overstaying his welcome had not young Mr

Campbell been in holy orders. And there is a peculiarly clerical timbre to the glacial bitchiness of Newman's letter to J. B. Morris. The accumulation of rebukes – that Morris has done carpentry in his own room but, apart from nailing down a carpet, not helped with general carpentry about the house; that he has been dilatory in his making of cocoa and coffee for other members of the community – bears the hallmarks of real ingrained *irritation*. There is much unconscious comedy in Newman's admission that he has written out this catalogue of Morris's shortcomings 'more than once over'. The details of clerical life, of which this letter of Newman's is not atypical, would never I think lead to widespread revolution, as happened in eighteenth-century France, but it might confirm Rose Macaulay's hunch in 1950 that many of the clergy 'seem rather chumps'.

This merriment of parsons is mighty offensive

He also disapproved of bishops going to routs, at least of their staying at them longer than their presence commanded respect. He mentioned a particular bishop. 'Poh! (said Mrs Thrale) the Bishop of — is never minded at a rout.' BOSWELL. 'When a bishop places himself in a situation where he has no distinct character, and is of no consequence, he degrades the dignity of his order.' JOHNSON. 'Mr Boswell, Madam, has said it as correctly as could be.'

Nor was it only in the dignitaries of the Church that Johnson required a particular decorum and delicacy of behaviour; he justly considered that the clergy, as persons set apart for the sacred office of serving at the altar, and impressing the minds of men with the aweful concerns of a future state, should be somewhat more serious than the generality of mankind, and have a suitable composure of manners. A due sense of the dignity of their profession, independent of higher motives, will ever prevent them from losing their distinction in an indiscriminate sociality; and did such as affect this, know how much it lessens them in the eyes of those whom they think to please by it, they would feel themselves much mortified.

Johnson and his friend, Beauclerk, were once together in company with several clergymen, who thought that they should appear to advantage, by assuming the lax jollity of *men of the world*; which, as it may be observed in similar cases, they carried to noisy excess. Johnson, who they expected would be *entertained*, sat grave and silent for some time; at last, turning to Beauclerk, he said, by no means in a whisper, 'This merriment of parsons is mighty offensive.'

Even the dress of a clergyman should be in character, and nothing can be more despicable than conceited attempts at avoiding the appearance of the clerical order; attempts, which are as ineffectual as they are pitiful. Dr Porteus, now Bishop of London, in his excellent charge when presiding over the diocese of Chester, justly animadverts upon this subject; and observes of a reverend fop, that he 'can be but *half a beau.*'

James Boswell, *The Life of Samuel Johnson* (1791)

A parson outstays his welcome

Aug 4 [1784]. . . . About 10 o'clock this Night a Clergyman by name Cam[p]bell (Vicar of Weasingham in this County and formerly of Oriel Coll: Oxford and afterwards Fellow of Worcester Coll: in the same University) came to my House and he supped and slept here – himself and horse. I remember him at Oriel Coll: but not so intimate as to expect that he would have taken such freedom especially as he never made me a Visit before. He slept however in the Attic Story and I treated him as one that would be too free if treated too kindly. It kept me up till after 12 o'clock.

Aug 5. . . . Mr Campbell breakfasted here on Milk only and after breakfast I took a ride with him to Norwich being Assize Week and there spent the Day – but returned in the Evening to Weston by myself, leaving Mr Campbell behind – and whom I saw nothing of all the Day after I left him on coming into Norwich.

James Woodforde, *The Diary of a Country Parson* (1926)

The Archbishop of Canterbury reproved

Then went this creature forth to London with her husband unto Lambeth, where the Archbishop lay at that time; and as they came into the hall in the afternoon, there were many of the Archbishop's clerks and other reckless men, both squires and yeomen, who swore many great oaths and spoke many reckless words, and this creature boldly reprehended them, and said they would be damned unless they left off their swearing and other sins that they used.

And with that, there came forth another woman of the same town in a furred cloak, who forswore this creature, banned her, and spoke full cursedly to her in this manner:

'I would thou wert in Smithfield, and I would bring a faggot to burn thee with. It is a pity thou art alive.'

This creature stood still and answered not, and her husband suffered it with great pain, and was full sorry to hear his wife so rebuked.

Then the Archbishop sent for this creature into his garden. When she came into his presence, she saluted him as best she could, praying him of his gracious lordship to grant her authority to choose her confessor and to be houselled* every Sunday, if God would dispose her thereto, under his letter and his seal through all his province. And he granted her full benignly all her desire without any silver or gold, nor would he let his clerks take anything for the writing or the sealing of the letter.

When this creature found this grace in his sight, she was well comforted and strengthened in her soul, and so she showed this worshipful lord her manner of life, and such grace as God wrought in her mind and in her soul, to find out what he would say thereto, and whether he found any default either in her contemplation or in her weeping.

And she told him also the cause of her weeping, and the manner of dalliance that Our Lord spoke to her soul; and he found no default in her, but praised her manner of living, and was right glad that Our Merciful Lord Christ Jesus showed such grace in our days, blessed may He be.

Then this creature boldly spoke to him for the correction of his household, saying with reverence:

'My lord, Our Lord of all, Almighty God has not given you your benefice and great wordly wealth to keep His traitors and them that slay Him every day by great oaths swearing. Ye shall answer for them, unless ye correct them, or else put them out of your service.'

Full benignly and meekly he suffered her to speak her intent, and gave her a fair answer, she supposing it would then be better. And so their dalliance continued till stars appeared in the firmament. Then she took her leave and her husband also.

* To go to Holy Communion

Margery Kempe (c. 1373–1439), *The Book of Margery Kempe*

Clerical envy of another man's book

Whenever anyone told a lie in his presence, Meilyr was immediately aware of it, for he saw a demon dancing and exulting on the liar's tongue. Although he was completely illiterate, if he looked at a book which was incorrect, which contained some false statement, or which aimed at deceiving the reader, he immediately put his finger on the offending passage. If you asked him how he knew this, he said that a devil first pointed out the place with its finger. In the same way, and again with a demon to help him, whenever he went into the dormitory of a monastery, he would point to the bed of any false monk whose religion was a pretext and did not come from the heart. He maintained that the vice of gluttony and greed was sordid beyond words; the vice of lust and libidinousness was perhaps more pleasing to the eye, but it was really even more foul. When he was harassed beyond endurance by these unclean spirits, Saint John's Gospel was placed on his lap, and then they all vanished immediately, flying away like so many birds. If the Gospel were afterwards removed and the *History of the Kings of Britain* by Geoffrey of Monmouth put there in its place, just to see what would happen, the demons would alight all over his body, and on the book, too, staying there longer than usual and being even more demanding. Barnabas, one remembers, or so we read in the stories told about him, used to place Saint Matthew's Gospel on people who were ill, and they were cured immediately. It is clear from this, and so it is, indeed, from the account which I have just given to you, how much respect and reverence we owe to each of the books of the Gospel. It is equally clear that anyone who knowingly perjures himself on one of the Gospels deviates from the path of truth with great danger to himself and with the risk of eternal damnation.

Giraldus Cambrensis (c. 1148–1220), *The Journey through Wales*

Blind mouthes!

Next *Camus*, reverend Sire, went footing slow,
His Mantle hairy, and his Bonnet sedge,
Inwrought with figures dim, and on the edge
Like to that sanguine flower inscrib'd with woe.
Ah; Who hath reft (quoth he) my dearest pledge?
Last came, and last did go,
The Pilot of the *Galilean* lake,
Two massy Keyes he bore of metals twain,
(The Golden opes, the Iron shuts amain)
He shook his Miter'd locks, and stern bespake,
How well could I have spar'd for thee, young swain,
Anow of such as for their bellies sake,
Creep and intrude, and climb into the fold?
Of other care they little reck'ning make,
Then how to scramble at the shearers feast,
And shove away the worthy bidden guest;
Blind mouthes! that scarce themselves know how to hold
A Sheep-hook, or have learn'd ought els the least
That to the faithfull Herdmans art belongs!
What recks it them? What need they? They are sped;
And whent they list, their lean and flashy songs
Grate on their scrannel Pipes of wretched straw,
The hungry Sheep look up, and are not fed,
But swoln with wind, and the rank mist they draw,
Rot inwardly, and foul contagion spread:
Besides what the grim Woolf with privy paw
Daily devours apace, and nothing sed,
But that two-handed engine at the door,
Stands ready to smite once, and smite no more.

John Milton, *Lycidas* (1637)

Keble's narrowness

To his immediate friends he was genial, affectionate, and possibly
instructive, but he had no faculty for winning the unconverted. If he
was not bigoted he was intensely prejudiced. If you did not agree
with him there was something morally wrong with you, and your

'natural man' was provoked into resistance. To speak habitually with authority does not necessarily indicate an absence of humility, but does not encourage the growth of that quality. If there had been no 'movement,' as it was called, if Keble had remained a quiet country clergyman, unconscious that he was a great man, and uncalled on to guide the opinions of his age, he would have commanded perhaps more enduring admiration. The knot of followers who specially attached themselves to him, show traces of his influence in a disposition not only to think the views which they hold sound in themselves, but to regard those who think differently as their intellectual inferiors. Keble was incapable of vanity in the vulgar sense. But there was a subtle self-sufficiency in him which has come out more distinctly in his school.

I remember an instance of Keble's narrowness extremely characteristic of him. A member of a family with which he had been intimate had adopted Liberal opinions in theology. Keble probably did not know what those opinions were, but regarded this person as an apostate who had sinned against light. He came to call one day when the erring brother happened to be at home; and learning that he was in the house, he refused to enter, and remained sitting in the porch. St John is reported to have fled out of a bath at Ephesus on hearing that the heretic Cerinthus was under the roof. Keble, I presume, remembered the story, and acted like the apostle.

J. A. Froude, Short Studies of Great Subjects (1867–83)

To a clergyman who would not pull his weight with domestic duties

To J. B. Morris

Mary Vale. May 8/[18]46

My dear Morris,

One is so seldom able in the common course of things to hear from others what concerns oneself, that I cannot bring myself to let slip the opportunity which now offers of begging you to hear me say about you what will be painful to me as well as to you, yet acceptable to you, I am sure, notwithstanding. Nay I feel confident, that, even though you should not see the justice of some things I am going to say, you will on the whole thank me still, from the chance of your learning something or other about yourself amid whatever I may say irrelevant or erroneous. Angel visits are said to be 'few and far between'; and speaking as I wish to do in Christian charity, I know, my dear Morris, you will pay me back that charity, and consider my words, in spite of their infirmity, as almost an Angel's, and a blessing.

Nor am I unmindful, as I do trust, of what may be the beam in my own eye while I venture to speak of the mote in another's; nor again do I forget the weakness of your general health, which may seem to account for the points which I am to notice. And here I am brought at once to my subject.

Weak health certainly has a tendency to make us selfish, unless we are watchful; and though I dare not use so hard a word of so good a person as you, yet I do think it has made you your own centre, more than is expedient, to the disparagement of the Scripture exhortations of yielding to one another, consulting for each other, and bearing one another's burdens.

And now, my dear Morris, comes my great difficulty, *how to bring this home to you*; for at first you will not see things in my light. And again, the evidence of it depends on a number of very small details which it is difficult, and almost frivolous to set down on paper. Each by itself may be explained away, whatever be the cumulative force of all together. Accordingly I shall give up absolutely any attempt to *prove* to you my impression; I shall but seek to *convey* it, by means of instances, which, however minute, nay though exaggerated, distorted, or unfounded here or there, and though abrupt in their sound, may on the whole gradually let you into my meaning on reflection. And now I begin.

Your first object apparently when you came here, was to get suitable rooms for yourself, and you have got such as no one else has. You wanted your books brought upstairs – several men cheerfully undertook at once what was a considerable labour. You took their services as a matter of course; you did not thank them, or feel that they were working for you. Then you set about carpentering for yourself; not for the house, except in one or two matters when you were directly asked, such as nailing down the parlour carpet. Then you ordered wood in my name at Mr Grove's; with my consent indeed, but you used it for yourself, not for the house. When we said you should be carpenter, you took the office, not as a duty towards the house, but as a sort of privilege. You kept the keys of the shop from us, while you made use of the shop only for yourself.

As you suffered your books to be brought up to you, so did you let us sweep your room, and attend to you when indisposed, as a matter of course, not showing that you felt the kindness. Each of us took his turn in the routine house business as Septenarius; it seemed never to occur to you that you ought to have a week too. I took yours for you during Lent, thinking you would be less wearied when Easter came. At Easter you were surprised to hear that you were to have two weeks together, nay that you were to have any week at all. You did not attend to either of them as a matter of duty. You went up to Oscott, leaving others to do your work, without asking them.

Instead of living with us, you have kept your own room. Nay you grudged us your company for any time however short, for a quarter of an hour after dinner, though you could go up *to Oscott* for the whole of Sunday. You could give us nothing of you, and nothing struck you but surprise that others did not leave the house on Sundays too. In consequence you knew nothing of our plans and rules, or what was going on among us; and when you made suggestions, they were out of place, from your not knowing how things stood with us. How could you, who never were with us but at meals? At breakfast and supper your one object was to make your own cocoa or tea, and get your meal. When you were septenarius, you thought it enough to engage another to make the coffee instead of you. Then you had the matter off your hands, and might sit down to your cocoa; as to standing by him, assisting him, doing what you could since you could not do all, seeing that every one was helped though you did not help them, in a word cultivating the spirit of *ministration*, as it may be called, it does not appear to have entered into your mind.

These are illustrations, my dear Morris, of what I mean to point out to you; and it distresses me to pursue the tokens of a similar habit of mind into other matters. I am reluctantly led to think that you like your way, more than you ought, generally. You have before now done serious things which ever seemed to me to be marks of something faulty in you, and for which I have not been able to account. I refer especially to that old matter, the letters in the English Churchman about the Vice Chancellor's election, as to which it avails very little to say that you consulted another person. You are apt too, without knowing it, to set up your own views as a standard, in indifferent matters, so as even to smile on those who measure things differently. You would be surprised to be made aware how frequent the word 'I' is in your mouth. E.g. your first remark on a book being mentioned is, 'This is a book I have never read,' though it is nihil ad rem to say so; or 'I have read part of that book,' or 'that is a book I don't think much of.' And as perhaps one remembers best, what has been personal to oneself, I will add my feeling, that you have been bent, more than you are aware of, on forcing your own judgment on me in my matters. E.g. in the case of the new bookshelves in the small library, you insisted that they should be grooved in at Birmingham, though you knew my own contrary view on starting, and I could hardly bring you to end the discussion. So again you took a view that I ought to go up to Oscott for the functions, which was no concern of yours. This made you insist on the Bishop's wish that we should be all there on Palm Sunday; and you told someone most erroneously that he was 'cut up' by my absence on Maundy Thursday.

And now, My dear Morris, I beg your pardon if I have not written this as kindly as I might have done. I have been anxious to do it well, and have written it more than once over; but I know well that had I more of the spirit of love, I should have written it better. While then I am giving you pain, I am not without some feelings of humiliation myself. That our most Merciful Father and Guide may ever be with you, show you his will, and direct you in your vocation is the earnest prayer of

Your affte Friend John H Newman*

* Newman preserved the first sheet of a letter from Morris, dating it 'May 1846,' written in the latter part of the month. It runs: 'The Bishop, [Wiseman], who, as my Confessor, is likely to be the best judge, is decidedly of opinion that I had better give up all hopes of continuing at Maryvale, at least for the present. . . . I am very sorry to add after all your kindness to me, that the same becomes more and more my own conviction. Since now I have been driven to resume comforts, which I hoped under the sunshine of your example I could have gone without with ease, after the great mercy shown me in bringing me into the Church.'

To Newman's own letter of 8 May Morris appended a note: 'I have read this over at five years interval and do not feel the truth of it: I have occasionally tried to do so at all sorts of times and failed – but this may be only proof of my self love.' The two remained friends and corresponded affectionately.

John Henry Newman, Letters and Diaries (1956)

A curate's polka

Once, when the athletic curate sang 'You should see Me dance the Polka' he accompanied the song with such violent action that he polked part of the platform down and left the double row of school-girls hanging in the air on the backmost planks while he finished his song on the floor:

> 'You should see me dance the polka,
>   You should see me cover the ground,
> You should see my coat tails flying
>   As I dance my way around.'

Edmund and Laura had the words and actions by heart, if not the tune, and polked that night in their mother's bedroom until they woke up the baby and were slapped. A sad ending to an evening of pure bliss.

Flora Thompson, Lark Rise to Candleford (1939)

Clerical smoking in the streets

This unseemly practice is particularly reprehensible in the case of clergymen who are foolish enough to walk about their parishes in their cassocks. My park-keeper at Auckland, a very level-headed and outspoken man and an ex-police sergeant, for whom I had great regard, said to me, when the local papers were commenting on the subject, '*You know, my Lord, we don't like it. The police on duty don't smoke, and a clergyman is, or ought to be, on duty when he is visiting the parish. Why should he smoke?*' It is a touching delusion of many clergymen that they commend their office to the people by an ostentatious disregard of the decent conventions which regulate the carriage and clothing of English clergy. They are mistaken, and lose more than they gain.

Hensley Henson, Retrospect of an Unimportant Life (1945)

The Rival Curates

List while the poet trolls
Of MR CLAYTON HOOPER,

Who had a cure of souls
　At Spiffton-extra-Sooper.

He lived on curds and whey,
　And daily sang their praises,
And then he'd go and play
　With buttercups and daisies.

Wild croquêt HOOPER banned,
　And all the sports of Mammon,
He warred with cribbage, and
　He exorcised backgammon.

His helmet was a glance
　That spoke of holy gladness;
A saintly smile his lance,
　His shield a tear of sadness.

His Vicar smiled to see
　This armour on him buckled;
With pardonable glee
　He blessed himself and chuckled:

'In mildness to abound
　My curate's sole design is,
In all the country round
　there's none so mild as mine is!'

And HOOPER, disinclined
　His trumpet to be blowing,
Yet didn't think you'd find
　A milder curate going.

A friend arrived one day
　At Spiffton-extra-Sooper,
And in this shameful way
　He spoke to MR HOOPER:

'You think your famous name
　For mildness can't be shaken,
That none can blot your fame –
　But, HOOPER, you're mistaken!

'Your mind is not as blank
  As that of HOPLEY PORTER,
Who holds a curate's rank
  At Assesmilk-cum-Worter.

He plays the airy flute,
  And looks depressed and blighted,
Doves round about him 'toot,'
  And lambkins dance delighted.

'*He* labours more than you
  At worsted work, and frames it;
In old maids' albums, too,
  Sticks seaweed – yes, and names it!'

The tempter said his say,
  Which pierced him like a needle –
He summoned straight away
  His sexton and his beadle.

These men were men who could
  Hold liberal opinions:
On Sundays they were good –
  On week-days they were minions.

'To HOPLEY PORTER go,
  Your fare I will afford you –
Deal him a deadly blow,
  And blessings shall reward you.

'But stay – I do not like
  Undue assassination,
And so, before you strike,
  Make this communication:

'I'll give him this once chance –
  If he'll more gaily bear him,
Play croquêt, smoke, and dance,
  I willingly will spare him.'

They went, those minions true,
  To Assesmilk-cum-Worter,
And told their errand to
  The REVEREND HOPLEY PORTER.

'What?' said that reverend gent,
  'Dance through my hours of leisure?
Smoke? – bathe myself with scent? –
  Play croquêt? Oh, with pleasure!

'Wear all my hair in curl?
  Stand at my door, and wink – so –
At every passing girl?
  My brothers, I should think so!

'For years I've longed for some
  Excuse for this revulsion:
Now that excuse has come –
  I do it on compulsion!!!'

He smoked and winked away –
  This REVEREND HOPLEY PORTER –
The deuce there was to pay
  At Assesmilk-cum-Worter.

And HOOPER holds his ground,
  In mildness daily growing –
They think him, all around,
  The mildest curate going.

W. S. Gilbert, *The Bab Ballads* (1869)

Two army padres

'Here is Iltyd Popkiss, the C. of E.,' said Breeze, 'and Ambrose Dooley
that saves the souls of the RCs, and is a man to tell you some stories
to make you sit up.'

Popkiss was small and pale. It was at once evident that he had a
hard time of it keeping up with his Roman Catholic colleague in
heartiness and avoidance of seeming straitlaced. Dooley, a large dark
man with an oily complexion and appearance of not having shaved
too well that morning, accepted with complaisance this reputation
as a retailer of hair-raising anecdote. The two chaplains seemed on
the best of terms. Bithel himself smiled timidly, revealing under his
straggling moustache a double row of astonishingly badly fitting false
teeth. He hesitantly proferred a flabby hand. . .

'But what about another round,' said Bithel. 'It's my turn, padre.' He addressed himself to the Anglican chaplain, but Father Dooley broke in vigorously.

'If I go on drinking so much of this beer, it will have a strong effect on my bowels,' he said, 'but all the same I will oblige you, my friend.'

Bithel smiled doubtfully, evidently not much at ease with such plain speaking in the mouth of the clergy.

'I don't think one more will do us any harm,' he said. 'I drink a fair amount of ale myself in civilian life without bad results.'

'You want to keep your bowels open anyway,' said Dooley, pursuing the subject. 'That's what I believe in. Have a good sluicing every day. Nothing like it.'

He held up his glass to the light, as if assessing the aperient potentialities of the contents.

'Army food gives me squitters anyway,' he went on, roaring with delight at the thought. 'I've hardly had a moment's peace since we mobilized.'

'It makes me as constipated as an owl,' said Pumphrey. 'I should just about say so.'

Dooley finished his beer at a gulp, again giving his jolly monk's laugh at the thought of man's digestive vicissitudes.

'Even if I'm all bound up, I always carry plenty of toilet paper round with me,' he said. 'Never be without it. That's my rule. You can't know when you're not going to be taken short in the army.'

'That's a good notion,' said Pumphrey. 'We must follow His Reverence's advice, mustn't we. Take proper precautions in case we have to spend a penny. Perhaps you do already, Iltyd. The Church seems to teach these things.'

'Oh, why, yes, I do indeed,' said Popkiss.

'What do you take Iltyd for?' said Dooley. 'He's an old campaigner, aren't you, Iltyd?'

'Why, yes, indeed,' said Popkiss, evidently pleased to be given this opening, 'and what do you think? In my last unit, when I took off my tunic to play billiards one night, they did such a trick on me. You'd never guess. They wrapped a french letter, do you know, between those sheets of toilet paper in my pocket.'

There was a good deal of laughter at this, in which the RC chaplain amicably joined, although it was clear from his expression that he

recognized Popkiss to have played a card he himself might find hard
to trump.

Anthony Powell, *The Valley of Bones* (1964)

Rather chumps

I rather wish the rising generation of clergy were more intellectual;
so many seem rather chumps; or do I generalize from inadequate
experience? I don't really know many. But I have a feeling that one's
scholarly clerical ancestors might rather turn in their graves at the
thought of them – or of many of them, for I know intelligent ones.

Rose Macaulay, *Letters to a Friend* (1962)

[15]

SOME ECCENTRICS

There can be few professions which have contained a richer spread of eccentrics than that of the clergy. Even among my own acquaintance, there have been dozens of really odd, creatively peculiar clergymen. I think of an old Jesuit – an extremely devout man, who would not have been able to say things merely 'for effect' – who once remarked to me that he had never been able to 'get anything out of the Gospels. I much prefer the writings of P. G. Wodehouse.' The remark was all the more striking since this ancient priest, with a severe gravelly voice, never said anything witty or amusing, and did not even appear to possess a sense of humour. Indeed, as the conversation about his favourite author proceeded, I became aware that he did not know that Wodehouse was supposed to be funny.

I think of another man, the incumbent of the same church for forty years, who was a distinguished numismatist. He preached on a variety of themes at his morning Mass, but thought it inappropriate, at the evening service of Benediction, to preach on any subject other than the Empress Josephine. He lived in a rotting, ivy-covered, gothic rectory, which connected to his church by a corridor. In latter years, he became so addicted to watching television that his congregation would start the service without him. The music of the opening hymn would vie with the strains of oriental music which came wafting down the corridor, at the end of which sat 'Father', fully vested, but unable to tear himself away from a programme designed for oriental immigrants learning English. It was not so inappropriate, since no new arrival in modern Britain from Bangladesh or Pakistan could have found twentieth-century secular society more 'foreign' than this pious and learned old man.

I am sometimes tempted to fear that modern training techniques for the clergy will iron out the eccentrics. It is certainly hard to imagine some of the figures in this section of the book feeling much at home in the modern church.

Eccentrics in the nineteenth-century church

The nineteenth-century Church attracted eccentrics. Or perhaps it would be truer to say that the Established Church, especially in rural areas, gave men thus inclined unique opportunities to cultivate their eccentricities. This was particularly true in the diocese of Exeter which was so large that the bishop could not exert any real degree of control over his clergy. Hawker described the effects on earlier generations of West Country ministers of their being severed from London, 'the great metropolis of life and manners', and of having their 'abode in wilds that were almost inaccessible', in such terms as make it clear that he was also giving an account of his own predicament.

The Cornish clergyman, insulated within his own limited sphere, often without even the presence of a country squire (and unchecked by the influence of the fourth estate, for until the beginning of this nineteenth century, Flindell's Weekly Miscellany, distributed from house to house from the pannier of a mule, was the only light of the west), became developed about middle life into an original mind and man, sole and absolute within his parish boundary, eccentric when compared to his brethren in civilized regions, and yet, in German phrase 'a whole and seldom man' in his dominion of souls ... These men were not, however, smoothed down into a monotonous aspect of life and manners by this remote and secluded existence. They imbibed, each in his own peculiar circle, the hue of surrounding objects, and were tinged into distinctive colouring and character by many a contrast between scenery and people.

This too bland account may explain why country clergymen became eccentric. But it gives no indication of just how very odd they could become.

A few examples, all from the West Country, will illustrate the assertion, made by Lord Hugh Cecil to the Church Assembly, that 'The Church of England is rich in eccentrics.' One parson did not enter his church for fifty-three years and kennelled the local foxhounds in his vicarage. Another varied the colour of his communion wine, sometimes red, sometimes white. Another refused to take services but, 'clad in flowered dressing-gown and smoking a hookah', greeted his parishioners in the churchyard. Another drove away his congregations, replaced them by wooden and cardboard images in the pews and surrounded his vicarage with a barbed-wire fence behind which savage Alsatians patrolled. Another spent his life searching for the Number of the Beast. Yet another, the rector of Luffincott, to whom Hawker gave friendly advice on the subject, devoted his energies to calculating the date of the millennium. These pastimes, all relatively tame when set against the exploits of hunting, fighting, drunken or adulterous parsons, of whom many West Country instances could be given, demonstrate that in being eccentric Hawker was anything but unique. Indeed he might almost be regarded as run-of-the-mill, if stories from other parts of the land are to be believed – of the incumbent who 'equipped his stall in Church with its own sanitary arrangements', or the one who 'professed himself a neo-Platonist and sacrificed an ox to Jupiter', or the entire clerical complement of the diocese of Lincoln which, so the new bishop Edward King was informed, 'could be divided into three categories: those who had gone out of their minds; those who were about to go out of their minds; and those who had no minds to go out of'.

Piers Brendon, Hawker of Morwenstow (1975)

The old-time parson

One of the most curious and eccentric characters that ever lived was the Rev. Joshua Brooks, chaplain of the old collegiate church of Manchester, who died in 1821... Once he was expelled from the chapter house on account of some fiery and hasty speech, and was not allowed to return until he made an apology. This he refused to do, but he put on his surplice in an adjoining chapel of the church, and then, standing outside the chapter-house door, exclaimed to all the persons who were passing on to attend the service, 'They won't let me in; they say I can't behave myself.' Sometimes he would during service box the ears of a chorister for coming late; and once he clouted a boy who was singing the Kyrie after the Fifth Commandment, saying, 'Hold thy noise, lad; what hast thou to do with the Fifth Commandment? Thou'st got neither father nor mother.'....

When reading the Burial Service he would break off in the middle, go to a neighbouring confectioner's shop, procure a supply of horehound drops, and then return to his neglected duties and conclude the service. Easter Monday was the great day for weddings at the old church, and large numbers flocked to be married, and with so many couples it was rather difficult to get them properly sorted, as one reading of the service sufficed for all. It was on one of these occasions that some of the bridegrooms got married to the wrong brides and the parson shouted out, 'Sort yourselves when you go out.' . . .

P. H. Ditchfield, *The Old-Time Parson* (1908)

The death of Montague Summers

Montague Summers died suddenly at his home in Dynevor Road, Richmond, on August 10, 1948. At his death his lawyers produced a will dated September 10, 1940, and at once notified Stuart-Forbes of certain instructions which it contained relating to his burial. These directions, which were duly carried out, were as follows:

> I DIRECT that my body be dressed in my soutane which will be found among my clothes and vested in amice alb and girdle and purple (violet) vestments all which garments will be found in the room which is generally known as my private oratory I FURTHER DIRECT that if it can conviently be done there be placed in the coffin my biretta the ivory and ebony crucifix which is over the altar in my private oratory the four volumes of my breviary a rosary (any one of the rosaries in my possession) and also I DESIRE that there be placed in my coffin the coat belonging to my dog Tango* which will be found among the vestments in my oratory . . .

> * Tango had died many years previously. He was the predecessor of Cornelius Agrippa and of Prince, the dog of Summers's later Oxford days.

Joseph Jerome, *Montague Summers* (1965)

Ronald Knox

Ronald's routine at Mells varied little. He was never called in the morning, and his Mass at eight o'clock came at the end of morning prayers, whose duration only he knew. After a long thanksgiving he returned to the house for breakfast, at which he left newspapers and letters untouched. He then retired to his study, where, unless there were guests to entertain, he spent his day. After luncheon he read *The Times* and answered his correspondence. He said his office and, rather rarely, read a new book. *The Tablet* and the *Clergy Review* were the only periodicals he studied regularly. Every afternoon he made the short walk to the village shop to post his letters and, when it was needed, buy tobacco. He worked again after tea. He never attempted at Mells the outdoor tasks he had performed at Beaufort, Keir, and Aldenham. Sometimes he walked up the village to visit the Hollises, but he preferred to be driven.

The evening was always devoted to recreation. There was often reading aloud. He devised a way of doing the crossword which some of his friends found too laborious. He allowed himself to read only the horizontal clues. When these were complete he filled in the perpendiculars by guesswork, and only then verified them from their clues. Every Christmas he composed a crossword which he copied out, not always quite accurately, and sent to his friends; they were expected to send him the solutions and held in disgrace if they neglected this duty. In Lent he denied himself the crossword entirely. In the last years of his life the American game 'Scrabble' greatly took his fancy. He made a copy in cardboard and paper of the first set which he saw. It was a mitigation for his friends when he acquired a real set, but the intensity with which he played and the solemn silence he demanded were especially trying to visitors who came to Mells in the hope of enjoying their host's and hostess's conversation.

He developed, without the discouragement they had sometimes met at Aldenham, a number of amiable crotchets. Once in his absence Mrs Asquith, finding herself without stamps, took some from the sheet on his table. Later he said: 'Of course, Katherine, I am delighted you should do so, but will you, please, in future, tear them horizontally *not* perpendicularly?'

Evelyn Waugh, Ronald Knox (1959)

Some clerical dons

Of all the senior members of the University Dr Homes Dudden was undoubtedly, and appropriately, the most striking in appearance. Always outstandingly good-looking he had acquired in the years which had elapsed since I had last seen him gracing the pulpit of St John's, Notting Hill, an added *gravitas*; the thick curly hair was now silvery-grey and the profile that of one of the more reputable Flavians. Although the longed-for bishopric had eluded him there had been impressive compensations – a canonry at Gloucester, the Mastership of Pembroke, and the Vice-Chancellorship of Oxford, all rôles in which he conducted himself with the utmost distinction and to which he brought an unrivalled panache. A powerful and moving preacher, he was also a man of the world and at least one rather *naif* undergraduate was startled to recognize in the relaxed, fur-coated figure lying full length in a first-class carriage on the last train back from London, smoking a large cigar and reading the final edition of the *Evening Standard*, the divine who in the University pulpit the previous Sunday had so feelingly described the trials and afflictions to which all flesh is subject in this vale of tears. However, although a Doctor of Divinity and a theologian of impeccable orthodoxy, it remains possible that he was not as unquestioningly reconciled to his lot as his appearance and performance suggested, for many years later a friend reported that on one occasion, when he had been dining at High Table in Pembroke, the Master had turned to him and remarked, *à propos des bottes*, 'As an ordained clergyman of the Church of England I am constrained to believe in a future life, but I don't mind admitting, my dear fellow, that personally I should much prefer extinction.'

If no one could quite rival the impressiveness of the Vice-Chancellor's passage through the streets there were many other passers-by who attracted almost as great notice and, maybe, roused an even livelier interest. There was Dr Phelps, the Provost of Oriel, the last clergyman habitually to wear a black straw boater, who was regularly visible tearing down The High bent almost double, hands clasped tight beneath the tails of his short cutaway, not infrequently talking to himself. As befitted an old Carthusian he was a staunch believer in *mens sana in corpore sano*, and greatly prided himself on the cold bath with which he started the day both winter and summer; that his enjoyment of this ritual may have been less spontaneous than he maintained is suggested by the experience of a visitor to the Provost's Lodgings who, on passing the bathroom door, was startled to hear his host exclaim in agonized tones, 'Come now, Phelps, be a man!' Unfortunately this pre-occupation with self-discipline and toughness (it is not, perhaps, irrelevant that at Charterhouse he was a near-contemporary of Baden-Powell) may finally have in some measure clouded his judgement and encouraged unwise enthusiasms, for on the last occasion that we met, in a railway carriage shortly before Munich, he passed the journey loudly regretting the political prejudice which had, in his opinion, coloured the University's decision not to send a delegation to the Third Reich on the occasion of the millenary celebrations at Heidelberg.

Osbert Lancaster, *All Done from Memory* (1953)

Bartle Starmer Hack

Hack was only a 'romanist' in his love of baroque vestments and ornaments. No one could have more disliked the title 'Father'. 'Nasty Roman Catholic habit', he would say disapprovingly, and yet he was known as Fr Hack by everyone in Oxford – dons, college porters, people in shops as well as his own congregation. He always wore a frock coat for he considered it an impropriety for a priest to show his bottom and he liked to think of himself as a Tractarian with Dr Pusey as his model. Every day his portly figure could be seen walking down the Cornmarket with a pile of books under his arm. It was commonly thought that like the learned Doctor, he read the Fathers for recreation but in fact he was an avid reader of novels and Boots Lending Library. Later he would be seen from the Broad sitting under a lamp in his drawing room, for he scorned electric light, and deeply absorbed in what he was reading. Those who saw him were convinced that it was the works of St Ambrose, but it was more likely to be the works of Miss Ethel M. Dell which were holding his attention.

His enormous belly must have reminded his parishioners of Canon Clayton, particularly when he preached on 'Fasting' at the beginning of Lent as he heaved it on to the edge of the pulpit. There was a story told of a woman dropping her handkerchief into his lap on a bus. She was too embarrassed to retrieve it but Hack could see her looking at something; to her horror he firmly tucked it inside his trousers as he thought it was his shirt sticking out.

They must also have been reminded of the Canon when someone asked Hack sentimentally what he would put into a 'Children's Corner' and he replied sharply: 'A birch rod.' He could indeed be very sharp in rebuke and once stopped in the middle of a sermon and said to a woman who was fidgeting: 'Either shut that handbag or leave the church.'

His greatest source of irritation was people who left the church doors open when they came in and he would rebuke them at once from the pulpit, or confessional and even from the altar if they paused on the threshold. One day a young man who had just finished his confession said timidly: 'I'm afraid that it was I who left the door open.' The waiting penitents were horrified to hear a loud voice from the box say: 'That is the unforgiveable sin.'

Colin Stephenson, Merrily on High (1971)

His Sacred Beatitude Mar Georgius I

Hugh George de Willmott Newman, M.A., D.D., D.C.L., LL.D., Ph.D., D.Litt., was born at Forest Gate, London, E7, on January 17, 1905, and was baptized in the Catholic Apostolic (Irvingite) Church, Mare Street, Hackney, E8. Both his father and grandfather had been deacons in the Irvingite Church. He himself performed the duties of an acolyte in this body from the age of seven until he was thirty, so he was well grounded in their elaborate ritual and ceremonial. In 1937 he was married in the Catholic Apostolic Church in Maida Hill, NW8, to Lola Ina del Carpio Barnardo, great-niece of the Founder of Dr Barnardo's Homes for Orphan Boys. The ex-acolyte was then acting as General Manager and Secretary of the National Association of Cycle Traders, an employer's trade association. He also edited the Cycle Traders' magazine, *The National Journal*.

De Wilmott Newman's interest in Old Catholic churches and kindred bodies resulted from a meeting with the Lord Patriarch Banks of Windsor in 1924. By 1938 he was convinced of a clear call to the priesthood. It would have been impossible for him to have been ordained in the Catholic Apostolic Church, for Henry Woodhouse, the last of its twelve Apostles, had died in 1901, so it must have been difficult for him to decide which bishop to approach. In the summer of 1938 he wrote to James McFall, who styled himself Regionary Old Catholic Bishop for Ireland, offering himself as a candidate for holy orders. This erratic prelate replied that he would be delighted to oblige, and it was arranged that he and one of his grandsons named Malachy should visit the Newmans at South Harrow. Accordingly Bishop McFall came over from Belfast, administered baptism *sub conditione*, confirmation, the four minor orders, the subdiaconate and diaconate to this former acolyte of the Catholic Apostolic Church, and raised him to the priesthood on October 23, 1938, using Mathew's *Old Catholic Missal and Ritual* for the ceremonies. At that date McFall was dreaming of reviving the Liturgy of the 'Illustrious Church of Sarum', for no other rite was rich enough to satisfy his passion for ornate ceremonial. He told Fr de Willmott Newman that he must turn one of the rooms in his house into an oratory, and gave detailed instructions about its furnishings. Only the Sarum colour sequence would be permitted. Before departing the Bishop presented a relic of the fourth-century martyr, St Vincent, to be enshrined in the oratory; otherwise all the ornaments would have to be paid for by the newly ordained priest. The Irish would-be Metropolitan of this new Sarum Rite Old Catholic Church, which as yet was only at the planning stage, promised to send plans for its organization once he returned to Ulster. But nothing ever materialized – not even faculties. McFall wrote that they were not necessary, and explained politely that it would be better to release this English priest from his jurisdiction!

De Willmott Newman now found himself in the position of a free-lance priest belonging to no Church, and subject to no ecclesiastical superior. Early in 1939 he heard of the existence of the so-called Old Catholic Orthodox Church, which consisted of a few layfolk who had broken away from Mgr Williams in 1925 after the latter had made Papal Infallibility an article of faith in the Old Roman Catholic Church (Pro-Uniate Rite). They had lost the services of a priest of the Vilatte-Lloyd American Catholic Church who had ministered to them at Hounslow, Middlesex, for a few years, and had nobody to say Mass for them. So it was arranged that the little groups at South Harrow and Hounslow should be linked up under de Willmott Newman, who did his best to look after both.

Peter F. Anson, Bishops at Large (1964)

St-John-the-Divine

It was in the winter of 1950–1 that the negro cleric named Denison Quartey Arthur arrived in Chelsea. He styled himself Mar Lukos, Bishop of Lagos, Acra, and Trinidad. He related that he had been brought up in Ethiopia and that later on he had found his way to North America, where on May 27, 1947, he had been consecrated by Archbishop St John-the-Divine Hickersayon, said to belong to the Coptic Orthodox Church, and in charge of its Foreign Missions.

It is rather unlikely that there were two bishops in the USA during the nineteen-forties both called 'St John-the-Divine', so it is a reasonable conclusion that Hickersayon was the same person as Hickerson, an American negro who worked as an evangelist in Baltimore in 1908, with Samuel Morris and George Baker. Rather later Baker acquired a world-wide notoriety as 'Father Divine', and claimed that 20,000,000 people called him God. By 1915 Hickerson had assumed the title of Bishop St John-the-Divine, and he was running an unconventional place of worship on 41st Street, New York City, known as 'The Church of the Living God'. Sara Harris writes:

'He must have been an impressive figure, for even today he is still imposing. Tall, ascetic, he looks like the old masters' painting of Jesus, except for his tan complexion and advanced age. He was a born preacher with an electrifying style when the spirit was in him. He would begin preaching in a low quiet tone, all the while walking slowly about. As his voice grew louder, and his words faster, he would break into a lope, and suddenly he would leap straight into the air and land shouting.'

The negro prelate – it is not certain who ordained or consecrated him – appears to have regarded himself more or less as God. He gathered round him lesser divinities (known as 'The Temples of God'). We are told that they 'wore crowns festooned with gold and silver, and they shouted: "God in you., God in me. Everybody he God. God lives in this Temple, and Ah'm so glad. Can't never die."'

Unfortunately St John-the-Divine got into trouble with the police. Some of the 'Temples of God' went beserk, even stabbing the ungodly. The result was that the Bishop had to disband his organization. It is not clear what were his subsequent activities until 1942, when he had chartered in the Borough of Manhattan, New York, a new sect called 'The Coptic Orthodox Church Apostolic Incorporated'.

Peter F. Anson (ibid.)

[16]

ODIUM THEOLOGICUM

'Violent zeal for truth hath an hundred to one odds to be either petulancy, ambition or pride', as Jonathan Swift observed over two hundred years ago. In the history of religion, there is no shortage of piety exciting the cruellest and most violent behaviour. It would be almost no distortion of the truth to say that the more a man believed, the nastier he would be to his fellow-mortals.

A book of 'church and clergy' which failed to give a taste of this phenomenon would be unrepresentative and untrue; but these are murky waters, and I have not chosen to immerse the reader in them for too long.

The causes of schism

Where the cause of Schism is necessary, there not he that separates, but he that is the cause of Separation is the Schismatick. Where the occasion of Separation is unnecessary, neither side can be excused from guilt of Schism. But who shall be the Judge? That is a point of great difficulty, because it carries fire in the Tail of it: for it brings with it a piece of Doctrine which is seldom pleasing to Superiours. You shall find that all Schisms have crept into the Church by one of these three waies, either upon matter of Fact, or upon matter of Opinion, or point of Ambition. For the first, I call that matter of Fact, when something is required to be done by us, which either we know or strongly suspect to be unlawful. Where he instances in the old great Controversy about EASTER, 'For it being upon error taken for necessary that an Easter must be kept, and upon worse than error (for it was no less than a point of Judaism forc'd upon the Church) thought further necessary that the ground of the time for the Feast, must be the Rule left by *Moses* to the Jews: there arose a stout Question, Whether 'twas to be celebrated with the Jews on the fourteenth Moon, or the Sunday following. This caused as great a Combustion as ever was; the West separating and refusing Communion with the East for many years together. Here I cannot see but all the World were Schismaticks, excepting only that we charitably suppose to excuse them from it, that all parties did what they did out of Conscience. A thing which befell them by the ignorance, for I will not say the malice, of their guides; and that through the just judgment of God, because, through sloth and blind obedience, men examined not the things they were taught, but like beasts of burthen patiently couched down, and indifferently underwent all whatsoever their Superiours laid upon them. If the discretion of the chiefest guides of the Church did, in a point so trivial, so inconsiderable, so mainly fail them: Can we without the imputation of great grossness and folly, think so poor-spirited persons competent Judges of the Questions now on foot betwixt the Churches? Where, or among whom, or how many the Church shall be, it is a thing indifferent: What if those to whom the Execution of the publick Service is committed, do something, either unseemly or suspicious, or peradventure unlawful; what if the Garments they wear be censured, nay, indeed be suspicious. What if the gesture or adoration to be used to the Altars, as now we have learned to speak? What if the Homilist have preached or delivered any Doctrine, of the truth of which we are not well perswaded, (a thing which very often falls out) yet, for all this, we may not separate, except we be constrained personally to bear a part in it our selves. Nothing can be a just cause of refusing Communion in Schism, that concerns Fact, but only to require the execution of some unlawful or suspected Act. For, not only in Reason, but in Religion too, that Maxim admits of no release, *Cautissimi cujusque præceptum, quod dubitas ne feceris*: That whatsoever you doubt of, that you in no case do.

Andrew Marvell, *The Rehearsal Transpros'd* (1672)

Hawker of Morwenstow's hatred of Wesleyanism

It has already been seen that Hawker blamed unchastity on 'that father of English fornication', John Wesley. What is clear from his unpublished writings is that Hawker considered that there was a direct relationship, indeed, a correspondence, between Methodism and sexual feeling. It was not just that he thought that Methodists were pre-eminently lascivious – though he did. His letters are studded with assertions like 'In Cornwall and in Wales, the thick places of Methodism, not one woman in 500 (and I speak from statistics verified from official authority) ever marries without disgrace . . . It is so general as to be no longer a reproach among themselves.' Or such announcements as 'On Saturday I marry Eliza Close, class-leader, pregnant and near child-birth, to Daniel Venning, class-leader and fornicator.' Nor was it simply that there was a strong association in Hawker's mind between servants, Methodists and sexual licence, as is illustrated in these three sentences which are linked by a logic apparent to no one but him:

In former times Methodist preachers expelled from their society any person of evil life. But they have long given up that discipline; one half or more of the depraved females are of that sect. But if I were asked what was the great grievance and sorrow of England I should answer at once, the servants.

No, Hawker's most visceral conviction about Methodism was that it was a nearly overt expression of sexual feeling and in particular the central, dramatic Evangelical experience – the conversion – was akin to an orgasm.

Hawker often described Methodism as a 'Spasm of the ganglions' and he declared that its central fallacy was the belief that conversion, a spiritual transformation, could be physically experienced. 'It is untruth that our forgiveness is made known to us senuously – *i.e.*, by a touch, or stroke, upon the ganglions.' Hawker, no physiologist, defined ganglions as 'the fibres of the diaphragm', 'a nervous centre [where] . . . Soul and Body as it were meet'. But there is a resonance about the word which, when juxtaposed with Hawker's many explicit remarks, such as his accusation that Methodism was 'the mother of the brothel . . . of modern England', suggests that in certain contexts he was actually thinking of the genitals. The following vituperative lines, addressed to the Methodist convert, are full of unmistakable sexual imagery.

Deem as thou wilt,
That filthy heart of thine is not the Vale
Of Armageddon: nor may thy ganglions
Thrill with the doom which He, the Son of Man,
Holds for the rapture of that utterance
Reserved, and for his own reward requited.
Lo! When thy carcase of foul flesh shall writhe
Fierce with its renal heat and wild with spasm
It is not He, the Paraclete, whose course [illegible]
Is like dove's and whose unconscious touch
Falls as the Dew's upon the fleece of wool,
Pure, soft and soundless.

It is difficult to avoid the conclusion that Hawker believed Methodist conversions, particularly when accompanied by ejaculations and ecstatic convulsions, by the quakings, shakings and holy rollings so often mentioned by Wesley and his followers, to be a form of sexual release.

Piers Brendon, *Hawker of Morwenstow* (1975)

Presbyterian Church Government

Synods are whelps of th' *Inquisition*,
A mungrel breed of like pernicion,
And growing up became the Sires
Of *Scribes, Commissioners,* and *Triers*;
Whose bus'ness is, by cunning slight
To cast a figure for mens *Light*;
To find in lines of Beard and Face,
The Phisiognomy of *Grace*;
And by the sound *and twang of Nose,*
If all be sound within disclose,
Free from a crack or flaw of sinning,
As Men try *Pipkins* by the ringing.
By *Black Caps* underlaid with *White*,
Give certain guess at inward *Light*;
Which *Serjeants at the Gospel* wear,
To make the *Spiritual Calling clear.*

The *Hand[k]erchief* about the neck
(Canonical *Cravat* of *Smeck*,
From whom the Institution came
When Church and State they set on flame,
And worn by them as badges then
Of *Spiritual Warfaring Men*)
Judge rightly if *Regeneration*
Be of the *newest Cut* in fashion.
Sure 'tis an Orthodox opinion
That *Grace is founded in Dominion*.
Great *Piety* consists in *Pride*;
To *rule* is to be *sanctifi'd*:
To domineer and to controul
Both o'er the Body and the Soul,
Is the most perfect *discipline*
Of Church-rule, and by *right divine*.
Bell and the *Dragons* Chaplains were
More moderate than these by far:
For they (poor Knaves) were glad to cheat,
To get their Wives and Children Meat:
But these will not be fobb'd off so,
They must have Wealth and Power too,
Or else with blood and desolation,
They'll tear it out o' th' heart o' th' Nation,
Sure these themselves from Primitive
And Heathen Priesthood do derive,
When *Butchers* were the only *Clerks*,
Elders and *Presbyters* of *Kirks*,
Whose *Directory* was to *Kill*;
And some believe it is so still.
The onely diff'rence is, that then
They slaughter'd only Beasts, now Men.
For then to sacrifice a Bullock,
Or now and then a Child to *Moloch*,
They count a vile Abomination,
But not to slaughter a whole *Nation*.
Presbytery does but translate
The Papacy to a *Free State*,
A *Commonwealth of Popery*,

Where ev'ry Village is a *See*
As well as *Rome*, and must maintain
A *Tithe Pig Metropolitane*:
Where ev'ry *Presbyter* and *Deacon*
Commands the *Keys* for Cheese and Bacon;
And ev'ry Hamlet's governed
By's *Holiness*, the *Church's Head*,
More haughty and severe in's place
Than *Gregory* and *Boniface*.
Such Church must (surely) be a Monster
With many heads: for if we conster
What in th' *Apocalypse* we find,
According to th' Apostles mind,
'Tis that the *Whore of Babylon*
With many heads did ride upon;
Which Heads denote the sinful Tribe
Of *Deacon, Priest, Lay-Elder, Scribe.*
Lay-Elder, Simeon to *Levi,*
Whose little finger is as heavy
As loins of Patriarchs, Prince-Prelate,
Archbishop-secular. This Zelot
Is of a mungrel, divers kind,
Clerick before, and *Lay* behind;
A Lawless *Linsy-woolsy Brother*,
Half of one Order, half another;
A Creature of amphibious nature,
On Land a Beast, a Fish in Water,
That always preys on Grace, or Sin;
A Sheep without, a Wolf within.
This fierce Inquisitor has chief
Dominion over Mens Belief
And Manners: Can pronounce a *Saint*
Idolatrous, or ignorant,
When superciliously he sifts,
Through coursest Boulter, others *gifts*.
For all Men live and judge amiss
Whose *Talents* jump not just with his.
He'll lay on *Gifts* with hands, and place,
On dullest noddle *light* and *grace*,

The manufacture of the *Kirk*,
Whose Pastors are but th' Handiwork
Of his Mechanick Paws, instilling
Divinity in them by feeling.
From whence they start up *chosen Vessels*,
Made by Contact, as Men get *Meazles*.

Samuel Butler, *Hudibras* (1663)

Now awaketh wrathe . . .

Now awaketh Wrathe, with two white eighen,
And nevelynge with the nose, and his nekke hangyng.   *running at*
'I am Wrathe,' quod he, 'I was som tyme a frere,   *friar*
And the coventes gardyner for to graffen impes.   *friary's; graft shoots*
On lymitours and listres lesynges I ymped,   *lectors; grafted*
Til thei beere leves of lowe speche, lordes to plese,   *produced; servile*
And sithen their blosmede abroad in boure to here shriftes.

blossomed; bedroom(s)

And now is fallen therof a fruyt — that folk han wel levere

i.e. result; much prefer

Shewen hire shriftes to hem that shryve hem to hir persons.

parish-priests

And now persons han parceyved that freres parte with hem,

are sharing

Thise possessioners preche and deprave freres;   *beneficed priests; revile*
And freres fyndeth hem in defaute, as folk bereth witnesse,

find fault (with)

That when thei preche the peple in many places aboute,
I, Wrathe, walke with hem and wisse hem of my bokes.   *teach (from)*
Thus thei speken of spiritualte, that either despiseth oother,

spirituality (C); each

William Langland (*c.* 1330–1386), *Piers Plowman*

William Prynne loses his years

A certain William Prynne, the son of a farmer living between Clifton and Henbury (probably a sheep-farmer on Durdham Downs, and later an agent for a property near Bath, belonging to Oriel College, Oxford), and his wife, Marie (a daughter of Sherston, Mayor of Bath, and member of Parliament for that city for four years), became an undergraduate at Oriel, and afterwards a student at Lincoln's Inn. He inherited from £150 to £200 a year from his father – a good income in those days – and had every prospect of a comfortable, prosperous, and honoured life.

Unfortunately, he could not leave well alone; but must needs write and publish a book of above one thousand pages, called *Histrio-mastrix*, against theatres, balls, hunting, 'Christmas-keeping,' May-poles, bonfires, public festivals, the erection of altars in churches, 'cringing and ducking to altars,' 'silk and satin divines,' and the 'barking,' and 'roaring' and 'grunting' of choristers.

As a specimen of the style, I may quote the following extract from the part which treats of theatricals: 'God forbedd that any whoe have beene dipped in the sacred laver of Regeneracion, any that have been bathed &c., should prove such desperate incarnate devills, such monsters of ympiety, such atheisticall Judases to their lord and Master, such perjured cutt throates to their Religion, such apostates or undeplored enimyes to their owne salvation, or such willfull bloody murtherers to their owne soules, as to approve or justifye or to practise these stage playes.'

For publishing this 'libellous volume,' Prynne was summoned before the Court of High Commission in the Star Chamber; his trial lasted three days, and, on the fourth, the Court proceeded to pass sentence.

Lord Cottington, Chancellor of the Exchequer, began. Mr Prynne, he said, had published a volume of libels expressing, in a manner, a malice 'against all mankind, and the best sort of mankind, against King, prince, peer, prelates, magistrates and governors, and truly in a manner against all things. But that which hath been more remark-able is, his spleen against the church and government of it.'

Lord Cottington's sentence was a very long one. When he came to the practical part, he ordered him to be disbarred, 'and because he had his offspring from Oxford ('now,' with a low voice, said the bishop of Canterbury, 'I am sorry that ever Oxford bred such an evil member') there to be degraded. And I do condemn Mr Prynne to stand in the pillory in two places, in Westminster and Cheapside, and that he shall lose both his ears, one in each place; and with a paper on his head, declaring how foul an offence it is.' 'And lastly (nay, not lastly) I do condemn him in £5000 fine to the King. And, lastly, perpetual imprisonment.'

The next judge fined him another £5000, and ordered him to 'be restrained from writing, neither to have pen, ink, or paper; yet let him have,' said he, 'some pretty prayer-book, to pray to God to forgive him his sins.'

The third judge fined him '£10,000, which is more than he is worth, yet less than he deserveth,' and ordered him to be branded in the forehead and slit in the nose, as he feared that he might conceal the disgrace of his cropt ears by forcing 'his conscience to make use of his unlovely love-locks on both sides.'

Laud merely remarked that he was 'sorrye that a man that hath been so prayerfull and had soe good breedinge should soe ill bestowe his labour to such haynous endes.'

J. Longueville, A Life of Archbishop Laud (1894)

Roast a Quaker

Quakers were being discussed. Sydney joined in:

'Though I am not generally considered an illiberal man, yet I must confess to one little weakness, one secret wish – I should like to roast a Quaker.'

'Good heavens, Mr Smith!' exclaimed a serious gentleman sitting nearby; 'roast a Quaker?'

'Yes, sir,' replied Sydney, with the utmost gravity; 'roast a Quaker.'

'But do you not consider the terrible torture?'

'Yes, sir, I have considered everything. It may be wrong, as you say; the Quaker would undoubtedly suffer acutely; but everyone has his tastes, and mine would be to roast a Quaker. *One* would satisfy me, only one. I hope you will pardon my weakness, but it is one of those peculiarities I have striven against in vain.

Stuart J. Reid, The Life and Times of the Rev. Sydney Smith (1884)

What is a Puseyite?
'At a recent trial Lord Justice Knight Bruce asked if any of the learned counsel could define a Puseyite, but none of the learned gentlemen attempted a definition.' – vide Morning Herald.

I
Pray tell me what's a Puseyite? 'Tis puzzling to describe
This ecclesiastic genus of a pious, hybrid tribe.
At Lambeth and the Vatican, he's equally at home,
Altho' 'tis said, he rather gives the preference to Rome.

II
Voracious as a book-worm is his antiquarian maw,
The 'Fathers' are his text-book, the 'Canons' are his law,
He's mighty in the Rubrics, and well up in the Creeds,
But he only quotes the 'Articles' just as they suit his needs.

III
The Bible is to him almost a sealèd Book,
Reserve is on his lips and mystery in his look;
The sacramental system is the torch to illumine his night,
He loves the earthly candlestick more than the heavenly light.

IV
He's great in punctilios, where he bows and where he stands,
In the cutting of his surplice, and the hemming of his bands,
Each saint upon the Calendar he knows by heart at least,
He always dates his letters on a 'Vigil' or a 'Feast.'

V
But hark! With what a nasal twang, betwixt a whine and groan,
He doth our noble liturgy most murderously intone;
Cold are his prayers and praises, his preaching colder still,
Inanimate and passionless; his very look does chill.

VI
He talketh much of discipline, yet when the shoe doth pinch,
This most obedient, duteous son will not give way an inch;
Pliant and obstinate by turns, whate'er may be the whim,
He's only for the Bishop, when the Bishop is for him.

VII

Others as weak, but more sincere, who rather feel than think,
Encouraging he leads to Popery's dizzy brink,
And when they take the fatal plunge, he walks back quite content
To his snug berth at Mother Church, and wonders why they went.

VIII

Such, and much worse, aye, worse! had I time to write,
Is a faint sketch, your worship, of a thorough Puseyite,
Whom even Rome repudiates, as she laughs within her sleeve,
At the sacerdotal mimic, the solemn Would-Believe.

IX

Oh, well it were for England, if her Church were rid of those
Half-Protestant, half-Papist, who are less her friends than foes.
Give me the open enemy, not the hollow friend;
With God, and with our Bible, we will the Truth defend.

Stuart J. Reid (ibid.)

Edmund Scambler
1517–94

Bishop of Peterborough, 1561; Norwich, 1584

For the Puritans in his diocese he had a great aversion, the reasons of which he expressed in a remarkable letter he wrote to Burghley, in which he set forth their neglect, if not abhorrence, of 'the divine servise sett owte by publique authoritye.' At Overston it was conspicuous by its absence, and 'in stede' of 'the booke of cõmen prayer,' two sermons – accompanied, we presume, with extemporaneous orisons – were delivered by two ministers who did not hold the episcopal licence to preach.

At Whiston great numbers assembled from the neighbouring towns and villages to receive the Communion, which they celebrated 'with preachers and ministers to their owne likinge, and contrarie to forme prescribed by the publique order of the Realme.' In all these unauthorised 'waies,' they were, as the bishop noted, 'verie bolde and stowte.' Part of that boldness, as appears elsewhere, was shown by the parishioners of this very Whiston putting their minister in the stocks. He may have deserved such treatment, but it was scandalous for them to have inflicted it.

In 1576 Bishop Scambler visited his cathedral, for which he published his Injunctions, and in 1584 he alienated to his patron, Lord Burghley, some of the best manors of his see, and was immediately afterwards translated, by way of reward it must be supposed, to the bishopric of Norwich. In that see he was conspicuous as a spoliator, and one of his successors, Montagu, described him as its '*calamitas.*' He devised a house in Ipswich, which had been given by Edward VI as a residence for the bishop, to his son James for three lives, with leave to pull down as much of it as he pleased, and James Scambler availed himself of the permission by pulling it all down. He made to the queen, for the benefit of Sir Thomas Heneage, sixty-one separate demises for a period of eighty years. It was commonly reported that when Bishop of Norwich he had embezzled the queen's subsidies, which he had collected from his clergy. He wrote to Walsingham denying the truth of the accusation, which he declared had no other foundation than 'the clamourous and unconscionable reportes of some lewde disposed persons.' Denial, however, especially from such a man as Scambler, is far from being disproof.

His episcopate at Norwich was sadly tarnished by the trial and condemnation of Francis Ket, formerly Fellow of Corpus College, Cambridge, who for his heterodox opinions about Christ's Atonement and the Divinity of the Holy Ghost was in 1588 cited into the Bishop's Spiritual Court, where he was convicted and sentenced. The trial having been thus concluded, Bishop Scambler wrote to Burghley pressing for immediate confirmation and execution of the sentence. His request was granted, and three months afterwards the unfortunate cleric was burnt at Norwich.

F. O. White, Lives of the Elizabethan Bishops (1898)

A brush with his brother, John Henry Newman

In the earliest period of my Oxford residence I fell into uneasy collision with him concerning Episcopal powers. I had on one occasion dropt something disrespectful against bishops or a bishop – something which, if it had been said about a clergyman, would have passed unnoticed: but my brother checked and reproved me –

as I thought, very uninstructively – for 'wanting reverence towards Bishops.' I knew not then, and I know not now, why Bishops, *as such*, should be more reverenced than common clergymen; or Clergymen, *as such*, more than common men. In the World I expected pomp and vain show and formality and counterfeits: but of the Church, as Christ's own kingdom, I demanded reality and could not digest legal fictions. I saw round me what sort of young men were preparing to be clergymen: I knew the attractions of family 'livings' and fellowships, and of a respectable position and undefinable hopes of preferment. I farther knew, that when youths had become clergymen through a great variety of mixed motives, bishops were selected out of these clergy on avowedly political grounds; it therefore amazed me how a man of good sense should be able to set up a duty of religious veneration towards bishops. I was willing to honour a Lord Bishop as a peer of Parliament; but his office was to me no guarantee of spiritual eminence – To find my brother thus stop my mouth, was a puzzle; and impeded all free speech towards him. In fact, I very soon left off the attempt at intimate religious intercourse with him, or asking counsel as of one who could sympathize. We talked, indeed, a great deal on the surface of religious matters; and on some questions I was overpowered and received a temporary bias from his superior knowledge; but as time went on, and my own intellect ripened, I distinctly felt that his arguments were too fine-drawn and subtle, often elaborately missing the moral points and the main points, to rest on some ecclesiastical fiction; and his conclusions were to me so marvellous and painful, that I constantly thought I had mistaken him. In short, he was my senior by a very few years: nor was there any elder resident at Oxford, accessible to me, who united all the qualities which I wanted in an adviser. Nothing was left for me but to cast myself on Him who is named the Father of Lights, and resolve to follow the light which He might give, however opposed to my own prejudices, and however I might be condemned by men. This solemn engagement I made in early youth, and neither the frowns nor the grief of my brethren can make me ashamed of it in my manhood.

Francis Newman, *Phases of Faith* (1857)

Gladstone's sister becomes a Roman Catholic

She wrote to Dr Wiseman in Birmingham asking to be received into the Roman Catholic Church. Wiseman, who had left Rome in 1840 to become Vicar Apostolic of the Midland District, was an eager welcomer of converts. In June 1842 Helen began a period at the Convent of Our Lady of Mercy in Birmingham. Wiseman received her submission. The newspapers reported Helen's conversion, conveying to the world what William called 'the record of our shame'.

He was stunned. In a memorandum for his father he urged that Helen be expelled from the family home. Romish priests, though it was 'impossible to exculpate them on the score of deceit', had not really been responsible. Helen herself, said William, was the guilty party. 'She has been acting from the first on a foregone conclusion.' John Gladstone, he believed, had 'not the power to act with determination' but had followed the fatal course of 'threats followed by a series of recessions from them'. 'God help her and us', groaned William. He told Helen flatly, 'the source of your malady is not religious. It is private will'. Not least of the evils Helen had caused was the danger that the enemies of the principles of the Church of England, noting William's position as the brother of an apostate, would 'endeavour to wound them through my sides'. He admonished her as 'the fruit of my mother's womb and the belovedest associate of my early years'.

S. G. Checkland, *The Gladstones* (1971)

Why John Betjeman should become a Roman Catholic

To John Betjeman
22 December 1946   Piers Court.

My Dear John
   Thank you very much for your Xmas card & the promise of *The Pavilion*. What you do not send & what I want very much is my article in *Life*.* Please please send it back.
   I have been painfully shocked by a brochure named 'Five Sermons by Laymen'. Last time I met you you told me you did not believe in the Resurrection. Now I find you expounding Protestant devotional

practices from the pulpit. This WILL NOT DO. You should be thinking of St Thomas More not of Henry Moore.

I understand that Penelope means to purchase you a years respite from uncongenial work. You must spend some of that time thinking. It is no good saying: 'I don't happen to be logical'. Logic is simply the architecture of human reason. If you try to base your life & hopes on logical absurdities YOU WILL GO MAD. No one goes mad because he works in a factory & eats tinned food, as you suggest, though these acts are symptoms of unreason. But people are going mad & talking balls to psychiatrists not because of accidents to the chamber-pot in the nursery, but because there is no logical structure to their beliefs. Vide Smarty-Boots-Connolly passim.

Your ecclesiastical position is entirely without reason. You cannot possibly be right. Marxist-Atheists might be. Zealous protestants may be (i.e. it is possible to say that from the word go the Church was all wrong & had misunderstood everything Our Lord told them, & that it required a new Divine Dispensation in the sixteenth century to put people on the right track again. That is just possible). What is inconceivable is that Christ was made flesh in order to found a Church, that he canalized his Grace in the sacraments, that He gave His promise to abide in the Church to the end of time, that He saw the Church as a human corporation, part of his Mystical Body, one with the Saints triumphant – and then to point to a handful of homosexual curates and say: 'That is the true Church.'

You & I cannot both be right. But every argument you can put forward for your little group in the Church of England is *a fortiori* an argument for me. This is so self-evident to me that I cannot expound it further.

You say you regard the question of Orders as the crucial question. Why? There is no conceivable doubt that the Catholic Church has valid orders; it is probable that the Orthodox have; also the various Eastern heretical bodies & the Ethiopians; it is highly improbable that the Church of England has. But even if they had they would not be free of the frightful sins of heresy & schism. Cranmer & Luther had valid orders. Did Calvin? I don't know. But valid orders do not confer impeccability or infallibility. Your communion would be sacrilegious if it were valid. A Church is a corporate human association. You cannot escape pollution from the blasphemous aberrations of most of your clergy by forming a little clique (even among whom I believe the most preposterous heresies are current).

You must not suppose that there is anything more than the most superficial resemblance between Catholics & Anglo-Catholics. They may look alike to you. An Australian, however well-informed, simply cannot distinguish between a piece of Trust House timbering and a genuine Tudor Building; an Englishman however uncultured knows at once.

The true Church is unique & indivisible & nothing is remotely like it. This may not be apparent from outside. But I think more violence is done to the Mystical Body by those who imitate it than by those who frankly hate it.

You will find an enormous number of features of the Catholic Church that are repugnant to you, for the very reason that it is sui generis. But I do implore you to spend your year in investigating. Then it will be a Year of Grace. You may not get another chance. It would be a pity to go to HELL because you prefer Henry Moore to Michelangelo.

THIS GOES FOR PENELOPE TOO

Evelyn

* 'Fanfare', published in *Life* in April, was an answer to his fan-mail, a defence of *Brideshead Revisited* and an attack on his critics, in particular Edmund Wilson.

Penelope Betjeman wrote to Waugh in April 1947:

'Dearest Evelyn

I am very grateful to you for writing those letters to John tho' it is very disloyal for me to write to you and say that still I hope you will pray very hard indeed during the next few weeks for him because he is in a dreadful state he thinks you are the devil and wakes up in the middle of the night and raves and says he will leave me at once if I go over ... However put yourself in his position: suppose Laura were to wake up and say to you tomorrow morning 'I have had a revelation of the TRUTH it is only to be found in A. Huxley's Yogibogi sect, I shall join it.' You would not unnaturally be a little put out. You might even threaten to leave the old girl should she persist. Well John feels just like that. He thinks ROMAN Catholicism is a foreign religion which has no right to set up in this country, let alone try to make converts from what he regards as the true catholic church of the country. Your letters have brought it out in a remarkable way.

The Letters of Evelyn Waugh (1980)

Grace abounding

Keel. But says Justice *Keelin*, what have you against the Common Prayer-book?

Bun. I said, Sir, if you will hear me, I shall lay down my reasons against it.

Keel. He said I should have liberty; but first, said he, let me give you one caution; take heed of speaking irreverently of the Common Prayer-book: For if you do so, you will bring great damage upon yourself.

Bun. So I proceeded, and said, my first reason was; because it was not commanded in the word of God, and therefore I could not do it.

Another. One of them said, where do you find it commanded in the Scripture, that you should go to *Elstow*, or *Bedford*, and yet it is lawful to go to either of them, is it not?

Bun. I said, to go to *Elstow* or *Bedford*, was a civil thing, and not material, though not commanded, and yet God's word allowed me to go about my calling, and therefore if it lay there, then to go thither, &c. But to pray, was a great part of the divine worship of God, and therefore it ought to be done according to the rule of God's word.

Another. One of them said, he will do harm; let him speak no further.

Just. Keel. Justice *Keelin* said, No, no, never fear him, we are better established than so; he can do no harm, we know the Common Prayer-book hath been ever since the Apostles time, and is lawful to be used in the church.

Bun. I said, shew me the place in the epistles, where the Common Prayer-book is written, or one text of Scripture, that commands me to read it, and I will use it. But yet, notwithstanding, said I, they that have a mind to use it, they have their liberty; that is, I would not keep them from it, but for our parts, we can pray to God without it. Blessed be his name.

John Bunyan, *Grace Abounding to the Chief of Sinners* (1666)

Protestants destroy the church at St Hilary, 193–

On the morning of the raid . . . I had saddled one of the horses, intending to ride there. A few minutes before I was to start, a woman rushed into my room exclaiming, 'They've come, Father, and Captain Hopes is locked up with them.' Hurrying across to the church, I met Norman Peters, a bell-ringer who lives close by. Together we tried to open the south door but found it locked. It was a strange experience to be standing knocking outside the door whose key had been entrusted to me at my induction more than twenty years before.

'We'll try the priest's door,' I said to Norman (this is a doorway leading into the chapel of Our Lady). After repeated knockings, the door was opened a few inches; stooping down – for the entrance is very low and narrow – I could see a number of strange men gathered there. I called to them through the opening that I was the Vicar of the parish and demanded admission. The door was then opened a little wider and we crept through. Norman Peters made a dash for the belfry to ring for help, but was overpowered. The three of us imprisoned there, an old man, a youth and myself, could do nothing against the forty or fifty men assembled. I attempted to withdraw into myself, to say my prayers and to repeat as much of the offices of the breviary as I knew by heart. I thought of Tregonning Hill where I might have been and the old donkey nibbling the tops of the furze bushes. But however much I tried, I could not escape from what was going on round me. I might shut my eyes, but I still saw men standing on the holy altar, hacking at the reredos or carrying away the image of Our Lady. I could not close my ears to the sounds of hammering which now filled the church.

I have not yet escaped from the scenes I witnessed that day and possibly never shall: whenever I enter an old country church and see the signs of destruction wrought there in the sixteenth century, I can hear the sounds of hammering and the crash of falling images. The men working this havoc have in my imagination the same faces as those who invaded St Hilary that morning in August. The old church, quiet and peaceful when I entered, is filled with the phantoms I have conjured up. I see them tearing down the figure of Christ upon the Rood and casting out the Mother from the House of her Son. Often on leaving, my eyes will rest on the broken face of a once-smiling cherub, a witness to all that happened there, and I am glad to escape . . .

There are two tabernacles in the church at St Hilary: one on the High Altar, condemned by the Chancellor; the other above the Chapel of the Sacred Heart, on which the Court had pronounced no judgement, since it was not there at the time of the hearing. In this tabernacle the Holy Sacrament was reserved. Now the guardianship of the Blessed Sacrament is part of the priest's office; the two men with me realized as fully as I did that the Holy Sacrament must be defended against profanation. While we were conferring together, a man who appeared to be in charge, approached me and suggested that if I surrendered the monstrance, now locked in the safe, he would be willing for me to remove the Sacrament. I could make no terms with him. Seeing that we were preparing to defend the Sacrament at all costs, he consented to my demands and allowed me to carry It to a place of safety. On my way to the house to fetch the key of the tabernacle, I spoke hurriedly to the people who had gathered outside and told them to procure candles. I returned and after vesting went to the altar and, opening the door of the tabernacle, took out the Sanctissimum.

Outside the church were a number of people who live close by – Johns, Hopes, Peters, Jenkins and their wives, a crowd of children returning from school and a few young labourers from the farm at Trevabyn. As I came from the little doorway of the Lady Chapel carrying the Holy Sacrament, I found them all on their knees lining the pathway through the churchyard, with lighted candles in their hands.

I had passed from the noise and tumult of passion to a quiet world of faith.

That night there was a service of reparation, when the Holy Sacrament was borne back to the church. All along the roadway from house to church were rows of people with bowed heads; as the procession passed slowly by they sang the hymn of St Thomas:

> Bow we then in adoration,
> This great Sacrament revere:

words in which the summit of man's faith is reached. Never had I so realized the God-given quality of faith as on that night when, together with this company of people, I entered the dismantled church.

During the week people were busy restoring the house of God;

carpenters and masons were repairing the damage; other images were substituted for those carried off and the church made gay with many flowers; so that by Sunday it was fit for the offering of the Holy Sacrifice. Everything was as it had been; but the cycle of peace which we had enjoyed for the past ten years had come to an end.

St Hilary was no longer hidden from the outside world by its circle of trees; its name appeared in newspaper head-lines; a sign-post was set up on the high-road pointing a finger to the Church-town; crowds came to visit the church and at times invaded our garden. The place had lost its old air of peace.

Bernard Walke, *Twenty Years at St Hilary* (1935)

A letter to John Caryll

(May the first [*sic*] 1714)

This miserable age is so sunk between animosities of party and those of religion, that I begin to fear most men have politics enough to make the best scheme of government a bad one, thro' their extremity of violence, and faith enough to hinder their salvation. I hope, for my own part, never to have more of either than is consistent with common justice and charity, and always as much as becomes a Christian and honest man, that is just as much as you. Tho' I find it an unfortunate thing to be bred a papist, when one is obnoxious to four parts in five as being so too much, and to the fifth part as being so too little, I shall yet be easy under both their mistakes, and be, what I more than seem to be, for I suffer for it. God is my witness, that I no more envy the Protestants their places and possessions than I do our priests their charity or learning. I am ambitious of nothing but the good opinion of all good men of all sides, for I know that one virtue of a free spirit is more worth than all the virtues put together of all the narrow-souled people in the world. If they promise me all the good offices they ever did, or could do, I would not change for 'em all one kind word of yours. I am entirely

dear sir

your obliged, and faithful
Friend and servant

A: P:

Alexander Pope, *Letters* (1946)

[17]

MONKS AND NUNS

Members of religious orders are sometimes regarded with puzzle-
ment, as some of the extracts in this section show. There must be
plenty of people who would echo Dora, in Iris Murdoch's *The Bell*,
when she realizes that the enclosed community of Imber Abbey are
never allowed out: 'How absolutely appalling.'

Those who 'live in the world' are tempted to think that there must
be something wrong with people who wish to bind themselves by
the vows of chastity, poverty and obedience. Monks and nuns are
easily dismissed as cases of arrested emotional development, or as
people too timid or too lazy to confront the difficult responsibilities
of marriage and earning a living.

My view of religious orders is rather different. Perhaps because I
had a happy time at a convent school, I have never thought that
there was anything particularly odd about the monastic vocation in
itself – even though some of those who have pursued such vocations
(such as Francis Kilvert's neighbour Father Ignatius) have been very
odd indeed. All civilizations in the world have produced men and
women who felt drawn to withdraw from it, for a life consecrated
to self-denial and contemplation. The results of such withdrawal are
not, of course, uniformly happy or edifying, but the impulse to
make it, captured so hauntingly in Gerard Manley Hopkins's poem
'Heaven-Haven', is one which will always make an appeal.

Caedmon receives the gift of poetry

He had followed a secular occupation until well advanced in years without ever learning anything about poetry. Indeed it sometimes happened at a feast that all the guests in turn would be invited to sing and entertain the company; then, when he saw the harp coming his way, he would get up from table and go home.

On one such occasion he had left the house in which the entertainment was being held and went out to the stable, where it was his duty that night to look after the beasts. There when the time came he settled down to sleep. Suddenly in a dream he saw a man standing beside him who called him by name. 'Caedmon,' he said, 'sing me a song.' 'I don't know how to sing,' he replied. 'It is because I cannot sing that I left the feast and came here.' The man who addressed him then said: 'But you shall sing to me.' 'What should I sing about?' he replied. 'Sing about the Creation of all things,' the other answered. And Caedmon immediately began to sing verses in praise of God the Creator that he had never heard before, and their theme ran thus:

> Praise we the Fashioner now of Heaven's fabric,
> The majesty of his might and his mind's wisdom,
> Work of the world-warden, worker of all wonders,
> How he the Lord of Glory everlasting,
> Wrought first for the race of men Heaven as a rooftree,
> Then made he Middle Earth to be their mansions.

This is the general sense, but not the actual words that Caedmon sang in his dream; for verses, however masterly, cannot be translated literally from one language into another without losing much of their beauty and dignity. When Caedmon awoke, he remembered everything that he had sung in his dream, and soon added more verses in the same style to a song truly worthy of God.

Early in the morning he went to his superior the reeve, and told him about this gift that he had received. The reeve took him before the abbess, who ordered him to give an account of his dream and repeat the verses in the presence of many learned men, so that a decision might be reached by common consent as to their quality and origin. All of them agreed that Caedmon's gift had been given him by our Lord. And they explained to him a passage of scriptural history or doctrine and asked him to render it into verse if he could.

He promised to do this, and returned next morning with excellent verses as they had ordered him. The abbess was delighted that God had given such grace to the man, and advised him to abandon secular life and adopt the monastic state. And when she had admitted him into the Community as a brother, she ordered him to be instructed in the events of sacred history. So Caedmon stored up in his memory all that he learned, and like one of the clean animals chewing the cud, turned it into such melodious verse that his delightful renderings turned his instructors into auditors. He sang of the creation of the world, the origin of the human race, and the whole story of Genesis. He sang of Israel's exodus from Egypt, the entry into the Promised Land, and many other events of scriptural history. He sang of the Lord's Incarnation, Passion, Resurrection, and Ascension into heaven, the coming of the Holy Spirit, and the teaching of the Apostles. He also made many poems on the terrors of the Last Judgement, the horrible pains of Hell, and the joys of the Kingdom of Heaven. In addition to these, he composed several others on the blessings and judgements of God, by which he sought to turn his hearers from delight in wickedness and to inspire them to love and do good. For Caedmon was a deeply religious man, who humbly submitted to regular discipline and hotly rebuked all who tried to follow another course. And so he crowned his life with a happy end.

The Venerable Bede (673–735), *History of the English Church and People*

Abbot Samson

We have heard so much of Monks; everywhere, in real and fictitious History, from Muratori Annals to Radcliffe Romances, these singular two-legged animals, with their rosaries and breviaries, with their shaven crowns, hair-cilices and vows of poverty, masquerade so strangely through our fancy; and they are in fact so very strange an extinct species of the human family – a veritable Monk of Bury St Edmunds is worth attending to, if by chance made visible and audible. Here he is; and in his hand a magical speculum, much gone to rust indeed, yet in fragments still clear; wherein the marvellous image of his existence does still shadow itself, though fitfully, and as with an intermittent light! Will not the reader peep with us into this singular camera lucida, where an extinct species, though fitfully, can still be

seen alive? Extinct species, we say; for the live specimens which still
go about under that character are too evidently to be classed as
spurious in Natural History: the Gospel of Richard Arkwright once
promulgated, no Monk of the old sort is any longer possible in this
world. But fancy a deep-buried Mastodon, some fossil Megatherion,
Ichthyosaurus, were to begin to speak from amid its rock-swathings
never so indistinctly! The most extinct fossil species of Men or Monks
can do, and does, this miracle – thanks to the Letters of the Alphabet,
good for so many things.

Thomas Carlyle, Past and Present (1843)

The Prioress

Ther was also a Nonne, a PRIORESSE,
That of hir smylyng was ful symple and coy;
Hire gretteste ooth was but by Seinte Loy;
And she was cleped madame Eglentyne.
Ful weel she soong the service dyvyne,
Entuned in hir nose ful semely,
And Frenssh she spak ful faire and fetisly,
After the scole of Stratford atte Bowe,
For Frenssh of Parys was to hire unknowe.
At mete wel ytaught was she with alle:
She leet no morsel from hir lippes falle,
Ne wette hir fyngres in hir sauce depe;
Wel koude she carie a morsel and wel kepe
That no drope ne fille upon hire brest.
In curteisie was set ful muchel hir lest.
Hir over-lippe wyped she so clene
That in hir coppe ther was no ferthyng sene
Of grece, whan she dronken hadde hir draughte.
Ful semely after hir mete she raughte.
And sikerly she was of greet desport,
And ful plesaunt, and amyable of port,
And peyned hire to countrefete cheere
Of court, and to been estatlich of manere,
And to ben holden digne of reverence.
But, for to speken of hire conscience,

She was so charitable and so pitous
She wolde wepe, if that she saugh a mous
Kaught in a trappe, if it were deed or bledde.
Of smale houndes hadde she that she fedde
With rosted flessh, or milk and wastel-breed.
But soore wepte she if oon of hem were deed,
Or if men smoot it with a yerde smerte;
And al was conscience and tendre herte.
Ful semyly hir wympul pynched eas,
Hir nose tretys, hir eyen greye as glas,
Hir mouth ful smal, and therto softe and reed;
But sikerly she hadde a fair forheed;
It was almoost a spanne brood, I trowe;
For, hardily, she was nat undergrowe.
Ful fetys was hir cloke, as I was war.
Of smal coral aboute hire arm she bar
A peire of bedes, gauded al with grene,
And theron heng a brooch of gold ful sheene,
On which ther was first write a crowned A,
And after *Amor vincit omnia.*
    Another Nonne with hire hadde she,
That was hir chapeleyne, and preestes thre.

Geoffrey Chaucer (*c.* 1343–1400), 'General Prologue',
The Canterbury Tales

The dissolution of the monasteries

The authorities in the abbey were accused of disaffection; and a commission of inquiry was sent down towards the end of the spring of 1536, to investigate. The depositions taken on this occasion are still preserved; and with the help of them, we can leap over three centuries of time, and hear the last echoes of the old monastic life in Woburn Abbey dying away in discord.

Where party feeling was running so high, there were, of course, passionate arguments. The Act of Supremacy, the spread of Protestantism, the power of the Pope, the state of England – all were discussed; and the possibilities of the future, as each party painted it in the colours of his hopes. The brethren, we find, spoke their minds in plain language, sometimes condescending to a joke.

Brother Sherbourne deposes that the sub-prior, 'on Candlemas-day last past (February 2, 1536), asked him whether he longed not to be at Rome where all his bulls were?' Brother Sherbourne answered that 'his bulls had made so many calves, that he had burned them. Whereunto the sub-prior said he thought there were more calves now than there were then.'

Then there were long and furious quarrels about 'my Lord Privy Seal' (Cromwell) – who was to one party, the incarnation of Satan; to the other, the delivering angel.

Nor did matters mend when from the minister they passed to the master.

Dan John Croxton being in 'the shaving-house' one day with certain of the brethren having their tonsures looked to, and gossiping as men do on such occasions, one 'Friar Lawrence did say that the king was dead.' Then said Croxton, 'Thanks be to God, his Grace is in good health, and I pray God so continue him;' and said further to the said Lawrence, 'I advise thee to leave thy babbling.' Croxton, it seems, had been among the suspected in earlier times. Lawrence said to him, 'Croxton, it maketh no matter what thou sayest, for thou art one of the new world;' whereupon hotter still the conversation proceeded. 'Thy babbling tongue,' Croxton said, 'will turn us all to displeasure at length.' 'Then', quoth Lawrence, 'neither thou nor yet any of us all shall do well as long as we forsake our head of the Church, the Pope.' 'By the mass!' quoth Croxton, 'I would thy Pope Roger were in thy belly, or thou in his, for thou art a false perjured knave to thy prince.' Whereunto the said Lawrence answered, saying, 'By the mass, thou liest! I was never sworn to forsake the Pope to be our head, and never will be.' 'Then,' quoth Croxton, 'thou shalt be sworn spite of thine heart one day, or I will know why nay.'

These and similar wranglings may be taken as specimens of the daily conversation at Woburn, and we can perceive how an abbot with the best intentions would have found it difficult to keep the peace.

J. A. Froude, *Short Studies of Great Subjects* (1867–83)

A mermaid in a convent

October 27

On this day the mermaid, (if she really was a mermaid), came to St Andrew's, Marrick, just as the Ladies were sitting down to their Mixtum, which to-day was of fried eggs, and salt herrings soused, because it was a Friday. There was a strong wind blowing from the west, so the sound of the pack-mules' bells did not reach even those Messes whose chamber windows looked down the Dale, until the mules were quite close. But as soon as any of the Ladies heard the bells they knew them for those on the harness of the two Priory mules, Black Thomas and the Bishop, and they knew therefore that Dame Margery Conyers the Chambress, and Dame Bess Dalton and the three servants were returning from York, where the Chambress had been to buy cloth for the Ladies' gowns.

Knowing this, more than one of the Ladies clapped a fried egg or a piece of herring between tranches of bread, and bearing these in one hand and a cup of ale in the other, made for the Great Court, to greet the arrival of the returning Ladies; those who had been to York had been, they considered, into the world, and brought back news of miracles, of fashions of gowns and coifs, of the Sweating Sickness, of the Scots, of the prices of cloth; and besides news on these important subjects, other news which might be called little better than tittle-tattle, but the Ladies loved it not less than any of the rest.

Dame Christabel was eating her Mixtum with the Prioress, and the Prioress's chamber faced up the Dale, towards Calva, humped and spined like a great beast under its brown heather and red-brown bracken. For this reason, and because of the great wind that was blowing, Christabel did not hear the mule bells; the Prioress did not hear them either, but that was because she was growing very deaf.

The first thing which Christabel heard above the noises of the wind, which rattled the casement, and made strange whistlings among the rushes on the floor, was the clack of the latch. Then the door burst open, dry bits of rush rose and flew about, the fire swirled out from the chimney, and Christabel had to catch the edge of the boardcloth to prevent it flapping back across the dishes on the table. Dame Elizabeth Close came in, like a great ship before the wind, wind in her skirts, wind in her veil. For a moment she looked far too big.

Then she caught the door and forced it shut behind her, and in the restored quiet of the room became her normal size again; which was big enough, Dame Christabel thought, for Dame Elizabeth was a very large woman.

'Our Lady!' cried she, casting up her hands. 'Our Lady! A marvel! Here's a marvel. Jesu! it is a marvel indeed!'

She went across to the old Prioress who was tremblingly trying to get up from her chair, for if she had not heard she had seen Dame Elizabeth's gesture.

'What is it?' she cried in her shaking old voice. 'Is is the Scots?'

'No, no. Not the Scots. Lord! no. It's a mermaid!'

'Where?' The Prioress looked vaguely round as if there might be one under the table.

'Here, in Marrick.'

The Prioress sank down again. She was not able to deal with such a situation. It was Christabel who asked, 'How did she come?'

'Dame Margery hath brought her from York.'

'She would!' Christabel murmured, but under her breath; and to herself she thought, 'At least if any of them would, she would.' But she had not expected that any of the Ladies should have had the opportunity of committing such a rare foolishness.

She said to the Prioress, 'Shall I go down and see?' And the Prioress nodded more vehemently than her ordinary ceaseless nodding, so Dame Christabel went.

The Great Court, as she went down the outer staircase from the Prioress's room, looked as if to-day were the great spring washing day, so full was it of the flapping white of the Ladies' veils. But besides the Ladies there were a great many of the serving women, and even some of the farm-men, and of course Jankin the porter in his green hood. And from the centre of the crowd came now and then the chime of the mule bells, or the ring of a hoof on stone as the beasts fidgeted.

None of them, not even the youngest girl that tended the hens, took notice of anything but what was in the centre of the mob, so, though Dame Christabel came to the outskirts of the crowd, she could see nothing, nor make any way in. 'Perdy!' and, 'Marry!' cried the wenches, and, 'By cock!' the men. But beyond them Dame Christabel could hear Dame Margery's taut, excited voice declaring that, 'Yea, truly she is a very mermaid and the Skinner's wife of

York would never have sold her to us but because of the great reverence her husband and she have for St Andrew. Two pounds I paid, and we are to pray for them both every St Andrew's Day.'

'Two pounds,' thought the Treasuress, 'for a mermaid!' She did not think that Dame Margery was one to have obtained at such a price a very mermaid. That would have cost far more, so the two pounds were sheer loss.

'Where,' cried Dame Anne Ladyman, 'shall we put her?'

'In the big fish-pond,' someone suggested.

'But she'll eat all the fish,' young Grace Rutherford piped up, forgetting in her excitement that it was no novice's place to speak aloud among the Ladies, still less so when there were men about.

'Little fool!' Dame Margery chid her, but not for the fault of speaking. 'It's pike, not mermaids, that eat fish.'

'Mass!' cried Dame Joan Barningham, with triumph in her voice. 'What will the Ladies of St Bernard say when they know that we have a mermaid in our House?'

H. F. M. Prescott, The Man on a Donkey (1952)

Cistercians

All things in the begining
    Before their Maker came,
The wheatfield for the winning,
    The furze-bush for the flame;

The cattle in the cow-land,
    The meadow-sweet and sedge,
The plover on the plough-land,
    The bullfinch in the hedge;

The sward the blackface browses,
    The stapler and the bale,
The grey Cistercian houses
    That pack the wool for sale;

The downland and the dewpond,
    The drainland and the dike,

The Friday-fishing stew-pond,
 The netting of the pike;

The grass on hillside ranges,
 The milk-froth in the pail,
The granaries and the granges,
 The echo of the flail;

The applegarth and vineyard,
 The Southern Cloister figs,
The dovecote and the kine yard,
 The fat December pigs.

All things in the beginning
 Before their Maker came:
Labour to keep from sinning,
 Fasting and Prayer to tame.

Compline with *Qui cisternas,*
 Exsurge with the lark;
The novice *Ad lucernas,*
 The old monk in the dark.

The old monk dreams and drowses,
 The young monk sings the scale;
The grey Cistercian houses
 Pack all the wool for sale.

     J. M. Falkner, *Poems* (1933)

Parson Woodforde meets a Benedictine monk

Nov. 10, 1786 ... Went out a Coursing this morning for an Hour or so, but saw no Hare. We dined and spent the Afternoon and part of the Evening at Weston House till after 9 o'clock with Mr and Mrs Custance, Mrs Collyer Sen[r] and a Mr Chamberlain who is a Roman Catholic Priest and lives with S[r] W[m] Jernegan and Family and what is most remarkable in him is, that he was bred up a Protestant, was at the University of Cambridge, had Preferment in the Church of England to the Value of £800 per Annum all of which he has lately given up, renounced the Protestant Religion, and has been made a

Monk. A very good kind of Man he appears to be and very sensible – has been in France &c. He is now Chaplain to Sr Wm Jernegan, that Family being of the Romish Persuasion. After Coffee and Tea, Mrs Custance, Mrs Collyer, Nancy and myself got to Cribbage at wch won o. 2. o. Nancy lost all that was lost being o. 5. o. Mr Custance and Mr Chamberlain did not play. It being Friday Mr Chamberlain eat no Meat only some Fish and some Rice Pudding.

James Woodforde, *The Diary of a Country Parson* (1926)

Father Ignatius

Friday, 2 September 1870
At 10.45 started across the fields to walk to Capel y Ffin. I came in sight of the little Capel y Ffin squatting like a stout grey owl among its seven great black yews. I hastened on, and in front of the Capel House farm there was the sunny haired girl washing at a tub as usual . . . 'Is Father Ignatius here?' I asked. 'Yes, at least he was here this morning.' I asked a mason at work upon the building if Father Ignatius was there. 'There he is with his brother,' said the mason. A black robed and cowled monk was walking fast along the bottom of the field towards a barn with Clavering Lyne. Clavering came up to me, but the monk walked quickly on without looking round. Clavering took me to his father and mother, who were sitting on a garden seat under a tree in a pretty little dingle. They had just arrived unexpectedly from Pontrilas having driven up the valley as I came down. It was curious, our meeting thus as it were by chance.

Mr and Mrs Lyne came up out of their dingle and Mrs Lyne brought up Father Ignatius and introduced us. He struck me as being a man of gentle simple kind manners, excitable, and entirely possessed by the one idea. He always spoke to his father and mother as 'Papa' and 'Mamma', and called me 'Father'. I could not persuade him that my name was not Venables. His head and brow are very fine, the forehead beautifully rounded and highly imaginative. The face is a very saintly one and the eyes extremely beautiful, earnest and expressive, a dark soft brown. When excited they seem absolutely to flame. He wears the Greek or early British tonsure all round the temples, leaving the hair of the crown untouched. His manner gives you the impression of great earnestness and single-mindedness . . .

Father Ignatius wore the black Benedictine habit with the two loose wings or pieces falling in front and behind, two violet tassels behind, the knotted scourge girdle, a silver cross on the breast, and a brazen or golden cross hanging from the rosary of black beads under the left arm.

We walked round the place and then climbed the steep bank above and looked down upon the building. Mrs Lyne gathered some whinberries and gave them to us to eat. They were very nice. They grew along the ground on tiny bushes among a very small delicately twisted pink heath. We saw the monks and novices below issuing from a barn where they had engaged for an hour or so in an 'examination of conscience'. One of the monks was gazing at us. He had conceived an irrepressible desire to see Mrs Lyne again. He did not wish to intrude upon her approach or address her. He simply wanted to see her at a respectful distance and admire her afar off. Mr Lyne said the monk was a man of few and simple wants, content with a little and thankful for small mercies. Because the monk had said that if he could see Mrs Lyne he would be perfectly happy.

Mrs Lyne not having much faith in the larder or resources of the monastery, especially on a Friday, had wisely taken the precaution of bringing with her an honest leg of mutton and two bottles of wine. The monasterial garden provided potatoes and French beans, very good, and we had luncheon under the tree in the dingle, waited on by the novices also cowled and robed in black like the monks. They addressed Father Ignatius as 'dear Father' whenever they spoke to him and bent the knee whenever they approached or passed him.

Whilst we were at luncheon we heard voices close to us proceeding from the bottom of a deep watercourse or lane, on the other side of the hedge. Then a man looked over the hedge and asked his way to Capel y Ffin. Father Ignatius had been sitting talking freely and at ease with his head uncovered, and his cowl lying back on his shoulders. But directly he heard the strange voices and saw the strange face peering over the hedge he dashed the cowl over his head and face and bolted up the bank among the shrubs like a rabbit . . .

One of the novices was a fine noble looking boy, a gentleman's son, with a sweet open face and fair clustering curly hair. He had been sent to the new monastery by his parents to learn to be a monk. The boy seemed to be devoted to Father Ignatius and came running up with a basket of mushrooms he had just bought to show them to the Father. His cowl was thrown back and his fair young head, bright face and sunny hair made a striking contrast with his black robe. 'Yes, dear Father. No, dear Father.' And off he went in high delight with his mushrooms and the approval of the Father, as happy as a king and much happier. Poor child. I wonder if he will ever become a monk. I hope he is reserved for a better fate. He shook hands with us all before he went off to the barn. His hand was as small, soft and white as a girl's. They called him 'Manny'. Another of the novices, of lower rank in life, one who waited on us at luncheon, had a peculiarly sweet and beautiful face. He is called Brother Placidus.

I stood in the lane near the Honddu bridge for some time talking with Father Ignatius. I asked him if he would not find an ordinary dress more convenient and practical and less open to insult and objection. But he scouted the idea of abandoning his distinctive monastic dress. He said he had once given it up for a few days, but he felt like a deserter and traitor till he took to the habit again. Then he again became happy. The Bishop of Gloucester and Bristol, he said, had suggested the same thing, but he turned the tables on the Bishop by asking him why he did not discard his own foolish and meaningless dress, far more irrational than the Benedictine habit, every part of which has its meaning. The Bishop laughed and said there was a good deal in what Father Ignatius said. He thinks the Bishops are coming round to his side. We shook hands and departed. 'Goodbye, Father,' he said with an earnest kindly look, 'and thank you for your good wish. You must come and see us again when we have our guest house ready.' When we had parted a little way and our roads had diverged he called out through the half screen of a hazel hedge, 'Father! Will you remember us the next time you celebrate the Holy Communion?' 'Yes,' I replied, 'I will.'

Francis Kilvert, Diaries (1974)

Heaven-Haven

A Nun Takes the Veil

I have desired to go
Where springs not fail,

To fields where flies no sharp and sided hail
And a few lilies blow.

And I have asked to be
Where no storms come,
Where the green swell is in the havens dumb,
And out of the swing of the sea.

Gerard Manley Hopkins (1844–89)

Abbot extraordinary*

His conception of the Contemplative Life involved, not only the building of this splendid monastery, but also the erection of an abbot's house, planned on late medieval lines, for his own use. This *prelatura* may have been inspired by one of the greater abbeys in Tuscany he had visited in the spring of 1910. No matter, there was and never has been anything comparable to the Anglican Abbot's House in any Roman Catholic Benedictine monastery in Britain erected since the Reformation.

As the founder of the Community of the Resurrection, Gore had such an extreme dislike of anything that might savour of autocratic government that he refused to accept the title of Superior, and insisted on being addressed as 'Senior.' Thus it is fairly certain that he would have found it difficult to appreciate the reasons for the re-creation of this outward symbol of abbatial autocracy. He would have wondered if it had any necessary place in the ministry and organization of the post-Reformation Church of England, which does not recognize minor prelates, only bishops and clerks in holy orders.

The large apsidal chapel was paved with black and white marble. The Renaissance altar was made of pink alabaster, the gift of the Earl of Plymouth. The six tall candlesticks and crucifix were hand-wrought silver. The tabernacle door was fashioned of solid silver. A most original sanctuary lamp, designed by Henry Wilson, hung from a silver galleon in full sail. The only furniture in the abbatial chapel was a massive carved oak prie-dieu, and an armchair. The six windows were filled with stained glass, depicting monastic saints who had lived the purely contemplative life, or who had propagated a reformed observance of the Benedictine Rule, such as we were supposed to be aiming at on Caldey. A small sacristy contained sets of costly vestments, most of them specially designed for the Abbot in Italian or Spanish Baroque shape. He possessed three croziers, one of them made of ivory and silver; several gold pectoral crosses and jewelled rings, and a number of mitres. One was embroidered with pearls and precious stones.

This Abbot's House was a far cry from the leaky bell tents in which the Brothers had spent the summer on Caldey in 1901. Also on the ground floor and leading out of an oak-panelled hall, were the private secretary's office and the abbatial reception room. The latter was immense, with a highly polished parquet floor, and oak panelled walls. A vast open fireplace, where logs blazed in winter, added to the warmth given by the central heating. In the far corner stood a roll-top desk – probably the one mentioned by Compton Mackenzie in *Sinister Street*, which had been part of the furniture in 'Dom Cuthbert Manners' room at Clere Abbey.' Behind it our Abbot was usually seated, fixing his eyes on anybody who walked towards him across the slippery parquet floor, when summoned to (or having sought) an interview. An oak staircase led up to the Abbot's bedroom, the same size as the reception room beneath it. When asked why it had been planned on such a scale, he replied that it was to enable all the community to stand around his death-bed! Adjacent was a smaller bedroom for distinguished guests. The fittings of the abbatial bathroom were in keeping with everything else in this splendid *prelatura*.

* Dom Aelred Carlyle, abbot of Caldey Abbey.

Peter Anson, *Bishops at Large* (1964)

Vocations

'My dear Sister Catherine.' Father Bernardine stepped forward briskly to greet her.

He dangled a purple stole in his left hand while he shook hands. 'Do you prefer here or the confessional? Perhaps you'd like to get rid of some of the burthen first by an absolution?'

'No thanks. I prefer, if it must be, just to talk.'

'Let us make ourselves comfortable. It is not for everyone I'd come away right in the middle of a retreat. But when you sought me – '

'You were sought for me,' Kitty said coldly, taking the chair he offered her.

'Ah!' He frowned slightly. 'You won't mind my taking this arm-chair? The journey down was rather fatiguing. A mere trifle, though, in a good cause,' he added, with a smile, settling himself well back in the chair with graceful negligence.

He rested his elbows on the arms of the chair and joined the tips of his long, slender fingers. His hair hung a little down on his forehead and gave him a look of fatigue. He gazed thoughtfully at his nails, frowned, sighed, smiled again and said with a nice blend of interest and affection:

'Now, my dear child, what is this temptation?'

Kitty gave a slight start. He had placed her chair straight in front of him, and in the short silence she watched him closely. How exactly would he begin? She knew most of his poses by now, but this was something new. The tightening of his lips helped to conceal the weakness of his mouth and gave it a note of sternness that was not yet severity. The general effect of the set of his head, of his tone, of his half-averted eyes was a slightly pained surprise. There was no doubt about his good looks. No wonder so many of the nuns were in love with him. When he spoke she was wondering vaguely if she had ever been in love with him, if that was why she had listened to him, been led by him?

'It's just that I grew up suddenly,' she said lightly.

For a moment he was disconcerted. Then the look of pain deepened. He turned his big brown eyes fully on her and said sadly and a little reproachfully:

'You mean you have allowed the world to whisper to your heart, to dim its beautiful freshness. A Greater than I has said, "Unless you become as little children you cannot come unto Me." But, thank God, the insidious temptation cannot yet have gained much foothold. We must strive with God's grace to restore your heart to its original innocence. You must again become as a little child with all its trust and confidence. Such only is the kingdom of heaven. Now what is the particular trouble?'

'It is everything. The whole life here. I don't believe in it. It's not life at all, but a mockery of it.'

He pursed his lips and frowned. 'The evil has gone deeper than I thought,' he remarked regretfully to a print on the wall. 'But we mustn't despair. We must try and get at the root of the trouble.'

He smiled. 'What is it *you* object to in life consecrated by the lives and deaths of innumerable saints of God?' he asked, with patronizing, half-bantering sarcasm.

'I'm not a saint of God – I'm only a woman,' she said bitterly.

His complacency annoyed her. For a week she had been subjected to hourly doses of intensive pietistic talk. It had come to seem a mere patter of meaningless words, repeated by rote. 'So are the others,' she added resentfully.

He looked pained and hurt, shuddered a little, closed his eyes and rested his hands on his knees as if making an effort to recover from a shock.

'This is serious,' he said. He joined his fingers again, looked at the ceiling with the expression of one of Guido's saints, and said:

'A convent to me is a vase of beautiful flowers filling the ambient air with the odour of their sanctity.'

She laughed. Half the nuns had this silly phrase from one of his sermons written in their Office books.

'Then when one of the flowers goes bad, the best things to do is to take it out of the bowl and pitch it away,' she said.

He frowned and said in a piqued tone, 'Please allow me to complete the figure. One mustn't deal crudely with metaphors. There is, perhaps, as yet only a slight wilting of a leaf, a tiredness in a petal. The precious flower of your vocation – '

She gave a sigh of relief, caught at the word, and interrupted eagerly:

'You were wrong about that. I never had a vocation.'

'Please allow me to be the judge of that,' he said sharply. 'I never make a mistake. The decision of your superiors here in admitting you to profession confirmed my judgement. You, yourself, are the final proof. Why else did you enter, take your vows?'

'Why, indeed?' she wondered blankly. 'I don't know. It was some sort of blindness. You all told me things that weren't true.'

He sat erect in his chair. His figure stiffened. He tried to smile, but his lips and eyes expressed anger and resentment.

'You were the worst,' she said, her anger kindled by his.

He laughed harshly. 'This is very serious, indeed, very serious.

After all my prayers, my labour. The careful study I gave to your soul. The counsel I've expended on you.'

'It was my own fault to be such a fool,' she returned. 'However, it is not yet too late. I can go.'

'It is too late,' he said sternly. 'I have no wish to be hard on you. But you speak foolishly. The Church can't alter its laws for the whim of a foolish girl. You've made a vow of obedience to your superiors, to your holy bishop, to our holy Church. I can't speak for his lordship, but I certainly could not recommend a dispensation in your vow of obedience. Your most excellent mistress of novices thinks there is some temporary aberration. You haven't given me one solid reason to justify your extraordinary conduct. Your superiors agree with me that you had a real vocation.' He stretched out his hand and took the stole off the table. 'You must have fallen into some sin. Come and remove the burthen from your soul. In the serene light of God's holy grace you will repent of this madness.'

'But I have committed no sin,' she protested.

She felt as if she was being enclosed in some new net.

His smile, half of superiority, half of pity, made her angry.

'You want to keep me here against my will,' she said.

He smiled again for a moment, and then said solemnly, 'My dear child, your will is no longer your own. You have given it up into the hands of your superiors, of your good bishop, of our holy mother the Church. You say you have committed no sin? You have already gravely broken your vow of obedience – at least in intention. If you leave this sanctuary of God's love,' he waved his hand towards the walls, 'you will sin daily against your vow of holy obedience. In a short time your soul will be a mass of corruption. *Facilis est descensus averni* – hell, will yawn wide in front of you. An eternity of torment for the gratification of a mere whim!'

She shut her eyes with a shudder. All the devils of her childhood seemed to rush at her. She put out her hand to ward them off. It fell limply through the empty air to her knee. She opened her eyes and smiled.

'I am counting the hours till I go,' she said.

Gerald O'Donovan, Vocations (1932)

The Carthusians

Parkminster, Cowfold, was founded by Carthusians when the religious orders were suppressed in France in the last century. They are an order of collective hermits, each monk living in an isolated house around a great cloister and joining together only in church and eating together only on Sundays and Feast Days. They keep silence except for their weekly walk, which I had seen them taking, but I have been told that they do not find much to talk about as they never see a newspaper or hear the radio.

After the Great War one of the monks, a German, simply refused to believe that Germany had been defeated, but there was no way of proving it to him. In 1940, during the Battle of Britain, a German plane was shot down in their grounds and the monk, who was still alive, said smugly: 'What did I tell you, the Fatherland still fights on!'

Colin Stephenson, *Merrily on High* (1971)

Nashdom

The community moved to Nashdom about 1923 and when I first visited them Abbot Denys had just died and had been replaced by Abbot Martin, a nice but rather pompous man who was very conscious of his position as the only abbot in the Church of England. When R.C. abbots retire they take titular abbacies from the ancient English abbeys and call themselves Abbot of Westminster, Glastonbury, etc. When Abbot Martin retired it was suggested that he might return the compliment and call himself 'Abbot of Downside'.

Nashdom Abbey was a great surprise to me as it was not what I expected a monastery to look like but a very grand house, designed by Lutyens for a Russian Princess who wished to have a *pied à terre* near Windsor. Even today if one lifts a pious picture on the great staircase one finds it covers a plaster roundel of the Princess's head. It is in fact a very beautiful house of lovely proportions and painted white with green shutters, which means that without constant and expensive renovation it can look rather shabby and seedy.

The gardens had a lovely broad walk of chestnut trees now, alas, fallen victims to the woodman's axe. People used to break through the fence to steal the chestnuts and I remember my cousin once saying that he now understood why the early monks went to live in the desert as there wasn't anything there anyone wanted to pinch!

Once inside the front door all my doubts at the secular appearance of the house were immediately dispersed. The porter was dressed in a black Benedictine habit and the entrance hall, from which a wide flight of steps led up to the chapel, was fragrant with the smell of incense, while a rather dramatic picture of the Sacred Heart hung at the head of the stairs.

The chapel had been constructed out of the ballroom of the house and visitors were allowed in the gallery where once the servants had crept in to peep over the edge and watch the Russian nobility waltzing below. The high altar was an effective baroque construction designed by an architect named Martin Travers who used his considerable talents in transforming many Anglo-Catholic churches into passable imitations of Italian places of worship, except that he worked in papier mâché, which cut the cost but rather gave the impression of a stage set.

The services were entirely in Latin and this was the first time I had heard its use in the Church of England but of course it reminded me of Cowfold Monastery and gave the place a feeling of authenticity. I was enchanted when one of the senior monks said: 'That rogue Bishop Frere defiled our high altar by using English at it.' Here, I felt, was the *crème de la crème* of Anglicanism.

All is now changed, for the chapel has been remodelled and the altar, without candlesticks, stands in the midst of the choir while visitors have been promoted to the principal position before it, the monks sitting in tiers on either side like a choral society. The last vestiges of the Latin tongue remain in the Anthems of Our Lady sung after Compline.

It used to be said that the only Book of Common Prayer to be found at Nashdom was in the library, filed under 'Comparative Religion', but this was untrue, for after my cousin's death I was sent a Prayer Book which had belonged to him and which showed signs of great use. Not that he was in the least in sympathy with the changes in the church and on my last visit before his death he said: 'Vespers still remains a fairly Christian service except that we have a whole chapter of the Bible read to us in the middle.'

Colin Stephenson (ibid.)

The Dolly Sisters

'The Darwell' (as Dr Darwell Stone, the former principal, was known) a learned, bearded figure, was still around and consulted by everyone in the Church of England like a Delphic oracle. There were many tales about him such as the undergraduate who told him he had been to see 'The Dolly Sisters' during the vacation to which 'The Darwell' replied: 'That is a religious community of which I have never heard'.

Colin Stephenson (ibid.)

Sister Ignatius

The war was secular agony completed. The more serious pain was reserved to eternity, and there was the promise of it every morning, not in words but in the practical demonstration of Sister Ignatius's strap. Sister Ignatius was a sort of Lancashire fishwife got up as a nun. She conducted morning prayers as though crying fresh halibut. Prayers were lengthy and featured the Virgin Mary more than her son or the great fuming dyspeptic God who raged round his punishment laboratory. Mary was there, visibly sweet and forgiving of words like 'arse' and 'bum', though it was assumed she was too well brought up to know what they meant. She was surrounded by candles which, on a dull day in the assembly hall on to which the classrooms disembogued, gave off a pleasant Christmassy feeling. We recited 'Hail Holy Queen' and many decades of the rosary. Occasionally a boy, never a girl, would faint from the long standing. ''Es chucked a dummy' would get into the Hail Mary. The boy, terrified of the strap for lateness, would probably have missed breakfast. Punishment for lateness was immediate, fired by the resentment of a nun who had had a foredawn mass call, and meted out in the cloakroom or on the run: black skirt arustle, she saw no indignity in chasing the reluctant. The strap hurt damnably, as she knew, and there was a kind of sinful logic in running away from it. She never once strapped empty air. It was a relief to turn from her to the Virgin Mary, dumb, puzzled but forgiving. 'Hail, our life, our sweetness and our hope. To thee do we cry, poor banished children of Eve. To thee do we send up our sighs, mourning and weeping in this vale of tears. Turn then, most gracious advocate, thine eyes of mercy towards us, and after this our exile show unto us the blessed fruit of thy womb.' I still think that is good prose.

Anthony Burgess, Little Wilson and Big God (1987)

Brother Oliver

MUGGERIDGE: How long have you been a monk, Brother Oliver?

OLIVER: Well, I entered Rosscrae in 1934, that's in Rosscrae, of course, in Tipperary, and I was there up until I came to Scotland in 1946.

MUGGERIDGE: When you are doing all this outdoor work on the farm, aren't you sometimes hungry?

OLIVER: Yes, you sometimes come home tired. And although the bed is a hard one, you know the old saying that the Cistercian bed is hard to lie on, but it's sweet to die on.

MUGGERIDGE: And you found it a bed hard to lie on?

OLIVER: Oh, indeed I always have done, and to this day I do. That's the one consolation you get when you go to a hospital – you get a lovely soft bed. You can sleep and sleep, and the last time I was in hospital the sister there said she thought I was never going to waken. She said I slept for six days without break – so there you are. That is a fact!

MUGGERIDGE: But sweet to die on?

OLIVER: Yes, it is sweet to die on. Well, that's the reward of a monk's life. I suppose he comes into the monastery to die, or to learn how to die perhaps.

MUGGERIDGE: Is that what you see as the purpose of living in a monastery – to learn how to die?

OLIVER: I think it is – now that's my purpose. I don't say it's everybody's perhaps, but if I didn't think I was going to get to heaven I wouldn't be here three days!

Malcolm Muggeridge, Muggeridge through the Microphone (1968)

The Abbey

They had crossed to the Abbey side of the terrace and were going down some stone steps, much riddled by long dry grasses, which descended to a path leading to the causeway. Dora, exasperated, kept silent.

The lake water was very quiet, achieving a luminous brilliant pale blue in the centre and stained at the edges by motionless reflections. Dora looked across at the great stone wall and the curtain of elm trees behind it. Above the trees rose the Abbey tower, which she saw in daylight to be a square Norman tower. It was an inspiring thing, without pinnacles or crenellations, squarely built of grey and yellowish stone, and decorated on each face by two pairs of round-topped windows, placed one above the other, edged with zigzag carving which at a distance gave a pearly embroidered appearance, and divided by a line of interlacing arches.

'A fine example of Norman work,' said Mrs Mark, following Dora's gaze.

They went on down to the causeway. This crossed the lake in a series of shallow arches built of old brick which had weathered to a rich blackish red. Each arch with its reflection made a dark ellipse. Dora noticed that the centre of the causeway was missing and had been replaced by a wooden section standing on piles.

'There was trouble here at the time of the dissolution, the dissolution of the monasteries, you know,' said Mrs Mark, 'and that piece was destroyed by order of the nuns themselves. It didn't help them, however. Most of the Abbey was burnt down. After the Reformation it became derelict and when Imber Court was built the Abbey was a deserted ruin, a sort of romantic feature of the grounds. Then in the late nineteenth century, after the Oxford movement, you know, the place was taken over by the Anglican Benedictines – it was formerly a Benedictine Abbey, of course – and was rebuilt about nineteen hundred. They acquired the manuscripts that interest your husband at about the same time. There's very little of the old building left now except for the refectory and the gateway and of course the tower.'

They stepped on to the causeway. Dora felt a tremor of excitement. 'Will we be able to go to the top of the tower?' she asked.

'Well, you know, we're not going *inside*,' said Mrs Mark, slightly scandalized. 'This is an *enclosed* order of nuns. No one goes in or comes out.'

Dora was stunned by this information. She stopped. 'Do you mean,' she said, 'that they're completely imprisoned in there?'

Mrs Mark laughed. 'Not imprisoned, my dear,' she said. 'They are there of their own free will. This is not a prison. It is on the contrary a place which it is very hard to get into, and only the strongest achieve it. Like Mary in the parable, they have chosen the better part.' They walked on.

'Don't they *ever* come out?' asked Dora.

'No,' said Mrs Mark. 'Being Benedictines, they take a vow of stability, that it they remain all their lives in the house where they take their first vows. They die and are buried inside in the nuns' cemetery.'

'How absolutely appalling!' said Dora.

Iris Murdoch, The Bell (1958)

Felixstowe or The Last of Her Order

With one consuming roar along the shingle
    The long wave claws and rakes the pebbles down
To where its backwash and the next wave mingle,
    A mounting arch of water weedy-brown
Against the tide the off-shore breezes blow.
Oh wind and water, this is Felixstowe.

In winter when the sea winds chill and shriller
    Than those of summer, all their cold unload
Full on the gimcrack attic of the villa
    Where I am lodging off the Orwell Road,
I put my final shilling in the meter
And only make my loneliness completer.

In eighteen ninety-four when we were founded,
    Counting our Reverend Mother we were six,
How full of hope we were and prayer-surrounded
    'The Little Sisters of the Hanging Pyx'.
We built our orphanage. We ran our school.
Now only I am left to keep the rule.

Here in the gardens of the Spa Pavilion
    Warm in the whisper of a summer sea,
The cushioned scabious, a deep vermilion,
    With white pins stuck in it, looks up at me

A sun-lit kingdom touched by butterflies
And so my memory of winter dies.

Across the grass the poplar shades grow longer
    And louder clang the waves along the coast
The band packs up. The evening breeze is stronger
    And all the world goes home to tea and toast.
I hurry past a cakeshop's tempting scones
Bound for the red brick twilight of St John's.

'Thou knowest my down sitting and mine uprising'
    Here where the white light burns with steady glow
Safe from the vain world's silly sympathising,
    Safe with the Love that I was born to know,
Safe from the surging of the lonely sea
My heart finds rest, my heart finds rest in Thee.

John Betjeman, Collected Poems (1958)

[18]

LAY PIETY

When I was a young ordinand, preparing to enter priesthood, I used to take exception when people said that I was 'going into the Church'. I would pedantically point out that I was 'in the church already'.

An anthology of this kind inevitably focuses on the clergy. 'The Church', however, is made up of what the Prayer Book calls 'the blessed company of all faithful people'.

It would be possible to compile an entire anthology of 'lay piety'. Even this short selection shows what a very wide range of different characters have been drawn to the Christian religion, and been diligent in its practice.

━━━━━━

Our Lord promises to slay her husband's lust

Another time, as she prayed to God that she might live chaste by leave of her husband, Christ said to her:–

'Thou must fast on Friday, both from meat and drink, and thou shalt have thy desire ere Whitsunday, for I shall suddenly slay (the fleshly lust in) thy husband.'

Then on the Wednesday in Easter week, after her husband would have had knowledge of her, as he was wont before, and when he came nigh to her, she said: – 'Jesus Christ, help me,' and he had no power to touch her at that time in that way, nor ever after with any fleshly knowledge.

It befell on a Friday before Whitsun Eve, as this creature was in a church of Saint Margaret at N . . . hearing her Mass, she heard a great noise, and a dreadful. She was sore amazed through fear of the voice of the people, who said God should take vengeance on her. She knelt on her knees, holding down her head, with her book in her hand, praying Our Lord Jesus Christ for grace and mercy.

Suddenly there fell down from the highest part of the church roof, from under the foot of the spar, on her head and back, a stone which weighed three pounds, and a short end of a beam weighing six pounds, so that she thought her back was broken asunder, and she feared she would be dead in a little while.

Soon afterwards, she cried 'Jesus, mercy!' and anon, her pain was gone.

A good man, called John of Wyreham, seeing this wonder and supposing she had been greatly injured came and pulled her by the sleeve and said:

'Dame, how fare ye?'

The creature, whole and sound, then thanked him for his cheer and his charity, much marvelling and greatly a-wonder that she felt no pain, having had so much a little before. For twelve weeks afterwards, she felt no pain. Then the spirit of God said to her soul:

'Hold this for a great miracle, and if the people will not believe this, I will work many more.'

A worshipful doctor of divinity, named Master Aleyn, a White Friar, hearing of this wonderful work, inquired of this creature all the details of the process. He, desiring the work of God to be magnified, got the same stone that fell on her back and weighed it, and then got the beam-end that fell on her head, which one of the keepers of the church had laid on the fire to burn. This worshipful doctor said it was a great miracle, and Our Lord was highly to be magnified for preserving this creature against the malice of her enemy, and told it to many people and many people magnified God much in this creature. Many also would not believe it, and thought it more a token of wrath and vengeance, rather than believe it was any token of mercy and kindness.

Margery Kempe (c. 1373–1439), *The Book of Margery Kempe*

When Faith and Love . . .

When Faith and Love, which parted from thee never,
Had ripened thy just soul to dwell with God,
Meekly thou didst resign this earthy load
Of death, called life, which us from life doth sever.
Thy works and alms and all thy good endeavour
Stayed not behind, nor in the grave were trod;
But, as Faith pointed with her golden rod,
Followed thee up to joy and bliss for ever.
Love led them on, and Faith, who knew them best,
Thy handmaids, clad them o'er with purple beams
And azure wings, that up they flew so drest,
And spake the truth of thee on glorious themes
Before the Judge; who thenceforth bid thee rest,
And drink thy fill of pure immortal streams.

John Milton (1608–74)

A Marching Song

Crist crucifyd
For thy woundes wide
Us commens guyde
   Which pilgrames be,
Thrughe godes grace,
For to purchache
Olde welth and peax
   Of the spiritualtie.

Gret godes fame
Doith Church proclame
Now to be lame
   And fast in boundes,
Robbyd, spoled and shorne
From catell and corne,
And clene furth borne
   Of housez and landes.

Whiche thynges is clere
Agaynst godes lere,

As doith appere
  In detronomio,
Godes law boke.
Open and loke,
As moysez spoke,
  Decimo nono.

Ther may be founde:
The lymyt grounde
May not lay dowyn
  Sesare nor kyng,
Which olde fathers
And the right heires,
For ther welfares,
  At theyr endyng

Gait to releif
Whome soraunce greve
Boith day and even,
  And can no wirke;
Ye this thay may,
Boith night and day
Resorte and pray
  Unto godes kyrke.
    .   .   .   .

Suche foly is fallen
And wise out blawen
That grace is gone
And all goodnes.
Then no marvell
Thoght it thus befell,
Commons to mell
  To make redresse.
    .   .   .   .

Bot on thing, Kynges,
Esayas saynges
Like rayn down brynges
  Godes woful yre,
Harrying the subject
Ther dewtis to forgett

And pryncez let
  Of suche disyre.

Alacke alacke
For the church sake
Pore comons wake,
  And no marvell.
For clere it is
The decay of this
How the pore shall mys
  No tong can tell.

    .   .   .   .

In troubil and care,
Where that we were
In manner all bere
  of our substance,
We founde good bate
At churche men gate,
Withoute checkmate
  Or varyaunce.

God that right all
Redresse now shall,
And that is thrall
Agayn make free,
  By this viage
And pylgramage
Of yong and sage
  In this countre.

    .   .   .

Church men for ever
So you remember,
Boith fyrst and latter,
  In your memento
These pilgramez poore,
That take such cure
To stabilisshe sure,
  Wiche dyd undoo.

Crim, crame, and riche
With thre ell and the liche
As sum men teache.
God theym amend!
And that Aske may,
Without delay,
Here make a stay
And well to end!

Anon, quoted in Ivor Gurney, *Recusant Poets* (1938)

Religio Medici

Yet have I not so shaken hands with those desperate Resolutions,
(who had rather venture at large their decayed bottom, than bring
her in to be new trimm'd in the Dock; who had rather promiscuously
retain all, than abridge any, and obstinately be what they are, than
what they have been,) as to stand in Diameter and Swords point with
them. We have reformed from them, not against them; for (omitting
those Improperations and Terms of Scurrility betwixt us, which only
difference our Affections, and not our Cause,) there is between us
one common Name and Appellation, one Faith and necessary body
of Principles common to us both; and therefore I am not scrupulous
to converse and live with them, to enter their Churches in defect of
ours, and either pray with them, or for them. I could never perceive
any rational Consequence from those many Texts which prohibit the
Children of Israel to pollute themselves with the Temples of the
Heathens; we being all Christians, and not divided by such detested
impieties as might prophane our Prayers, or the place wherein we
make them; or that a resolved Conscience may not adore her Creator
any where, especially in places devoted to His Service; where, if *their*
Devotions offend Him, mine may please Him; if theirs prophane it,
mine may hallow it. Holy-water and Crucifix (dangerous to the
common people,) deceive not my judgment, nor abuse my devotion
at all. I am, I confess, naturally inclined to that which misguided
Zeal terms *Superstition*. My common conversation I do acknowledge
austere, my behaviour full of rigour, sometimes not without
morosity; yet at my Devotion I love to use the civility of my knee,

my hat, and hand, with all those outward and sensible motions which may express or promote my invisible Devotion. I should violate my own arm rather than a Church; nor willingly deface the name of Saint or Martyr. At the sight of a Cross or Crucifix I can dispense with my hat, but scarce with the thought or memory of my Saviour. I cannot laugh at, but rather pity, the fruitless journeys of Pilgrims, or contemn the miserable conditions of Fryars; for, though misplaced in Circumstances, there is something in it of Devotion. I could never hear the Ave-Mary Bell without an elevation; or think it a sufficient warrant, because *they* erred in one circumstance, for me to err in all, that is, in silence and dumb contempt. Whilst, therefore, they directed their Devotions to *Her*, I offered mine to GOD, and rectified the Errors of their Prayers by rightly ordering mine own. At a solemn Procession I have wept abundantly, while my consorts, blind with opposition and prejudice, have fallen into an excess of scorn and laughter. There are, questionless, both in Greek, Roman, and African Churches, Solemnities and Ceremonies, whereof the wiser Zeals do make a Christian use, and stand condemned by us, not as evil in themselves, but as allurements and baits of superstition to those vulgar heads that look asquint on the face of Truth, and those unstable Judgments that cannot consist in the narrow point and centre of Virtue without a reel or stagger to the Circumference.

Thomas Browne, *Religio Medici* (1642)

Letter to Francis Atterbury

20 November 1717

Your Lordship has formerly advis'd me to read the best controversies between the Churches. Shall I tell you a secret? I did so at fourteen years old, for I loved reading, and my father had no other books. There was a collection of all that had been written on both sides in the reign of King James the second: I warm'd my head with them, and the consequence was, that I found my self a Papist and a Protestant by turns, according to the last book I read. I am afraid most Seekers are in the same case, and when they stop, they are not so properly converted, as out-witted. You see how little glory you would gain by my conversion. And after all, I verily believe your Lordship and I are both of the same religion, if we were thoroughly understood by one another; and that all honest and reasonable christians would be so, if they did but talk enough together every day; and had nothing to do together, but to serve God and live in peace with their neighbour.

As to the *temporal* side of the question, I can have no dispute with you. It is certain, all the beneficial circumstances of life, and all the shining ones, lie on that part you would invite me to. But if I could bring myself to fancy, what I think you do but fancy, that I have any talents for active life, I want health for it; and besides it is a real truth, I have less Inclination (if possible) than Ability. Contemplative life is not only my scene, but it is my habit too. I begun my life where most people end theirs, with a dis-relish of all that the world calls Ambition: I don't know why 'tis call'd so, for to me it always seem'd to be rather *stooping* than *climbing*. I'll tell you my politick and religious sentiments in a few words. In my politicks, I think no further than how to preserve the peace of my life, in any government under which I live; nor in my religion, than to preserve the peace of my conscience in any Church with which I communicate. I hope all churches and all governments are so far of God, as they are rightly understood, and rightly administer'd: and where they are, or may be wrong, I leave it to God alone to mend or reform them; which whenever he does, it must be by greater instruments than I am. I am not a Papist, for I renounce the temporal invasions of the Papal power, and detest their arrogated authority over Princes, and States. I am a Catholick, in the strictest sense of the word. If I was born under an absolute Prince, I would be a quiet subject; but I thank God I was not. I have a due sense of the excellence of the British constitution. In a word, the things I have always wished to see are not a Roman Catholick, or a French Catholick, or a Spanish Catholick, but a true Catholick: and not a King of Whigs, or a King of Tories, but a King of England. Which God of his mercy grant his present Majesty may be and all future Majesties! You see, my Lord, I end like a preacher: but this is *Sermo ad Clerum* not *ad Populum*. Believe me, with infinite obligation and sincere thanks, ever

Your, &c.

Alexander Pope, *Letters* (1946)

The difference between Presbyterians and RCs

I had hired a Bohemian as my servant while I remained in London, and being much pleased with him, I asked Dr Johnson whether his being a Roman Catholick should prevent my taking him with me to Scotland. JOHNSON. 'Why no, Sir. If *he* has no objection, you can have none.' BOSWELL. 'So, Sir, you are no great enemy to the Roman Catholick Religion.' JOHNSON. 'No more, Sir, than to the Presbyterian religion.' BOSWELL. 'You are joking.' JOHNSON. 'No, Sir, I really think so. Nay, Sir, of the two, I prefer the Popish.' BOSWELL. 'How so, Sir?' JOHNSON. 'Why, Sir, the Presbyterians have no church, no apostolical ordination.' BOSWELL. 'And do you think that absolutely essential, Sir?' JOHNSON. 'Why, Sir, as it was an apostolical institution, I think it is dangerous to be without it. And, Sir, the Presbyterians have no publick worship: they have no form of prayer in which they know they are to join. They go to hear a man pray, and are to judge whether they will join with him.' BOSWELL. 'But, Sir, their doctrine is the same with that of the Church of England. Their confession of faith, and the thirty-nine articles contain the same points, even the doctrine of predestination.' JOHNSON. 'Why, yes, Sir; predestination was a part of the clamour of the times, so it is mentioned in our articles, but with as little positiveness as could be.' BOSWELL. 'Is it necessary, Sir, to believe all the thirty-nine articles?' JOHNSON. 'Why, Sir, that is a question which has been much agitated. Some have thought it necessary that they should all be believed; others have considered them to be only articles of peace, that is to say, you are not to preach against them.' BOSWELL. 'It appears to me, Sir, that predestination, or what is equivalent to it, cannot be avoided, if we hold an universal prescience in the Deity.' JOHNSON. 'Why, Sir, does not GOD every day see things going on without preventing them?' BOSWELL. 'True, Sir, but if a thing be *certainly* foreseen, it must be fixed, and cannot happen otherwise; and if we apply this consideration to the human mind, there is no free will, nor do I see how prayer can be of any avail.' He mentioned Dr Clarke, and Bishop Bramhall on Liberty and Necessity, and bid me read South's Sermons on Prayer; but avoided the question which has excruciated philosophers and divines, beyond any other. I did not press it further, when I perceived that he was displeased, and shrunk from any abridgement of an attribute usually ascribed to the Divinity, however irreconcileable in its full extent with the grand system of moral government. His supposed orthodoxy here cramped the vigorous powers of his understanding. He was confined by a chain which early imagination and long habit made him think massy and strong, but which, had he ventured to try, he could at once have snapt asunder.

I proceeded: 'What do you think, Sir, of Purgatory, as believed by the Roman Catholicks?' JOHNSON. 'Why, Sir, it is a very harmless doctrine. They are of opinion that the generality of mankind are neither so obstinately wicked as to deserve everlasting punishment, nor so good as to merit being admitted into the society of blessed spirits; and therefore that GOD is graciously pleased to allow of a middle state, where they may be purified by certain degrees of suffering. You see, Sir, there is nothing unreasonable in this.' BOSWELL. 'But then, Sir, their Masses for the dead?' JOHNSON. 'Why, Sir, if it be once established that there are souls in purgatory, it is as proper to pray for *them*, as for our brethren of mankind who are yet in this life.' BOSWELL. 'The idolatry of the Mass?' JOHNSON. 'Sir, there is no idolatry in the Mass. They believe GOD to be there, and they adore him.' BOSWELL. 'The worship of Saints?' JOHNSON. 'Sir, they do not worship saints; they invoke them; they only ask their prayers. I am talking all this time of the *doctrines* of the Church of Rome. I grant you that in *practice*, Purgatory is made a lucrative imposition, and that the people do become idolatrous as they recommend themselves to the tutelary protection of particular saints. I think their giving the sacrament only in one kind is criminal, because it is contrary to the express institution of CHRIST, and I wonder how the Council of Trent admitted it.' BOSWELL. 'Confession?' JOHNSON. 'Why, I don't know but that is a good thing. The scripture says, "Confess your faults one to another," and the priests confess as well as the laity. Then it must be considered that their absolution is only upon repentance, and often upon penance also. You think your sins may be forgiven without penance, upon repentance alone.'

I thus ventured to mention all the common objections against the Roman Catholick Church, that I might hear so great a man upon them. What he said is here accurately recorded. But it is not improbable that if one had taken the other side, he might have reasoned differently.

James Boswell, *The Life of Samuel Johnson* (1791)

The Newcomes

When his father married, Mr Thomas Newcome, jun., and Sarah his nurse were transported from the cottage where they had lived in great comfort, to the palace hard by, surrounded by lawns and gardens, pineries, graperies, aviaries, luxuries of all kinds. This paradise, five miles from the standard at Cornhill, was separated from the outer world by a thick hedge of tall trees, and an ivy-covered porter's gate, through which they who travelled to London on the top of the Clapham coach could only get a glimpse of the bliss within. It was a serious paradise. As you entered at the gate gravity fell on you, and decorum wrapped you in a garment of starch. The butcher-boy who galloped his horse and cart madly about the adjoining lanes and common, whistled wild melodies (caught up in abominable play-house galleries), and joked with a hundred cook-maids, on passing that lodge fell into an undertaker's pace, and delivered his joints and sweet-breads silently at the servants' entrance. The rooks in the elms cawed sermons at morning and evening; the peacocks walked demurely on the terraces; the guinea-fowls looked more Quaker-like than those savoury birds usually do. The lodge-keeper was serious, and a clerk at a neighbouring chapel. The pastors who entered at that gate, and greeted his comely wife and children, fed the little lambkins with tracts. The head-gardener was a Scotch Calvinist, after the strictest order, only occupying himself with the melons and pines provisionally, and until the end of the world, which event he could prove by infallible calculations was to come off in two or three years at farthest. Wherefore, he asked, should the butler brew strong ale to be drunken three years hence; or the housekeeper (a follower of Joanna Southcote) make provisions of fine linen and lay up stores of jams? On a Sunday (which good old Saxon word was scarcely known at the Hermitage), the household marched away in separate couples or groups to at least half a dozen of religious edifices, each to sit under his or her favourite minister, the only man who went to church being Thomas Newcome, accompanied by Tommy, his little son, and Sarah his nurse, who was, I believe, also his aunt, or at least his mother's first cousin. Tommy was taught hymns very soon after he could speak, appropriate to his tender age, pointing out to him the inevitable fate of wicked children, and giving him the earliest possible warning and description of the punishment of little sinners. He repeated these poems to his step-mother after dinner, before a great, shining mahogany table covered with grapes, pine-apples, plum-cake, port wine, and Madeira, and surrounded by stout men in black, with baggy white neckcloths, who took the little man between their knees, and questioned him as to his right understanding of the place whither naughty boys were bound. They patted his head with their fat hands if he said well, or rebuked him if he was bold, as he often was.

'W. M. Thackeray, *The Newcomes* (1853–5)

Sir Walter Scott's last days

On the morning of Sunday the 15th, he was again taken out into the little *pleasaunce*, and got as far as his favourite terrace-walk between the garden and the river, from which he seemed to survey the valley and the hills with much satisfaction. On re-entering the house, he desired me to read to him from the New Testament, and after that he again called for a little of Crabbe; but whatever I selected from that poet seemed to be listened to as if it made part of some new volume published while he was in Italy. He attended with this sense of novelty even to the tale of Phœbe Dawson, which not many months before he could have repeated every line of, and which I chose for one of these readings, because, as is known to every one, it had formed the last solace of Mr Fox's deathbed. On the contrary, his recollection of whatever I read from the Bible appeared to be lively; and in the afternoon, when we made his grandson, a child of six years, repeat some of Dr Watts' hymns by his chair, he seemed also to remember them perfectly. That evening he heard the Church service, and when I was about to close the book, said – 'Why do you omit the visitation for the sick?' – which I added accordingly.

On Monday he remained in bed, and seemed extremely feeble; but after breakfast on Tuesday the 17th he appeared revived somewhat, and was again wheeled about on the turf. Presently he fell asleep in his chair, and after dozing for perhaps half an hour, started awake, and shaking the plaids we had put about him from off his shoulders, said – 'This is sad idleness. I shall forget what I have been thinking of, if I don't set it down now. Take me into my own room, and fetch the keys of my desk.' He repeated this so earnestly, that we could not refuse; his daughters went into his study, opened his writing-desk, and laid paper and pens in the usual order, and I then moved him through the hall and into the spot where he had always been accustomed to work. When the chair was placed at the desk, and he found himself in the old position, he smiled and thanked us, and said – 'Now give me my pen, and leave me for a little to myself.' Sophia put the pen into his hand, and he endeavoured to close his fingers upon it, but they refused their office – it dropped on the paper. He sank back among his pillows, silent tears rolling down his cheeks; but composing himself by and by, motioned to me to wheel him out of doors again. Laidlaw met us at the porch, and took his turn of the chair. Sir Walter, after a little while, again dropt into slumber. When he was awaking, Laidlaw said to me – 'Sir Walter has had a little repose.' – 'No, Willie,' said he – 'no repose for Sir Walter but in the grave.' The tears again rushed from his eyes. 'Friends,' said he, 'don't let me expose myself – get me to bed – that's the only place.'

With this scene ended our glimpse of daylight. Sir Walter never, I think, left his room afterwards, and hardly his bed, except for an hour or two in the middle of the day; and after another week he was unable even for this. During a few days he was in a state of painful irritation – and I saw realized all that he had himself prefigured in his description of the meeting between Crystal Croftangry and his paralytic friend. Dr Ross came out from Edinburgh, bringing with him his wife, one of the dearest *nieces* of the Clerks' table. Sir Walter with some difficulty recognised the Doctor – but, on hearing Mrs Ross's voice, exclaimed at once – 'Isn't that Kate Hume?' These kind friends remained for two or three days with us. Clarkson's lancet was pronounced necessary, and the relief it afforded was, I am happy to say, very effectual.

After this he declined daily, but still there was great strength to be wasted, and the process was long. He seemed, however, to suffer no bodily pain – and his mind, though hopelessly obscured, appeared, when there was any symptom of consciousness, to be dwelling, with rare exceptions, on serious and solemn things; the accent of the voice grave, sometimes awful, but never querulous, and very seldom indicative of any angry or resentful thoughts. Now and then he imagined himself to be administering justice as Sheriff; and once or twice he seemed to be ordering Tom Purdie about trees... But commonly whatever we could follow him in was a fragment of the

Bible (especially the Prophecies of Isaiah, and the Book of Job) – or some petition in the litany – or a verse of some psalm (in the old Scotch metrical version) – or of some of the magnificent hymns of the Romish ritual, in which he had always delighted, but which probably hung on his memory now in connexion with the Church servies he had attended while in Italy. We very often heard distinctly the cadence of the *Dies Iræ*; and I think the very last *stanza* that we could make out, was the first of a still greater favourite:

> 'Stabat Mater dolorosa,
> Juxta crucem lachrymosa,
> Dum pendebat Filius.'

. . . Perceiving, towards the close of August, that the end was near, and thinking it very likely that Abbotsford might soon undergo many changes, and myself, at all events, never see it again, I felt a desire to have some image preserved of the interior apartments as occupied by their founder, and invited from Edinburgh for that purpose Sir Walter's dear friend, William Allan – whose presence, I well knew, would even under the circumstances of that time be nowise troublesome to any of the family, but the contrary in all respects. Mr Allan willingly complied, and executed a series of beautiful drawings. He also shared our watchings, and witnessed all but the last moments. Sir Walter's cousins, the ladies of Ashestiel, came down frequently, for a day or two at a time; and did whatever sisterly affections could prompt, both for the sufferer and his daughters. Miss Mary Scott (daughter of his uncle Thomas), and Mrs Scott of Harden, did the like.

As I was dressing on the morning of Monday the 17th of September, Nicolson came into my room, and told me that his master had awoke in a state of composure and consciousness, and wished to see me immediately. I found him entirely himself, though in the last extreme of feebleness. His eye was clear and calm – every trace of the wild fire of delirium extinguished. 'Lockhart,' he said, 'I may have but a minute to speak to you. My dear, be a good man – be virtuous – be religious – be a good man. Nothing else will give you any comfort when you come to lie here.' – He paused, and I said – 'Shall I send for Sophie and Anne?' – 'No,' said he, 'don't disturb them. Poor souls! I know they were up all night – God bless you all.' – With this he sunk into a very tranquil sleep, and, indeed, he scarcely afterwards gave any sign of consciousness, except for an instant on the arrival of his sons – They, on learning that the scene was about to close, obtained anew leave of absence from their posts, and both reached Abbotsford on the 19th. About half-past one P.M. on the 21st of September, Sir Walter breathed his last, in the presence of all his children. It was a beautiful day – so warm, that every window was wide open – and so perfectly still, that the sound of all others most delicious to his ear, the gentle ripple of the Tweed over its pebbles, was distinctly audible as we knelt around the bed, and his eldest son kissed and closed his eyes.'

J. G. Lockhart, *The Life of Sir Walter Scott* (1840)

Gladstone at prayer

On 26 December, 1888, when the Gladstones were staying for two months with the George Rendels at their villa in Naples, Gladstone argued after dinner that occasional drunkenness, when it was solely due to 'social feeling and temptation', deserved to be treated with indulgence. Later that evening, Gladstone sat alone reading a theological book in German by Dollinger, in a small study which had been fitted up for him by his host. Stuart Rendel, watching his brother's guest through a chink in the door, could see the book firmly held up to the candle. Unwilling to go to bed before the guest, Rendel was making up his mind to disturb Gladstone, when he suddenly noticed the great arch of Gladstone's head so situated that it was obvious that he had dropped on to his knees, and was deep in prayer, bending low over the seat of the arm-chair in which he had been reading. Ten minutes passed, while Rendel waited, and then the light suddenly disappeared. Gladstone had slipped out by another door, 'shunning, I suppose,' Rendel noted, 'any break in his thoughts and acts by his usual bidding of me goodnight.'

Philip Magnus, *Gladstone* (1954)

General Gordon

Except for his boys and his paupers, he lived alone. In his solitude, he ruminated upon the mysteries of the universe; and those religious tendencies, which had already shown themselves, now became a fixed and dominating factor in his life. His reading was confined almost entirely to the Bible; but the Bible he read and re-read with an untiring, an unending, assiduity. There, he was convinced, all truth was to be found; and he was equally convinced that he could find it. The doubts of philosophers, the investigations of commentators, the smiles of men of the world, the dogmas of Churches – such things meant nothing to the Colonel. Two facts alone were evident: there was the Bible, and there was himself; and all that remained to be done was for him to discover what were the Bible's instructions, and to act accordingly. In order to make this discovery it was only necesssary for him to read the Bible over and over again; and therefore, for the rest of his life, he did so.

The faith that he evolved was mystical and fatalistic; it was also highly unconventional. His creed, based upon the narrow foundations of Jewish Scripture, eked out occasionally by some English evangelical manual, was yet wide enough to ignore every doctrinal difference, and even, at moments to transcend the bounds of Christianity itself.

Lytton Strachey, *Eminent Victorians* (1918)

'Tea or Eucharist, Sir?'

I suppose Halifax is the perfect example of the wealthy high church layman who has today almost disappeared from the ecclesiastical scene. He even took a chaplain with him on his honeymoon and for the Oxford Movement Centenary in 1933 when he was a very old man had a great altar pavilion designed and built in his garden at enormous cost for a single High Mass. It is said that if you were staying at Hickleton you were called in the morning by the butler who said: 'Tea or Eucharist, Sir?'

Colin Stephenson, *Merrily on High* (1971)

Butlin's holiday camp

25 September 1955
Butlin's was quite fun; rather like a visit to the moon, quite out of this world. Absurd, of course, for an adult, but having the two children made it fun; they loved every minute of it. One unexpected

thing was the little camp church, Anglican, with a chaplain of great geniality to one and all; Mass every day at 7.30 and 8.30, to which I went (at 8.30), and it was very well attended. A radio voice announced each morning at 7.29, 'In one minute there will be a celebration of Holy Communion in the camp church.' Disgusted and sleepy voice from the chalet on my left, '*What* an entertainment!' We all slept in nice little chalets in a row, or rather in many rows, for there were about 500 campers at a time. We had swimming pools (but I bathed in the sea myself) and every kind of game and diversion, and my younger charge, who is pony-mad, rode every day and helped to groom the horses. There was a repertory company, which acted exciting dramas, and television, which I saw for the first time and didn't think much of. Why is it so popular? One programme, which showed a panel of 4 famous people in a game of guessing 'Who wrote that?' to my surprise quoted something from me (but I don't know where I said it) – something about 'it is to the eccentrics that the world owes most of its knowledge'; no one guessed me; when they were told, they had to discuss its truth or otherwise, and on the whole agreed with me. My two children were delighted by this . . . By the way, on the way back (in the car) from Skegness, we turned aside to look at Yaxley church and village (Hunts). I wondered if that was *your* Yaxley, or is yours the one in Suffolk? It was a beautiful old church. There was no list of vicars, so I couldn't look for 'Johnson'. But I expect yours is Suffolk. However, I plucked a little flower from the graveyard and thought of you . . .

I am still being bombarded with little Catholic Truth pamphlets and long letters telling how I have no Mass, no sacraments, no priests. How rude they are! Imagine if I started writing in that vein to, say, Methodists. They are so stuck up and arrogant. Of course nothing *could* be so true as they think their Church is . . . I answered one of these priests who write to me that I thought Christians should tolerate one another's religions, and I was glad *they* had sacraments and thought they ought to be glad that I thought *I* had. The chaplain at Butlin's welcomed everyone to Communion – Church, Chapel, or whatever – though he was definitely Anglo-Catholic in his rites. That's the Christian spirit, surely. Imagine what our Lord would have said.

Rose Macaulay, *More Letters to a Friend* (1964)

Things you can do in London

Things you can do in London: Austerity meal (with wine) at St
Alban's Holborn.

Barbara Pym, A Very Private Eye (1985)

Doggerel by a Senior Citizen
for Robert Lederer

... *The Book of Common Prayer* we knew
Was that of 1662:
Though with-it sermons may be well,
Liturgical reforms are hell.

W. H. Auden (1969)

Tom Driberg

Over dinner Boothby told with great glee a wonderful story concerning Tom Driberg. Driberg, Boothby and Lady Violet Bonham-Carter
were all scheduled to take part in an *Any Questions?* programme in
the West Country on Good Friday. Boothby had thought the sensible
thing to do was for him to drive the other two down by car. He
telephoned Driberg to finalise the arrangements but Driberg was
appalled that Lady Violet should be travelling with them.

'Why do we have to have her with us, Bob?' Driberg protested. 'If
she *is* there it means I can't talk to you. And I want to talk to you.
I want to tell you about this marvellous new boyfriend of mine.' I
was told subsequently that the new boyfriend was American singer
Johnny Ray. 'It is the most wonderful thing that has ever happened
to me. I must talk to you about him.'

Whereupon Boothby, according to Boothby, said that he couldn't
possibly go back on his arrangement to give Lady Violet a lift and
that Driberg would just have to keep silent on the subject of his
boyfriend.

On the Friday morning on their way down to the West Country,
they were passing through a village when Driberg saw a church and
shouted, 'Stop, Bob! I want to go into that church. I want to make
the Stations of the Cross.'

Boothby stopped the car. And Driberg went into the church leaving Boothby and Lady Violet Bonham-Carter sitting twiddling their thumbs. But it was what Driberg said to them when finally he emerged from the church that had Boothby rocking with laughter.

'You may like to know,' Driberg said, 'that I have said a prayer for both of you.'

John Junor, *Listening for a Midnight Tram* (1990)

[19]

DOUBT

So many of those who have wrestled with the Christian faith, and produced the most devastating arguments against it, have done so from a Christian background. Those like A. J. Ayer or Bertrand Russell who devoted their lives to attacking Christianity from a position firmly outside the fold, perhaps made less imaginative impact than those, like Stevie Smith and Thomas Hardy, who saw the attractiveness of faith, and – in a *way* – loved the Church, while being unable to accept its teachings. It is often said that doubt is part of the life of faith – and that those who have not seen, but yet have believed, are more blessed than those who *have* seen. With such thoughts I have compiled a very short section on 'Doubt', knowing that for some doubters (Hardy was surely one such) it is hard to leave church behind even though he knew

> That with this bright believing band
> I have no claim to be . . .

Bible Christianity

There is something touchingly beautiful in the passion with which English and American Protestant divines cling to the letter of the Bible. It is an unconscious perception that in this Book, in some form or other, lies the solution of the enigma of existence. Their fault has been that they have assumed without reason that, while the truth is there, any one who can read will find it there; that it is as intelligible to the unlearned as the learned. They have seen in the Bible the meaning which their eyes brought with them. They have, I repeat, made the Bible into an idol. Their theories, being the work of their own minds, mortal like themselves, though dignified by the name of eternal verities, recoil on them, as superstitions always recoil, through the natural expansion of knowledge. The ground slips under their feet; religion loses its grasp. Materialism takes hold of philosophy; corruption takes hold of politics; speculative money-making and vulgar ambition, of the individual souls of the millions. They look on bewildered and helpless, while the Popery, which had been lying so long prostrate under the blows of the Reformation, lifts its unsightly limbs out of the grave, walks erect, and flings its shadow over the world once more.

J. A. Froude, *Short Studies of Great Subjects* (1867–83)

F. D. Maurice

I loved Frederick Maurice, as every one did who came near him; and have no doubt he did all that was in him to do of good in his day. Which could by no means be said either of Rossetti or of me; but Maurice was by nature puzzle-headed, and, though in a beautiful manner, *wrong*-headed; while his clear conscience and keen affections made him egotistic, and in his Bible-reading, as insolent as any infidel of them all. I only went once to a Bible-lesson of his; and the meeting was significant, and conclusive.

The subject of lesson, Jael's slaying of Sisera. Concerning which, Maurice, taking an enlightened modern view of what was fit and not, discoursed in passionate indignation; and warned his class, in the most positive and solemn manner, that such dreadful deeds could only have been done in cold blood in the Dark Biblical ages; and that no religious and patriotic Englishwoman ought ever to think of imitating Jael by nailing a Russian's or Prussian's skull to the ground – especially after giving him butter in a lordly dish. At the close of the instruction, through which I sate silent, I ventured to enquire, why then had Deborah the prophetess declared of Jael, 'Blessed above women shall the wife of Heber the Kenite be'? On which Maurice, with startled and flashing eyes, burst into partly scornful, partly alarmed, denunciation of Deborah the prophetess, as a mere blazing

Amazon; and of her Song as a merely rhythmic storm of battle-rage, no more to be listened to with edification or faith than the Norman's sword-song at the battle of Hastings.

Whereupon there remained nothing for *me* – to whom the Song of Deborah was as sacred as the Magnificat – but total collapse in sorrow and astonishment; the eyes of all the class being also bent on me in amazed reprobation of my benighted views, and unchristian sentiments. And I got away how I could, and never went back.

That being the first time in my life that I had fairly met the lifted head of Earnest and Religious Infidelity – in a man neither vain nor ambitious, but instinctively and innocently trusting his own amiable feelings as the final interpreters of all the possible feelings of men and angels, all the songs of the prophets, and all the ways of God.

John Ruskin, *Præterita* (1886–9)

How do you see?

How do you see the Holy Spirit of God?
I see him as the holy spirit of good,
But I do not think we should talk about spirits, I think
We should call good, good.

But it is a beautiful idea, is it not?
And productive of good?

Yes, that is the problem, it is productive of good,
As Christianity now is productive of good,
So that a person who does not believe the Christian faith
Feels he must keep silent, in case good suffers,
In case what good there is in the world diminishes.

But must we allow good to be hitched to a lie,
A beautiful cruel lie, a beautiful fairy story,
A beautiful idea, made up in a loving moment?

Yes, it is a beautiful idea, one of the most
Beautiful ideas Christianity has ever had,
This idea of the Spirit of God, the Holy Ghost,
My heart goes out to this beautiful Holy Ghost,
He is so beautifully inhuman, he is like the fresh air.

They represent him as a bird, I dislike that,
A bird is parochial to our world, rooted as we are
in pain and cruelty. Better the fresh air.

But before we take a Christian idea to alter it
We should look what the idea is, we should read in their books
Of holy instruction what the Christians say. What do they say
Of the beautiful Holy Ghost? They say

That the beautiful Holy Ghost brooded on chaos
And chaos gave birth to form. As this we cannot know
It can only be beautiful if told as a fairy story,
Told as a fact it is harmful, for it is not a fact.

But it is a beautiful fairy story. I feel so much
The pleasure of the bird on the dark and powerful waters,
And here I like to think of him as a bird, I like to feel
The masterful bird's great pleasure in his breast
Touching the water. Like! Like! What else do they say?

Oh I know we must put away the beautiful fairy stories
And learn to be good in a dull way without enchantment,
Yes, we must. What else do they say? They say

That the beautiful Holy Spirit burning intensely,
Alight as never was anything in this world alight,
Inspired the scriptures. But they are wrong,
Often the scriptures are wrong. For I see the Pope
Has forbidden the verse in Mark ever to be discussed again
And I see a doctor of Catholic divinity saying
That some verses in the New Testament are pious forgeries
Interpolated by eager clerks avid for good.

Ah good, what is good, is it good
To leave in scripture the spurious verses and not print
A footnote to say they are spurious, an erratum slip?

And the penal sentences of Christ: He that believeth
And is baptized shall be saved, he that believeth not
Shall be damned. Depart from me ye cursed into everlasting fire
Prepared for the devil and his angels. And then

Saddest of all the worlds in scripture, the words,
They went away into everlasting punishment. Is this good?

Yes, nowadays certainly it is very necessary before we take
The ideas of Christianity, the words of our Lord,
To make them good, when often they are not very good,
To see what the ideas are and the words; to look at them.

Does the beautiful Holy Ghost endorse the doctrine of eternal hell?
Love cruelty, enjoin the sweet comforts of religion?
Oh yes, Christianity, yes, he must do this
For he is your God, and in your books

You say he informs, gives form, gives life, instructs.
Instructs, that is the bitterest part. For what does he instruct
As to the dreadful bargain, that God would take and offer
The death of the Son to buy our faults away,
The faults of the faulty creatures of the Trinity?
Oh Christianity, instructed by the Holy Ghost,
What do you mean? As to Christ, what do you mean?

It was a child of Europe who cried this cry,
Oh Holy Ghost what do you mean as to Christ?
I heard him cry. Ah me, the poor child,
Tearing away his heart to be good
Without enchantment. I heard him cry:

Oh Christianity, Christianity,
Why do you not answer our difficulties?
If He was God He was not like us
He could not lose.

Can Perfection be less than perfection?
Can the creator of the Devil be bested by him?
What can the temptation to possess the earth have meant to Him
Who made and possessed it? What do you mean?

And Sin, how could He take our sins upon Him? What does it
    mean?
To take sin upon one is not the same
As to have sin inside one and feel guilty.

It is horrible to feel guilty,
We feel guilty because we are.
Was He horrible? Did He feel guilty?

You say He was born humble – but He was not,
He was born God –

Taking our nature upon Him. But then you say
He was perfect Man. Do you mean
Perfectly Man, meaning wholly? Or Man without sin? Ah
Perfect Man without sin is not what we are.

Do you mean He did not know that He was God,
Did not know He was the Second Person of the Trinity?
(Oh if He knew this and was,
It was a source of strength for Him we do not have)
But this theology of emptying you preach sometimes –
That He emptied Himself of knowing He was God – seems
A theology of false appearances
To mock your facts, as He was God whether He knew it or not.

Oh what do you mean, what do you mean?
You never answer our difficulties.

You say, Christianity, you say
That the Trinity is unchanging from eternity,
But then you say
At the incarnation He took
Our Manhood into the Godhead
That did not have it before,
So it must have altered it,
Having it.

Oh what do you mean, what do you mean?
You never answer our questions.

So I heard the child of Europe cry,
Tearing his heart away
To be good without enchantment,
Going away bleeding.

Oh how sad it is to give up the Holy Ghost
He is so beautiful, but not when you look close,

And the consolations of religion are so beautiful,
But not when you look close.
Is it beautiful, for instance, is it productive of good
That the Roman Catholic hierarchy should be endlessly discussing
  at this moment
Their shifty theology of birth control, the Vatican
Claiming the inspiration of the Holy Spirit? No, it is not good,
Or productive of good. It is productive
Of contempt and disgust. Yet
On the whole Christianity I suppose is kinder than it was,
Helped to it, I fear, by the power of the Civil Arm.

Oh Christianity, Christianity,
That has grown kinder now, as in the political world
The colonial system grows kinder before it vanishes, are you
  vanishing?
Is it not time for you to vanish?

I do not think we shall be able to bear much longer the dishonesty
Of clinging for comfort to beliefs we do not believe in,
For comfort, and to be comfortably free of the fear
Of diminishing good, as if truth were a convenience.
I think if we do not learn quickly, and learn to teach children,
To be good without enchantment, without the help
Of beautiful painted fairy stories pretending to be true,
Then I think it will be too much for us, the dishonesty,
And, armed as we are now, we shall kill everybody,
It will be too much for us, we shall kill everybody.

Stevie Smith, Collected Poems (1975)

Death and Judgement

I was much about this time tempted to content myself, by receiving
some false Opinion; as that there should be no such thing as a Day
of Judgment, that we should not rise again, and that sin was no such
grievous thing. The Tempter suggesting thus, *For if these things
should indeed be true, yet to believe otherwise, would yield you ease
for the present. If you must perish, never torment yourself so much
beforehand, drive the thoughts of damning out of your mind, by*

possessing your mind with some such conclusions that Atheists *and* Ranters *use to help themselves withal.*

But Oh! when such thoughts have passed thorow my heart, how, as it were within a step hath Death and Judgement been in my view! Methought the Judge stood at the door, I was as if 'twas come already: so that such things could have no entertainment; but methinks I see by this, that Satan will use any means to keep the Soul from Christ. He loveth not an awakened frame of spirit, security, blindness, darkness, and error is the very kingdom and habitation of the Wicked one.

I found it hard work now to pray to God, because despair was swallowing me up. I thought I was as with a Tempest driven away from God, for always when I cried to God for mercy, this would come in, *'Tis too late; I am lost, God hath let me fall, not to my correction, but condemnation: My sin is unpardonable, and I know, concerning* Esau, *how that, after he had sold his Birth-right, he would have received the Blessing, but was rejected.*

John Bunyan, *Grace Abounding to the Chief of Sinners* (1666)

Mr Prendergast

'I expect you wonder how I came to be here?'

'No, no,' said Paul soothingly. 'I think it's very natural.'

'It's not natural at all; it's most unnatural. If things had happened a little differently I should be a rector with my own house and bathroom. I might even have been a rural dean, only' – and Mr Prendergast dropped his voice to a whisper – 'only I had *Doubts.*

'I don't know why I'm telling you all this, nobody else knows. I somehow feel you'll understand.

'Ten years ago I was a clergyman of the Church of England. I had just been presented to a living in Worthing. It was such an attractive church, not old, but *very* beautifully decorated, six candles on the altar, Reservation in the Lady Chapel, and an excellent heating apparatus which burned coke in a little shed by the sacristy door, no graveyard, just a hedge of golden privet between the church and the rectory.

'As soon as I moved in my mother came to keep house for me. She bought some chintz, out of her own money, for the drawing-room curtains. She used to be "at home" once a week to the ladies of the congregation. One of them, the dentist's wife, gave me a set of the *Encyclopædia Britannica* for my study. It was all very pleasant until my *Doubts* began.'

'Were they as bad as all that?' asked Paul.

'They were insuperable,' said Mr Prendergast; 'that is why I am here now. But I expect I am boring you?'

'No, do go on. That's to say, unless you find it painful to think about.'

'I think about it all the time. It happened like this, quite suddenly. We had been there about three months, and my mother had made great friends with some people called Bundle – rather a curious name. I think he was an insurance agent until he retired. Mrs Bundle used very kindly to ask us in to supper on Sundays after Evensong. They were pleasant informal gatherings, and I used quite to look forward to them. I can see them now as they sat there on this particular evening; there was my mother and Mr and Mrs Bundle, and their son, rather a spotty boy, I remember, who used to go in to Brighton College by train every day, and Mrs Bundle's mother, a Mrs Crump, rather deaf, but a very good Churchwoman, and Mrs Aber – that was the name of the dentist's wife who gave me the *Encyclopædia Britannica* – and old Major Ending, the people's warden. I had preached two sermons that day besides taking the children's Bible-class in the afternoon, and I had rather dropped out of the conversation. They were all talking away quite happily about the preparations that were being made on the pier for the summer season, when suddenly, for no reason at all, my *Doubts* began.' He paused, and Paul felt constrained to offer some expression of sympathy.

'What a terrible thing!' he said.

'Yes, I've not known an hour's real happiness since. You see, it wasn't the ordinary sort of Doubt about Cain's wife or the Old Testament miracles or the consecration of Archbishop Parker. I'd been taught how to explain all those while I was a college. No, it was something deeper than all that. *I couldn't understand why God had made the world at all.* There was my mother and the Bundles and Mrs Crump talking away quite unconcernedly while I sat there wrestling with this sudden assault of doubt. You see how fundamental that is. Once granted the first step, I can see that everything else follows – Tower of Babel, Babylonian captivity, Incarnation, Church, bishops, incense, everything – but what I couldn't see, and what I can't see now, is, *why* did it all begin?

'I asked my bishop; he didn't know. He said that he didn't think the point really arose as far as my practical duties as a parish priest were concerned. I discussed it with my mother. At first she was inclined to regard it as a passing phase. But it didn't pass, so finally she agreed with me that the only honourable thing to do was to resign my living; she never really recovered from the shock, poor lady. It was a great blow after she had bought the chintz and got so friendly with the Bundles.'

Evelyn Waugh, *Decline and Fall* (1928)

A London curate

When I began hearing confessions at All Saints I discovered that a considerable number of husbands and wives felt extremely guilty about using contraceptives. They felt it put them on the wrong side of the church and hence cut them off from God. On the other hand it could be a matter of fundamental difficulty, perhaps even a danger to their marriage itself, to give up the practice.

I was myself unmarried and aged only twenty-seven. I thought it therefore essential to obtain advice from those I imagined most competent to give it. I wrote to two or three priests who were known as experienced confessors, including Raymond Raynes. In the nature of the case they were all Anglo-Catholics and they all gave the same reply: No artificial contraception could be allowed; it was against nature and so on. Raymond Raynes, I remember, said that he fully understood the difficulties which this prohibition might cause, but difficulties in life were the occasions of receiving the grace of God; and who knew what wonders of grace might be achieved by the endurance of these difficulties in marriage?

My opinions thus fortified, I went ahead in the confessional laying down the law. I was sure I could answer any question. I had it all taped.

But after six or nine months I began to be more and more severely shaken by what I increasingly considered to be the quite unnecessary frustration and misery and guilt caused by this relentless rule. And the moment came when I could no longer enforce or advocate it. It seemed to me exactly the kind of thing to which Jesus was referring when he said of the pharisees that they bound heavy burdens and grievous to be borne and laid them upon men's shoulders. Then, after a short time, I found that I was advocating the opposite of the rule in a quite positive manner. What I mean is that if a husband or wife felt a burden of guilt about this matter, I used to tell them that by mentioning it they had laid the responsibility squarely on my shoulders and could now go ahead with a clear conscience, and that, if I were mistaken, and artificial contraception was wrong after all, the guilt would be entirely on my head not theirs.

Now, thirty-five or so years later, and in view of the attitude taken by the Anglican communion since the Lambeth Conference of 1958, this must seem very much a storm in a tea-cup. But it certainly wasn't at the time, least of all for the couples concerned.

Today I should take the view that if people are silly enough to allow their conduct to be dictated by a bunch of clergymen, then they deserve whatever comes to them. If you opt for being a church mouse, you must be prepared to take the consequences. But at the time the issue made a very big dent in the armour of the professional priest and lecturer in theology I was trying to be, because the human being I also was, and the child within me, began to hint and more than hint, that the clear-cut definitions in which I put so much trust might turn out to be broken reeds, and that the solid rock which was meant to keep people safe did, in fact, the opposite by crushing and destroying them.

Harry Williams, Some Day I'll Find You (1986)

Debating *Honest to God*

Monday 13 May 1963

This evening went to St Mary-le-Bow, Cheapside, for a meeting of the Christian Agnostics to hear the Bishop of Woolwich, John Robinson, talking about his book *Honest to God*, which we had gathered to discuss. The Reverend Joseph McCulloch has organized this group, justifying its name by reference to the line (from Oranges and Lemons) which runs: 'I do not know – says the great bell of Bow'.

At this gathering were Canon John Collins of St Paul's Cathedral, Father Corbishley (a Jesuit writer), George Dickson (an industrialist),

Duncan Fairn (who took the chair), Gerald Gardiner, Dr Graham Howe (the humanist psychiatrist), the Earl of Longford, Canon and Mrs Milford, Mrs J. B. Priestley and a number of others.

The Bishop opened by saying that secularism was not basically anti-Christian and that Christians must understand and even welcome the revolt against dualistic supernaturalism, the mythological view of the world and the religiosity of the Church. He said his book was designed to help those who were in revolt to see the basic validity of the Christian message.

Mrs Priestley asked him if he was right to leave the mythological Christians to go on in the old way. Woolwich said he thought if they wanted to believe this sort of thing he saw no objection to it.

Canon Collins asked about Christ's resurrection and the empty tomb. Woolwich replied that he really was an agnostic on this. He did not know.

Father Corbishley pointed out that the witnesses to the resurrection believed in physical resurrection. Woolwich said that of course they also believed in the physical ascension and no one now accepted that. Corbishley replied that Jesus had to leave the world somehow and he could see no difficulty in his ascending into a cloud (a splendid Jesuit view). Woolwich said that he thought the concept of Christ beginning a space journey was not very helpful.

Graham Howe asked if Woolwich was concerned with communicating Christ or communicating reality. He thought we must communicate in terms of experience. Resurrection is not within the experience of a congregation but the idea of death and the idea of fatherhood are within human experience. The trouble with the Church is that it's all mother and no father.

Duncan Fairn asked whether God was Love, or Love was God. Woolwich replied that for him personal relationships were everything and he deified them and believed that Christians should say that they are the most important things.

Corbishley said that you must have some sort of mythology because you were trying to unscrute the inscrutable.

I said that I found the book a flood of light because having visited Jerusalem and having seen the Church of the Holy Sepulchre and Christ's last footprint in the Chapel of the Ascension, it had added nothing for me. Similarly, having spent three hours in the anti-religious museum in Leningrad which had mocked Christian mythology and riddled the record of the Church, I found it had detracted nothing.

I welcomed the idea that we had the right to think for ourselves about Christ and were not bound to take it or leave it. The idea of depth instead of height reconciled Christianity with the scientific method and substituted understanding for magic. But since it would lead to a new conception of Christian political commitment, it would challenge the supernaturalists in the Church and divide the Church, and Woolwich must be ready for a battle. As he had said in his foreword he suspected that he should have gone much further.

Canon Collins asked whether Christ was perfect, for if he was he was then God. Woolwich replied that he wanted to write a book about Christ and that the Virgin birth made Christ seem unreal. Woolwich's interest in Christ lay in his normality, not his abnormality. He felt he could not make sweeping statements about Christ's moral life, for what was significant was his obedience. Collins replied that if you simply say Christ was 'the best man I know', Christianity could never get started.

We broke up for supper and resumed for another hour and a half. Later we had a much deeper discussion about the supernatural in which I had a long confrontation with Corbishley about whether the evidence for the supernatural came really from external manifestations or the discovery of hidden depths. Corbishley was splendidly Jesuitical in saying that you had to have mythology 'to get people to pray'. Here is the real nub of the question. Is prayer a duty or a need?

I attacked the double standard by which the in-group of Christians know that the mythology is bunk but they don't discuss it publicly for fear of offending the faithful. Moreover, if the maintenance of the idea of the supernatural is justified on the grounds of practical necessity, it must be judged by results. And by results it has failed to stem the rising tide of secularism.

Woolwich summed up briefly. He is really an academic with guts but he is coming under such heavy fire now that I wonder if he can stand up to the pressure. The Anglican hierarchy is beginning to sense that his vibrations may start an avalanche and ruin its plans for Christian unity. But then unity on those terms is death. I hope he has the courage to go on and see it through. *Honest to God* is certainly the most helpful Christian theology that I've ever come across and I'm sure millions of others feel the same.

Tony Benn, *Out of the Wilderness* (1987)

The Impercipient

(At a Cathedral Service)

That with this bright believing band
    I have no claim to be,
That faiths by which my comrades stand
    Seems fantasies to me,
And mirage-mists their Shining Land,
    Is a strange destiny.

Why thus my soul should be consigned
    To infelicity,
Why always I must feel as blind
    To sights my brethren see,
Why joys they've found I cannot find.
    Abides a mystery.

Since heart of mine knows not that ease
    Which they know; since it be
That He who breathes All's Well to these
    Breathes no All's Well to me,
My lack might move their sympathies
    And Christian charity!

I am like a gazer who should mark
    An inland company
Standing upfingered, with, 'Hark! hark!
    The glorious distant sea!'
And feel, 'Alas, 'tis but yon dark
    And wind-swept pine to me!'

Yet I would bear my shortcomings
    With meet tranquillity,
But for the charge that blessed things
    I'd liefer not have be.

DOUBT

O, doth a bird deprived of wings
  Go earth-bound wilfully!
    .   .   .   .   .

Enough. As yet disquiet clings
  About us. Rest shall we.

Thomas Hardy, *Wessex Poems* (1898)

[20]

THE CHRISTIAN YEAR

One of the pleasures of church membership derives from the manner in which each season of the year is matched by the unfolding liturgical cycle. As the clocks change, and the year grows dark, the Church contemplates the Advent of Christ into the world. Not long after the shortest day is Christmas, when we hear again that 'the people that walked in darkness have seen a great light'. In the crisp, austere days of February and March, Christian people observe Lent, the time traditionally associated with Christ's period of fasting in the wilderness. As the bulbs come up and burst into life, they commemorate Christ's resurrection. The coming of May coincides with the Feast of Ascension, when the sun is high in the sky. And then, some time in high summer, there is Trinity Sunday, after which stretch the long, twenty-five weeks when, as John Meade Falkner wrote in his poem,

> We have done with dogma and divinity
> East and Whitsun past,
> The long, long, Sundays after Trinity
> Are with us at last.

It is appropriate that one of the best-selling books of the last century was John Keble's cycle, *The Christian Year*, since it was the Victorians who recovered the sense of liturgical seasons. It was they, homesick for their rural past, as the great manufacturing cities expanded and grew, who invented the Harvest Festival, nowadays one of the most popular services in the entire calendar. As some of the extracts here show, there is probably much 'folk religion', if not actually the remnant of half-forgotten paganism, in such customs as dressing graves on Easter Day or Beating the Bounds at Ascensiontide; but that is part of the appeal of such customs. The Church is one of our greatest links with the past, and by marking these rituals we also refresh our sense, each year, not only of 'dogma and divinity' but also of our common heritage, and of our common belonging to the world of nature. This surely explains why so many townspeople, who seldom go to church, and who have never seen a plough, flock to church each autumn to sing,

'We plough the fields and scatter
The good seed on the land!'

Hallow-tide

And now here we are in Hallow-tide. This morning Mass was very glorious and moving (to me) – one somehow felt the dim, candled chapel was full of the hallows, listening and joining. I do so love that introit 'Rejoice we all in the Lord, keeping holy day in honour of all the hallows, in whose solemnity the angels rejoice, and glorify the Son of God.'* I like it better, really, than in Latin – perhaps because of that lovely old English word 'hallows', which comes with its associations of poetry and ancient prose: 'the blessed company of hallows', 'Christ shall come, with all his hallows'. I even like the oath 'by all the hallows'. A pity it is gone out, except in All Hallows, Hallow E'en, Hallow-tide, etc. I think I shall swear 'by the Hallows' occasionally. Did you know that 'halibut' means 'holy flat-fish', because eaten on holy days ('butt' = flat-fish)? Well, anyhow, I like our version of that introit even better than the Latin 'sanctorum omnium',† though here you won't agree, I fancy. If we met, it would be interesting to go through a great number of the ancient Latin prayers and English translations, comparing the merits of each one. I think honours are about even; but I know you don't, being a more inveterate Latinist, and possibly less devoted to the 16th and 17th [century] vagaries and beauties of English? I don't mean you're *not* – only that I believe I have a very special doting on our language and its old modes.

* Introit for the Feast of All Saints.
† 'Of all the saints [or 'hallows'].'

Rose Macaulay, *Letters to a Friend* (1962)

A nocturnall upon S. Lucies day, Being the shortest day

Tis the yeares midnight, and it is the dayes,
Lucies, who scarce seaven houres herself unmaskes,
  The Sunne is spent, and now his flasks
  Send forth light squibs, no constant rayes;
    The worlds whole sap is sunke:
The generall balme th'hydroptique earth hath drunk,
Whither, as to the beds-feet, life is shrunke,
Dead and enterr'd; yet all these seem to laugh,
Compar'd with mee, who am their Epitaph.

Study me then, you who shall lovers bee
At the next world, that is, at the next Spring:
  For I am every dead thing,
  In whom love wrought new Alchimie.
    For his art did expresse
A quintessence even from nothingnesse,
From dull privations, and leane emptinesse:
He ruin'd mee, and I am re-begot
Of absence, darknesse, death; things which are not.

All others, from all things, draw all that's good,
Life, soule, forme, spirit, whence they beeing have;
  I, by loves limbecke, am the grave
  Of all, that's nothing. Oft a flood
    Have wee two wept, and so
Drowned the whole world, us two; oft did we grow
To be two Chaosses, when we did show
Care to ought else; and often absences
Withdrew our soules, and made us carcasses.

But I am by her death (which word wrongs her)
Of the first nothing, the Elixer grown;
  Were I a man, that I were one,
  I needs must know; I should preferre,
    If I were any beast,
Some ends, some means; Yea plants, yea stones detest,
And love; All, all some properties invest;

If I an ordinary nothing were,
As shadow, a light, and body must be here.

But I am None; nor will my Sunne renew.
You lovers, for whose sake, the lesser Sunne
 At this time to the Goat is runne
 To fetch new lust, and give it you,
  Enjoy your summer all;
Since shee enjoyes her long nights festivall,
Let mee prepare towards her, and let mee call
This houre her Vigill, and her Eve, since this
Both the yeares, and the dayes deep midnight is.

John Donne (1572–1631), Songs and Sonnets

The Christmas play at St Hilary

The Christmas Play at St Hilary goes back so many years that I have almost forgotten its origin.

At the time I could find no play suitable to the place and the people who were to perform it. I wanted an act of worship rather than a performance, a return to the old miracle play which was performed either in the church or in some open space, such as the field known at St Hilary as the Plain-an-guarry, 'the field of the play'.

Even in the modern theatre where the stage is separated from the auditorium, the audience is so important a factor that I believe the most skilful producer cannot estimate the whole possibilities of a play before the first night, when the indefinable relationship between actors and spectators will often produce a new situation. It was this combined action of players and spectators that I was looking for. The old Cornish miracle plays appeared to me to be too archaic and lacking in dramatic form for my purpose; and finding nothing among the more modern plays that corresponded to my conception, I determined that if there was to be one at St Hilary it must be written by myself.

The plan with which I started was that there should be no stage and that the players should pass, as in a measured dance, from place to place round the church among the people. In addition I planned that the Christmas crib should take the place of a character impersonating Our Lady with the Holy Child, and that there should be a dance of children before the crib, as an expression of joy in the nativity.

I had lately seen the Russian ballet and had been moved to tears at the tragedy of the dolls in 'Patroushka'. I had the same experience at a performance in Penzance of Giorno's marionettes. Those diminutive figures, with their illusion of being of the stature of ordinary men and women, conveyed a sense of the strange sadness of our lives that I have rarely experienced in the theatre.

It would seem that life is so secret and elusive that it is only by detaching it from reality, as in the Russian ballet and in these marionettes, that we can hope to enclose its form and substance.

The most notable example of this remoteness from imitation is found in the ritual of the Mass. Nothing could be more unlike the scene of the Last Supper than a High Mass according to the Roman rite. And yet any other method than the one employed by the Church would have resulted, as it often has among Protestants, in little more than the reproduction of the outward order in which, for a moment of time, God willed to give the freest and fullest expression of Himself. It may be that much of our modern painting and literature has, in its pursuit of realism, been betrayed by the same purpose – seeking to express what lies behind the actual phenomena by a slavish imitation of the facts that conceal it.

I have often been weary of this play 'Bethlehem', which has been produced so many times, and yet I never watch the grotesque figures of the shepherds with a fiddler at their head, followed by the children on their way to the dance before the crib, without experiencing a thrill of emotion. There is nothing in this crowd, in the music of the fiddler or the dances of the children, that is remotely related to the scene of the Nativity, and yet, as I watch them, I am more conscious of the joys of Christmas than I should be in witnessing the most realistic presentation.

I feel the same when the little girl arrives with the toy lamb in her arms. Children no longer care for woolly lambs as when I was a child. I searched the shops in Penzance to find one. 'We don't stock them,' was the answer I received. Teddy-bears were everywhere, but not a lamb to be found. At last I came upon a little toyshop kept by two old ladies in Market Jew Street. 'Yes,' said the elder of the two, who wore her hair in ringlets, 'I know what you want. Children used to be very fond of them when I was a girl, but we have not been asked for such a thing for years. Fancy now! children like one of these things,' she went on, pointing to a yellow Teddy-bear with a pink ribbon round its neck, 'rather than a little white lamb.' 'I do believe,' said the younger woman, 'we still have one put away somewhere. If the gentleman doesn't mind waiting we might find it. Or perhaps you will call again?' she said. I determined to wait while the two old ladies busied themselves in turning out cupboards and peeping into boxes. At last, when all the cupboards had been emptied out, a lamb was found in a box on the top shelf, a woolly lamb with crooked legs and a bell round its neck. I have never looked on greater innocency. 'We won't charge you the full price,' they said, 'for no one wants them to-day.' I am glad that others loved the lamb as I did. Gert Harvey, a painter in Newlyn, came to me after the play. 'O Ber,' she said, 'where did you get that lamb? His crooked legs made me cry.'

The play has seen many changes since its first presentation, each year adding something; but the use of the whole church as a stage, and the dance of the children before the crib, still give it any distinction that it may possess. Throughout the years it has retained its character as a religious play. All who take part make their confession and come to communion, pledging themselves to say daily during the weeks of rehearsal the Lord's Prayer, the Hail Mary and the prayer in the Prologue: 'Grant me, dear Lord, the power to act aright the beauties and the wonders of this blessed night, that all may see the tender mercy and the grace of Thy sweet coming to save our fallen race.'

Bernard Walke, Twenty Years at St Hilary (1935)

Christmas 1798

Dec. 25, Tuesday. Xmas Day. We breakfasted, dined, &c. again at home. Mr Cotman read Prayers and administered the Holy Sacrament this Morning at Weston-Church being Christmas-Day. Many People there, tho' none of Mr Custance's Family were there. The following poor People dined at my House, the Clerk, Willm. Large lately made so by me in the place of the late Thos. Thurston, Thos. Atterton Senr., poor old Mother Case, old Chris. Dunnell, Robt. Downing, and poor old Ned Howes who had his Dinner sent him (being ill) and also o.1.o. Gave each of the others also 1ˢ/oᵈ. o.5.o. To my Millers Man, Jⁿ̤ Shorter, Xmas Gift o.1.o. Dinner to day, Surloin of Beef rosted, plumb Puddings and Mince Pies &c. I gave the poor Folks after Dinner some old Beer. Very cold indeed to day with some Snow, it froze very sharply & shortly within Doors.

James Woodforde, *The Diary of a Country Parson* (1926)

Herne the Hunter

The night was so still that they, standing there in the snow, could hear the bells of nine churches ringing for Christmas. The Precentor, who had been a curate in that district, told Kay which village each bell belonged to:

'That one,' he said, 'with the tenor bell that needs recasting, is Naunton Crucis. Old Father Goodman has rung that bell for forty-nine Christmas Eves and this is his fiftieth.'

Above the noise of the bells Kay heard the jangling of lesser bells, or so it seemed. Then it died away so that he felt that he was mistaken, but immediately it broke out again louder than before. They were bells not ringing to any tune or time.

'They are sleigh-bells,' he said.

'Why, it's Father Christmas,' said the Precentor, 'coming with his team of reindeer.'

But it was not Father Christmas. Over the wall of the Roman Camp some lights appeared; the bells rang loud and clear. Leaping towards them, seeming hardly to brush the snow with their paws, came a magnificent team of harnessed lions drawing a long sledge driven by a lady whose eyes shone like sparks of fire. Kay saw at once that she was the Lady of the Oak Tree who had stood by Bob's shop waiting for a word from Cole Hawlings. Outside the glove of her left hand was the strange ring with the St Andrew's Cross upon it. Kay was amazed at the beauty and strength of the lions, their gleaming eyes, and the way in which they tossed back their manes and snarled, or scuffled the snow with their pads, or showed their teeth with coughing, terrifying roars. He had never seen lions so beautiful, so powerful, nor with eyes so full of yellow flame.

'Get in, Bishop,' the lady said. 'I can take half of you in this sleigh.'

The Bishop and some of the others got into the sleigh, which seemed to be made of bright gold. It was heaped with great scarlet rugs and the furs of strange beasts. As soon as they were snugly in the sleigh under the rugs, the lady called:

'I must start before my team starts quarrelling with the other team.'

She called to the lions, who bounded forward roaring. All the bells upon their traces and on the rim of the car jangled out clearly and seemed to Kay to strike now into a kind of tune. Kay saw them whirl round in a half-circle sending a great sheet of snow aloft, then they strode in to the night striking sparkles out of the air. Kay heard the Precentor, who was sitting with the Bishop, start singing, 'The First Noël', but they were out of earshot in half a moment; a second sleigh drew near.

Kay had been delighted by the first sleigh, though the lions had a little scared him, but what was his delight when he saw that the second sleigh was drawn by unicorns!

'Oh,' he said, 'unicorns! And they always told me that they never existed.'

But there was no doubt about these. It was a team of eight of the most beautiful unicorns that ever stepped. In build they were something like the very best white Arab stallions, only slimmer in the barrel and even neater in the leg. They had the same proud little heads and twitching nostrils. They were all snow-white except their hoofs, which were bluish. From their brows sprouted the most exquisite white horns about two feet long, sharp as needles and glowing, Kay thought, rather like mother-of-pearl, but perhaps that was the effect of the moonlight. Their traces and harness were of silver all studded with moonstones. They were driven by a man, whose sleeves were hung with little silver chains. In his helm there were antlers; over his glove a red cross glowed upon a ring.

'Oh, it is Herne again,' Kay said. 'I do love going with Herne the Hunter.'

'Jump in, the rest of you,' Herne cried. 'There will be room for all of you.'

The sleigh was heaped with Polar bear skins and great white fleeces from some mountain sheep. They all clambered on board and snuggled down into the fur. The driver called to his unicorns, who at once whinnied together and tossed up the snow with their hoofs. They, too, like the lions, whirled round and sent the snow flying in a cloud. Then away they went, whirling through the heaven, striking sparkles out of the air. Old Cole Hawlings touched something, all the side of the sleigh at once thrust out lighted Japanese lanterns attached to long streamers; smaller lanterns flew out from the reins of the unicorns as they sped. Cole Hawlings, who had a most beautiful voice, Kay thought, began to sing this carol:

'George took his lantern from the nail,
    And lit it at the fire-a;
He said, "The snow does so assail,
    I'll shut the cows in byre-a."

Amid the snow, by byre-door,
    A man and woman lay-a;
George pitied them, they were so poor,
    And brought them to the hay-a.

At midnight, while the inn kept feasts,
    And trump and whistle blew-a,
George heard a trouble in the beasts,
    And to the stable drew-a.

And there within the manger-bars
    A little child new-born-a,
All bright below a cross of stars,
    And in his brow a thorn-a.

The oxen lowed to see their King,
    The happy donkey brayed-a,
The cocks and hens on perch did sing,
    And George knelt down and prayed-a.

And straight a knocking on the door,
    And torches burning red-a,
The two great Kings with Melchior,
    With robes and wine and bread-a.

And all the night time rolled away
    With angels dancing down-a;
Now praise we that dear Babe today
    That bears the Cross and Crown-a.'

John Masefield, *The Box of Delights* (1935)

The Coming of the Wise Men

Lord when the wise men came from far
Led to thy Cradle by A Star,
Then did the shepheards too rejoyce,
Instructed by thy Angells voyce,
Blest were the wisemen in their skill,
And shepheards in their harmlesse will.

Wisemen in tracing natures lawes
Ascend unto the highest cause,
Shepheards with humble fearfulnesse
Walke safely, though their light be lesse:
Though wisemen better know the way,
It seemes no honest heart can stray.

There is no merit in the wise
But love, (the shepheards sacrifice).
Wisemen, all wayes of knowledge past,
To th' shepheards'wonder come at last;
To know, can only wonder breede,
And not to know, is wonders seede.

A wiseman at the Altar bowes
And offers up his studied vowes
And is received; may not the teares,
Which spring too from a shepheards feares,
And sighs upon his fraylty spent,
Though not distinct, be eloquent?

Tis true, the object sanctifies
All passions which within us rise,
But since no creature comprehends
The cause of causes, end of ends,
Hee who himselfe vouchsafes to know
Best pleases his creator so.

When then our sorrowes we applye
To our owne wantes and poverty,
When wee looke up in all distresse
And our owne misery confesse,

Sending both thankes and prayers above,
Then though wee do not know, we love.

Sidney Godolphin (1645–1712)

The New Year bells

Ring out, wild bells, to the wild sky,
  The flying cloud, the frosty light:
  The year is dying in the night;
Ring out, wild bells, and let him die.

Ring out the old, ring in the new,
  Ring, happy bells, across the snow:
  The year is going, let him go;
Ring out the false, ring in the true.

Ring out the grief that saps the mind,
  For those that here we see no more;
  Ring out the feud of rich and poor,
Ring in redress to all mankind.

Ring out a slowly dying cause,
  And ancient forms of party strife;
  Ring in the nobler modes of life,
With sweeter manners, purer laws.

Ring out the want, the care, the sin,
  The faithless coldness of the times;
  Ring out, ring out my mournful rhymes,
But ring the fuller minstrel in.

Ring out false pride in place and blood,
The civic slander and the spite;
Ring in the love of truth and right,
Ring in the common love of good.

Ring out old shapes of foul disease;
  Ring out the narrowing lust of gold;
  Ring out the thousand wars of old,
Ring in the thousand years of peace.

Ring in the valiant man and free,
  The larger heart, the kindlier hand;
  Ring out the darkness of the land,
Ring in the Christ that is to be.

Alfred Lord Tennyson, *In Memoriam* (1850)

Ceremonies for Candlemasse Eve

Down with the Rosemary and Bayes,
  Down with the Misletoe;
Instead of Holly, now up-raise
  The greener Box (for show.)

The Holly hitherto did sway;
  Let Box now domineere;
Untill the dancing Easter-day,
  Or Easters Eve appeare.

Then youthfull Box which now hath grace,
  Your houses to renew;
Grown old, surrender must his place,
  Unto the crisped Yew.

When Yew is out, then Birch comes in,
  And many Flowers beside;
Both of a fresh, and fragrant kinne
  To honour Whitsontide.

Green Rushes then, and sweetest Bents,
  With cooler Oken boughs;
Come in for comely ornaments,
  To re-adorn the house.
Thus times do shift; each thing his turne does hold;
New things succeed, as former things grow old.

Robert Herrick, *Hesperides* (1648)

A Spring Song of Love

When I see blossoms spring
  And hear fowlis song,
A sweet love-longing
  Mine heart throughout sprong,
All for a love new
That is so sweet and true,
  That gladdeth all my song;
I wot almid iwis   *with all certainty*
My joy and eke my bliss
  Of him is all along.   *all owing to him*

When I myself do stand
  And with mine heart see
Thurled foot and hand,   *pierced*
With great nails three;
Bloody was his head,
  Of him was nought bi-left   *remaining*
That was of painis free.
Well, well, ought mine heart
For his love to smart,
  And sigh, and sorry be.

Jesu, gentle and soft,   *tender*
  Give me strength and might
To long, sore and oft,
  To love thee aright,
Pine to thole and dree, *sorrow suffer and endure*
For thy son, Marie.
  Thou art so free and bright,
Maiden and moder, mild
  For love of thy child,
Ernd us heaven's light.   *earn*

Alas! that I' ne'er can
  Turn to him my thought,
And choose him as leman,   *lover*
  So dear he hath us bought,
With wounds deep and strong,
With pains sore and long.

Of such love know we nought.
His blood that fell to grounden
From his sweet wounden
From pain hath us i-brought.

Jesu, gentle and sweet,
    I sing thee my song,
Oft I thee greet
    And pray thee among   *in the meantime*
Let me sins leten,   *forsake*
And in this life atone
    That I have done wrong.
At our lives end
When we shall wend,   *die*
    Jesu, us underfong.

Anon, quoted in Ivor Gurney, *Recusant Poets* (1938)

Palm Sunday

Palm Sunday, known locally as Fig Sunday, was a minor hamlet festival. Sprays of soft gold and silver willow catkins, called 'palm' in that part of the country, were brought indoors to decorate the houses and be worn as buttonholes for churchgoing. The children at the end house loved fetching in the palm and putting it in pots and vases and hanging it over the picture frames. Better still, they loved the old custom of eating figs on Palm Sunday. The week before, the innkeeper's wife would get in a stock to be sold in pennyworths in her small grocery store. Some of the more expert cooks among the women would use these to make fig puddings for dinner and the children bought pennyworths and ate them out of screws of blue sugar paper on their way to Sunday school.

The gathering of the palm branches must have been a survival from old Catholic days, when, in many English churches, the willow served for palm to be blessed on Palm Sunday. The original significance of eating figs on that day had long been forgotten; but it was regarded as an important duty, and children ordinarily selfish would give one of their figs, or at least a bite out of one, to the few unfortunates who had been given no penny.

Flora Thompson, *Lark Rise to Candleford* (1939)

Holy Thursday

'Twas on a Holy Thursday, their innocent faces clean,
The children walking two & two, in red & blue & green,
Grey-headed beadles walk'd before, with wands as white as snow,
Till into the high dome of Paul's they like Thames' waters flow.

O what a multitude they seem'd, these flowers of London town!
Seated in companies they sit with radiance all their own.
The hum of multitudes was there, but multitudes of lambs,
Thousands of little boys & girls raising their innocent hands.

Now like a mighty wind they raise to heaven the voice of song,
Or like harmonious thunderings the seats of heaven among.
Beneath them sit the aged men, wise guardians of the poor;
Then cherish pity, lest you drive an angel from your door.

William Blake, *Songs of Innocence* (1789)

Good Friday Carol

I sigh when I sing
  For sorrow that I see
When I with weeping
  Behold upon the tree
And see Jhesu, my sweet,
His heart blood forlete   *drained*
  For the love of me,
His wounds waxen wete,
They weep still and mete;   *fittingly*
  Marie rueth thee.

High upon a down
  Where all folk it may see,
A mile from the town
  About the mid-day,
The rood is up-reared;
His friends are a-feared,
  And clingeth so the clay;
The rood stands in [the] stone,
  Marie stands alone
And saith: 'Wey-la-way!'

344

When I thee behold
  [With eye and heart both,]
And thy body cold;
  Thy face waxeth blue,
Thou hangest all of blood
So high upon the rood,
  Between thievës two;
Who may sigh more?
Marie thou weepest sore
  [Thou knowest all his woe.]

The nails be too strong,
  The smiths are too sley,   *skilful*
Thou bleedest all too long,
  The tree is all too high,
The stone be all wete.
Alas! Jhesu, the sweet,
  [Few friends hast thou nigh]
But saint Johan mourning,
And Marie weeping,
  [That all thy sorrow see.]

Well oft when I sike   *sigh*
  And make my moan,
Ill though it me like
  Wonder is it none
When I see, hang high
And bitter pains drei,   *endure*
  Jhesu, my lemon.
His woundës sore smart,
The spear is at his heart
  And through his sidës gone.

Often when I sleep
  With care I am through-sought,   *penetrated*
When I wake and weep
  Of sorrow is all my thought,
Alas! men be wode   *mad*
That sweareth by the rode
  And selleth him for nought

That bought us out of sin.
He bring us to wyn   *joy*
That hath us dearly bought.

Anon., quoted in Ivor Gurney (ed.) *Recusant Poets* (1946)

Goodfriday, 1613. Riding Westward

Let mans Soule be a Spheare, and then, in this,
The intelligence that moves, devotion is,
And as the other Spheares, by being growne
Subject to forraigne motions, lose their owne,
And being by others hurried every day,
Scarce in a yeare their naturall forme obey:
Pleasure or business, so, our Soules admit
For their first mover, and are whirld by it.
Hence is't, that I am carryed towards the West
This day, when my Soules forme bends toward the East.
There I should see a Sunne, by rising set,
And by that setting endlesse day beget;
But that Christ on this Crosse, did rise and fall,
Sinne had eternally benighted all.
Yet dare I'almost be glad, I do not see
That spectacle of too much weight for mee.
Who sees Gods face, that is selfe life, must dye;
What a death were it then to see God dye?
It made his owne Lieutenant Nature shrinke,
It made his footstoole crack, and the Sunne winke.
Could I behold those hands which span the Poles,
And turne all spheares at once, pierc'd with those holes?
Could I behold that endlesse height which is
Zenith to us, and our Antipodes,
Humbled below us? or that blood which is
The seat of all our Soules, if not of his,
Made dirt of dust, or that flesh which was worne
By God, for his apparell, ragg'd, and torne?
If on these things I durst not looke, durst I
Upon his miserable mother cast mine eye,
Who was Gods partner here, and furnish'd thus

Halfe of that Sacrifice, which ransom'd us?
Though these things, as I ride, be from mine eye,
They'are present yet unto my memory,
For that looks towards them; and thou look'st towards mee,
O Saviour, as thou hang'st upon the tree;
I turne my backe to thee, but to receive
Corrections, till thy mercies bid thee leave.
O thinke mee worth thine anger, punish mee,
Burne off my rusts, and my deformity,
Restore thine Image, so much, by thy grace,
That thou may'st know mee, and I'll turne my face.

John Donne, *Divine Poems* (1572–1631)

Easter Wings

Lord, who createdst man in wealth and store,
Though foolishly he lost the same,
Decaying more and more,
Till he became
Most poore:
With thee
O let me rise
As larks, harmoniously,
And sing this day thy victories;
Then shall the fall further the flight in me.

My tender age in sorrow did beginne:
And still with sickness and shame
Thou didst so punish sinne,
That I became
Most thinne.
With thee
Let me combine,
And feel this day thy victorie:
strengthen by grafting. For, if I imp my wing on thine,
Affliction shall advance the flight in me.

George Herbert, *The Temple* (1633)

347

Easter at Clyro (1)

Easter Sunday 1870

When I started for Cefn y Blaen only two or three people were in the churchyard with flowers. But now the customary beautiful Easter Eve Idyll had fairly begun and people kept arriving from all parts with flowers to dress the graves. Children were coming from the town and from neighbouring villages with baskets of flowers and knives to cut holes in the turf. The roads were lively with people coming and going and the churchyard a busy scene with women and children and a few men moving about among the tombstones and kneeling down beside the green mounds flowering the graves. An evil woman from Hay was dressing a grave. (Jane Phillips). I found Annie Dyke standing among the graves with her basket of flowers. A pretty picture she would have made as she stood there with her pure fair sweet grave face and clustering brown curls shaded by her straw hat and her flower basket hanging on her arm. It is her birthday to-day. I always tell her she and the cuckoos came together. So I went home and got a little birthday present I had been keeping for her, which I bought in the Crystal Palace in January, a small ivory brooch, with the carved figure of a stag. I took the little box which held it out into the churchyard and gave it to her, as she was standing watching while the wife of one of her father's workmen, the shepherd, flowered the grave that she came to dress, for her.

More and more people kept coming into the churchyard as they finished their day's work. The sun went down in glory behind the dingle, but still the work of love went on through the twilight and into the dusk until the moon rose full and splendid. The figures continued to move about among the graves and to bend over the green mounds in the calm clear moonlight and warm air of the balmy evening.

At 8 o'clock there was a gathering of the Choir in the Church to practise the two anthems for to-morrow. The moonlight came streaming in broadly through the chancel windows. When the choir had gone and the lights were out and the church quiet again, as I walked down the Churchyard alone the decked graves had a strange effect in the moonlight and looked as if the people had laid down to sleep for the night out of doors, ready dressed to rise early on Easter morning. I lingered in the verandah before going to bed. The air was as soft and warm as a summer night, and the broad moonlight made the quiet village almost as light as day. Everyone seemed to have gone to rest and there was not a sound except the clink and trickle of the brook.

Francis Kilvert, *Diaries* (1974)

Easter at Clyro (II)

Easter Sunday, 16 April 1876
Thank God for a bright beautiful happy Easter Day.

I waited for the postman thinking that Easter morning might bring me a line from dear Ettie to explain the sweet sad verses of Easter Eve. Soon I saw the postman coming by a meadow path across the sunny Common. He held several letters and a paper parcel and my heart beat with hope and expectation as he put them into my hand. But there was nothing from Ettie and I went sorrowfully back to the house.

There was a large congregation this morning. There were 41 Communicants beside the parson and clerk, the largest number that I or any one else had ever seen in Langley Church at once. The alms were £1.3.10.

When all the people had left the Church and no one remained but the Clerk putting away the sacred vessels I walked alone round the silent sunny peaceful Churchyard and visited the graves of my sleeping friends Jane Hatherell, Mary Jefferies, Anne Hawkins, John Jefferies, George Bryant, Emily Banks, John Hatherell, Limpedy Buckland the gipsy girl, and many more. There they lay, the squire and the peasant, the landlord and the labourer, young men and maidens, old men and children, the infant of days beside the patriarch of nearly five score years, sister, brother, by the same mother, all in her breast their heads did lay and crumble to their common clay. And over all she lovingly threw her soft mantle of green and gold, the greensward and buttercups, daisies and primroses. They they lay all sleeping well and peacefully after life's fitful fevers and waiting for the Great Spring morning and the General Resurrection of the dead. John Hatherell, the good old sawyer, now sleeps in the same God's acre to which he helped to carry the gipsy girl Limpedy Buckland to her burial more than sixty years ago.

Francis Kilvert (ibid.)

Easter Communion

Pure fasted faces draw unto this feast:
God comes all sweetness to your Lenten lips.
You striped in secret with breath-taking whips,
Those crooked rough-scored chequers may be pieced
To crosses meant for Jesus; you whom the East
With draught of thin and pursuant cold so nips
Breathe Easter now; you serged fellowships,
You vigil-keepers with low flames decreased,

God shall o'er-brim the measures you have spent
With oil of gladness; for sackcloth and frieze
And the ever-fretting shirt of punishment
Give myrrhy-threaded golden folds of ease.
Your scarce-sheathed bones are weary of being bent:
Lo, God shall strengthen all the feeble knees.

Gerard Manley Hopkins (1844–89)

Ascension Day rituals

The influence of the Ambarvalia, falling in May, must surely have been great: Rome herself kept it on the 29th, at a certain place in the old perimeter of Roman territory. Here a crowd assembled to move in procession around the cornfields, with singing and dancing, the sacrifice of animals, the driving away of Winter with sticks, and other enjoyable rites, intended to rid the cornlands of evil. Country people are stubborn about losing their customs, but do not object to keeping them for a better reason, or even on a different day. About the year 465 the Western world was suffering from earthquake, storm and epidemic. Mamertus, Bishop of Vienne, aware of the popular custom, ordered that prayers should be said in the ruined or neglected fields on Ascension Day or the three days preceding it. 'Beating the Bounds' had become a Christian ceremonial.

It was introduced into England early in the eighth century, and has remained with us ever since. During Rogationtide, at any period in history, including our own, a party might be seen setting out to trace the boundaries of the parish. At the head marched the bishop or the priest, with a minor official bearing the Cross, and after them followed a crowd of persons, including the schoolboys of the parish, led by their master. Most of them held slender wands of willow, like those of May Day, peeled white, and sometimes crowned, a little below the top, with a knot of flowers. At certain points along the route, at certain well-known landmarks – bridge or stile, or oftenest an ancient tree – the Cross halted, the party gathered about the priest, and a litany or rogation was said, imploring God to send seasonable weather, keep the corn and the roots and the boughs in good health, and bring them to an ample harvest. At one point beer and cheese would be waiting, provided out of small endowments made for that purpose. A rogation is no more than an 'asking', appropriate to any emergency, war, plague, drought or foul weather. The heathen perambulations of Spring had merely suggested a rogation of a fixed and perennial sort.

Then, beneath the 'Gospel Oak', or at the boulder on the hill, a curious duty was performed. The wand-bearers set to work to beat the landmark with their clashing wands. Suddenly, amid shouts of amusement, they transferred their attack to one of the boys, who offered himself, half-willing and half-reluctant. They rolled him in a briar bush, flung him in a pond, or, seizing him by shoulders and heels, bumped him several times against the boundary stone. Though lucky to escape without a scratch, a bruise or a wetting, the sacrificial victim did not show any great reluctance, for a new shilling was likely to be his reward. The Church will hardly have invented such a custom, and here we must surely see an element introduced by the Saxon peoples themselves, who are known to have had their vernal 'gang days', resembling, however roughly, the rites of the South.

Lawrence Whistler, *The English Festivals* (1947)

An Hymne of the Ascension

Bright Portalles of the Skie,
   Emboss'd with sparkling Starres,
  Doores of Eternitie,
   With diamantine barres,
  Your Arras rich up-hold,
  Loose all your bolts and Springs,
  Ope wide your Leaves of gold;

That in your Roofes may come the King of kings.
Scarf'd in a rosie Cloud,
  Hee doth ascend the Aire,
  Straight doth the Moone him shrowd
  With her resplendant Haire;
  The next enchristall'd Light
  Submits to him its Beames,
  And hee doth trace the hight
Of that faire Lamp which flames of beautie streames.

Hee towers those golden Bounds
  Hee did to Sunne bequeath,
  The higher wandring Rounds
  Are found his Feete beneath;
  The milkie-way comes neare,
  Heavens Axell seemes to bend,
  Above each turning Spheare
That rob'd in Glorie Heavens King may ascend.

O Well-spring of this All,
  Thy Fathers Image vive,
  Word, that from nought did call
  What is, doth reason, live;
  The Soules eternall Food,
  Earths Joy, Delight of Heaven;
  All Truth, Love, Beautie, Good,
To Thee, to Thee bee praises ever given.

What was dismarshall'd late
  In this thy noble Frame,
  And lost the prime estate,
  Hath re-obtain'd the same,
  Is now most perfect seene;
  Streames which diverted were
  (And troubled strayed uncleene)
From their first Source, by Thee home turned are.

By Thee that blemish old,
  Of *Edens* leprous Prince,
  Which on his Race tooke hold,
  And him exil'd from thence,
  Now put away is farre;
  With Sword, in irefull guise,

No Cherub more shall barre
Poore man the Entries into Paradise.
By Thee those Spirits pure,
First Children of the Light,
Now fixed stand and sure,
In their eternall Right;
Now humane Companies
Renew their ruin'd Wall,
Fall'n man as thou makst rise,
Thou giv'st to Angels that they shall not fall.
By Thee that Prince of Sinne,
That doth with mischiefe swell,
Hath lost what hee did winne,
And shall endungeon'd dwell;
His spoyles are made thy prey,
His Fanes are sackt and torne,
His Altars raz'd away,
And what ador'd was late, now lyes a Scorne.
These Mansions pure and cleare,
Which are not made by hands,
Which once by him joy'd were,
And his (then not stain'd) Bands
(Now forfeit'd, dispossest,
And head-long from them throwne)
Shall Adams Heires make blest,
By Thee their great Redeemer made their owne.
O Well-spring of this All,
Thy Fathers Image vive,
Word, that from nought did call,
What is, doth Reason, live;
Whose worke is, but to will,
Gods coeternall Sonne,
Great Banisher of ill,
By none but Thee could these great Deedes bee done.
Now each etheriall Gate,
To him hath opened bin;
And glories King in state,
His Pallace enters in;
Now come is this high Priest,

In the most holie Place,
Not without Blood addrest,
With Glorie Heaven the Earth to crowne with Grace.
Starres which all Eyes were late,
And did with wonder burne,
His Name to celebrate,
In flaming Tongues them turne;
Their orby Chrystales move
More active than before,
And entheate* from above,
Their soveraigne Prince laude, glorifie, adore.
The Quires of happie Soules,
Wakt with that Musicke sweete,
Whose Descant Care controules,
Their Lord in Triumph meete;
The spotless Sprightes of light,
His Trophees doe extole,
And archt in Squadrons bright,
Greet their great victor in his Capitole.
O Glorie of the Heaven,
O sole Delight of Earth,
To thee all power bee given,
Gods uncreated Birth;
Of Man-kind lover true,
Indeerer† of his wrong,
Who dost the world renew,
Still bee thou our Salvation and our Song.
From Top of *Olivet* such notes did rise,
When mans Redeemer did transcend the Skies.

* entheate: inspired (ad. L. entheätus).
† Indeerer: conciliator, atoner.

William Drummond, *Flowres of Sion* (1630)

The Whitsun ale

... we must not draw too rosy a picture of ancestral virtue. Obedience and generosity were not always uppermost in their minds. In the churchyard, on the North side of the church, a 'Robin Hood's

Bower' had been built out of branches, garlands and ribbons; and here the rustic 'Lord' and 'Lady' of the Whitsun Ale were enthroned, with a Mace-Bearer and Fool to attend them. This arbour was directly descended from those that St Augustine had been told to approve, and it probably looked much the same. It was in this part of the churchyard, where few were buried, that the people had always danced away the long Summer evenings, when the doors had been opened after Evensong; and Whitsun was above all the time of the Morris. For several weeks the young men who composed the local team had devoted an evening or two to rehearsal, and their leader had been in touch with the churchwardens. In the wardens' accounts of the fifteenth, sixteenth and seventeenth centuries there are many entries that concern them. Payment would be made for a hobby-horse, for dancing bells and beer, and for the dancing itself. The Morris men were held to be lawful entertainers – though not by all. Let us see them through the unloving eyes of Philip Stubbes, as they and their followers prepare to invade God's Acre on the Sabbath evening.

'First, all the wilde-heds of the Parish, conventing together, chuse them a Graund-Captain (of all mischeef) whome they innoble with the title of 'my Lord of Mis-rule', and him they crowne with great solemnitie, and adopt for their king. This king anointed chuseth forth twentie, fortie, threescore or a hundred lustie Guttes, like to him self, to waighte upon his lordly Maiestie, and to guarde his noble person. Then, everie one of these his men, he investeth with his liveries of green, yellow, or some other light wanton colour; And as though that were not (bawdie) gawdie enough, I should say, they bedecke them selves with scarfs, ribons & laces hanged all over with golde rings, precious stones, & other jewels: this doon, they tye about either leg xx or xl bels, with rich handkerchiefs in their hands, and sometimes lay a crosse over their shoulders & necks, borrowed for the most parte of their pretie Mopsies & looving Bessies, for bussing them in the dark.

'Thus al things set in order, then have they their Hobby-horses, dragons & other Antiques, togither with their baudie Pipers and thundering Drummers to strike up the devils daunce withall, then, marche these heathen company towards the Church and the Church-yard, their pipers pipeing, their drummers thundring, their stumps dauncing, their bels iyngling, their handkerchiefs swinging about their heds like madmen, their hobbie-horses and other monsters skirmishing amongst the rout; and in this sorte they go to the Church (I say) & into the Church (though the Minister be at praier or preaching), dancing & swinging their handkerchiefs over their heds in the Church, like devils incarnate, with such a confuse noise, that no man can hear his own voice. Then, the foolish people they looke, they stare, they laugh, they fleer, and mount upon fourmes and pews to see these goodly pageants solemnised in this sort. Then, after this, about the Church they goe again, and againe, & so foorth into the church-yard where they have commonly their Sommer-haules, their bowers, arbors and banqueting houses set up, wherein they feast, banquet & daunce at that day, & (peradventure) all the night too. And thus these terrestriall furies spend the Sabaoth day.'

Lawrence Whistler, *The English Festivals* (1947)

After Trinity

We have done with dogma and divinity,
Easter and Whitsun past,
The long, long Sundays after Trinity
Are with us at last;
The passionless Sundays after Trinity,
Neither feast-day nor fast.

Christmas comes with plenty,
Lent spreads out its pall,
But these are five and twenty,
The longest Sundays of all;
The placid Sundays after Trinity,
Wheat-harvest, fruit-harvest, Fall.

Spring with its burst is over,
Summer has had its day,
The scented grasses and clover
Are cut, and dried into hay;
The singing-birds are silent,
And the swallows flown away.

Post pugnam pausa fiet;
Lord, we have made our choice;

In the stillness of autumn quiet,
We have heard the still, small voice.
We have sung *Oh where shall Wisdom?*
Thick paper, folio, Boyce.

Let it not all be sadness,
Not *omnia vanitas*,
Stir up a little gladness
To lighten the *Tibi cras*;
Send us that little summer,
That comes with Martinmas.

When still the cloudlet dapples
The windless cobalt blue,
And the scent of gathered apples
Fills all the store-rooms through,
The gossamer silvers the bramble,
The lawns are gemmed with dew.

An end of tombstone Latinity,
Stir up sober mirth,
Twenty-fifth after Trinity,
Kneel with the listening earth,
Behind the Advent trumpets
They are singing Emmanuel's birth.

J. M. Falkner, Poems (1933)

Harvest Festival

To propitiate the Spirit of the Harvest by murdering a man was still the practice of many primitive peoples in the last century, and once it may have been universal. The Bible records it (II Samuel, 21): our own Teutonic ancestors perhaps did the same. The victim died 'for' the God in two senses, both as sacrifice and representative, and he was often treated with reverence before his execution. We may see in the holder of the sacred 'Neck' the spiritual descendant of that victim, who in some parts of England was still roughly handled after a thousand years of Christianity; while to souse him with water has been interpreted as an act of imitative magic, a charm to bring plentiful rain on the seed of the new year.

With these implications never wholly expunged from that abyss of memory where the archaic images survive, it is not surprising that there was some reluctance to cut those final haunted ears in which the wild Spirit had taken refuge. In South Wales and in the Midlands they used to tie them into a bunch and then throw at it with hatchets from a distance, as if to distribute the responsibility. In some counties it must have been thought that the Spirit withdrew, before the rhythmical advance of the reapers, from one farm to another, and took refuge and was finally executed in the last field of the most backward husbandman. For in modern times when a farmer finished before his neighbour there was much amusement in the field. Immediately a labourer sprang on the cart to shout the guilt-shifting formula amid applause. 'This be tu give notice that Mr Pickard has ge'un the hook a turn and sent th' owd Hare into Mr Easterbrook's standen corn!' A country God might well assume the body of that wild and fleetfoot creature. He was thought to do so at Easter. And now for a moment the God became visible again, bolting from the protection of the dwindling corn.

But the horror of blood had long since evaporated from the Saxon harvest-fields, even before the barbarians invaded, leaving only a nameless apprehension – and that by no means ubiquitous – to put a fine edge on the rejoicing. And how much a festival of joy was this, with its earthly flavour of accomplishment, unique among the festivals of promise! Twelfth Night, Plough Monday, Holy Thursday, Midsummer, Lammas – they all speak of the Harvest. The Harvest speaks only of itself, or of the Hand of Providence. 'They joy before Thee according to the joy in harvest,' said Isaiah. Between the 'Crying of the Neck' and the lifting of the corn there had been days of anxiety, but now the last load is about to be taken in, and there will be no serious work on the farm for a week. It is the hour of the Harvest Home.

Already the waggon has been drawn into the field behind a team of horses. There are garlands to their necks and ears, and sunflowers and scarlet ribbons to their blinkers. The captain of the reapers, crowned with flowers himself, directs the loading, and as soon as the last sheaf is lifted the children of the farm scramble on top, with the branches and festoons they have been preparing for this moment. On the leading horse is seated – surely in allusion to some half-remembered provincial Ceres? – the prettiest girl of the farm, dressed in white, with corn and flowers in her straw bonnet and a yellow sash to her waist. And high over all is raised up emblematically the 'Ivy Girl' or 'Corn Baby': a single sheaf from the best corn in the field, sometimes 'made into a human shape; curiously dressed by the women, and adorned with paper trimmings, cut to resemble a cap, ruffles, handkerchief, etc., of the finest lace'. Occasionally the load may support a life-sized figurehead. 'I have seen,' says Hutchinson in his *History of Northumberland*, 'in some places, an image apparelled in great finery, crowned with flowers, a sheaf of corn placed under her arm, and a sickle in her hand, carried out of the village in the morning of the conclusive reaping day, with music and much clamour of the reapers, into the field, where it stands fixed on a pole all day, and when the reaping is done, is brought home in like manner. This they call the harvest queen.' But their Nordic ancestors in Germany would have said that it represented the primordial monarch called 'Sheaf'.

And so the harvest came home, attended by all who had been at work in the fields, with flags and ribbons from the top, with pipe and drum beneath, and with songs and laughter. 'It is donne with great joy and merriment,' says Aubrey, 'and a Fidler rides on the loaded Cart, or Wayne, playing.' In the farmyard the mistress and her daughters and maids, busy all day about the evening's banquet, were out to see it arrive, and as the symbolic load came to a standstill, as likely as not a young man leapt on the shafts, to bawl –

> 'We have ploughed, we have sowed,
> We have reaped, we have mowed,
> We have brought home every load,
> Hip, hip, hip, Harvest Home!' –

and the last two words would be shouted by everyone. Then cake and beer were handed round by the girls, the load was driven away to the stackyard, the team unharnessed and put in the stable, and the men washed and spruced themselves up in new shirts and shiny boots for the supper. But first the Corn Baby was taken into the house, where it might remain for three or four years until its virtue was no longer remembered... In a few hours the harvest moon would be buoyant on the skyline, a prodigious gourd.

Lawrence Whistler, *The English Festivals* (1947)

Hay Fair

Thursday, 15 September 1870

Hay Fair. Roads lively with men, horses and sheep. We were busy all day dressing the Church or preparing decorations. Mrs Price and Miss Elcox had got a quantity of wild hops from their fields and were arranging bright red apples for ornament. Also they had boughs loaded with rosy apples and quantities of bright yellow Siberian crabs. At the school the children were busy leasing out corn from a loose heap on the floor, sitting among the straw and tying up wheat, barley and oats in small sheaves and bundles. Gipsy Lizzie was amongst them, up to her beautiful eyes in corn and straw. The schoolmaster, the boys and I gathering stringed ivy from the trees in the Castle Clump. The Miss Baskervilles dressing the hoops for the seven window sills with flowers and fruit. Mrs Morrell undertook to dress the reading-desk, pulpit, and clerk's desk, and did them beautifully. Then Cooper came down with his men carrying magnificent ferns and plants and began to work in the chancel. One fine silver fern was put in the font. Gibbins undertook the font and and dressed it tastefully with moss and white asters under the sweeping fronds of the silver fern. Round the stem were twined the delicate light green sprays of white convolvulus. The pillars were wreathed and twined with wild hop vine falling in graceful careless festoons and curling tendrils from wreath and capital. St Andrew crossed sheaves of all sorts of corn were placed against the walls between the windows, wheat, barley and oats with a spray of hop vine drooping in a festoon across the sheaf butts and a spray of red barberries between the sheaf heads. Bright flowers in pots clustered round the spring of the arches upon the capitals of the pillars, the flower pots veiled by a twist of hop vine. Mrs. Partridge returned from Worcestershire this afternoon and brought and sent us two magnificent branches of real hops from the Worcestershire hop yards. These we hung drooping full length on either side of a text Mrs. V. had made, white letters on scarlet flannel, 'I am the Vine. Ye are the branches. Without Me ye can do nothing.' And from the corners of this text Cooper hung two bunches of purple grapes. Two texts in corn on green baize. 'Praise ye the Lord' in wheat ears, and 'Thanks be to God' in oats were placed over the doors, inside. Outside the great door branches of apples and pears hung over the door. The gates were dressed with ferns, fruit and flowers. Following the outer arch, within a border of Spanish chestnuts, oak and acorn, elderberries, barberries and apples, was Mr Evans' text in scarlet letters on a bright blue ground, 'Enter into His Gates with Thanksgiving'. An avenue of tall ferns and coleus led up the chancel. A row of the same plants stood along the altar steps, and dahlias were laid on brae fern along the altar rail bars. On either side of the entrance to the altar hung a splendid cluster of purple grapes, and along the rails were tied at intervals small sheaves of wheat and tall heads of Pampas grass. On the altar stood two sheaves of all corn with a paten between them worked in scarlet flannel bordered with corn and IHS worked in wheat ears. Above this hung a cross covered with scarlet flannel and adorned with corn barberries. On the window sill above stood a larger sheaf of all corn in a moss field and upon the moss lay all fruit, plums, apples, pears.

Francis Kilvert, *Diaries* (1974)

Stir-up Sunday

(*In the choir stalls*)
Remember now thy Creator
  In the days of thy youth;
Perlege, siste, viator,
  Remember the days of ruth:
Days when we may not hearken
  To the music that they make;
When the window-panes shall darken,
  And the knees of the strong men shake.

Another year grows colder,
  The later months retire;
Our faces are twelve months older
  As we look across the Choir.
We come here Sunday by Sunday,
  To listen, or sleep, or pray;
Till they seek for our places one day,
  And we shall be away.

The lectern candles beacon,
  The morning is foggy and dark,

Bishop, and Dean, and Archdeacon,
    Precentor, Canon, and Clerk;
We are growing balder, and whiter,
    The morning is foggy and pale,
But we look for a place that is brighter,
    Where the light shall not fail.

Where the light of the Lamb is the one light,
    In streets of jasper and gold,
There will be no need of the sunlight,
    And no growing old.
Jesu, mundi salvator,
    There we shall know the truth;
Kneeling before the Creator
    We remembered in our youth.

J. M. Falkner, Poems (1933)

BIBLIOGRAPHY OF
WORKS CONSULTED

Andrews, William *Curious Church Gleanings* (Smith Elder & Co., 1896)
Anson, Peter F. *Bishops at Large* (Faber, 1964)
– *Fashions in Church Furnishings* (Faith Press, 1960)
Arnold, Matthew *Discourses in America* (Macmillan, 1885)
Auden, W. H. *Collected Poems* (Faber, 1989)
Austen, Jane *Pride and Prejudice* (OUP, 1930)
Baring-Gould, Sabine *The Vicar of Morwenstow* (Dent, 1876)
Barnes, William *The Poems of William Barnes* (Macmillan, 1931)
Bede, The Venerable *History of the English Church and People* (Penguin, 1965)
Belloc, Hilaire *Verse* (Duckworth, 1932)
Benn, Tony *Out of the Wilderness* (Century Hutchinson, 1987)
Betjeman, John *A Nip in the Air* (John Murray, 1974)
– *Collected Poems* (John Murray, 1987)
– *Summoned by Bells* (John Murray, 1965)
Blake, William *Collected Poems and Selected Prose* (Hart-Davis, 1957)
Blunden, Edmund *Poems of Many Years* (Chatto and Windus, 1957)
Boswell, James *The Life of Samuel Johnson* (OUP, 1980)
Brendon, Piers *Hawker of Morwenstow* (Secker and Warburg, 1975)
Browne, Thomas *Religio Medici* (Everyman's Library, Dent 1961)
Bunyan, John *Grace Abounding to the Chief of Sinners* (OUP, 1972)
Burgess, Anthony *Little Wilson and Big God* (Heinemann, 1987)
Butler, Samuel *Hudibras* (1663), in *Collected Works* Vols. I & II (OUP, 1912)
Cambrensis, Giraldus *A Journey through Wales* (Penguin, 1984)
Carlyle, Thomas *Past and Present* (John Murray, 1843)
Chadwick, Owen *Michael Ramsey: A Life* (OUP, 1990)
Challoner, Richard *Memoirs of Missionary Priests* (1745)
Chaucer, Geoffrey *Complete Poetical Works* (OUP, 1969)
Checkland, S. G. *The Gladstones* (OUP, 1971)
Coleridge, Samuel Taylor *Table Talk* (Everyman's Library, Dent 1910)
Comper, Frances M. M. (ed.) *Spiritual Songs* (SPCK, 1936)

Comper, Ninian *Of the Atmosphere of a Church* (Sheldon Press, 1947)

Crashaw, Richard *Poems* (OUP, 1972)

Crewe, The Marquis of, KG *Lord Rosebery* (John Murray, 1931)

Cupitt, Don *Only Human* (SCM, 1989)

Davidson, Randall and Benham, William *The Life of Archibald Campell Tait* (Longman, 1891)

Dearmer, Percy *The Parson's Handbook* (1903)

De-la-Noy, Michael *Michael Ramsey: A Portrait* (Collins, 1990)

Dickens, Charles *The Mystery of Edwin Drood* (OUP, 1975)

– *Our Mutual Friend* (OUP, 1975)

– *Reprinted Pieces* (OUP, 1975)

– *Sketches by Boz* (OUP, 1975)

Ditchfield, P. M. *The Old-time Parson* (1908)

Donne, John *The Divine Poems* (ed. Helen Gardner, OUP, 1971)

– *Songs and Sonnets* (1633)

Eliot T. S., *Collected Poems* (Faber, 1963)

Faber, Frederick William *Hymns* (1861)

Falkner, John Meade *Poems* (Westminster Press, no date)

Farrer, Austin *The End of Man* (SPCK, 1973)

Finlayson, Arthur R. M. *Life of Canon Fleming* (James Nisbet & Co, 1909)

Forster, E. M. *A Room with a View* (Penguin, 1960)

Froude, J. A. *Short Studies of Great Subjects* (Everyman, 1910)

– *Henry VIII* (Everyman, 1921)

Galt, John *Annals of the Parish* (Everyman's Library, Dent 1927)

Gaskell, Elizabeth *The Life of Charlotte Bronte* (OUP, 1936)

Gilbert, W. S. *The Bab Ballads* (Harvard UP, Cambridge, Mass, 1970)

Gladstone, W. E. *The Church of England and Ritualism* (Strachan and Co., 1873)

Godolphin, Sidney *The Poetical Works of Sidney Godolphin* (Cambridge University Press, 1931)

Goldsmith, Oliver *The Complete Works* (Nonesuch Press, 1958)

Greene, Graham *Brighton Rock* (Penguin, 1981)

Gurney, Ivor (ed.) *Recusant Poets* (Burns & Oates, 1946)

Hardy, Thomas *Collected Poems* (Macmillan, 1971)

Hare, Augustus *Memorials of a Quiet Life* (Macmillan, 1891)

Hawker, R. S. *Collected Verses* (Polperro Press, 1865)

Hazlitt, William *The Spirit of the Age* (Everyman's Library, Dent 1910)

Henson, Hensley *Retrospect of an Unimportant Life* (OUP, 1940, 1942, 1945)

Herbert, George *Poems* (OUP, 1965)

– *A Priest to the Temple* (Everyman's Library, Dent 1951)

Herrick, Robert *Collected Works* (OUP, 1970)

Hopkins, Gerard Manley *Collected Poems* (OUP, 1965)

Inge, W. R. *Diary of a Dean* (Hutchinson, 1949)

Jeafferson, John Cordy *A Book about Clergy* (The Avalon Press, 1870)

Jerome, Joseph (ps. Brocard Sewell) *Montague Summers* (Cecil and Amelia Woolf, 1965)

Joyce, James *Ulysses* (Penguin, 1990)

Junor, John *Listening for a Midnight Tram* (Chapmans, 1990)

Kempe, Margery *The Book of Margery Kempe* (OUP, 1961)

Kilvert, Francis *Diaries*, ed. William Plomer, (Cape, 1974)

Knox, Ronald *Enthusiasm* (OUP, 1939)

– *In Three Tongues* (ed. L. E. Eyres, Chapman & Hall, 1959)

Lancaster, Osbert *All Done from Memory* (John Murray, 1967)

Langland, William *Piers Plowman* ed. Schmidt, (Everyman's Library, Dent 1978)

Lawrence, D. H. *Collected Short Stories* (Heinemann, 1971)

– *The Rainbow* (Penguin, 1960)

'A Layman' *Life of Thomas Ken* (John Murray, 1854)

Lewis, W. H. *Brothers and Friends* (Harper & Row USA, 1987)

Lichtenberg's Commentaries on Hogarth's Engravings (trans. German, Innes and Gustav, 1966)

Lockhart, J. G. *Cosmo Gordon Lang* (OUP, 1949)

– *The Life of Sir Walter Scott* (Ballantyne, 1840)

Longueville, J. *A Life of Archbishop Laud* (1894)

Macaulay, Rose *Letters to a Friend* (Collins, 1962)

– *More Letters to a Friend* (Collins, 1964)

– *Personal Pleasures* (Gollancz, 1935)

– *The Towers of Trebizond* (Collins, 1956)

Mackenzie, Compton *The Parson's Progress* (Cassell, 1923)

Magnus, Philip *Gladstone* (John Murray, 1954)

Marshall, Arthur Calder *The Enthusiast* (Faber, 1962)

Marvell, Andrew *The Rehearsal Transpros'd* (ed. Smith, D. I., OUP, 1971)

Masefield, John *The Box of Delights* (Puffin, 1980)

Menzies, Lucy *Father Wainwright, A Record* (Longman, 1947)

Milton, John *The English Poems of John Milton* (OUP, 1942)

– *Milton's Prose* (OUP, 1925)

Montgomery, John *Abodes of Love* (Putnam, 1962)

Muggeridge, Malcolm *The Green Stick* (Collins, 1967)

– *Muggeridge through the Microphone* (Pan, 1968)

Murdoch, Iris *The Bell* (Chatto, 1958)

– *The Time of the Angels* (Chatto, 1960)

Newman, Francis *Phases of Faith* (Smith Elder & Co, 1852)

Newman, John Henry *Letters and Diaries* (OUP, 1956)

O'Donovan, Gerald *Vocations* (Chatto & Windus, 1932)

Panter-Downes, Mollie *One Fine Day* (Virago, 1985)

Pearson, Hesketh *The Smith of Smiths* (Penguin, 1958)

Pollard, A. W. *Thomas Cranmer and the English Reformation* (Smith Elder & Co., 1927)

Pope, Alexander *Letters* (OUP, 1946)

– *Poetical Works* (OUP, 1969)

Powell, Anthony *The Valley of Bones* (Heinemann, 1964)

Powys, John Cowper *A Glastonbury Romance* (1933)

Prescott, H. F. M. *A Man on a Donkey* (Eyre & Spottiswood, 1952)

Prior, Matthew *The Literary Books of Matthew Prior* (OUP, 1971)

Purcell, Edmund Sheridan *Life of Cardinal Manning* (Macmillan, 1895)

Pym, Barbara *Excellent Women* (Cape, 1958)

– *A Very Private Eye* (Macmillan, 1985)

Reid, Stuart J. *The Life and Times of the Rev. Sydney Smith* (Smith Elder & Co, 1951)

Ridler, Anne *A Matter of Life and Death* (Faber, 1959)

Ruskin, John *Praeterita* (Macmillan, 1912)

Scott, Sir Walter *Old Mortality* (Cassell, 1841)

– *Rob Roy* (Cassell, 1841)

Shorthouse, J. Henry *John Inglesant* (1881)

Simon, Ulrich *Sitting in Judgement* (SPCK, 1987)

Smart, Christopher *Selected Poems* (Penguin, 1990)

Smith, Stevie *Collected Poems* (Allen Lane, 1975)

Stanley, Arthur *Historical Memorials of Canterbury Cathedral* (Fellowes, 1861)

Stanley, Dean *The Life of Dr Arnold* (Fellowes, 1844)

Stephenson, Colin *Merrily on High* (DLT, 1971)

– *Walsingham Way* (DLT, 1969)

Stockwood, Mervyn *Chanctonbury Ring* (Hodder, 1982)

Strachey, Lytton *Eminent Victorians* (Chatto and Windus, 1918)

Swift, Jonathan *Poetical Works* (Oxford Standard Authors, OUP, 1967)

Teale, William Henry *Lives of English Divines* (London, 1846)

Tennyson, Alfred, Lord *In Memoriam* (Macmillan, 1850)

– *Northern Farmer Old Style* (Macmillan, 1861)

Tennyson Turner, Charles *Sonnets* (Smith Elder & Co., 1872)

Thackeray, William Makepeace *Complete Works* (Nelson, 1910)

Thomas, R. S. *Song at the Year's Turning* (Hart Davis, 1966)

Thompson, Flora *Lark Rise to Candleford* (Penguin, 1985)

Trollope, Anthony *Barchester Towers* (OUP World's Classics, 1910)

– *Framley Parsonage* (OUP World's Classics, 1941)

– *Is He Popenjoy?* (OUP World's Classics, 1943)

– *Last Chronicle of Barset* (OUP, 1980)

– *The Warden* (OUP World's Classics, 1975)

Vaughan, Henry *Collected Poems* (ed. Whistle, Revd. Hubert, OUP, 1931)

Von Hügel, Baron *Letters to a Niece* (Dent, 1933)

Waldegrave, Samuel *Life of Archbishop Tait* (Smith Elder & Co., 1891)

Walke, Bernard *Twenty Years at St Hilary* (Methuen, 1935; reprinted Anthony Mott Ltd, 1982)

Walker, Charles (ed.) *The Ritual Reason Why* (Mowbray, 1868)

Walpole, Horace *Selected Letters* (Everyman, 1968)

Walton, Izaak *Lives* (ed. House, Humphry, OUP, 1956)

Waugh, Evelyn *Decline and Fall* (Chapman & Hall, 1928)

– *Ronald Knox* (Chapman & Hall, 1959)

– *The Letters of Evelyn Waugh* (ed. Amory, Mark, Weidenfeld & Nicolson, 1971)

Whistler, Lawrence *The English Festivals* (Batsford, 1947)

White, F. O. *Lives of the Elizabethan Bishops* (Skeffingham & Son, 1898)

Wilde, Oscar *The Importance of Being Earnest* (Penguin, 1975)

Williams, Cicely *A Bishop's Wife but Still Myself* (Allen & Unwin, 1961)

Williams, Harry *Some Day I'll Find You* (Mitchell Beazley, 1986)

Wodehouse, P. G. *Mulliner Nights* (Barrie & Jenkins, 1980)

Woodforde, James *The Diary of a Country Parson* (ed. Beresford, John, OUP, 1926, 4 vols)

Woolf, Virginia *A Passionate Apprentice: The Early Journals* (Hogarth Press, 1990)

Wordsworth, William *The Prelude* (ed. De Selincourt, Ernest, Oxford Standard Authors Series, OUP, 1960)

ACKNOWLEDGEMENTS

We would like to thank all the authors, publishers and literary representatives who have given permission to reprint copyright material included in this anthology.

W. H. AUDEN: to Faber and Faber Ltd and Random House, Inc. for 'Doggerel by a Senior Citizen' from *W. H. Auden: Collected Poems*, ed. Edward Mendelson, copyright © 1969 by W. H. Auden; BEDE: to Penguin Books Ltd for extracts from *History of the English Church and People*, trans. Leo Sherley Price (Penguin Classics, 1986), copyright © Leo Sherley Price, 1955, 1968; HILAIRE BELLOC: to Peters Fraser & Dunlop Group Ltd for 'Ballade of Illegal Ornaments' from *The Complete Verse of Hilaire Belloc* (Pimlico Books, a division of Random Century Group); TONY BENN: to Curtis Brown Ltd on behalf of the author for an extract from *Out of the Wilderness* (Hutchinson, 1987), copyright © Tony Benn, 1987; JOHN BETJEMAN: to John Murray (Publishers) Ltd for 'Hymn', 'St Saviour's, Aberdeen Park, Highbury, N', 'Myfanwy at Oxford' and 'Felixstowe, or The Last of Her Order' from *Collected Poems* (1987); an extract from *Summoned by Bells* (1965); and 'Lenten Thoughts of a High Anglican' from *An MP in the Air* (1974); PENELOPE BETJEMAN: to John Murray (Publishers) Ltd for a letter to Evelyn Waugh (dated April 1947) reprinted in *The Letters of Evelyn Waugh*, ed. Mark Amory (George Weidenfield & Nicolson, 1971); PIERS BRENDON: to Curtis Brown Ltd for extracts from *Hawker of Morwenstow* (Secker & Warburg, 1975); ANTHONY BURGESS: to the author for an extract from *Little Wilson and Big God* (Heinemann, 1987); OWEN CHADWICK: to Oxford University Press for extracts from *Michael Ramsey: A Life* (1990); NINIAN COMPER: to the Society for Promoting Christian Knowledge for an extract from *The Atmosphere of a Church* (Sheldon Press, 1947); DON CUPITT: to SCM Press Ltd for an extract from *Only Human* (1989); T. S. ELIOT: to Faber and Faber Ltd and Harcourt Brace Jovanovich, Inc. for *Choruses from 'The Rock'* and *Little Gidding* from *Collected Poems 1909–1962* (1968); QUEEN ELIZABETH II: to Times Newspapers Ltd for 'George VI's Coronation' (*The Times*, 8 March 1990) by Simon Tait, copyright © Times Newspapers Ltd 1990; AUSTIN FARRER: to the Society for Promoting Christian Knowledge for

ACKNOWLEDGEMENTS

an extract from *The End of Man* (SPCK, 1973); E. M. FORSTER: to King's College, Cambridge and The Society of Authors as the literary representatives of the E. M. Forster Estate for an extract from *A Room with a View* (Penguin Books, 1960); GERALD OF WALES: to Penguin Books Ltd for extracts from *A Journey through Wales*, trans. Lewis Thorpe (Penguin Classics, 1978), copyright © the Estate of Lewis Thorpe, 1978; W. S. GILBERT: to Harvard University Press for 'The Rival Curates' from *The Bab Ballads*, edited by James Ellis (The Belknap Press of Harvard University Press), copyright © by the President and Fellows of Harvard College; GRAHAM GREENE: to David Higham Associates Ltd for an extract from *Brighton Rock* (Heinemann, 1938); HERBERT HENSLEY HENSON: to Oxford University Press for extracts from *Retrospect of an Unimportant Life* (1940); JAMES JOYCE: to the Estate of James Joyce represented by the Society of Authors and Random House, Inc for an extract from *Ulysses* (Penguin Books, 1960), copyright © 1934 and renewed 1962 by Lucia and George Joyce; JOHN JUNOR: to Chapman Publishers for an extract from *Listening for a Midnight Tram* (1990); MARGERY KEMPE: to Oxford University Press for extracts from *The Book of Margery Kempe*, ed. W. Butler-Bowdon (1954); OSBERT LANCASTER: to John Murray (Publishers) Ltd for extracts from *All Done by Memory* (1967); PHILIP LARKIN: to The Marvell Press for an extract from 'Church Going' from *The Less Deceived*; D. H. LAWRENCE: to Penguin Books USA, Inc. and Laurence Pollinger Ltd for an extract from 'Daughters of the Vicar' from *Complete Short Stories of D. H. Lawrence*, copyright © 1922 by Thomas Seltzer, Inc., renewed 1950 by Frieda Lawrence; W. H. LEWIS: to Harper Collins, Inc. for extracts from *Brothers and Friends* (1987); J. G. LOCKHART: to Hugh Lockhart for an extract from *Cosmo Gordon Lang* by J. G. Lockhart (Hodder & Stoughton, 1949); ROSE MACAULAY: to Peters Fraser & Dunlop Group for extracts from *Personal Pleasures* (Gollancz, 1935), *The Towers of Trebizond* (Collins, 1956), *Letters to a Friend* (Collins, 1962), and *More Letters to a Friend* (Collins, 1964); COMPTON MACKENZIE: to Random Century Group for an extract from *The Parson's Progress* (Cassell, 1923); JOHN MASEFIELD: to The Society of Authors as the literary representative of the Estate of John Masefield for an extract from *The Box of Delights* (Puffin Books, 1980); MALCOLM MUGGERIDGE: to David Higham Associates Ltd and William Morrow, Inc. for an extract from *The Green Stick* (Collins, 1967); and David Higham Associates Ltd for an extract from *Muggeridge through the Microphone* (Pan Books, 1968); IRIS MURDOCH: to Random Century Group for extracts from *The Bell* (Chatto & Windus, 1958) and *The Time of the Angels* (Jonathan Cape, 1960); JOHN HENRY NEWMAN: to Oxford University Press for extracts from *Letters and Diaries of John Henry Newman 1956–1990*, edited by Ian Ker; MOLLIE PANTER-DOWNES: to Virago Press for an extract from *One Fine Day* (1947; Virago, 1985); ANTHONY POWELL: to Octopus Publishing Group Library and David Higham Associates Ltd for an extract from *The Valley of Bones* (William Heinemann, 1974); H. F. M. PRESCOTT: to A. P. Watt Ltd, on behalf of Mrs S. C. Thedinga and J. W. Prescott, and Harper Collins Publishers Ltd for an extract from *The Man on a Donkey* (Eyre & Spottiswoode, 1952); BARBARA PYM: to Macmillan London Ltd for extracts from *A Very Private Eye*

ACKNOWLEDGEMENTS

(1985); and Random Century Group and E. P. Dutton, a division of Penguin, USA, Inc. for an extract from *Excellent Women* (Jonathan Cape, 1958); ANNE RIDLER: to the author for 'Cranmer and the Bread of Heaven' from *A Matter of Life and Death* (Faber and Faber, 1959); ULRICH SIMON: to the Society for Promoting Christian Knowledge for an extract from *Sitting in Judgement* (SPCK, 1978); STEVIE SMITH: to James MacGibbon and New Directions Publishing Corporation for 'Why Are the Clergy?' and 'How Do You See?' from *The Collected Poems of Stevie Smith* (Penguin Twentieth Century Classics), copyright © 1972 by Stevie Smith; COLIN STEPHENSON: to Darton Longman & Todd Ltd for extracts from *Merrily on High* (1971); R. S. THOMAS: to the author c/o Gwydion Thomas, 53 Gloucester Road, Kew, UK, for 'A Priest to His People' from *Stones of the Field* (1946) and 'In a Country Church' from *Song at the Year's Turning* (1956); FLORA THOMPSON: to Oxford University Press for extracts from *Lark Rise to Candleford* (1945); EVELYN WAUGH: to Peters Fraser & Dunlop Group for extracts from *Ronald Knox* (Chapman & Hall, 1959), *The Letters of Evelyn Waugh*, ed. Mark Amory (George Weidenfeld & Nicolson, 1971), and *Decline and Fall* (Chapman & Hall, 1929); CICELY WILLIAMS: to Harper Collins Publishers Ltd for an extract from *A Bishop's Wife but Still Myself* (Allen & Unwin, 1961); HARRY WILLIAMS: to Mitchell Beazley Publishers for extracts from *Some Day I'll Find You* (1986); P. G. WODEHOUSE: to Random Century Group and A. P. Watt Ltd for an extract from *Mulliner Nights* (Barrie & Jenkins, 1980); VIRGINIA WOOLF: to Random Century Group and Harcourt Brace Jovanovich, Inc. for extracts from *A Passionate Apprentice: The Early Years* (Hogarth Press, 1990);

Every effort has been made to contact or trace all copyright holders. The publishers will be glad to make good any errors or omissions brought to our attention in future editions.

INDEX

Abbot Samson, 2
Abodes of Love (Montgomery), 183–5
Acland, Henry, 60
Act of Supremacy, 276
Advent, 330
Agapemone, 183, 184
Albert, Prince Consort, 96
Alexandra, Princess of Wales (later Queen), 136, 137, 199–200
Aleyn, Master, 297
All Done from Memory (Lancaster), 63–4, 245–6
All Hallows, 331
All Hallows and S. Petrock, Exeter, 35
All Saints' church, Margaret Street, west London, 36
All Saints' church, Spitalfields, London, 35
All Saints Day *see* All Hallows
altar: Anglo-Catholic, 290; candlesticks on, 33–4; daily sacrifice at, 38; draping, 34; furnishings, 35
Alternative Service Book, 77
Alton Barnes church, Wilts, 214
Alton Priors church, Wilts, 202
Andrewes, Bishop, 111–12
Andrews, William, 25–6, 31–2
angels, 102, 109, 115
Anglican Deaconess Community of St Andrew, 217
Anglicanism, founding of, 102
Anglo-Catholicism, 208, 290, 312, 324
Annals (Annali d'Italia) (Muratori), 273
Annals of the Parish (Galt), 196–7
Ansford, Somerset, 61
Anson, Peter F., 35, 217, 247–50, 284–5
Anthemas of Our Lady, 290
Apostles, 167, 168, 273
Ark of the Covenant, 183

Arnold, Matthew, 88–9
Arnold, Dr Thomas, 90–91
Arthur, Denison Quartey (self-styled Mar Lukos), 249
Articles of Accusation, 108
Arundel Collection, 34
Ascension, 273, 326, 351–4
Ascension Day, 210, 330, 350–51
Astrey, Sir Samuel, 113
Atterbury, Francis, 302–3
Aubrey, John, 359
Auden, W. H., 313
Austen, Jane, 177–9
Ayer, A. J., 315

Bab Ballads, The (Gilbert), 234–7
Baddeley, Angela, 67
Baddeley, Hermione, 67
Baddeley, Rev. William Pye, 67
Baker, George ('Father Divine'), 249
banns, 67–8, 69, 157
baptism, 156–7, 202–3, 248
Barchester Towers (Trollope), 91–2, 210–11
Baring-Gould, Sabine, 26–8, 93–4, 156, 168–9
Barnado, Lola Ina del Carpio, 247
Barnes, Dr, Bishop of Birmingham, 123–4
Barnes, William, 20, 29–30, 154–5
Bath and Wells, Bishop of, 184
Baxter, Richard, 147
Beating the Bounds, 330, 350
Beauclerk, Topham, 225–6
Beaufort, Gwent, 244
Becket, Thomas à, Archbishop of Canterbury, 40, 43, 48
Bede, the Venerable, ix, x, 4–5, 272–3
Bell, The (Murdoch), 127–8, 271, 292–4

Belloc, Hilaire, 36–7
Benedictine Rule, 284
Benham, William, 95–7
Benn, Anthony Wedgwood (Tony), 325–8
Bennett, Trymer, Rector of St Levan, 159
Berkeley, Bishop George, 62
Betjeman, John, 1, 65–7, 68–9, 100, 173, 187–9, 220, 265–7, 294–5
Betjeman, Penelope, 265
biretta, 167, 217, 243
Bishop's Spiritual Court, 262
Bishop's Wife but Still Myself (Williams), 214–16
Bishops at Large (Anson), 217, 247–50, 284–5
Blake, William, 1–2, 8, 344
'Blame the Vicar' (Betjeman), 220
Blenheim Palace, 136, 137
Bonham-Carter, Lady Violet, 313, 314
Book about Clergy, A (Jeafferson), 144–7
Book of Margery Kempe, The (Kempe), 79–80, 226–8, 296–7
Boothby, Lord, 313–14
Boscawen, Rector of Ludgvan, 159, 160
Boswell, James, 61–2, 176–7, 225–6, 304–5
Box of Delights, The (Masefield), 336–8
Brady, Nicholas, 65
Bramhall, John, Bishop of Derry, 304
Brendon, Piers, 241–2, 253–4
Brideshead Revisited (Waugh), 266n
Brighton, Vicar of, 97
Brighton Corporation, 97, 98
Brighton Rock (Greene), 204–6
Brontë, Charlotte, 89, 116–17, 181–2
Brontë, Rev. Patrick, 89, 116, 117, 182
Brooks, Rev. Joshua, 242–3
Brothers and Friends (Lewis), 56
Brougham, John Cam Hobhouse, 1st Baron, 86
Browne, Thomas, 301–2
Bruce, Lord Justice Knight, 260
Bruton church, Somerset, 61
Buchan, Countess of, 83
Bude, 94
'Bugler's First Communion, The' (Hopkins), 53–4
Bunsen family, 117
Bunyan, John, 267, 321–2
Burgess, Anthony, 291–2
Burghley, William Cecil, 1st Baron, 261, 262
Bury St Edmunds, Suffolk, 45–7, 273
Butler, Samuel, 254–7
Butlin's holiday camp, Skegness, 311–12

Caedmon, 272–3
Caldey Abbey, 284–5
Calvin, John, 265
Cambrensis, Giraldus, 44–5, 228
Campbell, Rev., Vicar of Weasingham, 224–5, 226
Candlemas Eve, 341
candlesticks, 33–4
Canning, George, 86
Canterbury, Archbishop of, 108, 114, 226–8
    see also under individual names
Canterbury, See of, 102, 110
Canterbury Cathedral, 47–8
Canterbury Tales (Chaucer), 143–4, 274–5
Canute (Knut), King, 21
Carlyle, Dom Aelred, 284–5
Carlyle, Thomas, 2, 19, 45–7, 273–4
Carthusians, 289
Caryll, John, 270
Catholic Apostolic Church, 248
Catholic Apostolic Church, Maida Hill, London, 247
Catholic Apostolic (Irvingite) Church, Hackney, London, 247
Catholic Truth pamphlets, 312
Cato, 58
Cecil, Lord Hugh, 241
Cefn y Blaen, 348
Cerinthus, 230
Chadwick, Owen, 164, 216
Chamberlain, Colin Mackenzie (Fra Filius Domini), 217
Chamberlain, Neville, 99
chapel, church and, 70–72
Chapel Royal, St James's Palace, London, 67
Charles I, King of England, 26, 148
Charles II, King of England, 103, 132, 133
Charteris, Francis (later Lord Wemyss), 60
Chaucer, Geoffrey, 143–4, 274–5
Checkland, S. G., 264
Chester, diocese of, 226
Chesterton, G. K., 19
Chichester, Bishop of, 129
children, catechizing, 203–4
Children of the Resurrection, 183
Christ Church, Oxford, 59–61, 147n, 188
christening, 156–7
Christian Year, The (Keble), 330
Christmas, 330, 333–8, 356
church and chapel, 70–72
Church Assembly, 159, 160, 241
Church Mystical Union, 63–4
Church of England: 'abolished', 103; on

being Anglican, 11–13; dignity of, 92; use of Latin in, 290; and Newman, 88; and Orders, 265; and Trial of the Seven Bishops, 103
Church of England and Ritualism, The (Gladstone), 33, 167
'Church of the Living God', New York City, 249
Church of the Resurrection, Brighton, Sussex, 97
'Church's One Foundation, The' (Stone), 3–4
Churchill, Sir Winston Spencer, 100
Cistercians, 292
Clapton, London, 174, 183, 184
Clarke, Dr, 304
Coggan, Dr Donald, Archbishop of Canterbury, 210
Coggan, Jean, 210
Coifi, Chief Priest of King Edwin, 4
Cole, Dr, 105–6
Cole, Somerset, 61
Coleridge, Samuel Taylor, 83, 86
Collected Poems (Betjeman), 187–8, 294–5
Collected Poems (Smith), 76, 317–21
Collins, Canon John, 325, 326, 327
Commentaries on Hogarth's Engravings (Lichtenberg), 166
Common Prayer, Book of, viii, 53, 57, 58, 66, 76, 77, 115, 261, 267, 290, 296, 313
communion, 53–4, 156, 207, 210, 228n, 261, 312, 350
Community of the Resurrection, 284
Comper, Sir Ninian, 19, 37–9
confession, 204–6, 305, 324
confessionals, 123
confirmation, 52, 215, 248
Confraternity, 217
Consecration Feasts, 38
contraception, 324–5
Convent of Our Lady of Mercy, Birmingham, 264
Convocation of Canterbury, 217
Coptic Orthodox Church, 249
Coptic Orthodox Church Apostolic Incorporated, 250
Corbishley, Father, 325, 327
Cornwall, 253
Corpus Christi, Oxford, 137
Cosmo Gordon Lang (Lockhart), 117–18, 221
Cottington, Lord, 258–9
Council of Constantinople (692), 25
Council of Trent, 305

Court of High Commission, 108, 258
Covent Garden Market, 92
Cowfold Monastery, 290
Crabbe, George, 307
Cranmer, Thomas, Archbishop of Canterbury, 76, 102, 105–8, 147n, 265
Crashaw, Richard, 111–12
Crewe, the Marquis of, 118–19
Cromwell, Oliver, 276
Croxton, Dan John, 276
Cuddesdon Theological College, 56
Cupitt, Don, 76–7
Curious Church Gleanings (Andrews), 25–6, 31–2

Daladier, Édouard, 99
'Daughters of the Vicar' (Lawrence), 161–2
David II, Bishop of St David's, 45
Davidson, Randall, 95–7
Dearmer, Percy, 33–4, 53, 169
Decline and Fall (Waugh), 322–4
Dedication Festivals, 19–20, 38
De-la-Noy, Michael, 17, 129
Delights of the Muses, The (Crashaw), 111–12
Dell, Ethel Mary, 246
Denys, Abbot (of Nashdom Abbey), 289
Desart, Earl of, 60
Deserted Village, The (Goldsmith), 148–50
Dew, Rev. Henry, 52
Diary of a Country Parson, The (Woodforde), 61, 198, 224–5, 280–1, 335–6
Diary of a Dean (Inge), 140–41
Dickens, Charles, 16, 30–31, 70–72, 209, 211–13
Dickson, George, 325
Dijon Cathedral, 37
Diocesan Home Mission, 92
Discourses in America (Arnold), 88–9
D'Israeli, Benjamin, 136, 137
'Dissertation sur les Porches des Eglises' (Thiers), 26
Ditchfield, P. H., 155–6, 157, 242–3
Divine Poems (Donne), 346–7
Dix, Dom Gregory, 107
Dock Strike, London (1898), 119–22
Dr Barnado's Homes for Orphan Boys, 247
Dollinger, Johann Joseph Ignaz von, 310
Donne, John, 2, 10, 133–4, 332–3, 346–7
Dowsing, William, 44
Driberg, Tom, 313–14
Drummond, William, 351–4

Dudden, Dr Homes, 245
Dugdale, Sir William, 21, 23n

Easter, 252, 330, 347–50
Easter Monday, 243
Eastern Church, 168
Ecclesiastical History (Bede), 4–5
Ecclesiologist, The, 35
Edmund, St, 21, 45–7
Edward VI, King of England, 262
Edward VII, King of England, 96
Edwin, St, King of Northumbria, 4
Elijah, prophet, 40
Eliot, T. S., 20–21, 40, 48–9
Elizabeth II, Queen, 12, 77
Eminent Victorians (Strachey), 310–11
Emlyn, Earl of, 60
End of Man, The (Farrer), 11–13
English Festivals, The (Whistler), 350–51,
    354–6, 357–9
Enthusiast, The (Marshall), 179–81
Episcopal Church, 12
Eucharist, 123
Evensong, 143, 174
Excellent Women (Pym), 189–93
Exeter, diocese of, 241

Faber, Frederick William, 28–9
Fairn, Duncan, 326
Falkner, John Meade, 14–16, 279–80,
    330, 356–7, 361–2
'Fanfare' (Waugh), 266n
Farrer, Austin, 2, 11–13
Farrington, Father, 101
Fashions in Church Furnishings (Anson),
    35
Father Wainwright: A Record (Menzies),
    206–7
Fearon, Rev., 63
Feast of All Saints, 331n
Feversham, Earl, 114
Finlayson, Arthur R. M., 199–200
First Communion, 53–4
Fitton, Hedley, 26
Fitzgerald, Lord, 151
Fleming, Canon, 199, 200
Flowres of Sion (Drummond), 351–4
fonts, 27, 35, 156
Forster, E. M., 185–6
Four Quartets (Eliot), 48–9
Fox, Dr, 133
Foxe, John, 147n
Francis of Assisi, St, 25, 208
Frere, Bishop, 290
Freud, Sigmund, 123
Frideswide, St, 60

Froude, James Anthony, 87–8, 103–5,
    224, 229–30, 275–6, 315–16
Fulham, south west London, 92

Galt, John, 196–7
Gardiner, Gerald, 326
Gaskell, Elizabeth, 89, 116–17, 181–2
Geoffrey of Monmouth, 228
Gilbert, Sir William Schwenck, 234–7
Gladstone (Magnus), 310
Gladstone, Helen, 264
Gladstone, John, 264
Gladstone, W. E., 33, 167, 264, 310
Gladstones, The (Checkland), 264
Glastonbury Romance, A (Powys), 40
Gloucester and Bristol, Bishop of, 283
Glyn, the Hon. Edward Carr, Bishop of
    Peterborough, 68n
Godolphin, Sidney, 339–40
Goldsmith, Oliver, 143, 148–50
Good Friday, 34, 65, 344–7
'Good Friday Carol' (Anon.), 344–6
Gordon, General Charles George, 310–11
Gordon, Osborne, 60
Gore, Bishop Charles, 284
Grace Abounding to the Chief of Sinners
    (Bunyan), 267, 321–2
Graham, Dr Billy, 100–101
Grail, Holy, 40
Green Stick, The (Muggeridge), 123–4
Greene, Graham, 204–6
Guards' Chapel, Wellington Barracks,
    Birdcage Walk, London, 67
Gurney, Ivor, 301, 342–3, 344–6
Gwynn, Nell, 132–3

Hack, Bartle Starmer, 246–7
Halifax, Edward Wood, 1st Earl of (2nd
    creation), 99, 311
Hallow-tide, 331
Hampden church, 46
Hardenburg, Friedrich von see Novalis
Hardy, Thomas, viii–ix, 23–4, 65, 97, 122,
    160–61, 200–202, 315, 328–9
Hare, Augustus, 142, 157–8, 202–3,
    213–14
Hare, Mrs Augustus, 213–14
Hare, Julius, 157–8
Harvest Festival, 330, 357–9
Hawker, Rev. (of Morwenstow Church),
    27–8, 93, 156, 168–9, 241–2, 253–4
Hawker of Morwenstow (Brendon),
    241–2, 253–4
Hazlitt, William, 84–7
'Heaven-Haven' (Hopkins), 271
Heenan, John Carmel, Cardinal, 128

Heneage, Sir Thomas, 262
Henrietta Maria, Queen Consort of
    Charles I of England, 26
Henry VIII (Froude), 103–5
Henry VIII, King of England, 40
Henson, Hensley, Bishop of Durham, 41,
    44, 98, 234
Herbert, George, 25, 78–9, 144–5, 195–6,
    210, 347
Hereford, Bishop of (Atlay), 52
Herrick, Robert, 341
Hesperides (Herrick), 341
Hickersayon, Archbishop St John-the-
    Divine, 249–50
high church, 54–6, 100, 165, 170
High Mass, 311, 334
Himmler, Heinrich, 100
*Historical Memorials of Canterbury
    Cathedral* (Stanley), 47–8
History of Henry Esmond, The
    (Thackeray), 174–6
History of Northumberland (Hutchinson),
    359
History of the English Church and People
    (Bede), 272–3
History of the Kings of Britain (Geoffrey
    of Monmouth), 228
Histriomastrix (Prynne), 258
Hitler, Adolf, 99, 100
Holy Ghost/Spirit, 262, 273, 317–21
Holy Thursday, 25, 344, 358
Honest to God (Robinson), 325–8
Hooker, Richard, 102, 109–10
Hooper, John, 110
Hope Patten, Alfred, 41, 43
Hopkins, Gerard Manley, 53–4, 271,
    283–4, 350
Hounslow Heath (army camp), 113–14
House of Commons, 103
House of Lords, 92
Howden church, N. Humberside, 45
Howe, Dr Graham, 326
Hubert, Archbishop of Canterbury, 46
Hügel, Baron Friedrich von, 2, 13–14
Hugh, St of Avalon (St Hugh of Lincoln),
    43
Human Shows (Hardy), 160–61
Huntingdon, Countess of, 243
Hurstmonceaux Rectory, 142, 157–8
Huss, John, 147
Huxley, Aldous, 266
Hymns (Faber), 28–9
Hymns Ancient and Modern, 96

Ignatius, Father, 271, 281–3
Ignatius, Sister, 291–2

Imitations of English Poets (Pope), 148
Importance of Being Earnest, The (Wilde),
    94–5
In Memoriam (Tennyson), 340–41
In Three Tongues (Knox), 134–5
Incarnation, 156, 273
inductions, 214, 215
Inge, Dean William Ralph, 130, 140–41
Inglis, Sir Robert, 117
Irvine, Father, 59
Irving, Rev. Edward, 84–6
Irvingite Church, 247
Is He Popenjoy? (Trollope), 131
Istanbul, 50

James the Just, St, Bishop of Jerusalem,
    168
Jeafferson, John Cordy, 144–7
Jerome, Joseph, 243–4
Jerusalem, 326
Jesus Christ: Atonement, 262; Church's
    mediation of, 13; and company of
    saints, 11; and foundation of the
    Church, 1; and man's fallen nature,
    203; and pharisees' burdens, 325; and
    sacraments, 265; and secular use of
    church buildings, 25
Jewel, John, Bishop of Salisbury, 171
Jocelin de Brakelond, 46–7
John, St (Apostle), 168, 230
John Inglesant (Shorthouse), 54–6
John of Dice, 45, 46
John of Wyreham, 297
John the Baptist, St, 27–8
Johnson, Dr Hewlett, Dean of Canterbury,
    123
Johnson, Dr Samuel, 61–2, 176–7, 224
Journey through Wales, A (Cambrensis),
    44–5, 228
Joyce, James, 72–5
Jubilate Agno (Smart), 10–11
Junor, John, 313–14

Keats, John, 140
Keble, John, 143, 152, 153, 224, 229–30,
    330
Kempe, Margery, 80, 226–8, 296–7
Ken, Thomas, 114, 132–3
Kensington, London (Potteries), 92
Kensit, 44
Ket, Francis, 262
Kildare, Marquis of, 60
Kilvert, (Robert) Francis, viii, 34, 52, 69,
    93, 131–2, 142, 156–7, 167, 203–4,
    220, 271, 281–3, 348–9, 360–61
Kilvert, Maria, 131–2, 182–3

King, Edward, Bishop of Lincoln, 242
King, Dr Henry, 134
Knock, 73
Knox, Ronald Arbuthnott, 134–5, 244–5

Laidlaw, William, 308
Lambeth Conference (1958), 325
Lambeth Palace, 146, 226
Lammas, 358
Lancaster, Osbert, 63–4, 245–6
Lang, Cosmo Gordon, Archbishop of Canterbury, 118, 221
Langland, William, 5–6, 41–2, 257
Langley church, 349
Lark Rise to Candleford (Thompson), 208, 234, 343
Larkin, Philip, vii
Last Chronicle of Barset, The (Trollope), 209, 217–19
Last Supper, 334
Latimer, Hugh, 83
Laud, William, Archbishop of Canterbury, 259
Lawrence, D. H., 143, 161–2, 186–7
Lawrence, Friar, 276
Leningrad anti-religious museum, 326–7
Lent, 244, 330, 356
'Lenten Thoughts of a High Anglican' (Betjeman), 188–9
Leskov, 130
Letters of Evelyn Waugh, The (Waugh, ed. Amory), 264–7
Letters to a Friend (Macaulay), 59, 239, 331
Letters to a Niece (Hügel), 13–14
Lewis, Sir Gilbert, Canon of Worcester, 131–2
Lewis, Lady, 132
Lewis, W. H., 56
Liddell, Alice, 136–7
Liddell, Dean Henry George, 60, 136
Life and Times of the Rev. Sydney Smith, The (Reid), 150, 151, 198–9, 259–61
Life of Archbishop Laud, A (Longueville), 257–9
Life of Archbishop Tate (Waldegrave), 92–3, 135–6
Life of Archibald Campbell Tait (Davidson and Benham), 95–7
Life of Canon Fleming (Finlayson), 199–200
Life of Cardinal Manning (Purcell), 119–22
Life of Charlotte Brontë, The (Gaskell), 89, 116–17, 181–2
Life of Dr Arnold, The (Stanley), 90–91

Life of Dr John Donne, The (Walton), 133–4
Life of Samuel Johnson, The (Boswell), 61–2, 176–7, 225–6, 304–5
Life of Sir Walter Scott, The (Lockhart), 307–10
Life of Thomas Ken ('A Layman'), 112–14, 132–3
Lincoln, Dean of, 99
Lincoln, diocese of, 242
Lincoln Cathedral, 99
Listening for a Midnight Tram (Junor), 313–14
Little Gidding, Cambs, 40, 48–9
Little Wilson and Big God (Burgess), 291–2
Littlemore, Oxon, 89
Liverpool, Robert Jenkinson, Earl of, 86
Lives (Walton), 109–10
Lives of the Elizabethan Bishops (White), 108, 171, 261–2
Llangorse, 69
Llewelyn (Dean of St David's, previously Principal of Lampeter), 69
Lockhart, J. G., 117–18, 221, 307–10
London, and missionary clergy, 92
London Hospital, east London, 207
Longford, Earl of, 326
Longueville, J., 258–9
Lord Rosebery (Marquis of Crewe), 118–19
Lourdes, 44, 73
Lukos, Mar, see Arthur, Denison Quartey
Luther, Martin, 31–2, 265
Lutyens, Sir Edwin Landseer, 289
Lycidas (Milton), 224, 229
Lyne, Clavering, 281, 282

Macaulay, Rose, 2, 17–18, 57–9, 100–101, 225, 239, 311–12, 331
Macaulay, Thomas Babington, 1st Baron Macaulay, 117
McCulloch, Rev. Joseph, 325
MacDonald, Ramsay, 123
McFall, Bishop James, 248
Mackenzie, Compton, 160, 165, 170, 285
Magnus, Philip, 310
Malmesbury Abbey Church, 26
Mamertus, Bishop of Vienne, 350
Man on a Donkey, The (Prescott), 277–9
Manchester, collegiate church of, 242
Manchester Cathedral, 124
Manning, Cardinal Henry Edward, 119–22, 153
Marshall, Arthur Calder, 179–81
Martin, Abbot (of Nashdom Abbey), 289

Martineau, Harriet, 151
Martinmas, 357
Marvell, Andrew, 222–3, 251–2
Marx, Karl, 123
Mary, Queen (wife of King George V), 77
Masefield, John, 336–8
Mass, 72–5, 170, 240, 244, 249, 305, 312, 331, 334
Matins, 46–7, 67–8, 142
Matter of Life and Death, A (Ridler), 107–8
Maurice, Frederick Denison, 316–17
Mells, Frome, Somerset, 244
Memorials of a Quiet Life (Hare), 142, 157–8, 202–3, 213–14
Menzies, Lucy, 206–7
Mercadante, Saverio, 74
Mercer (hymn writer), 96
Merrily on High (Stephenson), 97–8, 246–7, 289–91, 311
Methodism, 253–4, 312
Michael Ramsey: A Life (Chadwick), 164, 216
Michael Ramsey: A Portrait (De-la-Noy), 17, 129
Middleton, Marmaduke, Bishop of Waterford, 108
Midsummer, 358
Milton, John, 1, 6–7, 51–2, 58, 102, 103, 110–11, 165–6, 171–2, 224, 229, 298
mitre, 165, 167–8
Moments of Vision (Hardy), 23–4, 65
monasteries, dissolution of, 275–6
Montagu, Richard, Bishop of Chichester, then Norwich, 262
Montague Summers (Jerome), 243–4
Montgomery, John, 183–5
Moral Rearmament, 100
More Letters to a Friend (Macaulay), 311–13
Morris, J., of Reading, 183
Morris, Rev. J. B., 225, 230–33
Morris, Samuel, 249
Morwenstow, Cornwall, 93, 94
Morwenstow church, Cornwall, 26–8, 168
Mowbray, A. W., 167–8
Mozart, Wolfgang Amadeus, 74
Muggeridge, Malcolm, 123–4, 128, 292
Muggeridge through the Microphone (Muggeridge), 128, 292
Mulliner Nights (Wodehouse), 124–7
Munich agreement, 99
Murdoch, Iris, 127–8, 271, 292–4
music, church, 140–41
Mussolini, Benito, 99

Mystery of Edwin Drood, The (Dickens), 16

Nashdom Abbey, 289–90
National Gallery, London, 34
Neville, Father, 118
New Year, 340–41
Newcastle, Duke of, 36
Newcomes, The (Thackeray), 306–7
Newman, Francis William, 262–3
Newman, Hugh George de Willmott, 247–9
Newman, Cardinal John Henry, 87, 88–9, 118–19, 143, 152–3, 225, 230–33, 262–3
Newton, Charles, 60
Nicene Creed, 141
Nicholls, Rev. Arthur Bell, 181–2
Nip in the Air, A (Betjeman), 188–9
Norwich, Bishop of, 44
Notre Dame, Cathedral of, Paris, 25, 26
Novalis (Friedrich von Hardenburg), 47

O'Donovan, Gerald, 285–8
'Of Reformation in England and the Causes that Hitherto Have Hindered It' (Milton), 110–11, 171–2
Of the Atmosphere of a Church (Comper), 37–9
Old Catholic Orthodox Church, 248–9
Old Mortality (Scott), 80–82
Old Catholic Missal and Ritual (Mathew), 248
Old Roman Catholic Church (Pro-Uniate Rite), 249
Old-time Parson, The (Ditchfield), 155–6, 157, 242–3
Oliver, Brother, 292
On the Death of Doctor Swift (Swift), 138–9
One Fine Day (Panter-Downes), 163–4
Only Human (Cupitt), 76–7
Order of Deaconesses, 217
Orders, 265
ordination, 195
Ornaments Rubric, 33
Orthodox Church, 265
Osana, St, 45
Oscott (St Mary's College), 232, 233
Osred, King, 45
Our Mutual Friend (Dickens), 209, 211–13
Oxford, Bishop of, 117
Oxford Group, 100
Oxford Movement, 87–8, 143, 311

Oxford University, 136, 147n, 187–8, 262, 263

Palestrina, Giovanni Pierluigi da, 74
Palm Sunday, 56, 220, 233, 343
Palmer, Mr (of Eardisley), 52
Panter-Downes, Mollie, 143, 163–4
papal infallibility, 12, 249
Paradise Lost (Milton), 6–7
Parson's Handbook, The (Dearmer), 33–4, 53, 169
Parson's Progress, The (Mackenzie), 170
Passion, 79, 88, 273
Past and Present (Carlyle), 21–3, 45–7, 273–4
Patmore, Coventry, 173–4
Paul, St, viii, ix, 89, 99
Paulinus, Archbishop of York, 4
Pearson, Hesketh, 193
Peel, Sir Robert, 151
Penseroso, Il (Milton), 51–2
Pentecost, ix, 165, 168
Pepys, Samuel, 103
Personal Pleasures (Macaulay), 57–9
Peters, Norman, 268
Phases of Faith (Newman), 262–3
Phelps, Dr, Provost of Oriel College, Oxford, 246
Phillips, Jane, 348
Phipps, Mary, 129
Phipps, Simon, Bishop of Horsham, 129
Piers Plowman (Langland), 5–6, 41–2, 257
Placidus, Brother, 283
Plough Monday, 358
Plymouth, Earl of, 284
Poems (Falkner), 14–16, 279–80, 356–7, 361–2
Poems in the Dorset Dialect (Barnes), 29–30, 154–5
Pollard, A. W., 105–7
Pope, Alexander, 148, 270, 302–3
Pope, Rev. (curate of Cusop), 52
Porteus, Dr, Bishop of London, 226
Pounsett, Samuel, 61
Powell, Anthony, 224, 237–9
Powys, John Cowper, 40
Praeterita (Ruskin), 59–61, 117, 136–7, 316–17
prayers: church v. chapel, 70, 71; posture for, 63; St Theresa on, 56
Preece, Ruth Annie, 184
Prelude, The (Wordsworth), 84
premunire, 103, 104–5
Presbyterian church, 165, 304

'Presbyterian Church Government' (Butler), 254–7
Prescott, H. F. M., 277–9
Pride and Prejudice (Austen), 177–9
Priest to the Temple, A (Herbert), 78–9, 144–5, 195–6, 210
Priestley, Mrs J. B. (Jacquetta Hawkes), 326
Prince, Brother Henry James, 183
Prior, Matthew, 114–15
prison chapel, 30–31
Promised Land, 273
Protestant Meeting Houses, 38
Prynne, Marie, 258
Prynne, William, 257–9
psalms, 54–5, 57, 65, 174, 197, 203
Psalter, 55
Purcell, Edmund Sheridan, 119–22
Purgatory, 305
Puritans, 261
Pusey, Dr Edward Bouverie, 143, 152–3, 246
Puseyites, 151, 260–61
Pym, Barbara, x, 65, 67, 129, 189–93, 313

Quakers, 259

Radcliffe, Ann, 274n
Rainbow, The (Lawrence), 174, 186–7
Ramsey, Arthur Michael, Baron, Archbishop of Canterbury, 2, 17, 102, 129
Ray, Johnny, 313
Raynes, Father Raymond, 36, 324
Reformation, 76, 166, 316
Rehearsal Transpros'd, The (Marvell), 222–3, 251–2
Reid, Stuart J., 150, 151, 198–9, 259–61
Religio Medici (Browne), 301–2
Rendel, George, 310
Rendel, Stuart, 310
Reprinted Pieces (Dickens), 70–72
Reresby, Sir John, 113
Resurrection, 264, 273, 326, 330
retreats, 173
Retrospect of an Unimportant Life (Henson), 44, 98, 234
Rheims Cathedral, 38
Ridler, Anne, 107–8
Ridley, Nicholas, 110
Ripon, Bishop of, 116–17
Ritual Reason Why, The (Mowbray), 165, 167–8
Ritual Revival, 96
Rob Roy (Scott), 62–3

Robinson, John, Bishop of Woolwich, 325–7
Rock, The (Eliot), 20–21
Rogationtide, 350
Rogers (Vicar of Penzance), 159
Roman Catholicism: and altar candlesticks, 33, 34n; and bishops, 103; and Dr Johnson, 304–5; harmful practices of, 14; and orders, 265; and Papacy, 12
Ronald Knox (Waugh), 244–5
Room with a View, A (Forster), 185–6
Ruskin, John, 59–61, 117, 136–7, 316–17
Russell, Bertrand, 315

sacrament, 55, 109, 123, 265, 269, 305, 335
St Alban the Martyr, Holborn, London, 313
St David's church, Llanfaes, 44
St Edmundsbury Abbey, 21–3
St Gabriel's church, Pimlico, London, 101
St George's Hospital, London, 206
St Hilary, Cornwall, 160, 268–70, 333
St James chapel, Lynn, 79
St James church, Bermondsey, London, 35
St James' Proprietary Chapel, Ryde, 35
St James's, Piccadilly, London, 67, 92
St John's church, Notting Hill, London, 245
St Lucy's Day, 332–3
St Martin in the Fields, London, 101
St Mary Abbots, Kensington, London, 67–8
St Mary-le-Bow, Cheapside, London, 325
St Mary's church, Oxford, 88, 105, 119
St Mary's College, Oscott, 232, 233
St Michael's church, Isle of Man, 115–16
St Patrick's Cathedral, Dublin, 140
St Paul's Cathedral, London, 104, 130, 134, 151, 325
St Saviour's, Highbury, London, 68–9
saints: and Anglicanism, 12–13; invocation of, 305; produced by the Church, 18
Salisbury, 135, 214
Samson, Abbot (St), 2
Sanctuary, The, Basil Street, London, 64
Saravia, Dr, 109
Sarum Rite Old Catholic Church, 248
Satires of Circumstance (Hardy), 97
Scambler, Edmund, Bishop of Peterborough, then Norwich, 261–2
Schism, 251, 252
Scott, C. P., 123, 124
Scott, Miss Mary, 309

Scott, Mrs, of Harden, 309
Scott, Thomas, 309
Scott, Sir Walter, 62–3, 307–10
secularism, 326, 327
Sheldon, Gilbert, Bishop of London, later Archbishop of Canterbury, 146
Sherbourne, Brother, 276
Short Studies of Great Subjects (Froude), 87–8, 229–30, 275–6, 315–16
Shorthouse, Henry 54–6
shrines, 40–49
Sibthorpe, Richard Waldo, 35
Silex Scintillans (Vaughan), 8–9
Simon, Ulrich, 99–100
Sinister Street (Mackenzie), 285
Sitting in Judgement (Simon), 99–100
Sketches by Boz (Dickens), 30–31
Slipper Chapel, Walsingham, 44
Smart, Christopher, 10–11
Smith, Stevie, 76, 315, 317–21
Smith, Sydney, 150, 151, 193, 198–9, 259
Smith of Smiths, The (Pearson), 193
Smyth-Pigott, Rev. John Hugh, 174, 183, 184
Some Day I'll Find You (C. Williams), 35–6, 101, 324–5
Song at the Year's Turning (Thomas), 32–3, 221–2
Songs and Sonnets (Donne), 332–3
Songs of Experience (Blake), 8
Songs of Innocence (Blake), 344
Sonnets (Turner), 32
South, Robert, 304
Southampton Dock, 152
Spirit of the Age, The (Hazlitt), 84–7
Stanley, Dean Arthur Penrhyn, 40–41, 47–8, 90–91, 157–8
Star Chamber, 258
Stephenson, Colin, 41, 43, 97–8, 246–7, 289–91, 311
Stockwood, Mervyn, 210
Stokesley, John, Bishop of London, 104–5
Stona of Sancreed, 159
Stone, Dr Darwell, 291
Stone, S. J., 3–4
Stonehenge, 40
Strachey, Lytton, 310–11
Suckling, Sir John, 58
Suffolk, Lady, 138
Summers, Montague, 243–4
Summoned by Bells (Betjeman), 65–7, 68–9
Sunderland, Lord, 113
Swift, Dean Jonathan, 130, 138–9, 148, 251

'Dr Swift: The Happy Life of a Country Parson' (Pope), 140

Table Talk (Coleridge), 83
Tait, Archibald Campbell, Bishop of London, 92–3
Talgarth, Vicar of, 69
Tate, Nathum, 65
Taylor, Thomas (of St Just), 159
Teale, William Henry, 115–16
Temple, The (Herbert), 25, 347
Ten Commandments, 70, 100, 242–3
Tennyson, Alfred, 1st Baron, 199, 340–41
Thackeray, William Makepeace, 174–6, 306–7
Theresa, St, 56
Thiers, Jean Baptiste, 26
39 Articles, the, 59, 151, 214, 304
Thomas, R. S., 32–3, 221–2
Thomas, Rev., Vicar of Disserth, Powys, 93
Thomas, St, 269
Thomas Cranmer and the English Reformation (Pollard), 105–7
Thompson, Flora, 208, 234, 343
Thoughts on Religion (Swift), 130
Time's Laughing Stocks (Hardy), 200–202
Tomkinson, Cyril, 35–6
Towers of Cybele, 40
Towers of Trebizond, The (Macaulay), 17–18, 100–101
Travers, Martin, 290
Trevelyan, Lady, 117
Trial of the Seven Bishops, 103, 112–14
Trinity Sunday, 330
Trollope, Anthony, 91–2, 131, 142, 153–4, 209, 210–11, 217–19
Turner, Charles Tennyson, 32
Twenty Years at St Hilary (Walke), 158–60, 268–70, 333–5

Ulysses (Joyce), 72–5

Valley of Bones, A (Powell), 224, 237–9
Vatican, 44
Vaughan, Henry, 8–9
Verses (Belloc), 36–7
A Very Private Eye (Pym), 65, 67, 129, 313
Vespers, 290
Vicar of Morwenstow, The (Baring-Gould), 26–8, 93–4, 168–9
Victoria, Queen, 95–7, 98
Vilatte-Lloyd American Catholic Church, 249
Vincent, Rev. W., 93

Vincent, St, 248
Vocations (O'Donovan), 285–8

Wagner, Fr Arthur, 97–8
Wainwright, Father, 194, 206–7
Waldegrave, Samuel, 92–3, 135–6
Wales, 40, 253
Walke, Bernard, 158–60, 268–70, 333–5
Walpole, Horace, 82–3
Walsingham, Our Lady's Shrine at, 40–44
Walsingham, Sir Francis, 262
Walsingham Way (Stephenson), 43
Walton, Izaac, 109–10, 133–4
Wapping, London, 194, 206
Ward, Archbishop, 217
Warden, The (Trollope), 142, 153–4
Watt, Dr, 307
Waugh, Evelyn, 243–4, 264–7, 322–4
weddings, 243
Wells Cathedral, 184
Wemyss, Lord (Francis Charteris), 60
Wesley, John, 82, 83, 243, 253, 254
Wesley, Samuel Sebastian, 4
Wessex Poems (Hardy), 328–9
Westminster Abbey, 47
Westminster Hall, Parliament Square, London, 112, 114
Whately, Archbishop Richard, 98
Whippingham Parish Church, Isle of Wight, 96
Whistler, Lawrence, 350–51, 354–6, 357–9
White, F. O., 108, 171, 261–2
White, Robert, 61
Whitsun, 330, 354–6
Wilberforce, Archdeacon Samuel, 63
Wilde, Oscar, 94–5
William Albert Victor, Duke of Clarence (Prince Edward), 199–200
Williams, Harry, CR, 35–6, 101, 324–5
Williams, Cicely, 214–16
Williams, Lord, 106–7
Williams, Mgr, 249
Williams, Ronald, Bishop of Leicester, 214, 215
Wilson, Edmund, 266
Wilson, Henry, 284
Wilson, Joyce, 129
Wilson, Roger, 129
Wilson, Thomas, Bishop of Sodor and Man, 102, 115–16
Windsor Castle (Private Chapel), 95, 96
Winter Words (Hardy), 122
Wiseman, Dr Nicholas Patrick Stephen, Bishop (later Archbishop of Westminster and Cardinal), 233n, 264

Woburn Abbey, 275, 276
Wodehouse, P. G., 124–7, 240
Woodforde, Fanny, 61
Woodforde, James, 61, 198, 224–5, 280–81, 335–6
Woodhouse, Henry, 248

Woolf, Virginia, 67–8, 143, 162–3
Wordsworth, William, 84
Wroth, Jane, 133

Yaxham, Norfolk, 313n
Yonge, Charlotte Mary, 142